The Life and Times of KRISHNA

The Deity who Lived as Man

THE LIFE AND TIMES OF KRISHNA

THE DEITY WHO LIVED AS MAN

JB PATRO

First published 2013
Reprinted 2015

ISBN 978-81-8328-329-8

Published by
Wisdom Tree
4779/23, Ansari Road
Darya Ganj, New Delhi-110 002
Ph.: 23247966/67/68
wisdomtreebooks@gmail.com

Printed in India

Twadiyam Vastu Govind Tubhyamev Samarpayami

I, Brahman and Krishnapada, and my beloved wife, Kusum, dedicate this work at Govinda's lotus feet in Tirumala Kshetra, the abode of Govinda, where hundreds of millions chant Govinda Nama!

Om Tat Sat

Contents

ACKNOWLEDGEMENTS

I am grateful to the couple at Iris Graphics, Shri TR Rajaraman and his wife, Smt Sita, for taking the trouble to decipher the manuscript and bring out a digital version of the voluminous manuscript on Krishna.

I am also grateful to S/S Krishnanand Koppiker (Bengaluru) and Chandrakanth Kadambari (Canada) for sparing their valuable time and energy to format the original manuscript. But for their devotion and assiduous efforts, this book would not have taken its present shape.

My wife, Kusum, has been an asset to me throughout my life, and during these four years spent in bringing out this work, she not only supported me, but also co-authored the book.

I thank Ms Rachna Pandey Donthi, who skilfully copy-edited the vast material of the text into lucid narration. Her excellent command over English and understanding of my passion for the subject, made the story easier to read, while still holding on to the crux of the content.

A very special thanks to our daughter Krishna and her spouse, Dr Yashveer Bhatnagar, to have piloted the effort to get the book published. And it so happened, Lord Krishna, the epitome of knowledge and wisdom, guided me to Wisdom Tree, headed by Shri Shobit Arya, Founder-CEO. I must compliment the talented editors who have polished the text for a smooth narration of Krishna's story.

Finally, I am indebted to Lord Krishna, the Great Spirit, for having prompted me from time to time as to how His life's saga unveiled. It has helped me immensely in sifting through the vast material on His 'Life and Times'.

Vanaprastha, Coimbatore
JB Patro
2 May 2012

HINDU CHRONOLOGY

Chronology is the backbone of history! Going by that, I would say that we, in India, particularly the Hindu community, have strong muscles, but a weak backbone. Though there is enough material to reconstruct past events, our chronology is ambiguous. The sequence of events presented to us could be historical or bordering on the ridiculous. Incidents often get magnified to absurd levels in order to attract the 'lightless masses' towards Hinduism. Actual history has nothing to do with yugas, incongruous chronology and its associated legends. Even when based on astronomical calculations, such chronology does not serve any historical purpose. The Europeans who came to India in the seventeenth century appreciated the wisdom in Upanishadic philosophy, but ridiculed our chronological ambiguities.

Five different calendars were prevalent in ancient India. Of these, the Solar Calendar, comprising 365 and a quarter days, and the Lunar Calendar, comprising 354 days, were the most prominent. For most matters, the Lunar Calendar was used. Bhaskara, in his *Siddhanta Siromani*, stated: The measurement of month, days and year is regulated by the course of the moon.

According to the Vedas, the age of Kali—Kaliyuga, begins in 3102 BC (2950 BC Solar). Hindu writings mention three Kaliyugas: Aryan, War and Astronomical. Of these, the first is based on historical facts and, therefore, considered genuine; the second is a clever invention of the later brahmanas to magnify Krishna and popularise his worship; the third is said to last 4,32,000 years, which is an imaginary period and, as such, falls beyond the domain of history.

Incidentally, the Mahabharata and the Bhagavata Purana were the first to preach about War Kaliyuga. Therefore, the Kaliyuga epoch is usually identified with the era of Yudhisthira and the Mahabharata War. Such false notions have greatly distorted Hindu chronology. Historians mark 3102 BC as the Aryan Kaliyuga epoch. This claim is validated in the Mahabharata—Shantiparva, chapter fifty-nine, talks of the moral decline of the Aryans then living in the Kashmir Valley.

As per the Vishnu Purana, from the birth of Arjuna's grandson, Parikshit, to the coronation of Dhana Nanda of Magadh, this period consists of 1015 lunar years. This places the crowning of Dhana Nanda at 405 BC (Solar). If we add 983 solar years to this, we arrive at 1388 BC. Therefore, it is highly probable that the war took place in November or December 1389 BC. The Bhagavata Purana fixes the Great War at 1000 Lunar or 1374 BC.

Krishna lived for another thirty-six years after the war and, therefore, his exit falls in the year 1338 BC. Having lived, as per the Bhagavata Purana, for over a hundred solar years, we can assume Krishna was in his mid-sixties at the time of the conflict.

Foreword

Here is an extraordinary book by Sri Brahmanaanda Patro and Smt Kusum Patro, presenting Sri Krishna against the background of history. In this book, one would find the land's cultural riches, spiritual heights, the royal intrigues, feuds, battles, and strategies—all emerging in one colourful language, in the narration of the life and times of Krishna.

The authors have gathered all the material for the book from the Mahabharata, Harivamsa, Vishnu Purana and the Bhagavatam. We are used to referring to Sri Krishna as *bhagavan* or lord and his entire life as *leela* or play. Here is a refreshingly new narrative, taking into account all available historical and geographical facts relating to Sri Krishna as a person, whom the reader can look up to as a role model.

This book will prove to be the most significant contribution to the rich literature already in circulation on Sri Krishna. The reader is bound to undergo an inner transformation. I congratulate the authors for this painstaking and brilliant work, rendered with love and dedication.

—Swami Dayananda Saraswati

BHARATVARSHA

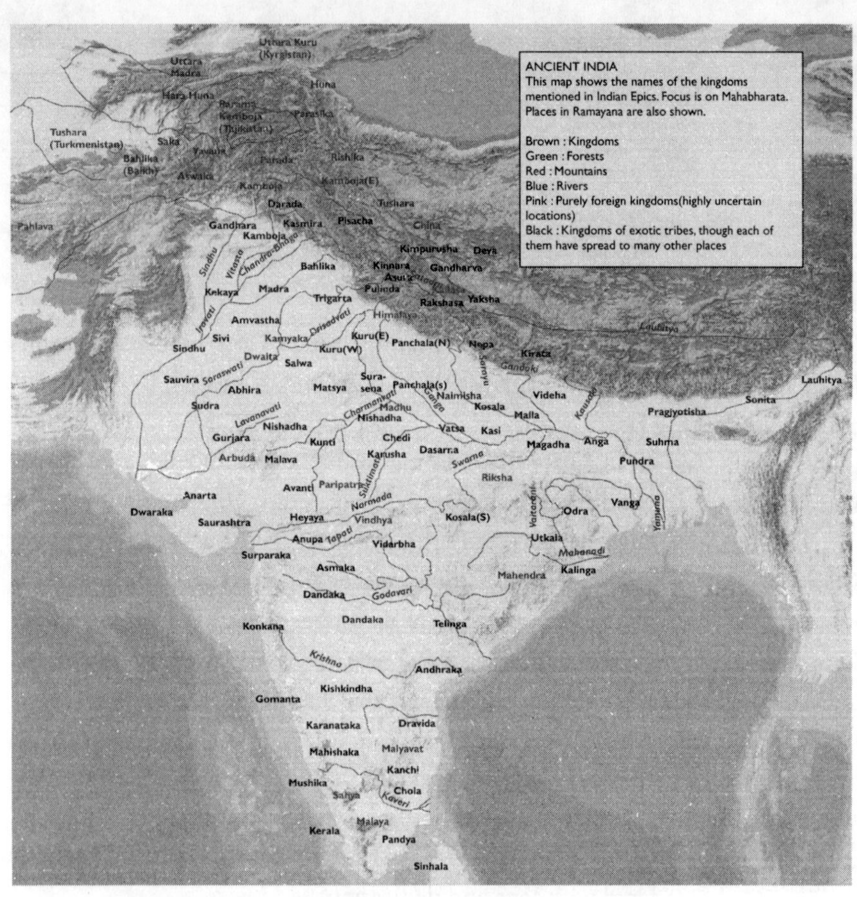

Preface

Human migration in ancient times played a significant role in shaping the current destinies of the world. In this instance, lured by the fertile soil and perennial rivers of the Indian subcontinent, a group of visiting Aryan tribes decided to settle down here. This land then came to be known as Aryawartha. In time, they emerged as an agrarian society, comprising various clans.

Aryans assigned a pivotal place to the elders of their clan, believing that they had the advantage of experience and could function as advisors to society at large. In dispensing their wisdom, these elders soon acquired immense power and wealth, which predictably led to envy and conflict. To counter this, a system based on popular consensus was evolved for decision-making. People began consulting leaders of various groups to settle their issues. These leaders were known as brahmanas as they had *brahma vidya* or knowledge. The decision of the majority was held as binding.

As smaller clans had to defend themselves from aggressive neighbouring tribes, young men were then trained to be warriors. Each warrior group had its own captain or commander. But the elders and the warrior groups often differed on the policy to be adopted for dealing with a particular social situation. In time, the warrior class, called kshatriyas—those who carried *kshatra*s or arms, increasingly felt that they were more competent to take decisions on behalf of society and thus, began asserting their role. The leader of the warrior group then became the monarch or Raja. The king began taking the brahmanas' advice to ensure peace in his kingdom.

Conflicts occurred when kings grew arrogant and placed themselves above all social rules. Fearing the wise men as obstacles in their drive for power, the ambitious monarchs began to systematically eliminate the brahmanas. As a result, society lost its moral moorings. With no laws binding the people or their rulers, there was anarchy. Life turned unbearable for the weak and poor.

When things get out of hand in the mortal world, Nature is expected to interfere and set the balance of life. Bhagwan Parashurama, son of Sage Jamadagni, took up the task of punishing the evil kings and carried out twenty-one campaigns to destroy the kshatriyas who were terrorising the populace.

At the end of his campaign, there was a sudden vacuum in the Aryan social structure. The brahmanas had been removed earlier and Bhagwan Parashurama eliminated the kshatriyas. Having suffered cruelty under monarchy, the general public developed an aversion to the rule of kings or those who bore arms. Instead, they began to periodically elect representatives from amongst themselves to provide just leadership and guidance on all matters governing their life. This was the birth of what the Greeks later termed as democracy.

The tribes elected five people to the panchayat, a governing body that heard all issues and offered solutions after much debate. Several such panchayats were then grouped together in *gana sabha*s for easy commerce and safety. Several *sabha*s united to raise a protection force and frame common laws for governance. They emerged as republics, each having an elected leader from among their representatives. This leader had king-like powers, but was made accountable to the other representatives. This form of governance continued for a long time.

Any institution of governance based on consensus is susceptible to manipulation by the shrewd, ambitious and selfish among those who take decisions. Such individuals manipulated the people's representatives and hijacked the institution, declaring themselves as kings and giving rise to an amalgam of kingdoms all over Aryawartha.

Some of these rulers, especially those who migrated to the eastern part of the Ganga basin, used force to expand their territories. On the other hand, some of the kingdoms, especially those formed by tribes that arrived in Aryawartha much later, had wise kings who retained noble-minded advisors. The Kuru clan, settled in Hastinapura, was one such prominent kingdom ruled, at the time, by Pururava.

The Kuru empire extended west of the Yamuna-Saraswati river basin and was the most powerful kingdom in Aryawartha. It constantly faced attacks from tribes of the northwest mountain regions and from the waves of fresh migrant clans settling down in their kingdom. This continuous change in the composition of the population led to varying interpretations of laws, which gave rise to conflicts within society. The brahmanas in the Kuru court realised that it was necessary to codify the laws of conduct and educate society on how to follow them.

Following their advice, Shantanu, the ruling Kuru king, set up a centre on the banks of River Yamuna, where learned men and women could share knowledge and help codify their interpretations of Nature's laws. This centre or ashram was named Dharma Kshetra, or the place where dharma or the law of good conduct was to be recorded in written form.

Dharma Kshetra was founded with great expectations. All wise men keen to reside in the campus were welcomed. One of the last to arrive was Rishi Atharvan. He came from the far-off lands, bordering the Armenian mountains. He was a master of applied sciences and soon achieved much fame and fortune by impressing both the king and the people with his novel solutions. Envious scholars, however, forced Shantanu to exclude Atharvan's knowledge, compiled as the Atharva Veda, from the final version of the Vedas. He was subsequently expelled from the campus. A departing Atharvan cursed that savages would soon kill all the sages in the ashram, leaving behind only jackals to howl forever.

His prophecy came true, with only two young students surviving the downfall. One of them was Parashara, son of Rishi Vasishta, who was the head of Dharma Kshetra. Parashara had been studying under Rishi Atharvan and was saved by the fishermen living on the banks of the Yamuna river. Parashara later fell in love with the daughter of the head fisherman and had a son named Krishna Dwaipayana.

The unfinished task of writing the Vedas and codifying the knowledge base was completed by Krishna Dwaipayana, who came to be known as Veda Vyasa. He became the prime mover in enforcing dharma in Aryan society, which was codified in the four Vedas—Rig, Sama, Yajur and Atharva.

Helping Vyasa enforce the dharmic codes was another luminary of this era, Krishna Vaasudeva of the Yadava clan, better known as Lord Krishna. This joint effort by the son of a fisherwoman and a cowherd was indicative of a classless and casteless Hindu society.

Their efforts also had a profound effect on the ongoing tussle between the Kauravas and the Pandavas, the two branches of the Hastinapura-based Kuru clan. In order to implement dharma, the immoral Kauravas had to be eliminated. This led to the war of the Mahabharata, where most of the able-bodied men died, fighting for one of the two Kuru branches. This colossal loss of life crippled the Aryan civilisation in such a way that it could never rise again to reclaim its lost glory.

The populace was disgusted with the mass massacre in the battlefield. The war provoked people to question the 'right way of living' and they found themselves increasingly drawn towards a non-violent society, where ahimsa—non-violence—was the path to attain the goal of dharma. This line of thought later gave birth to Jainism, which became the prominent religion for two millenniums. Jainism was displaced by its variant, Buddhism, which also exhorted people to seek refuge in dharma.

It was Adi Shankaracharya who reversed this tide and spurred society towards seeking Govinda, Lord Krishna. This took people back to the Hindu way of life as enunciated by Veda Vyasa and explained by Lord Krishna.

The role played by Krishna Vaasudeva in establishing dharma in Aryawartha was all-encompassing. To appreciate it, one must learn about Krishna's life and actions. The story of Krishna, as it unfolds in the following chapters, will help us understand his actions and achievements. We will also realise what we have missed and should strive to achieve in our lives.

The essence of the 'Philosophy of Life' as enunciated by Lord Krishna to warrior Arjuna, popularly known as the Bhagavad Gita, is today one of the most coveted documents of human civilisation. We admire the great efforts made by Lord Krishna and are left wondering whether he truly succeeded in guiding Hindu society to a permanent state of dharma. Krishna had also revealed to Arjuna that *parivartan* or continuous change was a basic character of Nature and one has to accept it. He said, 'He will be born again and again to protect those who follow dharma and punish the evil.'

The present state of disenchantment in society underlines how much we need Krishna's presence once again to guide the world and instil love and respect for dharma in us. We hope that reading Krishna's story will revive his presence in our lives and inspire us to lead a richer life, full of love and respect for humanity.

As a divine reincarnation, Krishna absorbed in himself everything that is life, denoting it as Vasudeva Sarvamiti—the very inclusiveness, which was the central theme of his life. His easy accessibility has put him on the high pedestal of Poornavatar or a complete reincarnate, all other incarnations being partial, incomplete and contextual.

In Chapter X of the Bhagavad Gita (verse 40/41), Lord Krishna teaches His disciple that 'There is no limit to My divine manifestation; this is only a brief description of Me and the extent of My glory. All that is glorious, brilliant and powerful is only a small manifestation of My glory.'

In his anthropomorphic form, Krishna gets divided—one part accepting him emotionally as simply the religious icon and ignoring the second part, the essence, which the form represents in reality. He himself narrates in Chapter VII of the Bhagavad Gita (verse 19) that only, 'In the very last of all births the enlightened soul worships Me realising that all this is God, Vasudeva Sarvamiti—the dweller within. Such a great soul is indeed *sudurlabhaha*—rare.'

It is apparent that organised religion has created a dichotomy between his 'form' and 'essence'. His 'form' eloquently represents Vishnu, the all-pervading and comprehensive divinity, whereas the 'essence,' the illumining factor, is the 'dweller within', the living Universal Spirit.

The Gita expounds that He is the *Sarva Boothastamaatnaam Sarva Bhootaanichatmani,* and Vyasa believed Him to be *Krishnasya charaacharam*, both denoting the universal presence of Krishna in the living and otherwise.

While explaining his General Theory of Relativity, Einstein said, 'The most beautiful and most profound emotion we can experience is the sensation of the mystical...to know that what is impenetrable to us really exists, manifesting itself as the highest wisdom, and most radiant beauty which our dull faculties can comprehend only in the most primitive form. This knowledge, this feeling, is at the centre of the religiousness.' Krishna fits into this concept. Knowing that emotive receptivity is stronger than the intellectual, Krishna says *yo yo yam tanum tanum bhaktah*—whichever form that one desires to be in communion with him, he shall be that. Krishna stood for the perpetual principle of the righteousness, the immutable cosmic law, Dharma Rita. In his entire life, he strived to establish dharma, which can connote different things to people.

The authors have relied heavily upon Vyasa's Srimad Bhagavatam, Mahabharata, Harivamsa Purana, Vishnu Purana, Kulapathi and KM Munshi's *Krishnavatara*. Krishna's birth and childhood is beautifully portrayed in the Bhagavatam. He is introduced to the world at Draupadi's *swayamvara* in the Mahabharata.

While the Pandavas recognised and acknowledged Krishna's divinity and accepted him as a friend, advisor, intellectual guide and the mastermind behind all their actions, the Kauravas neither recognised nor respected Krishna's divinity. At best, they accepted him as the leader of a clan, a universally acknowledged statesman, who could be a powerful ally or a dangerous adversary.

When Vyasa recorded the events in *Jaya,* in prosaic and traditional bardic form, narrating the Kuru family legacies, Gandhari's righteousness, the Pandavas' truthfulness and Kauravas' misdeeds, he transformed the tale to bring out Krishna's greatness and divinity, as the ancient seer Narayana born again. He had no pretensions about characters—the Pandavas were never accepted as the quintessence of virtue nor were the Kauravas shown as an embodiment of evil. Both were portrayed as conscious of the principles of righteousness, though the Pandavas were more upright and divinely ordained. On the other hand, the Kauravas were rarely righteous, influenced often by basic instincts and desires, and reeling under the impact of dark and obscure forces.

Krishna was born from the Divine Consciousness and established himself in *prakriti,* the human form, with all the imperfections of *purusha* or humans rather than the Brahmana, the Supreme Being and the ultimate reality.

Vyasa's principle disciple Vaisampayana's austere and noble imagination transformed Krishna's personality into a striking divine status associated with the Vedic Vishnu. Krishna then ceased to be a historical figure and emerged more as a Divine Consciousness.

This book treats the life of Krishna as divine babe and enchanter; extraordinary man; consummate statesman and nation builder; warrior and teacher of divine wisdom; philosopher and mystic. Krishna's uniqueness lies in being beyond man's empirical understanding and reaching to great spiritual heights, while retaining his 'form' as the undisputed icon of a wondrously graceful personality.

He has been the subject matter of legends and literature, political and theosophical dissertations, controversies and conflicts. His image has changed over time in the minds of believers and sceptics, poets and artistes, reflecting the tenor of each age and time and so, it is difficult to separate the historical from the mythical Krishna.

THE MAN THAT WAS LORD KRISHNA

Whether Krishna Vaasudeva was human or God-incarnate, there is no denying the fact that he has been ruling the hearts of millions for over three millennia. When an individual can have such a profound impact on a vast group of people, affecting their psyche and ethos for centuries, He has to be the Supreme Being. What else is the concept of God? After all, it is man that perceived God—a timeless concept. Hindu scriptures declare that Krishna is an avatar, God in human form, who came among mortals to save mankind and its society from the morass it had created for itself. Vyasa says in the Bhagavata Purana, '*Krishnastu Bhagvan Swayam*'—Krishna, you are God Himself, though this does not connote that God has a gender!

An incarnation is not a product of history, but someone who creates and shapes history. The primary purpose of an avatar, as Krishna himself stated in the Bhagavad Gita, is to establish dharma or righteousness.

This means protecting and strengthening the hands of the people who defend dharma and, if need be, by subduing and eliminating the evil ones bent on destroying it. That is the reason Krishna chose Yudhisthira as Dharmaputra, or the one who will uphold dharma. Though extremely virtuous and steadfast, he was indecisive, fatalistic and fond of gambling with dice. But Krishna was certain that only he could establish an order based on righteousness and justice.

Krishna strived throughout his life to achieve that goal, never deviating from his just and benevolent nature. A study of Krishna's character and personality keeping these traits in mind will not only be worthy of him and the values he stood for, but also inspire mankind.

Krishna's sole concern as an avatar was dharma: To uphold and protect it, to reassert its supremacy and to unravel its mystery, whenever it became inscrutable. Unless it lives in our minds and is expressed through our actions, dharma becomes just an ethereal concept. Krishna was concerned about our society, especially the weaker sections of the community. Caring tenderly for the cowherds of Vrindavan, curing Kubja and Vainateya of their handicaps, coming to the rescue of Draupadi when her honour was at stake in the Kuru court, and lavish bestowal of wealth on Sudama who never asked for it—these illustrate Krishna's concern for the distressed, who had intense faith in him.

Krishna, though possessing a heart softer than a flower—*karunya sindho Krishna*—could exercise a decisive will and great valour when required, especially in defence of dharma and *dharmic* people. In fact, in his time, Krishna was the strongest in personal combat and the greatest warrior and charioteer in Aryawartha. He was adept at martial arts and *vyuha*—battle strategy and statecraft, but at the same time he never misused his immense strength and power for selfish pursuits. He was a master statesman who advocated peace, but not at the expense of dharma.

Krishna was said to be a child prodigy with an outstanding intellect, great understanding and *yeka samtagrah*—phenomenal memory. His scholarship of Vedic lore and the secular sciences and arts was renowned. His philosophic expositions in the form of the Bhagavad Gita, Anu Gita and Uddhava Gita validate his superior intellect.

Krishna had an intuitive insight that helped him override intriguing situations, solving them in the interest of the common good. His intuitiveness was evident in his mission to Hastinapura as a peace emissary, his attempt to win over Karna to the side of the Pandavas and his apparently questionable strategies during the Kurukshetra war.

Intelligence and learning often make a man arrogant and egoistic. But Krishna was an embodiment of humility—unruffled, pleasing and bewitchingly charming, with his trademark smile. When Krishna met Kamsa as a boy of fourteen years, he approached the king with a smile, hands on his hips and said, 'Hello Uncle, I have come.' Kamsa could not believe that this charming lad was destined to slay him. The Mahabharata reveals that Krishna wore the same smile when Bhima killed Jarasandha.

Krishna lived by the doctrine he preached, unaffected by material wealth. He even returned the throne of Mathura to Ugrasena and crowned Sahadeva as the crown prince of Magadh after Jarasandha's killing. Even in the face of grave provocation, Krishna remained calm and nonchalant, sporting just a deceptive smile.

He was God-incarnate, the universal teacher, a philosopher par excellence, a repository of yogic powers and a mystic. In the Mahabharata, Vyasa calls Him *Maha Yogeswaro Hari*—Great Yogi Hari, the all-pervading Spirit, Vishnu.

The Bhagavata Purana narrates several incidents wherein Krishna displayed his yogic powers. He was the sole master of the eight prime siddhis that no avatar possessed before him (Bhagavata, Chapter XI and XII). He granted the vision of Vishnu to Akrura, the Yadava emissary of Kamsa who came to Vrindavan; stunned the royalty in the Kuru court at Hastinapura with a brilliant flash of light that made Dushassana and others faint and finally, revealed His cosmic form to Arjuna at the battlefield of Kurukshetra.

A three-year-old Krishna overwhelmed his mother, Yashoda, with his divine prowess when he opened his mouth. The Bhagavata Purana says, 'Yashoda, for a flash of a moment, witnessed *bhuvana bhandas*—the Fourteen Universes, a cosmic phenomenon, which none else had seen and was only described by Vyasa.'

Mysticism and activism rarely go together, but Krishna dwells in them. Krishna means Chaitanya—eternally active. His life was a 'continuum of dynamic activity' and his actions were selfless. Perhaps, this singular quality has made his personality unique and immortal. The Mahabharata says, *Krishnaya klista karmane*—unceasing action was Krishna Vaasudeva.

Krishna, as a rule, respected tradition and old customs, but did not make a fetish of them. If, in his judgement, any such custom needed to be altered or even given up or replaced with another, he never hesitated to do so. He stopped the worship of Lord Indra, an archaic Vedic ritual, practised by the cowherds of Vrindavan and instead promoted the worship of Nature and cows, which were the backbone of their agrarian society. He willingly became Arjuna's charioteer, a job usually meant for the ordinary.

Krishna responded to every human emotion appropriately, ensuring that people felt comfortable with him. An ecstatic mystic sang, *manasa sancharare Brahmani manasa sancharare*, claiming that the hallmark of a born leader is that he lives in the hearts of the people devoted to him. Being the enchanter that he was, everyone was drawn towards Krishna. The learned rishis were elated to meet him; Vyasa, therefore, addressed him as Purushottama, the best among humans. His charisma was overpowering and perhaps, that is why, in his time, Krishna was referred to as the all-knowing, omniscient.

Though the fountainhead, he was never imposing, dejected or desolate. He viewed life as a panorama, filled with dance and love. Unlike many eminent personalities before him who preferred to watch from the periphery, Krishna plunged into life and participated in it like it were a festival.

As his time drew to an end and he lay wounded by the hunter Jara's arrow, Krishna showed compassion to Jara, insisting that the hunter had only done his duty. Jara was, however, grief-stricken when he realised his prey was none other than Krishna. When he tried to remove the arrow from Krishna's bleeding foot, a feeble voice in excruciating pain stopped him, 'Let it be, my friend. I was waiting for you. What took you so long? You have lived by your karma, and so, you will go to heaven.' Krishna folded his hands and shut his eyes, his face suffused with pain. He seemed ready for his exit and the phenomenon that was Krishna was gone, only to live on in our hearts.

Principal Characters

Krishna: The God-incarnate.
Balarama: His older brother.
Subhadra: His younger sister; Arjuna's wife.
Vasudeva: His father.
Devaki: His mother.
Yashoda: His foster mother.
Nanda: His foster father, a cowherd.
Radha: His favourite *gopi* in Vrindavan.
Gargacharya (Sage Garga): His family preceptor and High Priest of the Yadavas.
Acharya Sandipani: His teacher, with his ashram at Avanti.
Shvetaketu: His tutor, Sandipani's, principal disciple.
Kamsa (Bhojaraja): His maternal uncle, and Ugrasena's son; also king of the Bhoja clan.
Trivikraa (Kubja): His devoted maidservant.
Satyabhama (Satyaa): Daughter of Satrajit, and Krishna's wife.
Jambavati: The girl rescued from the Bear world and Krishna's wife.
Daruka: His charioteer. Krishna's chariot was called Nandi Ghosha, driven by four horses: Saibhya, Sugriva, Megha Pushpa and Blaahaka.
Vainateya: His Garuda bodyguard and standard bearer.

HIS WEAPONS:

Sudarshana Chakra: Discus.

Kaumudaki: Mace.

Saranga: Bow.

Panchajanya: Conch that evokes a primordial sound and whose music hangs in the air eternally.

HIS ALLIES:

Vinda and Anuvinda: The twin princes of Avanti (Ujjain).

Chekitana: A Yadava chief, ruler of Pushkar.

HIS FOES:

Shalva: Ruler of Saubha

Shishupala: Son of Damaghosha.

Dantavaktra: Ruler of Karusha.

YADAVAS:

Ugrasena: Head of the Andhaka clan and king of Yadavas.

Akrura: The saintly chief of the Vrishni clan of Yadavas.

Devabhaga: Vasudeva's younger brother.

Kamsa: Devabhaga's wife and Ugrasena's daughter.

Brihadbala: Devabhaga's second son.

Uddhava: Devabhaga's third born and Krishna's intimate friend.

Damaghosha (Chedi Raj): King of Chedi.

Shrutashrava: Damaghosha's queen and sister of Vasudeva.

Satrajit: An elderly Yadava chief.

Kritavarma: Krishna's friend, a Yadava Atiratha (captain of chariot force).

Yuyudhana Satyaki: A young Yadava chief, Krishna's aide.

Jarasandha (Magadha Naresh): Emperor of Magadha, Kamsa's father-in-law.

OTHER PRINCIPAL CHARACTERS:

Shrigalava Vasudeva: King of Karavirapura, who was killed by Sri Krishna in a fight.

Saibhya: Shrigalava Vasudeva's niece.

Bhishmaka: Bhoja king of Vidarbha.

Kaishika: Father of Bhishmaka.

Rukmi: Son of Bhishmaka

Rukmini (Vaidarbhi): Bhishmaka's daughter and Krishna's principal wife.
Bhishma (Gangeya): Eldest son of Kuru emperor, Shantanu.
Satyavati: Stepmother of Bhishma and dowager empress of Hastinapura.
Krishna Dwaipayana: Great grandson of the Vedic rishi, Vasishta; son of Parashara and Satyavati; generally known as Veda Vyasa.
Dhaumya: One of the disciples of Vyasa and the preceptor of the Pandavas.
Narada: A celestial bard, great musician and evangelist of Krishna's philosophy—a scion of the Gandharva tribe in the Himalayas.

PANDAVAS

Pandu: Son of Princess Ambalika by Krishna Dwaipayana Vyasa; king of Hastinapura.
Kunti: Pandu's wife, sister of Vasudeva, Krishna's father.
Yudhisthira (Dharmaraja, Dharmaputra): Pandu's son by Kunti.
Bhima: Pandu's second son by Kunti.
Arjuna (Partha, Kuntiputra, Falguna): Pandu's third son by Kunti.
Madri: Pandu's second wife.
Nakula and Sahadeva: Pandu's twin sons by Madri.
Draupadi (Krishnaa, Yajnaseni, Panchali): Daughter of Drupad Yajnasena and wife of the Pandava brothers.
Karna: Eldest son of Kunti by the Sun God, born when she was still a maiden; Duryodhana's bosom friend and king of Anga Desa.

KURUS:

Dhritarashtra: Blind son of Princess Ambika, begotten by Krishna Dwaipayana Vyasa; father of the Kauravas.
Gandhari: Dhritarashtra's wife.
Shakuni: Dhritarashtra's brother-in-law.
Duryodhana (Suyodhana): Dhritarashtra's eldest son.
Dushassana: One of Dhritarashtra's sons.

OTHERS IN KURU CAMP:

Dronacharya (Drona): A pupil of Parashurama and the teacher of the Pandavas and Kurus.
Aswathama: Dronacharya's son.
Kripacharya: Dronacharya's brother-in-law and also a teacher to the princes.

Vidura: Son of a maidservant, begotten by Krishna Dwaipayana Vyasa; the Principle Minister at the Kuru court.
Drupad Yajnasena (Panchala Naresh): King of Panchalas with his capital at Kampilya.
Drishtadyumna and Satyajit: Drupad's sons.
Virata: King of Matsyadesa.
Uttara: Virata's daughter and wife of Abhimanyu.

DESCENDANTS OF KRISHNA:

Pradyumna: Son of Krishna by Rukmini.
Samba: Son of Krishna by Jambavati.
Aniruddha: Son of Pradyumna.
Vajranabh: Son of Aniruddha.

DESCENDANTS OF PANDAVAS:

Abhimanyu: Son of Arjuna by Subhadra.
Parikshit: Son of Abhimanyu and Uttara.
Janamajaya: Son of Parikshit, the last king of Hastinapura.

Nearly five thousand years ago, the Supreme Being Himself was born in the form of Krishna. He was the embodiment of dharma and fought for a just society, throughout his life. An event such as this was never to occur again: *Na bhooto na bhavishyati*—neither in the past nor in the future.

Kaalah pibati tadrisam—Time, without exception, empties everything of its essence. Today's memorable event is forgotten tomorrow. However great the event may be, with the passage of time, it is forgotten and buried in history. But the life of Krishna is so timeless and eternal, that Time has not been able to destroy its essence and relevance even today. In fact, the past decades have witnessed a surge in the popularity of Krishna and His consciousness across the globe, especially in the materialistic West.

The Divine Power that is formless and indefinable, assumed a human form as Krishna. For thousands of years, people have been singing and chanting how gloriously Krishna led his life, as though it all happened just yesterday.

Krishna's story is popular not just among the common folk. Ancient saints and sages too sang his glory with fervour. Krishna is also known as Yaduveera, warrior of the Yadus. The Yadavas looked upon him as God and experts in statecraft acknowledged him as a great statesman. His contemporary and confidant, Rishi Narada says in the Bhagavatam:

Gopyah, Kamat bhayat Kumso dveshachaidhadaugo nrpate
Sambhandat Vrishnayah, sucto yuyam bhavatya vayam, vibho

(Looked at from any angle, the life of Lord Krishna confers benefits on us.)

One should not read the lives of great men with blind faith. Even Krishna ends his sermon to Arjuna on the battlefield of Mahabharata saying, '*Vimrsyaitadasesena yathechasi tatha kuru*' (Gita 18.63)

(Arjuna, I have told you what I believe to be true, but in this matter you think for yourself and decide what you want to do.)

The presented story is just one of the many interpretations of his life. It is up to you to take from it what you will and incorporate it in your life, so that you too can follow the path of dharma.

EPISODE 1

KRISHNA'S BIRTH AND CHILDHOOD

Anandarupa! Bhagnavannayi te avataare
Prapte pradiptabhavadanganiliya maanai
Kanti vrajairiva ghanaaghana mandalyrdya
Maavrunvati viruruche kila varsha velaa velaa

O Lord! Thou bliss personified! As thy incarnation approached, the rainy season enveloping the skies with masses of clouds, is said to have transformed as if from the light emitting forth from the limbs of thy brilliant self.

THE REPUBLIC OF YADAVAS

The state of Yadavas was a republic ruled by the people themselves; Babhru (Shoorasena) and Ugrasena were its leaders. In a dialogue between Rishi Narada and Krishna, Narada points out that although a republic is the best form of government, it could, however, disintegrate under extenuating circumstances like internal dissensions.

Ancient scriptures advise that our passions should be ruled by noble thoughts and all powers which are exercised without compromising ethics or religion are broadly denoted by dharma. At the time of Krishna's birth, the republican states were demoralised. They functioned neither for the welfare of the citizens nor were they guided by religion. 'Might is right' was the rule of the day. This gave rise to kingdoms where kings resorted to aggressive imperialism and threatened the very existence of democratic republics.

Jarasandha, the Emperor of Magadha, was the leader of such an imperialist state. He had defeated eighty-six republican rulers, annexing their territories and imprisoning the vanquished kings. He was a great intellectual and an extraordinary ruler. He was also the sworn enemy of the republican state in which Krishna was born.

Ignoring the pitfalls of his imperial policy, Jarasandha strived to bring fourteen more kingdoms under Magadha. After winning these battles and capturing 100 kings, he wanted to hold a Naramedha Yagna—human sacrifice as a part of a Rudra Yagna—a Tantric ritual to attain invincibility, if not immortality.

Jarasandha was a powerful monarch, great wrestler and merciless tyrant. He maintained a huge army with several war elephants. But, he was also a shrewd diplomat. He maintained very cordial ties with the neighbouring kingdom of Chedi. The Chedi king, Damaghosha, as well as his son, Shishupala, were his close allies. So were Shalva, the king of Saubha, which lay near the Sindhu river; and the Mlechha, Kalayavana, who was a barbarian and ruled over the western desert. At the time of Krishna's birth, Jarasandha's imperialism had emerged triumphant and he sought to consolidate his empire.

Jarasandha proclaimed that he was absolute and his aim in life was to show that the principles of dharma held no ground before his might and intelligence. Emboldened by his allies, Jarasandha proclaimed that the only principle that worked was to snatch what belonged to others and become richer. He stated that the concept of justice and injustice existed solely for ordinary people, not emperors.

People, too, began to consider wealth and material power as everything in life. Coupled with the downfall of brahmanas, who were the learned class, it resulted in the very backbone of society breaking. The entire Aryawartha and land of Bharata was in a state of chaos and became morally decadent. Krishna revealed to Arjuna in the Gita that He had to take birth amidst humanity in order to steer the world back on to the true path of dharma.

Yada Yada hi dharmasya glanirbhavati bharata
Abhyudhanamadharmasya, tadatmanam srijamyaham

(I will be born again and again; every time evil grips this world
I will come to restore dharma).

The advent of Sri Krishna had immediate precedents, which are incorporated in the ancient texts.

Sri Krishna was born to Devaki and Vasudeva. But he grew up in the house of Nanda at Gokul; spending most of his childhood there. He later went to Mathura, killed Kamsa, the ruthless son of Ugrasena and thereafter, revealed his Yadava identity. Until he killed Kamsa, Krishna was known as Nandagopatanaya, the son of Yashoda and Nanda.

The Yadavas were believers in a republican form of government called Gana

Sanghas or the people's democracy. There is a story in the Puranas narrating how Yayati had asked his son, Yadu, to gift him his youth in exchange for old age. When Yadu refused, Yayati cursed him, saying that no progeny of Yadu will ever become king. Most people believe that it is due to this curse that there has been no monarch from the Yadu clan since then.

However, research reveals that in those days new experiments were being tried in statecraft. The Puru dynasty ruled as monarchs, whereas the Yadavas believed in a republican form of government. At a later stage in Krishna's life, Shishupala, who was an ally of Jarasandha and Kamsa, stopped Krishna from performing the Agrapuja at the conclusion of Yudhisthira's Rajasuya yagna because the Yadavas were not monarchs. Although elected by the majority, a president in the republican government enjoyed as much power as the king, whose rule was hereditary.

The Yadavas had a republican form of government and Krishna was never a king, but a *Sangha Pramukha*—present-day CEO—of the republic. This post did not confine him to side with any one family branch. Kautilya, in his *Artha Shastra,* referred to the Yadava institutions as Vrishni Sangha.

The republic of Yadavas consisted of two groups: Vrishnis and Andhaka. The Andhaka group was based in the area around Mathura. Ugrasena was the president of the republic and was often referred to as king. Similarly, in the Vrishni republic, the leader was Akrura. Vasudeva, Krishna's father, belonged to the Vrishni group. Both these republics had a great deal to fear from the aggressive imperialism of Jarasandha, whose power was spreading rapidly. Jarasandha aimed to include as many territories as possible under his hegemony.

He was a constant threat to the republics, for they lacked the strength to resist his imperial power. Realising that mutual cooperation could help the two Yadava republics fend off an impending attack, Ugrasena gave his daughter, Sutanu, in marriage to Akrura. He also gave Devaki, his cousin Devak's daughter, to Vasudeva. They held a common assembly, and Ugrasena and Akrura presided jointly to administer the republics.

Wary of these republics putting up a united front, Jarasandha, too, built a strategic relationship by marrying off his two daughters, Asti and Prapti, to Kamsa, the son of Ugrasena. Kamsa was dictatorial and ambitious by nature and soon turned into Jarasandha's close ally in establishing an autocratic form of government.

The support of Jarasandha increased Kamsa's thirst for absolute power. He tried to destroy the republic and convert it into a police state, with spies and mercenaries. Jarasandha fully exploited Kamsa and used him to divide the Yadava republics. This unleashed a reign of terror. Kamsa arrested Ugrasena, usurped power and declared himself king.

Akrura and Vasudeva were both men of mettle. Related to Kamsa by marriage, Akrura had to reluctantly accept him. Vasudeva, on the other hand, firmly opposed Kamsa's tyrannical rule. Kamsa, therefore, strongly disliked him.

Vasudeva was the shining example of a person devoted to dharma. He was unselfish and principled, willing to sacrifice his life than deviate from the path of justice. Vasudeva was dedicated to the welfare of his people and much loved.

Though equally dedicated to righteous living, Akrura was not so selfless. He too set out to safeguard his republic from Kamsa, but could not resist the lure of power. Akrura had his worldly weaknesses. As the story unfolds, we will see that he even doubted the divinity of Krishna, till the time he received Krishna's grace.

Such were the times when Krishna was born. The brahmanas had been subjugated and the social climate had deteriorated. It was an indulgent, amoral society that had sunk into a deep pool of despair and decay.

In this society, Krishna was born to Devaki: It was midnight and the Abhijit constellation was in the sky.

KRISHNA KATHA, THE TRADITIONAL NARRATIVE

Harivamsa, the adjunct to the Mahabharata, treats Krishna as a historical figure who was a complete statesman, diplomat and nation builder, whereas the Bhagavatam espouses the divinity that is Krishna Vaasudeva, the dweller in the hearts of his devotees—the all-pervading Vishnu incarnate.

KAMSA, THE RULER OF MATHURA WHEN KRISHNA WAS BORN

Ugrasena, the Yadava chieftain and also king of the Bhojas of Mathura, was a pious devotee of Vishnu and a follower of *Sanatana Dharma*. He was a just ruler, patron of sages and Vedic learning. Ugrasena had a beautiful wife named Pavanarekha who gave birth to two sons, Kamsa and Mahanaman. Of the two, Kamsa, the crown prince, did not imbibe any noble quality from his father. He was unpredictable, cruel and overambitious.

King Ugrasena was aware of his son's ambition and evil intentions, but could not rein him in. In order to safeguard his kingdom, Ugrasena married Kamsa to Jarasandha's twin daughters. Kamsa was averse to Vishnu worship. The Vishnu Purana says that Kalanemi, who hated Vishnu, was reborn as Kamsa. Backed by his troops, Kamsa began oppressing the followers of Vishnu and Vedic culture. He obstructed Vedic ceremonies and recitations, polluted sacrificial altars and compelled the devotees of Vishnu to follow Jarasandha and him in worshipping only Shiva as Rudra.

The pious bhaktas complained to Ugrasena about the atrocities of his son. When Ugrasena chastised him, Kamsa, on the advice of Jarasandha, deposed his father and seized the throne for himself after imprisoning him.

After assuming kingship, Kamsa's atrocities increased manyfold. His terror machine included evil entities such as Mahanemi, Pancha Jana, Bana Sambara, Valkala, Dantavaktra and Putana. He ordered all the Yadava chiefs to implicitly obey him. Those who were meek readily submitted to him. Others migrated to neighbouring kingdoms, fearing assassination. The diplomatic Akrura toed the line of Kamsa, but not Vasudeva. Kamsa needed the political backing of both his cousins, but failed to win the loyalty of Vasudeva.

One day, in a show of arrogance, the sadistic Kamsa forced the great sage Madhuka to drag his chariot. The sage warned Kamsa, 'Mend your ways, O king, for the sake of God who created you, for Truth which will prevail in the end, else you will have to reap the painful consequences. The wage of sin is death.'

Intoxicated with power, the conceited Kamsa merely laughed and replied, 'Don't talk to me of God and Truth. This universe is without God or Truth. Men are born by the union of sexes, promoted by naught but lust. What have I to fear? Who is equal to me in this entire world? I am strong, I enjoy as I like, and I give largely to my friends and dependents. I sacrifice to the great Mahadeva as Rudra and the gods. I have slain or conquered all my enemies so far. I shall slay or conquer my enemies who may turn up hereafter. Who will be able to fight or kill me?'

'Vishnu,' said Madhuka. 'He came as Narayana, white as milk in the Krita Age; he came as Trivikrama, yellow as gold; and as Rama, blue as sapphire in the Treta Age. He will come as Krishna, black as collyrium in this Dwapara Age and finish you off. You are an incarnation of evil, you demon.'

Gritting his teeth, the enraged Kamsa then whipped the gentle sage and ran him over with his chariot. After this incident though, an unknown fear gripped Kamsa's heart. Conscious of his guilt, he grew increasingly paranoid of meeting his end at the hands of Vishnu, the all-pervading God.

THE ADVENT OF KRISHNA

As per the Srimad Bhagavatam: The events on Earth have their origin in Heaven. When the demons were defeated in the battle and thrown out of Heaven, they retreated in a body and sought refuge on Earth. In course of time, they multiplied enormously, captured power and began to oppress the virtuous in various ways. Their oppression became verily intolerable. And Kamsa was the epitome of this tyranny.

Mother Earth, in the form of a cow, with tears rolling down her cheeks, then implored Brahma the Creator, to put an end to Kamsa's oppression. Brahma took the cow to Lord Narayana—Sri Maha Vishnu, the Sustainer, who was in a cosmic Yoga Nidra on a sea of milk. Brahma addressed the lord, 'You promised to descend to the world from age to age to save the virtuous, to destroy the wicked and to uphold dharma. Pray do so now. Kamsa's atrocities cannot be stopped by a mere man. He is another Ravana in might and can only be defeated by an avatar.'

Narayana plucked two locks of hair from his head, one black and the other white and said, 'These will go out into the world, the white hair as Balarama the fair, the black hair as Krishna, and shall be born as sons to my noble devotees. These divinities, along with many of my devotees, will be born as contemporaries to establish dharma.'

Back on Earth, the events proceeded to fulfil the lord's prophecy. As Vasudeva and Devaki's wedding celebrations ended, Vasudeva prepared to take his bride home. A large dowry of men and gifts accompanied the royal bride, and displaying great affection for his sister, Kamsa himself charioteered the couple. On the way, Kamsa suddenly recalled Rishi Madhuka's curse, and in his mind's eye, the chariot's horses turned into Madhuka. The sage had perished under the wheels of Kamsa's chariot. Burdened by guilt, Kamsa panicked as he heard the sage cry out, 'You fool, this woman whom you are taking to her husband's place is going to be the cause of your death. The eighth child born to her will kill you.'

In a flash, Kamsa jumped down from the chariot, caught his sister by her braided hair and drawing his sword to behead her, screamed, 'Devaki!

Since you will be the cause of my death, I will slay you right here.' Vasudeva ran towards Kamsa, gripped the upraised arm brandishing the sword and tried to pacify him. 'Kamsa, you are the scion of a reputed house, the house of Shurasena, and you are a noble-minded prince. Would you kill your own sister and earn eternal disgrace for killing a woman?' But Kamsa remained unmoved.

In order to avert a tragedy, Vasudeva then promised Kamsa that whenever a child is born to him, he would himself hand over the baby to Kamsa. Vasudeva also reminded Kamsa that he was at peril only from the eighth child of Devaki and there being no immediate danger, he should let Devaki live. The tyrant Kamsa relented and lowered his sword, saying, 'So be it.'

In due course, a son was born to the couple and Vasudeva named him Kirtiman. Though distressed, he carried the newborn to Kamsa as promised. Vasudeva was a man blessed with equanimity and wisdom and it was possible for him to take the child to the cruel Kamsa saying, 'Here is my child. I promised to deliver him to you as soon as he was born.' Impressed by this noble gesture, a smiling Kamsa returned the child to Vasudeva saying, 'Please take this child back with you. I am not going to kill it. After all I have been told that it is your eighth child, which will bring death to me. This is your firstborn. I have no fear from him.'

Vasudeva went back with the child in his arms, unsure of Kamsa's split personality. It so happened that Kamsa did not touch the next five sons of Devaki. But he remained mortally afraid of Vasudeva's progeny. Exploiting this paranoia, Kamsa's counsellors provoked him that any of the sons of Vasudeva might pose a danger, and it would be best to eliminate them all. They also reminded Kamsa of his previous birth, when he was the asura Kalanemi, who was eventually slayed by Narayana. In a moment of rage and extreme fear of death, Kamsa rushed to Vasudeva's house and mercilessly killed all the six children of Devaki. Vasudeva and Devaki were then sent to the dungeons and chained to prevent them from escaping.

Devaki was about to deliver her seventh child. With some divine intervention, Adisesha, an esoteric name for Time and one of Vishnu's aspects, entered her womb to bring joy to the mother who bore him. Kamsa's cup of sins had at last become full, so God descended on this world to bring an end to *adharma*. Narayana commanded his alter ego, Yoga Maya, to transfer the six-month-old foetus from Devaki's womb to that of Rohini, Vasudeva's other wife. Rohini lived safely in Gokul, away from the cruel world of Kamsa.

Rohini delivered a fair-complexioned, healthy baby boy who was brought up by Nanda and his wife Yashoda. Nanda was a cowherd chief from Vrajabhoomi across Yamuna. Kamsa was told that Devaki had aborted the child. On hearing this, Kamsa laughed hysterically, believing that Devaki had aborted her child out of fright. He now waited for the eighth child to be born.

THE BIRTH OF KRISHNA

Lord Vishnu entered the mind of Vasudeva, bestowing on his face, a divine glow. Devaki was about to give birth to the Lord of Lords and, thus, looked as radiant as the full moon in Sharad Ritu.

On a visit to the prison, Kamsa noticed the divine glow on his sister's face. Despite her terrible sorrow, she smiled at Kamsa. Haunted by guilt, Kamsa said to himself, 'Devaki has never looked like this before. It seems to me that the strange glow is because of the child that is to be born. I think it is Narayana who will be born. I must take proper precautions lest I meet my end. I could kill her now, but it is a terrible sin to kill a woman who is also my sister, and that too while she is carrying a child. For such a heinous crime, the world will condemn me forever. All my fame and wealth and power will then suffer an irreparable damage.' Absorbed in his self-introspection, Kamsa resembled a walking corpse. Growing fearful, he began hallucinating about the unborn child.

The auspicious time for the lord's birth had come. It had the charm of all the six seasons. The planets and stars were on the ascendant and the four quarters were clear and placid. Rohini, the star governed by Prajapati, was in the ascendant, as the clouds rumbled in the sky and the ocean roared below. It was midnight and the *muhurata* was Abhijit when Narayana, the Supreme Lord Himself, was born to Devaki.

Vasudeva looked at the newborn and was amazed. It was not an ordinary child. He couldn't help staring at the newcomer's lotus eyes and the four arms beholding the *shankha*, *chakra*, *gada* and *padma*—Narayana had appeared in His true form. Vasudeva gazed in wonder at Srivatsa, the auspicious mark adorning the chest of the new arrival. The baby was draped in yellow silk and the Kaustabh jewel gleamed around his neck. Dark as a rain cloud, the little marvel lit up the entire place with the splendour of his crown. His earrings were shaped like fish, with the glory that was He. Vasudeva stood transfixed by this extraordinary form.

As a kshatriya, Vasudeva was expected to perform certain rites to mark his respect for the lord, but being a prisoner he was restricted. He, therefore, placed the child on the ground and with folded palms and head bowed in humble worship, chanted a prayer to the Parama Purusha.

> Oh Lord of the Lords, in Your infinite kindness to the Earth and to poor Vasudeva and Devaki, You have assumed the form of a human being. How can I describe, the thrill of being the father of this divine baby? It makes me speechless and nervous. I am no longer a miserable prisoner. I am the most fortunate among men and my wife is the mother of the Lord Himself. Great is Your mercy towards us.

Devaki too came out of her stupor and prayed:

> You are the sole destroyer of all evil. Please have pity on Mother Earth and put an end to the tyranny of Kamsa and please let not Kamsa see You in this form because, to see Your True Form, yogis spend endless time in penance. It is not meant for ordinary eyes to dwell on Your Divine Form. Your birth has made me sad, because unlike other mothers, I cannot keep You for myself. Kamsa has killed my children. Having been informed of Your arrival, the killer must be rushing to this place. Lord, Kamsa does not deserve to see You in this form.

The lord then replied:

> Devaki, you are the purest among women. In your previous birth, you were born in the line of Swayambhu Manu, and your name was Prishni. Vasudeva was known as Sutapa. Both of you were great yogis who did great penance for my darshan and when I granted this grace, instead of asking me for moskha, you sought a boon that I be born as a son to you. Now that I am born as a son to you both, hereafter you may attain my loka and moksha.

Having said this, even as the two looked on, the lord changed His divine form into that of an ordinary child. The lord had instructed Vasudeva to take the newborn to Nanda's house in Gokul and return with the child of Yashoda. But Vasudeva and Devaki wondered how they would complete this feat in their imprisoned state.

This was the hour of change in the duty of the prison guards. As it was raining heavily, the night guards couldn't make it to work. The guards, on duty since early morning, were, by now, tired and sleepy. They were also very reluctant to inform Kamsa about the birth of the baby boy. Like most of the people in Mathura, the guards too were tired of Kamsa's killings and had no heart to witness the gruesome murder of another innocent child.

Vasudeva was amazed to see his shackles unclasp on their own. As he placed his child in a small wicker-basket and covered him with his upper cloth, the locked prison gates slid open. To Vasudeva's surprise, he found all the guards fast asleep. Walking out unhindered with the baby, Vasudeva soon reached the banks of the Yamuna. The river was flooded and the sky was dark. Having faith in Narayana, Vasudeva began wading through the waters, but felt the rush of the waterflow suddenly recede as if he had reached a high ground. In his anxiety to reach his destination safely and in time, Vasudeva did not even notice that the serpent, Adisesha, had spread out its hood to guard the child from the torrential rains.

When Vasudeva reached Gokul, he found everyone asleep in Nanda's house. Yashoda lay in a swoon in the hall, her baby girl by her side. Quickly placing baby Krishna beside the unconscious Yashoda, Vasudeva rushed back to the prison with the girl child instead. She was none other than Yoga Maya. Right after he re-entered the prison cell, the gates closed on their own. Vasudeva clasped back the iron shackles on his ankles and hands and awaited the arrival of Kamsa.

The cries of the newborn now roused the guards. Awakening from their stupor, they finally decided to inform Kamsa about the birth. Though initially reluctant, they feared his wrath and realised this was, after all, a call of duty.

Kamsa was lying on his bed. Sleep had deserted him long ago; every night he lay awake, knowing that the child who was coming, would be his nemesis. The moment Kamsa heard his guards announce the birth, he snatched his sword and rushed to the prison, his hair flapping threateningly around him.

Alarmed by his menacing approach and terrible appearance, Devaki fell at his feet:

> My dear brother, please do not kill this child. Spare her because it is a girl who has been born to me. Every one of my sons I gave to you and you killed them. But this is a girl, and what can a poor girl do? I am sure she is incapable of fulfilling the prophecy, which has frightened you. Spare her. Killing a woman is a terrible sin. Do not commit that folly. I was once dear to you. In the name of that love, I plead you; please leave this one child to me.

Imploring thus, Devaki held the child to her bosom as tears welled in her eyes.

Kamsa was like a man possessed and the fear of death had made a beast of him. Rudely, he snatched the child from his sister's frail hands. Grasping her tender legs, he tried to smash the child against a protruding stone on a pillar in the dungeon.

But the child slipped from his grip and flew into the sky. Stunned by what had happened, everyone looked upward and were amazed to see Devi in Her divine form, high up in the sky. She held weapons of destruction in her eight hands—a bow, trident, arrows, sword, discus and mace. She was also holding a conch in one of her hands; her neck was adorned with a garland of bright flowers, jewels gleamed around her neck, arms and feet. Siddhas, Charanas, Gandharvas, Apsaras, Kinnaras and other celestial beings were all present, worshipping her.

Kamsa was shaken out of his wits when this celestial being laughed aloud and said to him, 'What avails you, Kamsa, to have hauled me to the ground? He is born who shall kill you, the mighty one amongst the gods who was formerly your destroyer. Now quickly secure him and provide for your own welfare.' Thus having spoken, the goddess vanished before the eyes of Bhojaraja.

These events happened in such quick succession that Kamsa grew more panicky. He was also suddenly ashamed of himself for taking out his spite on Vasudeva and Devaki. Scared of divine retribution, Kamsa then himself removed the handcuffs and chains that had bound his sister and Vasudeva's hands and feet like common criminals for many long years. Filled with regret, Kamsa folded his hands and addressed both of them:

> Oh! My dear sister, my dear Vasudeva! I feel extremely sorry for all that has happened to both of you because of my anger and cruel nature. In my self-obsession, I became a demon and killed all your children. My heart had become empty of all compassion and love for others. I dread to think of the future, about the special hell, which will be waiting for me when I am dead. I am guilty of murdering children.

For a while, Kamsa fell silent and then spoke again.

> I know that human beings speak lies to serve their own purpose. But till now, I was unaware that even the gods lie. Believing the words of an unknown voice from the skies, I killed my sister's children. Devaki, please forgive me.'

With tears flowing from his eyes, Kamsa fell at the feet of his former captives and then hugged them.

Devaki and Vasudeva, being noble and good-natured, thought Kamsa was genuinely repentant and distressed by the heinous crimes he had committed. Lifting Kamsa up, the two told him that they had bowed before their fate and accepted the loss of their children. Devaki said with a sad smile:

> My dear brother, we forgive you. Lead a life of virtue and banish fear from yourself. Brother, when the sky is overcast with dense clouds, it is not possible for the sun to be seen. At times, the clouds do part for a moment and the eye catches a gleam of sunlight. But the clouds cover it again and darkness reigns. The gleam of sunlight is just a memory which fades only too soon.

This was so with Kamsa. He was in the presence of good people like Vasudeva and Devaki, who were noble souls. Their goodness was contagious and Kamsa felt that he finally understood the truth surrounding one's life on earth—about the foolishness in aspiring for immortality and also about loving every being, since we are all the reflections of the same light.

Once he left their presence, the demon in Kamsa was back and he became his cruel and dubious self again. As soon as he reached his palace, he summoned his principal counsellors and said to them:

> O valiant chiefs! Hear my words. The vile and contemptible denizens of heaven are assiduously plotting against my life, for they dread my prowess. But, O heroes, I hold them of no account. What can the impotent Indra or the ascetic Hara perform? Or, what can Hari accomplish, except the murder of his foes by fraud? What have we to fear from the Adityas, Vasus, Agnis, or any other of the immortals who have all been vanquished by my irresistible arms? Have I not seen the king of the gods* when he had ventured into conflict, quickly retreat from the field with my shafts piercing him?

Kamsa, further ranted:

> Are not all the monarchs on earth in terror of my prowess and subject to my orders, save only Jarasandha, my sire? And now listen, chiefs of the

---

*King of the gods is Indra; in Vedic times, also referred to as Varuna, the Rain God: A source of water for sustenance.

> Daitya race. It is my determination to inflict serious blows to the devotees of Hari and followers of the Vedas and associated sacrifices, and starve the gods by punishing and, if need be, kill the brahmana priests who are the perpetrators of these sacrifices. Kill all the devotees of Hari. The goddess who has been born as the infant child of Devaki has announced that he is alive, who in a former life was my death. Let, therefore, active search be made for whatever young children there may be upon earth, and let every boy in whom there are signs of unusual vigour, be slain without remorse.

Having issued these commands, Kamsa retired to his palace and liberated Vasudeva and Devaki from their captivity and said to them, 'It is in vain that I have slain all your children, since he who is destined to kill me has escaped. It is of no use to regret the past. The children you may have hereafter may enjoy life unto its natural close; no one shall cut it short.' Having reassured them, Kamsa withdrew into the inner chambers of his palace.

When Vasudeva was freed, he learnt that Nanda was in Mathura and went to meet him. He found the cowherd chief with his folks, all rejoicing that Nanda had become a father at such a late age. Vasudeva congratulated him. Nanda revealed that the annual tribute had been paid to the king and they were ready to leave for Gokul. A tense Vasudeva requested, 'Do not delay your departure now that your affairs are settled. Please move on with haste and reach your village immediately. Along with your son, bring up the son of Rohini, who is also under your care.'

Vasudeva also cautioned Nanda against celebrating the birth of the children, especially his own son, as Kamsa had evil designs on Gokul and its neighbourhood. 'Keep the happy tidings subdued and treat them as an ordinary event.' Nanda was surprised, but he knew about Vasudeva's travails and promised to refrain from any celebrations.

Kamsa, meanwhile, began killing all newborns in his kingdom and beyond.

The wife of one of his councillors, Putana, was a dreadful Asura woman. She was endowed with occult powers and could transform herself from one form to another. Summoning Putana, Kamsa confided in her, his plan to hunt down and kill the children. Having no qualms, Putana immediately agreed to carry out his order. She began prowling the countryside, killing all newborns by suckling them from her poisoned breasts.

Turning herself into a bird, she flew around and, spotting Gokul, landed there. Taking the form of a beautiful woman, she then entered the large household of Nanda and saw the little dark baby in a cradle. Putana looked around and, when no one was watching, picked up the babe for suckling. The lord started suckling the wholesome breasts of Putana. After a few seconds, she realised that the child was sucking her life out. Krishna held the breast with both hands and sucked with such violence that He drained it of life. The hideous Putana fell to the ground, screaming, and died.

Startled by the terrifying cry of the demoness, everyone in Vraja ran to the spot and found Putana lying on the ground with Krishna in her arms. Yashoda snatched up Krishna and quickly waved a cow tail brush over him to guard against evil, whilst Nanda applied dry cowdung powder upon the child's head. Nanda also tied an amulet with a prayer to ward off all evil.

The whole of Gokul stared in shock at the dead woman, whose body resembled that of a huge elephant. Suddenly, Nanda remembered Vasudeva's warning to rush back home. He told everyone, 'Indeed, my friend Vasudeva has divine powers, else how could he predict that there would be danger here? He had warned me that there could be evil in Gokul and asked me to hurry home.'

Even with all the *gopa*s helping, it took a lot of time to move the body of Putana and light her pyre after piling it high with wood. When the body was burning, something unusual occurred—it exuded the fragrance of sandalwood and divine scents. No one could explain it. Putana was evil, but it appeared that the lord had sucked all her sins out of her. Touching the lord had purified her. Putana was very fortunate indeed! In her pure form, Putana became Punita.

The Bhagavatam says: 'Whoever listens to the story of the liberation of Putana is blessed by the good fortune of having their mind eternally set on Krishna. Such a person will have unsparing devotion to Krishna.'

Hearing the stories of Krishna avatar rids the mind of its misery and the many desires that make a man unhappy. The mind, cleansed of all its impure thoughts, then thinks of only the lord and craves only the company of devotees of Narayana!

SAKATASURA: THE TRIPPING OF THE BULLOCK CART

Yashoda's little son was growing up fast. He was now three months old and had just learnt how to turn over on his belly. Watching him do so made Yashoda ecstatic and she would run to her baby, smiling. When her child was tired,

Yashoda would place him in a makeshift cradle made out of her sari. She would hang this cradle to the yoke of a bullock cart—even today, in villages, this is a common practice among peasant folk. This cradle was so snug, Krishna would immediately fall asleep.

The first sign of a child recognising his mother indeed calls for celebration. In Gokul, it usually meant a ceremonial bath for the babe, along with music, dancing and feasting for the whole community on the banks of the Yamuna. Therefore, when Krishna responded to his mother's approach, Yashoda ran to share her joy with the other womenfolk. In her excitement, she overlooked that baby Krishna was crying for a feed. When no one noticed his tantrum, Krishna kicked the cart, from which the cradle was hung, to attract attention. Cradle still hanging, the cart then rolled over and one of its wheels came off the axle. All the pots of milk and water in the cart tumbled over and broke.

Another mercenary of Kamsa, who had been trying to kill the child in the cradle, met his death when the wheel of the cart rolled over and knocked him dead. As per the Bhagavatam, this demon was known as Sakatasura, and the incident occurred twenty days after the Putana story.

TRINAVARTA: THE INCIDENT OF THE WHIRLWIND

Kamsa had employed an animal trapper called Trinavarta whose name meant 'as silent as the wind.' He was commissioned by Kamsa to kill Nanda's baby. Ever since the death of Putana, Kamsa had been certain that his nemesis was alive in Gokul, in the form of a dark-complexioned child.

Yashoda, after bathing her five-month-old son, was sitting in the courtyard with the child on her lap. All of a sudden, she found the child tense and heavy. She thought she was imagining it, but when the baby grew very heavy she placed him on the ground, wondering what had caused this strange feeling. Finding him asleep, she went inside to finish her household chores.

Trinavarta was hiding and watching all this from a nearby grove. The hunter was waiting for the right moment to kidnap the baby and do away with him. Just then, a dust storm advanced towards Gokul, covering the entire area in a haze. It grew dark with desert sand. The fine dust blowing all over offered Trinavarta the perfect opportunity to kidnap the child. But as he ran with the baby, Trinavarta found the child growing heavier and heavier, and his pace getting slower and slower. Blinded by dust and haze, he crashed headlong into a boulder that lay ahead and broke his neck.

After the dust storm subsided, Yashoda and her friends began a frantic search for the child and found him a little farther away, playing by himself. Lifting the infant, she went on kissing him and wondered how the little one had got so far. Krishna had escaped from the hunter's arms and lay beside the dead man.

COSMIC FORM

One day, Yashoda saw Krishna putting some earth into his mouth, a common thing for a six-month-old baby to do. She ran to him to try and get the mud out, but the boy clenched his mouth shut. Yashoda was annoyed and demanded that the child open his month. She was about to give him a flick with her finger when the baby opened his mouth to avert the sting. At first glance, Yashoda found his mouth clean with no dirt, but suddenly the hollow of the mouth grew pitch dark. Yashoda then saw, to her amazement, the sun, moon, planets, stars and the earth, swirling around along with its mountains, oceans, rivers, trees and other living beings, in her baby's mouth. She almost fainted from shock. A concerned Krishna then withdrew His cosmic vision. When Yashoda came out of her stupor, she found her son's mouth filled with some mud, which he spat. Yashoda washed his mouth, gave him a spanking and said, 'Never do it again!'

NAMING OF THE CHILDREN: *NAMAKARANA*

The initiation rites for the boys, Balarama and Krishna, were performed by Rishi Garga, the family priest of the Yadavas. Vasudeva sent the world-renowned sage to name them as per the religious practices.

Nanda welcomed the wise old sage and planned to hold a big ceremony. But Garga cautioned Nanda to maintain the utmost secrecy, as Kamsa was going on killing every newborn, relentless in his goal. Nanda understood and performed the *namakarana* or naming ceremony secretly in his house, without informing any of his kinsmen.

Garga looked at Rohini's child and said, 'This young child of Rohini charms everyone with his beauty and will, later in life, charm everyone with his outstanding qualities. I will name him Rama. But since he will also be very powerful, he will be known as Bala. He is also to be called Sankarshana.' Thus, the elder boy came to be known as Balarama.

'Nanda,' began the sage, then paused and gathered his emotions before continuing, 'this other son of yours is dark in complexion and I name him Krishna. My studies of the Jyotishamyanam tell me that in his previous birth, he was the son of your friend Vasudeva and so we can also call him Vaasudeva. But do not let that name be used. Let it be a secret known only to you, and extreme caution is the need of the hour. This baby will be most handsome and he will be the enchanter of minds. His personality will be so attractive that whoever sees him once would instantly get drawn to him!'

The sage continued, 'This child Krishna will bring you good fortune. He was born earlier as the king of the country and delivered it of all its troubles. He was then known as Prithu, as our world is called Prithivi. I am short of words when it comes to talking about this baby. He is *akarshanat*, always a cynosure of attraction! Those who love this son of yours will not be troubled by enemies, just as asuras who were devoted to Narayana were not troubled despite their *asuric* birth. Nanda, Krishna will perform great things for the good of all. He is truly an extraordinary child!'

THE BUTTER THIEF

Many cowherds in Nanda's clan were friendly with Krishna and they loved to spend their days with him, in endless play and frolic. From time to time, Krishna and his gang of friends were gifted fresh butter by the *gopi*s. But this mischievous band of boys kept craving for more and would sneak into the houses of these cowherds and run away with however much butter they could lay their hands on. The *gopi*s would then complain to Yashoda, as Krishna was usually the leader of the gang of butter thieves. Though she scolded him many times, he kept stealing butter.

Yashoda would ask Krishna to take as much butter as he liked from his own house, but she refused to give enough for his friends too. Krishna would then tease her, saying that butter stolen from other houses tasted sweeter.

The Bhagavatas call Krishna *Navneeta Chora*—the butter thief. A curious fact was that after Krishna had raided, the leftover butter acquired a finer flavour and was, therefore, in great demand in the market of Mathura. Though they kept accusing Krishna of stealing butter from their houses, the *gopi*s then secretly wished he would continue to do so and would deliberately leave their doors ajar.

THE FRUIT SELLER

One day, when Krishna was playing in the courtyard, he heard a voice in the street, 'Fruits! Jambul fruits!' He rushed to the door and saw a *nishada* woman with a basketful of the purple fruit. Krishna called out to her and said, 'Give me some of these fruits. I am fond of them.' She smiled at him and said, 'My darling child! Of course you can have as many as you want, but what will you give me in return?' The little fellow did not know what to give, so he went inside and returned with a handful of grains in his tiny palms, dropping most of it on the way. Going to her, he held out his hands and said, 'See, I have got grains for you. Now give me the fruits.' Charmed by this little boy, she hugged and kissed him with great affection and filled his palms with the delectable fruits. Krishna happily shared his find with Balarama and others.

When the fruit seller reached home, she found that her basket was heavy, even after selling all the fruits. Placing it on the ground, she removed the cloth covering the basket and found, to her amazement, nuggets of gold within. As she tried to recall how she had come by this fortune, the pink palms of a beautiful child with lotus eyes danced before her eyes and she knew the answer at once!

THE SAL TREES

Early one morning, when Krishna was a little over five years old, he went up to his mother and asked her to feed him. She told him to wait, as she was busy churning butter out of the milk collected during the day. Krishna was annoyed and broke the butter pot with a stick. Yashoda lost her temper and decided to tie him up. But while she was chasing him, his monkey friends helped themselves to the spilt butter and further infuriated Yashoda.

When Yashoda could not run anymore and sat down exhausted, Krishna surrendered, saying, 'I was naughty. Tie me up and I promise not to break any more butter pots.' So Yashoda brought a rope to bind him around his waist, but it turned out to be too short. Annoyed with herself for not knowing her darling son's waist size, she then took another rope and joined them. Even then, she could not bind him. Yashoda now looked sternly at her son's mischievous eyes and brought a longer rope, but still failed.

Frustrated and utterly tired, as she sat down, it dawned on her that there was something odd about the whole situation. Noticing this, Krishna immediately offered himself to be tied. Emerging from her stupor, Yashoda tied the child Krishna to a wooden pounding mortar and warned him to remain there till she was back. But the baby started dragging the wooden mortar into their kitchen garden and the block soon got stuck between two young sal trees. With Krishna dragging the mortar with all his strength, the two trees were pulled down.

Two angels then emerged from the bushes; they circled the Divine Baby and left. The Bhagavatam says that they were the two sons of Kubera, the god of wealth—Nalakoobara and Manigriva. They had been transformed into trees when cursed by the celestial sage, Narada.

Alarmed by the racket of trees falling, Nanda and other elders rushed to the scene. Finding Krishna safe, they dismissed the commotion as another demon sent by Kamsa. Suddenly remembering that she had left Krishna tied up, Yashoda rushed back and lifting the baby into her lap, began suckling him. Everyone arose as if from a trance, and soon forgot the incident. However, after this incident, Krishna got a new name—Damodara. The Bhagavatam mentions that the name was framed due to the binding of *dama*—rope around his *udara*—belly.

VRINDAVAN

Of late, Gokul was bothered at night by wolves that sometimes took away the villagers' calves. Besides being terrified of the wolves' fierce howling, the cowherds looked upon this as a bad omen. Therefore, in an assembly of the elders, headed by Nanda, the cowherds decided to move out of Gokul. They found a new place across the Yamuna, which had better pasture lands. There was also a small hill, lush with vegetation and many rock caves. The area abounded in herbs, especially basil, whose leaves emanated an exhilarating fragrance. Basil, in Sanskrit, is called *vrinda* or *tulsi*, hence the place was named Vrindavan.

Having found the perfect solution to their problem, the elders in Vraja then told their families to move out without delay. Accordingly, they set off with their wagons and cattle, driving before them their cows and calves, and household stores. At nightfall, they parked their wagons in a crescent formation for safety, and lit bonfires to keep wild animals away. Thus they reached Vrindavan, full of joy and excitement.

The two boys, Balarama and Krishna, grew up together, indulging joyously in their simple hobbies. They made crests out of peacock plumes, garlands from forest flowers, and musical instruments with leaves and reeds. They even played the bamboo pipes used by the cowherds. Their hair was trimmed like the wings of the crow. Krishna, with curly hair that reminded one of a bumble bee, learned to play the flute and would enchant the whole community, often sending the young girls into ecstasy!

Calves jumped playfully, hearing Krishna play his flute. When evening came, the cowherds would drive their cattle back to their pens and jump into the waters of the Yamuna for a refreshing bath. Tired and hungry, Krishna would then cuddle into the lap of his mother and fall asleep, and Yashoda would gaze lovingly at her lotus-eyed little one. She would say a silent prayer to Narayana for the safe keeping of her treasure. Life at Vrindavan was all song and dance for the two boys.

VATSA AND BAKA

One day, while Balarama and Krishna were tending their cattle on the banks of the Yamuna, Vatsa—an asura mercenary sent by Kamsa from Mathura—assumed the form of a big calf and joined the herd of cows that were grazing peacefully in the meadows. Animals have a great instinct for smell. When they sensed an unfamiliar scent, they alerted the rest of the herd that something was wrong.

Krishna, with his acute sense of perception, noticed a foreign calf. He, in turn, warned Balarama, who approached the animal, pretending to be friendly, even patting the calf affectionately to allay its fears. The next instant, he caught hold of the calf's hind legs, lifted it high up and smashed it on the ground. The calf died instantly, regaining its original asura form.

A few days later, the cowherds took their cattle to a tank, in a remote part of the meadow, for water. They saw a huge crane-like bird resting on the banks with its beak wide open. Growing curious, some of the mischievous boys peered into the beak of the giant bird. The creature did not harm the boys even as they poked around. The huge crane was Baka, the younger brother of the slain Vatsa. He had come to avenge his brother's death.

Krishna guessed that the bird was a demon sent to kill him. He, therefore, joined his friends in peeping into the open beak. As soon as Krishna entered, the bird closed its beak to swallow him. Krishna entered the bird's throat, which was quite long, and stayed put. The crane began to suffocate and vomited Krishna out. Krishna then grasped the two beaks and tore them apart, killing the bird.

DHENUKASURA VADHA

Krishna was also known as Keshava by the loving maidens of Vrindavan because of his flowing curly black hair that fell on his beautiful eyes. Yashoda, having tried many times, finally managed to keep his unruly curls in check by tying a silk band around his forehead. One day, Krishna found a handful of peacock feathers and his loving brother made a plume out of them and fixed it in his headband. This became Krishna's signature and even as an adult, he would always decorate his crown with a peacock plume.

Wandering through the woods once, Krishna and Balarama reached a pleasant grove of palms where they saw a large herd of wild asses grazing on the fallen palm fruits. The animals had devoured too much of the intoxicating fruit and had turned quite aggressive. The leader of the herd, an alpha male, was a fierce-looking and large-toothed creature that did not like the intrusion of the cowherds.

It started charging at the boys, who ran shouting, 'Dhenuka, the terrible demon—run for your lives.' Balarama and Krishna were busy shaking the palm trees for its fruits and did not heed the warning. The angry Dhenuka attacked Balarama, kicking on his breast with its hind heels. But Balarama seized Dhenuka by his hind legs and whirled the animal around till it died. He then tossed the carcass to the top of a palm tree, causing a shower of palm fruits on the ground, much to the delight of the boys.

The other asses then started chasing the boys, but Balarama gave them the same treatment, until the trees were laden with dead asses and the ground was strewn with ripe fruit. The remaining asses ran off, leaving behind the cowherds who, along with their cattle, had a grand feast.

PRALAMBA VADHA

The wild asses in the palm forest were owned by an asura named Pralamba. He was one of Kamsa's loyal guards and a distant cousin of the slain Putana. Upon learning how his herd had been slaughtered, he went wild with fury and decided to seek revenge.

Pralamba was adept in *asura vidya*—knowledge of changing into different forms. One day, in the forest, Krishna noticed an unknown cowherd in their group. That day, instead of playing the usual games, Krishna suggested that everyone should wrestle. He divided the boys into two groups, one headed by

Balarama and the other by himself. The rule of the game was that the loser in the contest would carry the winner on his back for some distance.

Pleased that no one had questioned where he came from, Pralamba readily agreed to participate in the game. He cunningly opted to be on Krishna's team. Moving towards the shade of a large Aswatha tree, known as Pandarika, the two teams began their wrestling match in right earnest.

Krishna wrestled with Sridama of Balarama's party and was defeated. So he carried Sridama on his back and walked some distance, much to the amusement of all the boys who shouted and clapped, saying, 'Krishna! Enough, enough! Now, let Sridama dismount.' It was now Pralamba and Balarama's turn to wrestle. Balarama won easily, which meant that Pralamba had to carry Balarama. Krishna quietly cautioned Balarama; divulging Pralamba's true identity, he asked him to do the needful.

The asura had lost the bout. The rules of the game now presented him the perfect opportunity to fulfil his evil design. Pralamba readily carried Balarama deep into the forest. When the other boys were out of sight, he put Balarama down and stood before him in his dreadful, dark and hairy form. Then began the real duel; they fought hard. Finally, Balarama used his fist to land a crushing blow on Pralamba's head, cracking his skull. The asura fell on the ground with a thud and died.

Krishna called the boys to run with him, to see the fight. When they reached the spot, they found the mountain of a man, Pralamba, lying in a pool of blood. The boys were amazed at the strength of Balarama. They embraced him and tried to lift him up, but found that they could not. Balarama had truly lived up to his name.

QUENCHING THE WILD FOREST FIRE

It was late spring and the trees were decked in fragrant flowers. The mango trees were in full bloom; the water in the Yamuna was soothing and refreshing; cuckoos were singing and the green pastures had begun to turn yellow under the hot afternoon sun. Only patches of green pastures on distant foothills were available for the cattle to graze. The distant rumble of thunder clouds, the occasional rainbow and the smell of rain on dry earth was exhilarating as Krishna rested on a bough and played the flute peacefully.

His divine music rode on a gentle breeze across the dry plains and brought with it the smell of burning grass. The boys were busy in their usual games and failed to realise that their cattle had strayed far and beyond in search of greener pastures. Also, no one noticed that the dry grass and bushes had caught fire, which was spreading rapidly and engulfing the cattle. When their eyes fell on the flames, the boys called out to Krishna, who asked them not to panic. 'Close your eyes, each one of you, and do not open them, until and unless I ask you to do so,' he said. The cowherds implicitly followed his instructions. They stood with their eyes tightly shut and their minds set on Krishna and Krishna alone! The melodious music of Krishna's flute then filled their ears, captivating all. A cool, soothing breeze began to blow, followed by a sudden drizzle.

A heavy shower of rain quenched the fire and the cattle began jumping in glee, as if inviting Krishna to join them. Krishna led his friends to the cattle resting under the comfort of an Aswatha tree. He said, 'Open your eyes, my friends.' At that moment, the enchanted cowherds felt that they were in the presence of Divinity. The feeling was transient and vanished soon. A few still stood transfixed, charmed by the melody of the music and the cool ambience. Krishna revealed that he played a melody that induced the thunder clouds to rain. The boys were jubilant as Krishna proposed, 'The clouds danced to this music, so let us call this music Megh Malhar.'

KALIA NAGA

In search of new pastures, Krishna and Balarama often took their cattle to far-off places, along with the other cowherds.

To develop and maintain a healthy body, Krishna played games and this endeared him to the children of Vrindavan. He ensured that no child of the neighbouring villages was deprived of either food or play. Through his fun and frolic, this little boy fostered a sense of brotherhood that brought all the sections of the Yadava community together.

One day, Krishna took his cattle out for grazing, without Balarama. It was a hot summer day and the thirsty cattle and their keepers alike searched high and low for a water source. In their hurry to drink water, the cowherds left Krishna behind and headed towards the Kalindi lake, which lay in an unfrequented part of the forest. This lake filled up only during the monsoons when the Yamuna flooded. The rest of the year, it stayed stagnant and was overrun with weeds. The place was eerie and had a foul, overpowering smell. The boys were frightened and ran back to Krishna, narrating all they saw.

An enormous and ferocious snake, Kalia Naga, happened to live in the pool with his brood. His presence stopped others from venturing near the lake. The foul gas emanating from the stagnant pool, poisoned its shiny and greenish waters.

As the legend goes, one day, Rishi Sambhari was performing *tapasya* on the banks of Kalindi. He noticed that all the fish in the lake were mourning. He came to know that Garuda, the majestic golden eagle, who was not just the king of birds, but also the celestial vehicle of Lord Vishnu, was eating all the fish. Out of compassion for the fish, the sage forbade Garuda from appearing anywhere near the lake. He threatened the bird with death if it should disobey. Garuda respected the sage, for he was a devotee of Vishnu. Thus obeying him, he stopped flying over the Kalindi waters.

In Nature, snakes are prey for eagles, who use their excellent sight to swoop down from great heights and pick up their food. It was customary in those days for people to prepare a feast for serpents every month and leave it at the base of a special peepul tree. The serpents would come together and gather all the offerings, setting apart a good portion of the offering for Garuda, their enemy, so that he might not harm them. They would then eat the rest to their hearts' content.

Once, Kalia Naga ate the food which was kept aside for Garuda. Then he hid himself in his underground pit. When Garuda learnt of this act of defiance, he hunted Kalia Naga and wounded him severely. Hearing that Rishi Sambhari had banished Garuda from the lake, the serpent decided to migrate to the safe haven of the landlocked Kalindi lake.

The lake turned poisonous with the venomous secretions of Kalia Naga and his brood. In the absence of any fresh inflow of water, the pool turned inhospitable and was avoided by everyone. The lake came to be known as the 'water of instant death' and none dared to go near it.

Krishna had heard the Naga's story from the elders in the village when they had cautioned the boys from venturing near the lake. Krishna had long wanted to rid the pool of this menace, as many cows and calves had died after drinking its water. Deciding it was time to end this environmental hazard, Krishna climbed on to the branch of a Kadamba tree that stood beside the lake and peered down quietly. His eyes were fixed on the huge snake as it glided in and out of the water. Before his companions could understand what he was up to, Krishna had tucked up his dhoti, gripped a rope in his hand and jumped into the pool. The boys standing on the bank, screamed in terror. Sridama and Uddhava, the most devoted of his friends, ran all the way to Vrindavan to warn Nanda and Yashoda.

The waters of the pool were slimy with tangled weeds, so Krishna found it difficult to swim across and reach Kalia. He, however, remained cool as ever, supremely confident of his own strength and skill, the divinity in him sparkling. The pool bore a blue haze. The snake awakened, furious to see someone trespass on his domain. Raising his hood in rage, Kalia began to approach Krishna. But as he swam away, Krishna straightened himself, made a lasso of the rope and dragged the snake's neck in the noose. The frantic snake struggled to get away, but there was no escape. The noose grew tighter every time Kalia tried to get out of it. The frightened crowd on the banks of the pool watched this fearsome struggle in agony and with bated breath.

Kalia was now getting tired and started fuming; blood oozed from his swollen fangs. Krishna then ordered the snake to get out of the pool and return to the wide ocean, where he originally belonged, or else death would be certain for his brood.

Then, swimming back to the shallows on the farther side of the lake, Krishna loosened the noose, but held the rope taut. Kalia's mates began to slither out; they entered the main stream of the Yamuna that led out to the ocean. All the *gopa*s and *gopi*s were thrilled with this dramatic development and began chanting, 'Jai Krishna!'. The angry Kalia Naga coiled around his attacker to throttle him, but Krishna enlarged his body and suffocated the snake.

Stretched too far, the serpent loosened his grip on Krishna's body. Though Kalia had to let go of Krishna, the serpent stood threatening, tense on his tail and wild with fury, his fangs spraying venom. Krishna then strangled the snake's neck and pulled it out of the waters, swinging him around like a rope before throwing him down with a huge thud.

Regaining control over his body, the serpent stood up again on his tail and spread out his hood such that his five hoods appeared to be one. Krishna came back to his normal size. As the snake lunged at him, Krishna jumped aside and Kalia crashed to the ground. Krishna then stepped on the serpent's hood and began to dance. He jumped and did somersaults on the stricken hoods as if it were a stage. Balarama witnessed the celestial dance of his brother and, to his surprise, saw a number of smaller snakes dancing and bowing before the small feet of Krishna. It looked as if they were imploring him to forgive and release their mate. Kalia, the mighty hydra of the ocean, had been subdued at last.

Once Krishna came out of the water, Kalia slowly regained consciousness and obeyed him by vacating the Kalindi lake, along with his brood. From then on, this species of snakes came to be known as Krishna Sarpa. These cobras have a twin footmark on their hoods and are native to Bharatvarsha.

There was great jubilation and, in this commotion, a beautiful *gopi* came forward and started kissing Krishna, calling him, 'My Kaanha! I am bewitched by your beauty. I heard your flute in the forest and was eager to know you. At last, I can hug you. Will you not please call me when you play the flute next?'

Krishna smiled and said, 'You called me Kaanha. I like it. Who are you?'

'I am Radha from Barsana village, daughter of Veerabahu.'

The next day, the elders met and took stock of the events of the previous day. Though the snake pit in the Kalindi lake was cleared of reptiles, the water remained poisonous and harmful. In order to reclaim the lake, the people, under Nanda's leadership, decided to drain out its water before the next monsoon. Nandagopa asked all the able-bodied men to clear Kalindi and increase the flood plains during the next monsoons. The flood waters of the Yamuna rejuvenated the lake; lotus flowers began to bloom, birds started chirping and the swarming fish gave new life to Kalindi.

The location of the lake was ideal for womenfolk to bathe and frolic in. Therefore, it was decided to set aside this lake for the exclusive use of *gopi*s. Male members were barred from visiting this lotus pool.

AN ACT OF INDISCRETION

It was the Margashirsa month, early December, and the skies were clear. The Yamuna, with its deep blue waters, was placid. The grove around Kalindi was lush with wild flowering bushes and Kadamba trees. The scene was idyllic.

The *gopi*s of Vrindavan were busy appeasing goddess Katyayini—the eternal mother Parvati—also the spouse of Lord Mahadeva. They would get up early in the morning to bathe in the cold waters of Kalindi, then dry their hair and the clothes, partially worn to cover their modesty.

This was part of the Katyayini Vrata, the belief that their wishes for a good husband will be granted by the Mother Goddess. Usually, no menfolk were allowed to go near the lake during this month and taking advantage of this rule, the girls would bathe nude in the lake with gay abandon.

Krishna noticed this indiscretion and wanted to make a point, cautioning the maidens to be careful and not tempt the young boys of the community. As a party of ten girls left their clothes at the foot of Kadamba tree and waded into the waters stark naked, a ten-year-old Krishna stealthily sneaked in and took all the garments up the tree where he reclined and gently played his flute—the music of bliss in the form of Mohana Raga.

The maidens, engrossed in bathing, were suddenly alerted by the flute and were shocked to see Krishna. They then pleaded with Krishna to leave immediately and allow them to come out and collect their garments.
Krishna replied:

> You have no respect for the waters of Kalindi, which is Yamuna itself. Young as you are, you ought not to leave your modesty on the banks. If some menfolk come to this place, what will they do? They will not leave without harming you. You should be thankful to goddess Katyayini that I, who am only a boy, had come; who will marry you, if you are so careless and casual of your modesty? Today your indiscreet behaviour has to be punished. If you want your clothes, come up as you are, with your arms raised over your head and palms clasped as an *anjali* to the goddess and collect your clothes.

The maidens agreed, 'Yes, we will do as commanded, but you should close your eyes, please Krishna, we beg of you.'

Radha heard of this episode and was upset that she was not a part of it. Radha had attained puberty and, as was the custom, no girl of marriageable age could go out without the consent of her parents. Radha had two stepmothers and the younger one, Kapila, was a very difficult woman to deal with. Radha was also betrothed to a soldier named Ayyan of Kamsa's army, who was expected to be back at Barsana, at any moment, to wed her.

INDRA MAKHA FESTIVAL

Vrindavan was getting ready for an ancient Vedic sacrificial festival called Indrotsava. Indra was the Rain God and, according to the ancient Aryan culture, he had to be appeased with sacrifices to keep him in good humour so as to ensure bountiful rains, good pastures for the cattle and abundant crops for the people.

Learned priests would prepare sacrificial altars on which mounds of butter, ghee and grain had to be offered. Occasionally, to satisfy the baser elements in Vedic lore, a male heifer would be sacrificed and the flesh of this animal would be the main offering to Indra. The flesh was also offered to the *yajamana*, or the presiding person.

It was a custom in the pastoral community of Vrajabhoomi, of which Vrindavan was also a part, to elect a prominent person to preside over this Indra Makha festival which fell towards the end of the peak winter season. During this time, there would be winter rains and heavy snowfall in the Himalayas. Winter rains ensured a good harvest and greener grazing grounds for the cattle in the torrid summer months.

The festival was so important that Vasudeva asked Nanda to invite their Kula Gurus—preceptors—Rishi Garga and Acharya Sandipani, to the event. Sandipani was also adept at teaching martial arts to kshatriya princes. He had set up his ashram and *gurukul* (hermitage and residential school) in Avanti, present-day Ujjain.

Gargacharya, the family priest, had been told by Rishi Vyasa that the blue boy of Vrindavan is none other than Narayana himself. Sandipani was thrilled to meet the boy Krishna and instantly recognised the Divinity and yogic aura around him.

At Nanda's camp, the learned priests assembled to decide who was to officiate as *yajamana*. The chosen one would have to go through a purificatory fast for three days and, thereafter, perform the essential rituals for seven days. Balarama had officiated in the previous years, but this time Gargacharya suggested that Krishna should perform this role. Everybody unanimously approved Gargacharya's suggestion.

Young Krishna, however, did not show any interest. When the village was busy with preparations, he would withdraw into the shadows of Mount Govardhan along with his flute and favourite cows. Only Radha was aware of her Kaanha's emotions.

One evening, as Krishna returned with the cattle, Gargacharya called him and said, 'My son, we have decided that this year you shall be the *yajamana* at the festival and undergo the purificatory fast.'

Krishna was very reticent and sullen; he replied, 'Learned Acharya, I think it is not right for me to preside over the sacrifice when my brother Balarama is around.' Upon being reminded that Balarama had fulfilled the responsibility in the previous years, Krishna suggested Sridama's name. 'I would like others to have the honour, venerable Acharya,' requested Krishna with folded hands.

Gargacharya then asked him, 'Krishna, what is in your mind? The whole of Vrindavan wants you to be the sacrificer, and yet you are unwilling?'

'Acharya, you know I am not fit for the job,' replied Krishna. He then said:

> Please forgive me, O learned one, because I do not believe in Indrotsava. Who is Indra? Why do we lavish so much milk, honey, butter, grain and fuel over him? Is it because we are afraid of Indra? Do we fear that he will be angry and destroy us if we do not observe the festival? Respected Acharya, God is love, not fear. I do not like festivals prompted by fear. I do not find any joy in them. I only want to rejoice in those I love and who love me.

Gargacharya was taken aback and said, 'Krishna, it is an ancient custom and rejecting it will be blasphemy, my son!' But Krishna insisted that it was blackmailing by the gods and, with a mischievous gleam in his eyes, emphasised, 'I would be happy if a festival was held in honour of our *gopa*s and *gopi*s; our cows which bless us with milk, butter and ghee, and dung too, for our fires and fields; our trees too, which give us shade, fruit, fuel and the wood for our homes.' The sage smiled in admiration and Sandipani was amazed at the wisdom of this boy. Others agreed with him, but feared the wrath of Indra.

Krishna was annoyed and said, 'Is it not our dharma to resist the angry? Never yield to blackmail, never be meek and never spare *adharma*.'

Sandipani then got up and addressed Nanda, 'O Chief, what your son says has a great bearing on all of us who are present in this assembly and also for the time to come. This young boy has extraordinary wisdom for his age and we should do what he suggests.'

In full acceptance, an ecstatic Nanda pronounced, 'My son, you are absolutely correct! The cows, the trees and Mount Govardhan give us everything; we are pastoralists and we should worship Nature and its bounty. The sacrificial ceremonies will be a mere ritual and the offerings only symbolic.' So, in the same assembly, it was decided to worship Mount Govardhan and preparations began amidst great jubilation and excitement.

Ayyan's father, Stokakrishna, though, was petrified at the prospect of offending Indra. Moreover, he didn't like Radha's constant meetings with Krishna and was clearly annoyed at her indiscretion. Stokakrishna was anxiously waiting for his son to come back after Kamsa's victorious return from Jarasandh's Ashwamedha sacrifice. He felt that Radha's wedding with

Ayyan would definitely put an end to her clandestine meetings with Krishna. Hence, he thought of staying aloof from the rest of the group.

Soon the nominated day arrived and people left for Mount Govardhan; all the cattle was washed and fed. Most of the cows had been decorated with coloured powder and shells. Krishna and Balarama led the procession. Balarama, being taller than the rest by half a cubit, carried a small *hal (*plough) on his broad shoulders. Krishna was dressed in *pitambar* (yellow silk), a flower garland decked his neck and a crown of peacock feathers adorned his head. His flute was secure in his waistband. He was the life of the celebrations, the centre of fun and frolic.

The wise eyes of Gargacharya and Sandipani witnessed the change in festivities brought about by Krishna and were anticipating great events to follow. At noon, the procession reached Mount Govardhan and families settled down under the shade of ancient trees to enjoy the meal they had brought. The next morning, the cows were milked and the calves had their extra fill. The cattle were cleansed, watered and bedecked once again. Adults and children gathered around the milch cows to drink their potful of fresh milk.

When everyone in the gathering had adorned themselves with flowers and red powder, they climbed up to the top of Govardhan. Everyone felt elated as Gargacharya and Sandipani prepared to worship the mount. They realised that hereafter, Govardhan would not only be the lord of hills, but also a god. Such was the significance of its consecration in the presence of Krishna and Balarama.

The *aarti* was about to begin when Krishna saw Ayyan and two of his friends climbing up the hill from the rear. His keen eyes did not miss their furtive looks or the way they sneaked up to the group of girls where Radha stood. A quiet smile played on his handsome lips. The crowd of men and women gathered there too saw Ayyan and his friends. They grew increasingly angry and suspicious.

'Shridama!' Krishna called out, loud enough to be heard by all. 'Ayyan and his friends have come to join the festivities. Invite them here. Ayyan, please join me in worship,' requested Krishna. Shridama took a step towards them, but Ayyan and his friends quickly retreated down the path they had come.

Gargacharya not only worshipped Govardhan, the cows and the trees, but also ended by venerating Krishna himself. Balarama was thrilled to see Krishna as the Divinity—sitting surrounded by a halo, dark as a rain cloud, with the Kaustabh jewel gleaming around his neck. Smiling up at him, Balarama offered a prayer to Narayana, his other self. Gargacharya then invoked the Vedic chants: *Brahamaarpanam Brahmahavi Brahma magnau, Brahamnaavritam Brahmainagantavyam Brahma karma samadhina.*

> The means of offering is Brahman. The oblation is Brahman, and is offered by Brahman into the fire, which again is Brahman. Brahman indeed can be reached by him who sees everything as Brahman.

On the last day of the festival, everyone was enjoying themselves. Suddenly they felt a chill in the air, unusual for that time. However, the bonfire warmed the breeze and the sky was clear. The cowherds were planning the return trip in the morning and many looked crestfallen as the festivities were drawing to an end. As darkness fell, each family went to sleep near their carts and cattle. It was quiet, but for the distant rumbling of thunder in the north. It was after midnight that one dark cloud after another rose in the sky. The wind grew chilly and people turned in their sleep. As lightning flashed and thunder struck nearby, the cows and bullocks grew restive and the startled people woke up. Seeing the overcast sky, they were overtaken by sudden fear. The cowherds thought Indra had been offended and was going to punish them for being foolish enough to listen to Krishna and deny Indra his worship.

The Rain God was angry indeed, for the sky grew darker towards dawn. The lightning came in flashes, with loud thunder, and it rained in torrents with the winds blowing in fury and claps of thunder shattering the peace of the mountain. The small rivulets began to overflow and the ground turned to slush. Men and women had to crawl under the uplifted carts for shelter. It was impossible to return to Vrindavan with the forest paths submerged and the rains threatening to be incessant. Everyone began to pray to Indra, asking for forgiveness and vowing to perform Indrotsava, if only the Rain God would rescue them from this perilous storm.

Krishna measured the sky with his eagle eyes and called out to his friends. Then looking at Balarama, he pronounced, 'Indra has to be fought and taught a lesson.' Balarama nodded in agreement and smiled.

At the first faint glimmer of dawn, Krishna led his friends towards some hollows which the rain and wind had carved out in the belly of Mount Govardhan over time. On his earlier visits, Krishna had played in these caves with Balarama and his friends; they used to hear the echoes of their voices here. Krishna said, 'Balarama, Indra is out to fight us. We will now have to fight him.'

Helped by the mighty Balarama and others, Krishna tried to roll a boulder away and open the entrance to a cave where women and children could hide in safety.

As the storm grew in strength, there was a clap of thunder, which shook the hill and the huge boulder rolled downhill, revealing a fairly large cavern from which rainwater gushed out. Another clap of thunder made the earth tremble and the loose soil in the cavern caved in along with the bedrock. It appeared as though the hill rose by a couple of cubits. Krishna and Balarama now jumped on the bedrock to test its firmness. It was perfect!

Krishna then commanded everyone, including the cattle, to come under the cover of the cavern. Standing in the middle and assuring one and all that they would be safe under the canopy of the hill, Krishna then lifted the little finger of his left hand to support the roof of the cavern—a symbolic gesture of his faith in himself. This gesture gave the impression that he was lifting the Govardhan itself on his little finger—a divine hallucination. From then on, Krishna was called Govinda, the saviour of cows. The One who knows, finds or tends cattle, *Gam Vindati iti*—Govinda, the protector of the entire world and all living beings.

The Bhagavatam says that the storm continued for seven days and all this time, Krishna looked after his people. At the end of the ordeal, everyone realised that Krishna was indeed a god who was living among them. However, this feeling was transient and the moment they came down the hill, the people forgot all about the miracle and started praising Krishna and Balarama as two very strong boys.

When the rain stopped, people yoked the bullocks to their carts. All of them were wet and wanted to reach their homes as quickly as they could. The path had become slushy and muddy, yet everyone was euphoric; they managed to wade through and return to their hearths.

KRISHNA AND HIS FLUTE

It was a moonlit night. The atmosphere was ethereal and blissfully calm. Krishna knew that the sublime life at Vrindavan would not last long. Nonetheless, he wanted to live in the present and enjoy life in the idyllic countryside.

Often, Krishna would walk into a grove next to the Yamuna and play his flute. His enchanting music left the whole village enthralled. The *gopis* of Vraja would abandon their chores and run towards the moonlit banks of River Yamuna.

Krishna welcomed the damsels with delight and enquired about the welfare of their families, perhaps to remind them of their primary duty. The *gopi*s would reply that he was the lord of their hearts and none could replace him. As per the Bhagavatam, Krishna used his Yoga Maya to create an illusion in their homes so that no one noticed their absence. This was one of his *leela*s often referred to as Leela Manushapurasha. He also used his Mohana Roopa Siddhi, which sent the *gopi*s into an ecstasy, as if they were in his physical presence; each *gopi* felt that she was locked in an embrace with the Divine for a moment, and emptiness engulfed them as Krishna disappeared. They would then search for him on the banks of the Yamuna, a vain search in the external world for the One that dwells in the heart of every creature.

While searching, the *gopi*s would begin singing the ballad of his childhood deeds and adventures and plead, 'O Govinda! Please have pity and come back to us.' Responding to their call, Krishna would suddenly make himself visible in his radiant form, sitting cross-legged and playing the flute. He made the wind dance to his tunes and these melodies were, later on, called ragas—harmonious tunes such as Sarang Shuddha Malhar, Megh Malhar, Malasri, Dev Gandhara, Vibhas, Bilaval, Kedar and many more. Krishna's favourite was the Mohana Raga and he dedicated this to his beloved Radha. This music is sung as *Geeta Govinda* in many households even today.

On the clear sands of the Yamuna, he commenced a Divine Dance called Raasa Leela, where Krishna, the Divine incarnate, stood in the centre playing the flute, encircled by the *gopi*s. The lord manifested himself between two *gopi*s so that every alternate figure was Krishna, standing cross-legged and playing the flute. Everyone danced to the rhythm in absolute bliss. The Bhagavatam describes it such:

Anganaa, Anganaa Antaare Maadhavam, Madhavam Maadhavam
Antaare Anganaa

The lord appeared at the centre as a mere witness to this divine play, unconcerned, except for the music covering all the ragas, a *raga malika*—the string of melodies. This was when Krishna made Radha his Divine Consort. Radha occupied the pride of place in his heart as she loved him intensely, yet never tried to possess him. This became Krishna's philosophy: *Sarvasya bhootanichaturani*—He belonged to no one exclusively, but everyone belonged to him.

EVENTS AT MATHURA

Ayyan was furious when he heard about Radha's clandestine meetings with Nanda's son. He also learnt that Radha's younger sister, Anuradha, too was in love with the dark boy and was jealous of the attention her sister received from the object of her affection.

Before leaving for Mathura, an angry Ayyan went to Veerabahu's house and demanded Radha's hand as had been promised. He shared his discomfiture about Radha and Krishna with Veerabahu. But having reconsidered his earlier decision, Radha's father replied angrily, 'No father would give his daughter in marriage to a soldier. Who knows what will happen to him in the next war? He could be dead. Every girl in Vraja wants to marry Krishna—can I help it? If Radha agrees to the union, you can marry her.'

Ayyan was now more curious than ever about this enchanter. He had heard rumours about how Kamsa was to be slain by the eighth son of Vasudeva and now suspected that Krishna could be that son. Keen to take this news to Kamsa himself, Ayyan sought an audience with him.

When Kamsa heard about Krishna, he was terrified and thought of summoning his prime minister, Pralamba. He was the one who managed the affairs of the kingdom when Kamsa went on his campaigns. Pralamba was experienced in statecraft and his loyalty towards the Bhoja kings kept him in good stead with Kamsa. When Kamsa realised that Pralamba was unwell, he decided to pay him a visit.

To better understand Kamsa's frame of mind at the moment, we need to review the prevailing situation. When Kamsa returned after twelve years of campaigning, he was dejected to learn that the thirty-one Yadava clans had become practically independent, which meant he could no longer rule over them. His return to Mathura was also devoid of celebration as the people had turned sullen and passive. Even his father did not welcome him, and the prime minister lay paralysed on his deathbed.

Pradyota, his trusted general of the palace guards, informed him that the prime minister had taken the path of least resistance in the matter, and the Yadu clans were the most defiant against Kamsa. Kamsa now regretted releasing Vasudeva from prison.

In an attempt to regain past glory, Kamsa stationed the Magadha warriors at several vantage points of the city. It was also announced that his victorious return would be celebrated by Dhanuryagna, a ritual comprising a bow sacrifice to propitiate Lord Shiva. He thought this would showcase his might and he would also get an opportunity to display his superiority over the clans.

Interestingly, as a token of appreciation for his son-in-law's efforts during his Ashwamedha sacrifice, Jarasandha had ceded some more territories to Kamsa. Jarasandha also proclaimed Kamsa as the king of Mathura, which was earlier only a principality with Kamsa as the crown prince. In celebration, Kamsa had granted some pasturelands to the surviving soldiers, and Ayyan was one of them.

Hearing Ayyan describe the boy's extraordinary god-like looks, Kamsa was frightened and, at the same time, furious. Though he was over fifty years old, Kamsa still feared death more than anything else. He was not afraid of death in battle, but the prospect of dying at the hands of a young Yadava and that too a blood relation, galled him greatly. He still had great ambitions of crushing the defiant Yadava chiefs, consolidating his newly acquired territories and calling himself a Chakravarti someday. Pradyota also told him that the ailing prime minister was aware of these events. The next morning he went to the house of the ailing minister, who lay prostrate on the bed.

Kamsa shook the frail, semi-conscious old man and asked him what he knew about Krishna. The old minister admitted knowing about the extraordinary Yadava boy. This admission infuriated Kamsa so much that he threatened to kill Pralamba, but the minister was too weak to protest. Kamsa demanded to know the whole story.

The old man made a supreme effort; his eyes widened and there was a gleam in them as he began to speak, 'O King, Rishi Vyasa said that Devaki's eighth son Krishna, is Narayana Himself,' and with those words, the minister dropped dead. Kamsa panicked. He commanded Pradyota to summon the Yadava chiefs at once, for he could not rest till Krishna was eliminated once and for all.

It was announced that after a fortnight, on the full moon day of Kartik, Kamsa was going to celebrate his triumph by holding a Dhanuryagna. It was to be a week of festivities with display of warlike feats, elephant fights and wrestling.

Such was the extent of his paranoia that Kamsa now had no confidence in his palace guards. Therefore, he placed the Magadhan captain, Vritrighna—a cousin of Kamsa's favourite wife Asti—in sole charge of the palace guards. Pradyota and their ilk were out of favour with Kamsa.

Pradyota, however, was scared even though he was now in charge of the Bow Sacrifice. He was also hurt at being sidelined. He was also a chieftain of the Yadava clan and feared that he might be made a scapegoat in Kamsa's warped plans. His sister, Putana, had already met a gory end in Gokul. At that moment, he was summoned by Kamsa, who said, 'My friend, I want you to go to Akrura, the chief of Vrishnis, and extend an invitation to all the Yadava chiefs for tomorrow afternoon.' Pradyota looked skeptical and asked, 'All the chiefs?'

'Yes,' said Kamsa.

'I want to make peace with all of them, including my revered father, Ugrasena.'

Pradyota was amused and said, 'My lord, you want me to be present as well?'

'Of course! How can I meet them in your absence? You are one of the Yadavas!' he said, rather sarcastically.

Pradyota himself went to meet the most respected chief, Akrura, whose flowing white hair and beard and kindly eyes bespoke of his great experience and wisdom. When Pradyota bowed at Akrura's feet, the Vrishni chief was surprised, yet received his guest cordially. Pradyota told the chief about the festivities and Kamsa's invitation to all the Yadava chiefs, and requested Akrura to meet the king in his palace. Akrura was perplexed and asked Pradyota, 'Why this, so suddenly? What is cooking in your master's mind?'

Pradyota replied, 'I do not know his plans. I was just told to convey his message.' He then continued, 'Akrura, is it true that Devaki's eighth son is alive?' Taken by surprise, Akrura asked, 'Who told you this? Please do not question me about it. I shall come to see your Kamsa whenever he bids. Tell him I am too old to be afraid of anything. Let God take care of us!'

With folded hands, Pradyota bowed before Akrura and said, 'I am told that Devaki's eighth son is God Himself. He will be our saviour.' He then prostrated on the floor and began weeping uncontrollably before Akrura, as though repenting his past sins. The Vrishni chief lifted Pradyota and told him, 'I have also heard this rumour, but I do not know where he is.'

AKRURA'S DIPLOMACY

Kamsa, in twenty-five years of his rule, had never once called a gathering of the Yadava chiefs. The fact that he did so now, aroused suspicion; some even predicted a sinister plan to assassinate them! They were also apprehensive that the virtuous Vasudeva may be harmed once again. To add to their woes, Bow

Sacrifices were usually known to end in violence; invariably, rival wrestlers got massacred during their bouts.

The fifty chiefs assembled, fully armed to defend themselves against Magadha soldiers. Ugrasena, though seated next to his son, was trembling with fear. There was a commotion in the assembly when Bahuka, the revered nonagenarian chief of Andhaka clan, who was an uncle of Ugrasena and the grandfather of Pradyota, arrived at the scene. He sat next to Ugrasena. The chiefs were astounded that a person who had retired from active politics and who was a great devotee of Lord Shiva had chosen to come out of recluse.

The others in the assembly were Bahuka, Vasudeva, Devak and Akrura. Pradyota sat beside him, feeling guilty about being Kamsa's hatchet man. Kamsa addressed the assembly:

> Worshipful father, grand uncle, noble Yadava chiefs, please accept my greetings. It is with great pleasure I invite you all, along with your clans, to the festivities of the Bow Sacrifice on the occasion of my acquiring several territories for Mathura, now a kingdom. Let us rejoice.
>
> The city will be lit with bright lights; there will be music, dance and fun. We will have archery and wrestling bouts, with champions from the neighbouring kingdoms participating as well. I shall reward the victor in each of the events handsomely. On the seventh day, the sacred bow of Lord Shiva will be put into action. Whoever shoots the farthest with this formidable bow will be the victor and will be personally honoured as the hero of this event.
>
> The bow I am going to prepare for this occasion is a mighty weapon, one that few men can lift and none can bend. Yet, there might be one who can handle it—after all, Yadavas are skilled archers. Yadavas are also renowned wrestlers, and I am a good one myself. But as king, I will not participate. My favourite wrestlers, Chanura and Mushtika, will represent me.

Akrura was the only one to speak after this. 'Oh great one, as per our ancient custom, the king should preside over these festivities; so, may I humbly request Your Highness to invite your father, His Majesty, Ugrasena?' Kamsa gave consent.

At the entrance, Vritrighna gave a command and about fifty armoured warriors of Magadha surrounded the hall. The audience grew uneasy and old

Bahuka demanded to know who these foreigners were and why were they interrupting their meet.

'Uncle, please don't be angry,' Kamsa replied coolly. 'They are the Magadhan warriors and were with me for twelve years in the Ashwamedha wars. I invited them to boost security during the festivities.' A nonchalant Kamsa also introduced Vritrighna to the assembly as a very able warrior and his constant companion for over a decade.

Kamsa then said to Vasudeva:

> You had promised that you would hand over to me every newborn son of Devaki, and I trusted you. But now I have come to know that you breached my faith. You sent off the eighth son of Devaki. I know that son of yours is in Vrindavan, living as the son of Nanda. Is this the dharma of a kshatriya?

The whole assembly was aghast at this revelation. Before Vasudeva could open his mouth, Andhaka, a much-respected Yadava chief, got up to reply:

> Son of Ugrasena! You, of all people, are invoking kshatriya dharma? You, being the descendent of a noble kshatriya family, imprisoned your sister Devaki and her husband Vasudeva on the day of their marriage without any reason; was it kshatriya dharma? Was it dharma to kill six sons of one mother? Was it dharma to destroy newborn children?

Bahuka joined in the tirade against Kamsa, saying, 'Kamsa, I am too old to care for my life, and you are a disgrace to the name of Yadavas. Why are you so concerned about Vasudeva's son? Vasudeva suffered enough at your hands, and I will not allow you to torture him any further.'

Kamsa lost his composure and his hand involuntarily reached the hilt of his sword. Akrura noticed this and said:

> Oh the mighty one, do not let your anger override your wisdom. Anger is madness! You want to know about Vasudeva's eighth child? Devaki's eighth child was a son. Your prison guards were vexed with your cruelty and allowed Vasudeva to smuggle out his eighth born. You came from a noble family, yet have become a victim of your anger and cruelty, causing people to loathe you. It is not too late to mend your ways, I advise you as one elder to you. I do not have anything to lose but my life. You may take it right now!
>
> The eighth child of Devaki is in Vrindavan. If anyone has deceived you, it is me.

> I arranged for the exchange of Devaki's son for Nanda's daughter to save you from the wickedness of killing all of Devaki's sons! I wanted to save you from yourself.

Kamsa composed himself and asked Akrura, 'Venerable sir, am I that cruel? That story is a thing of the past and we must forget it. Now that we know Devaki's son is alive, I would like to invite him here to participate in the Bow Sacrifice and wrestling contests. I heard he has an elder brother. Please bring him as well.'

'Is this some sinister plot to lure him here?' asked Bahuka.

'Why should I trick anyone? Devaki's son is my nephew. I am told he is very powerful, almost like God. It will enhance my prestige if my nephews also participate in the games. Do you not agree, respected father?' Kamsa then asked Ugrasena.

'*Eashwarecha*—as is God's wish,' replied Ugrasena.

Kamsa assured everyone present that no harm would come to the boys.

Vasudeva instructed two of his confidants, Sadhaka and Madhaka, to rush to Nanda's house with the urgent message. Nanda called an emergency meeting of the village elders and informed them of Kamsa's invitation, asking all to prepare to leave for Mathura the next day. They were disheartened to learn that Krishna was a kshatriya.

Krishna retreated to the moonlit banks of the Yamuna and reflected on his carefree life in Vrindavan and Gokul, and the life which awaited him in Mathura and beyond.

KRISHNA'S LAST NIGHT IN VRINDAVAN

As the entire town prepared for the journey, there was a sense of sadness in every heart, for their beloved boy was to leave them soon. All of a sudden, the moonlit night was filled with music. The melody of Krishna's flute was so familiar and enchanting that no *gopi* could resist his call. They all went running to the banks of the Yamuna.

On his last night here, Krishna wanted to have a dance that would be remembered forever and he, therefore, asked Radha to assemble thirty-six *gopi*s and form a *mandala*. He requested Radha to join him in the centre as he played the flute. 'The whole world will remember this night, my beloved Radha, as Radha Madhav Leela Lalana or the "dance of love",' he told her.

Balarama, who was more interested in wrestling than romance, also joined in on this special occasion. Soon, the young boys and girls formed a circle around Krishna with Radha at his side, smiling blissfully, her eyes fixed with rapturous devotion on her Kaanha's face.

In the midst of this revelry, Radha and Krishna quietly retreated into the woods. Radha was inconsolable at the prospect of losing her Krishna. She begged him not to go as it was definitely a plot to kill him. Moreover, she was sure that he would forget her and marry a princess.

Krishna gently drew her into an embrace and said, 'Radha, you are my beloved and I am nothing without you. I will marry you right now in a Gandharva ceremony and take you to Mathura.' She wiped her tears and said, 'Gandharva style? It is nothing short of eloping with you. After you leave, I will be doomed. Now, let me go into the Yamuna before your eyes.'

Krishna put a garland around her neck and urged her to do the same to him. 'I will take you to Guru Sandipani who will consecrate our marriage and inform all the elders. Please keep my flute to remind you of my presence. I have no music when you are not by my side.'

Sandipani solemnised their wedding and Krishna took his bride to seek the blessings of his parents. He told his mother that he would leave Radha in her care. He reassured her that he will soon return victorious from Mathura.

Yashoda was most upset upon learning that her beloved son was not her own. Nonetheless, Krishna pacified her, saying that she will always be his mother, and he her Nandagopal. She was in tears.

'Ma!' implored Krishna. 'Do not cry. I will always be with you. I may be Devakiputra, but before that I am Yashoda Nandan. To commemorate Vrindavan for ever, I will henceforth be called Nandagopal.'

PROPHECY COMES TRUE

Akrura started for Vrindavan the next day, anxious to see Krishna. An aroma of tulsi leaves greeted him as he approached the Yamuna at Vrindavan. He saw two exceptionally bright lads, one with a flute and the other with a small plough on his shoulder. Guessing that they were the sons of Vasudeva, he alighted from the chariot and set foot on the sacred soil of Vrajabhoomi.

Akrura fell at the feet of the boys and looked up into the eyes of Krishna. The boys embraced him, saying, 'You are learned, wise and elderly. You should not fall at our feet.' To which Akrura replied, 'I have fallen at the feet of gods.'

Akrura introduced himself as the Andhaka chief and told them that their mother, Devaki, is with him at Mathura, and so is their father, Anakadundubhi. Hearing this, Krishna responded, 'I thought we belong to Nanda and Yashoda and Rohini Ma. Then who is this Anakadundubhi, because I have heard that my real father is Vasudeva?'

'Both are the same, and you will come to know why in good time,' replied Akrura.

The next morning, after the usual rituals, the caravan of carts started their journey. Akrura invited Krishna and Balarama to join him in his chariot. Balarama declined, saying that Krishna was God, whereas he was just an ordinary boy and would prefer to be with others like him.

On the way, Akrura told Krishna that he would continue the journey only after offering prayers to the Sun God. During the ritual, as Akrura chanted Vedic hymns near a pool, he saw Krishna and Balarama's image in the water, smiling at him tenderly. He was stunned and thought he was hallucinating. Then the image changed to show Krishna lying on a huge serpent that sheltered Him under its enormous hood. Akrura looked back at the other bank and saw Krishna and Balarama frolicking with their friends. He then realised that he had just been blessed with the vision of the lord in His true form.

When they reached the gates of Mathura, Akrura requested the brothers to come to his abode and meet their parents. But both the boys wanted to first have a look at the festivities, after which they promised to return for the meeting.

Krishna and Balarama started on foot—admiring the magnificent palaces, wide roads, high fort walls, the richness and beauty of the whole city and its landscape. While they were walking along the main thoroughfare of Mathura, they came across a group of washermen carrying a load of freshly-laundered clothes. Krishna stopped the chief and asked for some fresh clothes to wear, as they were to meet Kamsa. The washerman ridiculed him, saying, 'You country brutes! Our high born ruler has no place for rustics like you. Leave me, I am in a hurry and I do not have any clothes for people like you who smell of cowdung and sweat!' The otherwise calm Krishna was enraged, and hit the washerman on his head, instantly killing him. One of the soldiers ran to the palace to inform the king that Krishna had killed the royal *dhobi*. Meanwhile, out of fright, the other washermen unloaded their bundles and offered that the two choose clothes according to their liking. Balarama called his friends and asked them to help themselves too.

As they headed for the palace, they met a weaver who was so taken by their divine presence that he offered them *saropa*s, made out of the finest silk, to wear around their necks. Similarly, a flower seller gifted them garlands as a token of his respect.

Krishna later confessed to Balarama that he did not mean to kill the *dhobi*. He only wanted to slap him and did not realise that it would kill him.

KUBJA

At Kamsa's court, a beautiful young maiden, named Trivakra, had been struck by polio, which had left her crippled. People used to call her Kubja, the hunchback. She would reply that she was born beautiful, but fate had been unkind to her. Her husband, the royal *mahout*, abandoned her after she took ill. Trivakra's mother, a *sairandhri*—cosmetic girl in the royal household—had taught her daughter all the secrets of the trade after this twist of fate. Trivakra had acquired great expertise in preparing perfumes from exotic flowers and herbs. During the night, she would burn fragrant powders and incense in the royal chambers to keep away mosquitoes and other pests.

Krishna overheard people bantering about her and approached Kubja. He asked her what exactly she did at the palace. Kubja replied, 'Sir, I supply sandal paste, *kasturi* and all other unguents to King Kamsa and his wives every day. Could I apply some on your chest? You seem to have such a divine presence about you!' Krishna was more than happy to accede to her request. She then wanted to know if she would ever be able to stand erect.

Krishna replied, 'Why not? You must have faith in yourself.' Krishna then held Kubja by both hands, kept his right wrist under her chin, both his feet pressing Kubja's feet and toes. 'And now, my dear young lady, lift and stretch yourself,' he said. Kubja followed Krishna's instructions and, in a miracle, she was cured of her deformity.

Krishna then named her Sulakshana and asked her to leave, as she now had to perform her duties at the palace. He however, agreed to grant her another wish as he was in such a happy mood. The girl was overjoyed and asked him to visit her home. 'Alright Sulakshana,' promised Krishna. 'I shall come to your place, but not now.' Balarama and Krishna then moved on further, enjoying the attention they were getting in this fascinating city.

KAMSA'S RAGE

Kamsa was a worried man even though he had never been as strong as he was now—with Mathura a powerful kingdom, subservient neighbouring kings, and 3,000 Magadhan soldiers deputed for his security. Now the only concern was to keep the Yadavas under his thumb and crush their spirit, swiftly and decisively. But first, he had Devaki's son to deal with, which left him more nervous than ever.

An anxious Kamsa had assigned Pradyota to keep an eye on the boys while they were in Mathura and had ordered him that under no circumstance were they to enter the palace or be brought in front of him. While Pradyota was keeping a lookout, Bahuka Andhaka came to visit Kamsa about an urgent matter. The old man complained that Kamsa's security troops had been terrorising the people of the city. But an unperturbed Kamsa argued, 'They are the gift from my father-in-law for my safety. Mathura is no more a principality. It is a kingdom of Yadavas, respected uncle, and therefore, I am under threat from my enemies. I need these troops for my protection.'

'Is that why I hear you want to kill Nanda's boys tomorrow during the festivities?' the Andhaka chief shouted back.

Kamsa was shocked that the prophecy of his death and his plans to prevent it had become public knowledge. 'Uncle, I am not so weak as to be killed by a mere boy.'

The old man reprimanded:

> Kamsa, mend your ways and seek the pardon of Devaki and Vasudeva for all your brutal massacres of their sons. People say that Krishna and Balarama are their sons too. If that is so, show some repentance, forget your needless enmity and bring harmony. Release your old father from house arrest and let Devaki and her sons remain fearless in your kingdom.
>
> You also need to get rid of these alien soldiers, return the confiscated lands of Vasudeva and make peace with him! I seek your welfare—I want you to be a benevolent ruler. Please listen to me for your good.

Kamsa dismissed the old man and his advice. When Bahuka implored, Kamsa assured him that he would not harm Krishna. As the old man was leaving, Kamsa gestured to Vritrighna to carry out a sinister command.

Kamsa reiterated his promise to Pradyota of not harming the boy as long as he saw to it that Krishna did not come in front of him.

As Pradyota was leaving the palace, disgusted by the orders given to him, he heard a scuffle and then saw the dead body of the revered old man. He, at once, realised the consequences of going against Kamsa's orders. Pradyota was stunned by this atrocity and pledged that Kamsa will be killed the next day. He would bring Krishna face to face with the cruel ruler of Mathura so that the prophecy could be fulfilled.

THE SACRED BOW

Everyone had gathered for the main festivities to begin and were admiring the miraculous transformation of Trivakra and the two divine looking boys. Suddenly, in the marketplace, there was a clatter of horse hooves and the rider cracked a whip, yelling, 'Give way for the royal party of Vidarbha!' One whiplash brushed Balarama and the usually quiet boy reacted instantly with anger, 'Who is this fool and why is he disturbing the peace?' He saw the rider ploughing through the crowd and instinctively held the horse to a halt. At the same time, he pulled the whip from the rider. The rider tripped and fell and the crowd burst into laughter. Meanwhile, Balarama pushed the horses back, right into the bullock cart that carried the princesses of Vidarbha. The two ladies seated inside the cart shrieked in terror.

The rider was furious and shouted at Krishna, 'You fool! Do you not know who I am? I am Rukmi, the prince of Vidarbha and the guest of your master Kamsa.'

'I know who you are,' replied Krishna, with nonchalance. 'You better get back to your womenfolk and stop harassing the people of this city with your arrogance.'

At this provocation, Rukmi began to unsheathe his sword; but in a flash, Krishna twisted his hand with expert skill and threw the prince off balance. Before Rukmi could get a grip of himself, Krishna lifted him up and threw him into the chariot. The women screamed in terror, and one of the girls shouted at Krishna, 'Let go of my brother, you wicked fellow!'

With a charming smile, Krishna responded, 'O beautiful one! It is a pity this prince is your brother. Take care of him. It is not cultured to be so arrogant, young princess. Your brother has not lost anything except his conceit.'

The moon-faced beauty, whose name was Rukmini, then blushed and her anger soon melted away. 'Who are you, the dark one?' she asked.

'Aha! Only now you noticed my colour, noble princess. I am but a cowherd from Vrindavan. This fair fellow, the mighty one, is my brother Balarama, and we are the guests of Kamsa.'

Krishna then walked up to the frightened bullocks and said gently into their ears, 'Please be gentle, my lovely ones. Behave yourselves and take care of the beauty inside.' The bullocks gave a friendly nod as if they understood his request. Krishna winked mischievously at Rukmini and said, 'You can now safely reach your host's palace, young lady!' The cart departed, followed by a much humbler Rukmi on his horse.

The large crowd was now more in awe of these boys than ever. People began whispering that these two were their saviours, but when Krishna heard this, he modestly said, 'Why do you embarrass your guests? Please, I am like you, except that I cannot tolerate injustice and neither should you. Be bold, my friends, don't tolerate *adharma*. Resist it.'

Just then, the crowd heard soldiers heading their way, so they soon dispersed. It was Pradyota, who on reaching the boys, dismounted and asked, 'Are you the sons of Nanda of Gokul?'

'Yes,' replied Krishna.

'The king has asked me to look after you well. I shall be with you throughout your stay at Mathura.'

Krishna replied, 'Sir, we can look after ourselves. But your master has invited all ill-mannered people for the festivities. The prince of Vidarbha was very rude with one and all and we had to punish him.'

Pradyota felt secretly glad when he heard this. He introduced himself, 'I am Pradyota. I belong to the Andhakas and I am sorry that Prince Rukmi was annoying. My apologies to this tall, fair boy. I can see the whiplash on his cheek.'

Krishna was all smiles and said, 'General, this means that you are an uncle to us. Can we address you as such?'

Pradyota looked around and said in hushed tones, 'Yes, your father is like a brother to me, but be careful my lovely nephews, for you do not know the perils that await you. Allow me to accompany you around the city as are my orders.'

Krishna understood and agreed to be escorted by the general as long as Trivakra could come along as well because they had already asked her to show them the city.

'Uncle, can we see the *mandapa*, the special platform where you are displaying the Sacred Bow?'

'Of course!' But Pradyota cautioned him again, 'You know Krishna, the place is supposed to be sacred. However, you can look at the bow since you are one of the contestants.'

They all proceeded to the *mandapa* where priests were chanting Vedic hymns and offering oblations to the Fire God. The *homa kund*, the sacred fire, was a little away from the *mandapa*, which was canopied and beautifully decorated. The bow was placed on a raised platform, its string let loose.

Pradyota said, 'You know, this bow is very difficult to string; it has been specially made by the Magadhan artisans. Special green bamboos were sliced, layer after layer was bent and bonded with a fine twine of wires and coated with amber resin. The several layers are thus laminated, making the bow very powerful. I understand that an arrow shot from this bow can strike any animal dead even from a distance of a hundred cubits. It is heavy too—it took several men to carry it to the platform. Krishna, are you as powerful as they say?'

'I do not know Uncle, but I will try my best if I am asked to participate by your king.'

Pradyota warned Krishna again:

> Be careful though! Kamsa is not a good man. I am the unfortunate servant of his who imprisoned your parents—the noble Vasudeva and princess Devaki. Please forgive me. I had to obey my master's orders. I will atone for my sins at an opportune time and I shall fall at the feet of your parents, asking them to forgive my sins.

Krishna admired the general's repentance and replied, 'Uncle, it is our destiny that guides us. Only the great Mahadeva can forgive us. Have faith in Him.'

As they neared the *mandapa*, Krishna could see that the bow represented Kamsa's power and arrogance. He decided to demonstrate to everyone that this symbol of evil could be conquered, and that he was challenging his arrogant uncle.

Krishna examined the bow; it looked mighty indeed with the smell of resin still fresh, and the bamboo fibres too formidable to yield and bend. Krishna told Pradyota that he felt none could handle this remarkable weapon. Trivakra then asked if Krishna would like to have a try.

Krishna smiled at her and said, 'I am but a cowherd who does not know anything about weapons. In Vrindavan, we do make some bows and arrows to kill small game when they trouble our cattle, or for our safety. This seems to be a weapon of mass destruction. Yet, I could try.' He then looked at Pradyota and asked, 'Am I to be called to string the bow on the last day?'

Trivakra suggested, 'Why not try to do so now?'

'Alright,' said Pradyota, 'but be careful!' Krishna stared at the bow for some time very closely to gauge its weight. People gathered around, tense but curious.

Krishna noticed a flaw in the joints of the bow, this boosted his confidence and he lifted it with ease. Holding the bottom part of the bow between his toes, Krishna bent down to string it, but ended up cracking the bow into two pieces. Krishna dropped the two pieces on the ground and said calmly, 'General, the bow is broken!'

This led to an uproar with the priests crying, '*Ashubham*, it is an ill omen!' The head priest screamed, 'Inform Kamsa at once and postpone the festivities!'

Pradyota had a smile writ on his face that he tried to conceal. He was now certain that Krishna was their saviour, but was worried that the Magadhan soldiers might kill him with a sniper arrow. Therefore, he ordered his soldiers to surround Krishna and Balarama and escort them to safety.

Pradyota conveyed the details of what had transpired to Kamsa and, as expected, infuriated him. 'Who asked you to take Krishna to the *mandapa*? How could he break it? There is a trick in this Pradyota. I will not pardon you; you are a traitor.' Pradyota reminded him that it was the Magadhans who had crafted the weapon and Kamsa himself had inspected it, and declared it to be formidable. Kamsa accepted that, but was left wondering how a mere boy could snap it into two. More scared than ever, he repeated his order that the boy not be allowed to come near him.

'But my lord, everyone from Nanda's camp will be here to watch the wrestling matches. How can I prevent Krishna from accompanying them? Instead, I have placed four guards around the boys so that they cannot roam free.'

'Yes, we cannot prevent him from coming to the match. Announce that the Dhanuryagna will be held the day after tomorrow. Only the wrestling matches will be held tomorrow.'

Kamsa was nervous and enquired about Trivakra. He was told she was with the princesses. He then called for Vritrighna. Kamsa wanted to know what had been done with the dead body of his old uncle. 'We have dumped him in the Yamuna, tied to a big boulder, at a spot that is infested with crocodiles. By now, they would have consumed his body. You need not worry, my lord. But, the Yadava camp does suspect some foul play in the disappearance of Bahuka Andhaka.'

'Alright, I will attend to it,' said Kamsa. 'Keep your forces on alert, and at the appropriate moment, wait for my signal. The attack should be sudden and quick. Now summon Angaraka from the elephant stables.'

Meanwhile, in the princesses' chambers, Trivakra was wild with joy. She could not stop talking about the two boys. Kamsa's queens were frightened. They were aware of the prophecy and his fear. Rukmi's wife found it unacceptable that a *sairandhri*—cosmetic girl—should talk in this way and said, 'The cowherds were arrogant. How they insulted the Vidarbha prince! If it happened in my country, they would have been beheaded.'

Rukmini giggled as she teased her sister-in-law and said, 'The boys were not wrong. Why did my brother hit the fair one with his whip? He deserved what he got. We should be thankful that they did not harm my brother.'

As Trivakra was leaving, Rukmini went after her and asked, 'Who is Kuvalyapida?' Trivakra grew pale, and replied, 'He is not a person, but the most wild and rogue elephant in the royal stable. A huge beast! It has to be kept chained at all times. But why do you ask?'

'I ask because plans are afoot to kill Krishna tomorrow when he comes to attend the games. I heard the prince talking to a stable man called Angaraka.'

'Angaraka! He was my husband till he left me.'

Rukmini asked anxiously, 'Can you save Krishna, Trivakra?' Trivakra became tense and said, 'My lady, that boy is a god. Nobody can harm him. Leave it to me and do not mention our conversation to anyone.'

THE END OF TYRANNY

Trivakra decided to pay a visit to her former husband after her conversation with Rukmini. When she reached his house, she found Angaraka lying intoxicated, his two wives applying herbal oils and hot compresses on his tired limbs. As she entered, the two women shrieked in shock as if they had seen a ghost. Angaraka could not recognise her.

'Have you forgotten me, Aryaputra?' asked Trivakra with a mischievous laugh that rippled through the room. He was staring at the beautiful maiden in disbelief, and recollected that only his first wife Malini used to address him with such civility.

'Are you cured? How did you become so tall all of a sudden?'asked Angaraka.

'My god made me what I am,' replied Trivakra nonchalantly.

'Who is this god you speak of? I have heard that Nanda's sons performed some miracles in the town square. It seems the dark one even had a scuffle with the prince of Vidarbha.'

'You have heard rightly, except that they are the sons of Vasudeva, not Nanda. The dark one is Devaki's eighth son,' revealed Trivakra. 'Is it true that the King ordered you to kill the boy with the help of Kuvalyapida?'

Angaraka narrated his conversation with Kamsa earlier that day.

> He called and praised me, saying that I was his best stable keeper, one whom even the rebel Kuvalyapida obeys. I told him, I feed Kuvalyapida palm jaggery which he likes, and also rice liquor. It keeps him calm. Then he said that he wanted to assign an important task to me. Once I complete it, he will ensure I get so much land and gold that I do not have to work any more and can retire.

'What is this task?' She enquired.

> Tomorrow I have to block the main entrance gate to Mathura with Kuvalyapida and prevent Nanda's camp from entering the wrestling arena. Then I should instigate the wild beast to crush the dark skinned boy to death. If I fail, I will pay for it with my head. I do not wish to carry out these heinous orders, but what choice do I have?

Trivakra got up and said, 'No one can kill Devaki's son—he is God. Now let me go to my quarters and when I come back, we shall go to the stables of Kuvalyapida. I have a plan. Will you do as I say?' Angaraka gave his word that he would.

Trivakra returned with a large bundle of herbs and asked Angaraka to feed it to the elephant along with grass and lots of toddy. He did as he was told.

In the meantime, the Yadava chiefs were getting perturbed with Kamsa's tactics and feared for their lives. They had pinned their hopes on a child, and some still had doubts if he was indeed the one who would fulfil the prophecy. But they all went to meet Devaki and assured her that they would not let her sons be harmed.

Kamsa was equally tense and disturbed. When he woke up the next day, he saw a beautiful damsel standing in his room with a silver casket of unguents and perfumes. 'Who are you?' he asked.

'My lord, do you not recognise me? I am Trivakra, cured by Nanda's son,' she said. Kamsa's mind clouded over, as Narada's prophecy loomed large over his head.

He was now impatient to hear from Angaraka. He went and stood by the window that overlooked the main gate through which Kuvalyapida would be let in. The brahmana priests, the kshatriyas, vaishyas and shudras had occupied their respective seats in the enclosures. The Magadhan soldiers were stationed at vantage points, especially around the enclosure occupied by the Yadava chiefs. Even the women's exclusive enclosure was full. The entire city wore a festive look and all were eager to see Nanda's sons.

The blowing of the conches signalled the start of the wrestling competition. The royal athletes entered the arena, slapping their biceps and thighs, challenging those present to enter the ring and fight them. Kamsa's favourites, Chanura and Mushtika, greeted him along with the other athletes. Finally, Kuvalyapida entered the arena with his rider, Angaraka, resplendent in gold embroidered robes, worn only on special occasions, exclusively by the Master of Elephants; Kuvalyapida too appeared magnificent and was bedecked in gold. The elephant proudly walked up to a spot near his quarters, raised his trunk in salute, and trumpeted cheerfully.

Kamsa was surprised. Kuvalyapida, who always stomped with heavy, sharp strides, was moving with leisurely and unsteady steps. His eyes were groggy and appeared listless. The elephant was lumbering through the parade, not marching.

Kuvalyapida ambled across the wide court in a jolly mood and shifted his weight first on to one leg and then the other as if he was dancing. Angaraka positioned himself at the entrance as was directed. Right then, Nanda's group came towards the gate with the two boys wearing garlands. This was the first time Kamsa laid eyes on his nemesis and he became more impatient to crush him.

The young men reached the elephant, but instead of rushing at the boys, Kuvalyapida saluted them with his mighty trunk. It, however, stopped them from passing the gate by swaying his mighty trunk from one side to the other. Krishna whispered something into the giant ear of the elephant, following which Kuvalyapida gazed hard at Krishna as if he was a long-lost friend, then rolled his body and uttered a loud grunt as if snoring, and kneeled. Krishna patted his trunk and the elephant picked him up in the crook of his trunk. People were terrified, thinking that Krishna will be crushed, but the elephant slowly raised the boy as if in salute and then lowered him gently on the ground, only to fall asleep.

Krishna removed one of his flower garlands and placed it on the trunk of the sleeping elephant. The jubilant crowd cheered, seeing this mighty beast submit to a boy. Kamsa, on the other hand, was busy working out another strategy to achieve his goal of getting rid of the boy.

Kamsa summoned Agha, his advisor, and enquired how the boy managed to enter the courtyard when the elephant should have crushed him. 'They say the elephant was killed by him, my lord,' replied Agha. 'Some say that he tamed the beast by a mere touch! I will send for Angaraka, and ask him what went wrong.'

Kamsa was furious. 'There is no need for Angaraka; he is finished as far as I am concerned. They are all traitors; they failed me. Send word to Chanura to choke Krishna in the wrestling bout.' An exasperated Agha pointed out, 'My lord, it is against the shastras that a veteran wrestler should challenge a mere boy.'

'I do not care about the shastras—do as I say!' Kamsa insisted with a frown.

Kamsa then went down to the platform and took his place as the presiding king on the podium in front of the wrestling arena. The others were seated, as per their rank, in the royal enclosure.

Kamsa glanced towards the enclosure where Krishna sat and found the boy staring at him. A shiver ran down his spine, but he composed himself soon enough. He felt reassured when he saw Vritrighna standing behind Vasudeva.

As the matches began, Chanura, Mushtika and Toshala—the city's three master wrestlers—entered the arena to loud claps of admiration. Their twelve disciples were walking behind them. A fairly large contingent of participants followed.

The wrestlers were all dressed in *langota*—tight string thongs, their bodies well oiled and their necks decked with marigold garlands. Chanura had the honour of covering himself with the golden shawl presented by Kamsa when he hailed Chanura as the Master of Bahu Yuddha or hand combat, as wrestling was known at that time.

Skilful wrestlers always had a pride of place amongst royals. Kamsa himself was an expert wrestler. For kshatriyas, it was an important part of their training, and even Krishna and Balarama indulged in mock bouts on the sand bars of the Yamuna. But Chanura and others were professionals and very disciplined, observing every rule and regulation stated in the shastras.

When Agha told Chanura what the king had commanded, he was reluctant, but had to obey him. He signalled for the bouts to start. Each bout lasted a short while and the victors were then separated from the vanquished. As the spectators cheered, Chanura went around the arena and reached the enclosure where Krishna and Balarama were seated. Chanura slapped his biceps and thighs and called out, 'So you are the boy-god?'

Chanura was a bald and very heavy man. His massive body and drooping paunch were well oiled; his biceps and thighs were very muscular and fleshy, making him look like a lumbering giant. 'Nandaraj, are these your boys?' Chanura asked Nanda. 'They look like princes. I think they should join the tournament.' Nanda would not hear of it.

'You are a professional! They are just cowherds.'

'Come along, sons of Nanda,' said Chanura, directly addressing the boys. 'I have heard that both of you are great heroes, now prove yourself.' The audience was also not happy with Chanura's challenge.

'I am not afraid, but my father forbids it,' said Krishna.

'Of course, it is natural,' jeered Chanura. 'He knows that you can only dance with milkmaids and seduce them, doesn't he?'

Krishna stood up and addressed his father, 'Please permit me, I will win.' And with that he entered the arena. Balarama was very angry at this obvious plot to harm his brother. When Mushtika challenged him, Balarama removed his headdress, stood up and punched the arrogant champion on his face. Mushtika reeled from the blow and could barely help falling.

Taking advantage of this, Balarama stepped into the arena. Recovering his balance, Mushtika jumped upon him like a tiger and the two were locked in a fierce combat. Within minutes, Balarama had hurled Mushtika on the ground with such force that the champion's skull broke like a clay pot. Kamsa grew tense and looked nervously at Vritrighna.

Meanwhile, Krishna was closely observing his opponent's moves. Chanura's eyes and movements reminded Krishna of a hungry python that invariably paralysed its victim. Krishna noticed that the athlete's greatest asset was his enormous body, which could overwhelm his opponents and suffocate them to death or result in broken ribs.

He also detected a slight limp in Chanura's left leg; his heel and ankle seemed to be weak. Krishna kicked his weak spot causing Chanura to stagger. The wrestler regained his composure, but seemed to be writhing in pain. Krishna was elusive and moved swiftly like a deer to kick Chanura repeatedly at the same spot, pushing him towards the royal enclosure where Kamsa sat. Chanura was tottering and began to breathe heavily, enraged at being beaten by a boy.

With a final blow to his opponent's ankle, Krishna brought down Chanura. Collecting the last vestiges of his strength, Chanura stood up and turned to swoop on Krishna when the boy jumped back and the wrestler fell on his face. Then, before Chanura could get up, Krishna jumped on him and pinned him to the ground. Not relinquishing his hold, Krishna sat astride the wrestler's chest and proposed, 'Chanura, admit defeat and save yourself.'

Chanura reacted by trying to overthrow his opponent, who then hit him hard—broke his nose and smashed his teeth. The mighty champion fell on the ground. Just then Krishna saw a Magadhan pointing a sword at his father, but Pradyota came to the rescue and struck him down. Akrura, meanwhile, stopped the other soldiers from declaring war on the assembled Yadava chiefs. This angered Kamsa so much that he was instantly on his feet, sword drawn, and hit Akrura to bring him down.

Seeing this, Krishna rushed at Kamsa like a falcon swooping down from the sky and grabbed him by his hair. Dragging him to the floor, Krishna severed Kamsa's head with his own sword. Kamsa was dead. Pradyota's soldiers then killed all the Magadhan guards. The mayhem was complete. Krishna blew the conch lying near Kamsa and declared an end to tyranny.

Throwing down the sword, Krishna then walked up to where Vasudeva stood, protected by Balarama's mace. He prostrated before his father and said with humility, 'Father, bless me. Where is my dear mother?'

'I will take both of you to her, my sons. The prophecy has come true; twenty-five years of tyranny have finally ended,' said Vasudeva.

Vasudeva, with the help of other Yadava chiefs, revived Akrura, who had a concussion on his head. The gentle chief slowly regained consciousness and awakened to the good news of Kamsa's death. Akrura was overwhelmed.

Krishna now turned to address the gathering: 'Respected elders, never tolerate *adharma* such as my uncle unleashed. It is our duty to eliminate *adharma* from the world.'

Balarama and Krishna reached Akrura's house where Devaki, looking emaciated, yet beautiful, was waiting to welcome her sons with a plate of water, lime and turmeric to ward off the evil spirits that had hovered over her family for so many years.

Seeing her, Krishna and Balarama fell at her feet; Devaki was inconsolable on being reunited with her sons. 'My sons! How I have longed to see you! I have missed telling you stories and singing lullabies.'

Vasudeva then said to his wife:

> Devaki, we have to thank Nandagopa and Yashoda for bringing up our boys. I know you have suffered for long, but imagine their plight. It was not Yashoda's fault that she was the mother of Krishna, and now she has had to part with him. Let the boys spend time with them and their friends. After the ceremonial farewell, Krishna and Balarama will return to you.'

Devaki bathed and fed the boys; Krishna had butter with beaten rice and jaggery, while Balarama enjoyed the freshly leavened bread, cooked vegetables and sweet meats.

THE KINGDOM UNDER A NEW RULE

After Kamsa's death, Krishna sensed a power vacuum and spoke to Balarama, 'Brother, a kingless state will turn into anarchy! Soon we must appoint a leader.' Balarama agreed.

After consulting Vasudeva and Akrura, it was decided that the kingdom should be restored to Ugrasena. Vasudeva was proud of his sons' maturity at such a young age. They approached Ugrasena, who had grown feeble after being confined for so long. But Ugrasena refused, saying that he was too old and his mind was no longer sharp enough to rule the kingdom. He turned to Krishna and said, 'You should be the king, not me. You are the victor and the land is yours by right, O son of the Shoora Chief!'

Krishna replied humbly, 'Grandfather, I am a Yadava and you are Bhoja. Have you forgotten the curse of Yayati that no Yadava would sit on the throne? My brother and I will stand beside you and help you discharge your duties.' Krishna then asked those chiefs who had fled Mathura to return to a reformed city.

Many days had passed since the wrestling match and Nanda wanted to leave for Vrindavan, so he sought Vasudeva's permission. Krishna embraced his foster father and then fell at his feet with tears in his eyes. He said, 'My dearest father, we have been your sons ever since we became aware of our surroundings. You have given us the unconditional love that only parents can. It is not easy to bid farewell. You will be remembered forever, my dear father!' Nanda hugged him and Balarama. His grief was immense, but Nanda knew his sons would be better off in the palace of Mathura.

The caravan left for Vrindavan after a teary farewell; Krishna and Balarama stood watching the slow, meandering procession of carts until the dust swallowed up everything. Krishna grew pensive and said to his brother, 'Our lives will never see the carefree happiness that we have left behind!'

With a sigh of sadness, they walked back to the palace.

THE EDUCATION OF BALARAMA AND KRISHNA

Vasudeva had not been able to celebrate his sons' birth as he was in prison, but now he wanted to make up for that. He gave away cows, gold and silk to poor brahmanas, as was the custom in the royal families. He then approached Garga and asked him to initiate the two boys with the sacred Gayatri mantra in a ceremony called Upanayanam. A sacred thread was tied around the boys' left shoulders, which looped down to touch their waists. There was a divine glow around the two boys who were, however, amused that they would now have to be educated like princes after being cowherds all their lives.

Krishna now reflected on the current political scenario. 'King Ugrasena is feeble. Though he is a good man, he is diffident and therefore, indecisive. This is a major drawback in a leader. How can one overcome that?'

Vasudeva and Akrura were the only stable forces in the new Mathura. One was sober-minded and the other saintly, but even they were incapable of quick decision or prompt initiative. Pradyota was effective in his own way, but only as second in command. Yuyudhana Satyaka, son of the slain Andhaka chief, though old, commanded universal respect. The other Yadava chiefs had spent most of their lives resisting Kamsa and lacked the ability and training in statecraft. They were only interested in laying claim to their properties and lands seized by Kamsa.

The Yadavas or Bhojas, as they were sometimes called, were a loosely woven confederacy of tribes. They were irrepressible; fighting, killing and being killed all the time, pushing their way into unknown lands and making it their own. They were proud of their descent from the great emperor Yayati and his son Yadu, but they also married women from non-Aryan tribes.

Krishna was curious to know about his ancestry. He learnt that Haryashva, son of Kuvalayashva, who killed the demon Dhundhi, was their ancestor. It is said that the country of Panchala was named after *pancha*—his five sons. Haryashva married the daughter of Madhu, a demon, and gained Anarta, present day Gujarat and Saurashtra, as an inheritance. He then built the mountain fortress of Girinagar. Its original name was Kushasthali. Yadu himself married Naga princesses who bore him five brave sons; one of them was Madhava from whom all the clans—the Andhakas, the Vrishnis, the Shooras and others claimed descent. Krishna and Balarama therefore had Naga ancestry.

Krishna found that though his ancestors were aggressive, they never failed to uphold Arya Dharma, wherever they might be. Their zeal gave them a sense of mission and made them respect Vedic priests by supporting their hermitages and sacrificial sessions. Kamsa was a descendent of King Madhava who had established himself at Mathura.

Another branch of Bhojas settled in Chedi, towards the east and closer to the coast, in present day Odisha, had become more powerful. The Chedi kingdom was ruled by Damaghosha, who married Shrutashrava, the sister of Vasudeva. Krishna was eager to meet the Chedi king and his son Shishupala, so Vasudeva invited them for the Upanayanam ceremony of his sons. Vasudeva was aware that Damaghosha and his impetuous son, Shishupala, were very close to the Chakravarti, Jarasandha.

With his astute grasp of statecraft and deep political insight, Krishna fully realised the crushing blow he had dealt to the mighty monarch of Magadha. Jarasandha would never pardon Krishna for the murder of his son-in-law. He also knew that the Chakaravarti was a formidable enemy who was far from the path of dharma.

Vasudeva wanted to placate, to some extent, the wrath of Jarasandha, through his brother-in-law, Damaghosha. The King of Chedi was a key ally in the current scenario. However, Shishupala was not only impulsive, but also a favourite of the imperial court.

Rukmi's father, Bhishmaka, who was the King of Vidarbha, was also an ally of the emperor. Rukmi too, like the Chedi prince, was arrogant and Krishna had already earned his wrath on the streets of Mathura. Rukmi was still smarting from the insult meted out by Krishna.

Vasudeva's strategy threw up a surprising twist. Only his sister, Queen Shrutashrava, arrived along with her son, Shishupala. The shrewd and diplomatic Damaghosha excused himself by saying that matters of state bound him to his palace.

A congenital deformity made Shishupala resentful of Krishna and Balarama's good looks. Shishupala had been born with an ugly black mark on his right cheek. Damaghosha consulted many physicians to get rid of this ugly mark, but was unsuccessful. His astrologers predicted that the mark would disappear when Shishupala touched the person who would eventually kill him. The queen grew very protective of her son and overindulged him despite his wicked nature. When Krishna and Balarama were introduced to him, Shishupala objected and said, 'I do not want to mix with cowherds. Are there no princes in Mathura? Moreover, these cowherds murdered my uncle. I understand Prince Rukmi of Vidarbha has come. Please take me to his palace.' Vasudeva arranged to take him and his mother to the palace. Balarama was seething with anger and wanted to hit the prince, but Krishna restrained him, saying that Shishupala was a guest of their father.

Vasudeva had also sent a messenger named Sunku, who was a close confidant of Akrura, to Hastinapura to invite his sister Kunti—wife of late King Pandu, along with her five sons, better known as Pandavas or Panduputra. Vasudeva requested Akrura to accompany Kunti and her sons on their return journey to Hastinapura and find out what was happening at Dhritarashtra's court. Dhritarashtra was blind and weak, but very cunning. The kingdom of Kurus was dominated by a mighty warrior named Bhishma who was a staunch protector of dharma, very steadfast and a more formidable warrior than Jarasandha.

Vasudeva realised that their relationship with Hastinapura, which was governed by Bhishma, was crucial for their existence. Rukmi and Shishupala were likely to instigate Magadha Naresh to attack Mathura at the earliest, whereas Bhishma's support would delay the plans of Jarasandha and give them time to consolidate their position. A friendly Hastinapura could be of great help.

Jarasandha had never dared to annex any part of the kingdom of Hastinapura. Similarly, he was afraid of the ruler of Panchala, Drupada. Panchala was a very prosperous state with an equally powerful army. The mighty Jarasandha was mortally afraid of Bhishma who was the greatest pupil of Parashurama—the jewel of the Bhrigu clan of the ancient Aryans.

Krishna learnt about Bhishma Pitamah, the grandfather, and his principled stand—not to occupy the throne of Hastinapura due to a promise given to his father, Shantanu. His great vow of *brahmacharya*—to remain celibate for life, his invincible military prowess and his god-like valour was legendary. He was the guardian of all the princes of Hastinapura who were being trained and led by Acharya Drona, who himself was a great warrior and a pupil of the venerable Parashurama. Krishna grew eager to meet him.

Minister Vidura was asked by Bhishma to accompany Kunti and her sons to Mathura. Vidura was the son of Vyasa by a chambermaid. A very humble scholar, he specialised in the moral codes of statecraft—called Vidura Neeti—and was known as the conscience-keeper of the King of Hastinapura.

Upon the arrival of the Pandavas, Vasudeva confided in his sons:

> Balarama, you have a match in Bhimasen, the second son of your aunt Kunti. He is called Bhima, the mighty; and you are my Balarama, the mightier. Krishna will find his match in the third son of Pritha, called Arjuna. Your aunt's maiden name was Pritha and after being adopted by King Kuntibhoja of Kuntala, she was renamed Kunti. I have heard that her brother-in-law, King Dhritarashtra, is not treating them well. After their father, King Pandu's death, they have all been ill-treated by Duryodhana, the eldest son of Dhritarashtra and Queen Gandhari.

Queen Shrutashrava of Chedi was taken to the royal chambers where the princesses of Vidarbha were lodged. Unlike their aunt from Chedi, Kunti treated Krishna and Balarama as her own sons. All her five sons were also handsome and well built and faultless in their behaviour. The eldest, Yudhisthira, carried himself with quiet dignity and was three years older than Krishna. The second one, Bhima, who happened to be a year older than Krishna, was a strong and muscular lad, very jovial and full of fun. Her third son, Arjuna, was younger than Krishna, and always carried a bow. The twins, Nakula and Sahadeva, were the youngest of the brood—both were lean and intelligent.

Although Krishna soon grew fond of them all, he developed a close bonding with Arjuna. During one of their conversations, Arjuna confided in Krishna that he had taught himself to shoot at a target in the dark, but pleaded with Krishna not to mention this to Dronacharya. Puzzled, Krishna asked the reason for keeping such a talent hidden. Arjuna explained:

> One day while I was eating, a strong gust of wind blew out the candle flame, leaving me in the dark. As I continued to eat, I wondered why can I not hit a target in the dark with the same instinct that leads my hand to my mouth? I practised on my own, night after night, shooting at a target in the dark and acquired this skill. I do not want him to know because I am afraid that once my Kuru cousins find out about this they would blame him for not teaching them this skill. Secondly, my guru is extremely fond of his son Aswathama who, though a great expert in arms, is haughty and ill-tempered. Even he might cast aspersions on his father for the same reason.

Krishna admired the transparency of Arjuna and thought to himself that Arjuna not only has all the ingredients of a legendary archer, but also, with his keen intellect and concentration, he could become an invincible warrior and a deep thinker. When he learnt that Arjuna was the son of Indra, Krishna, in turn, confessed to him how he had rebelled against the sacrifices for Indra. He also added that one day Indra had appeared before him in his dream and asked him to take care of his son. At that time, Krishna had dismissed it, but now that he had met Indra's son, he knew it was fate that had brought them together.

As was the custom in those times, after the Upanayanam ceremony, Krishna and Balarama were to live in learned Sandipani's *gurukul*. The boys were excited. Balarama wanted to hone his fighting skills and he was told that Sandipani was skilled in the use of mystic *astra*s or weapons, besides being proficient in logic, prosody, grammar, phonetics, astronomy and etymology. Balarama teased his brother that he need not bother learning about mystical weapons, as he was one himself! To which Krishna replied, 'It is true. With you by my side, I do not need weapons, only logic.'

Both the teacher and the students were glad to have come together. Sandipani was especially fond of Krishna, whom he believed to be the creator of the Vedas. Krishna learned many new things during his tutelage under the great guru. He also understood the full depth of his responsibilities, in the coming years, as the upholder of dharma.

THE UPANAYANAM CEREMONY

The *yagnopavitha* or thread ceremony was held without much fanfare, as the princes were still mourning their uncle's death. With the permission of their parents and Gargacharya, the two brothers and their cousin, Uddhava, wore the sacred thread to the chant of mantras. Each of them was given a deerskin to wear over his shoulder by day and to lie on at night. They were also given a staff, a *kamandalu*—bowl hewn out of wood, and a pair of wooden sandals. As per the shastras, Krishna, Balarama and Uddhava were now *dvija*—twice born. Their initiation into the Aryan clan was complete. Krishna and Balarama had entered the stage of *brahamacharya.* All through their life as students, they were to observe strict discipline.

BRAHMACHARI BHIKSHA

It was customary after the thread ceremony to touch the feet of elders and ask for *bhiksha*, or alms. The three boys accordingly touched the feet of their elders, seeking blessings and taking the offerings. Balarama, being the eldest, was the first to do so, followed by Krishna and Uddhava. Balarama started with his parents, and then approached Akrura, Kunti, Shrutshrava, Shishupala and other elders to collect alms.

When Krishna touched Shishupala's feet, the ugly mark on his face disappeared. His mother shrieked in alarm that the prophecy would come true, and immediately requested Vasudeva to arrange for her departure. When she explained her reason for leaving, Krishna tried to placate her saying that he had no enmity with her son.

Krishna continued:

> My cousin should control his temper and alter the lifestyle that he currently follows in the company of Magadha Naresh. Else he is bound to commit grave errors, which will ultimately bring him in conflict with me and land him in great peril. Aunt Shrutshrava, I will forgive ninety-nine of his faults. But if he exceeds this number, he will meet his fate.

Shrutshrava hastened for Chedi, more worried than ever for her son.

As *brahmacharis*, the brothers were to beg for their food. They stood before Devaki with bowls in their hand and chanted, '*Bhavati bhikshan dehi, mata annapoorneswari.*' Devaki gave them a potful of fresh milk each and was upset as her sons were supposed to leave her, yet again.

Sandipani had entrusted Balarama, Uddhava and Krishna to his nephew, Shvetaketu. He was equally handsome and as dignified as his celebrated uncle. Besides the three of them, the twin princes of Avanti, Vinda and Anuvinda, were also in Shvetaketu's group. The princes were not too happy to be in the company of commoners. They also felt offended in seeking alms for food. The other three had no such qualms. They visited Trivakra with their bowls and were duly rewarded with a hearty meal.

Lately, whenever they visited Trivakra, Rukmi's sister was sure to be there as well. She insisted on serving Krishna, and it was plain to see that she was fond of Krishna. He too seemed to have developed a liking for her, but was bound to follow the path of *brahmacharya* till his education was complete.

Sandipani's travelling school was preparing to leave Mathura and move towards Prabhasa Kshetra. Krishna remembered his promise to mother Yashoda and Radha that he would visit them soon and realised that now it would not be possible. He heard from Nanda's representative, who had come from Vrindavan, that Yashoda was very sad at the turn of events in Mathura. She grieved more because her Krishna would be leaving for Avanti, which was far away from her. Krishna then requested Uddhava to visit Yashoda and Radha, and explain to them how the current situation prevented him from fulfilling his promise. Uddhava, Krishna's dear friend and confidant, returned after a five-day stay at Vrindavan and narrated:

> Krishna, I could not control my sorrow upon seeing the state of all those who love you in Vrindavan. Father Nanda rarely speaks to anyone. Mother Yashoda is inconsolable. Radha kept talking to herself, going from tree to tree, calling out to you. I have heard people say that ever since you left, the yield of milk from the cows had dropped. Time, it seems, has stood still at Vrindavan.

THE TRAVELLING SCHOOL OF SANDIPANI

On the twenty-fifth day after Kamsa's death, Sandipani decided to leave Mathura by road along the banks of the Yamuna. Krishna was sixteen years old and Balarama was nearing eighteen, both were in their prime.

Sandipani ran his school with strict discipline, unmindful of the status of his students. They camped for the night near a village with a water source. The pupils, after completing their morning ablutions, would chant Vedic mantras as prescribed by Veda Vyasa, and retire for their morning meal. Carrying their bowls in silence, they would go to the village for alms.

After the morning meal, the students would take a break for *vishram* or rest. When the heat turned bearable, they would begin their education. In the evening, they would camp under the cover of a grove of trees. The students would wrestle, then bathe, offer their prayers, have food and spreading their deerskins on the bare earth, retire for the night.

Krishna enthusiastically took in all the knowledge on offer. His body and mind were soon attuned to the new routine. Shvetaketu had never seen a pupil with such a receptive mind. Krishna would repeat every chant with meticulous accuracy. Once a canon of conduct was explained to him, he would never forget it and imbibing its spirit, would follow it to the minutest detail. Krishna was always cheerful, sincerely completed his chores and made friends easily. His education had been neglected so far and now he was determined to make up for it with a passionate intensity.

Krishna once noticed some students teasing a physically weak student. He went up to them and gently chided them, saying they should help the student overcome his weakness rather than mocking him. 'The principle of survival of the fittest is not the highest form of civilisation. One should cultivate a habit of helping the underprivileged and create harmony in the society.'

Due to his impressive leadership qualities, Krishna was entrusted with the task of organising provisions for the daily affairs of the school. Once, when they ran out of firewood, the students volunteered to collect some for him, but Krishna pointed out that it was his duty to do so and asked the rest to return to their own chores. He emphasised that each one must do his duty and this will ensure that dharma prevails. Sandipani watched Krishna's progress with deep admiration and respect for the boy.

No one could match Krishna and Balarama in running and at wrestling. Wrestling with Krishna was a struggle. The skill of a champion was pitted against an intuitive mind, which foresaw every mood and thrust of his opponent.

During his stay in the *gurukul*, Krishna had taken a great liking to an eighteen-year-old brahmana boy, Sudama. He was nicknamed Kuchela because he was lean and weak. Sudama was very intelligent and humble. His late father hailed from the west, somewhere near the sacred Prabhasa Tirtha, a great pilgrimage centre for the worship of Lord Shiva as Somnatheswar.

He had been Sandipani's friend and colleague and was adept at chanting the Sama Veda.

Sudama, too, flawlessly chanted hymns from the Sama Veda, whose music was set by Lord Shiva—the God of Gods himself. Krishna requested Sudama to teach him these hymns and Sudama happily agreed. Krishna became so fond of this music that he would listen to Sudama sing almost every verse with great feeling and devotion.

Balarama, on the other hand, was not much interested in *brahmacharya*. He was an outgoing person. Although very intelligent, he stayed away from academics at every opportunity, but thoroughly enjoyed the evening martial arts classes.

Under the direction of their guru, the students practised archery and learnt to wield the mace and the battleaxe proficiently. Balarama, with his great height and muscular frame, became adept at wielding the mace. He had the temperament of a tornado when aroused. When he grew older, Balarama came to be known as Gadadhar, or the one that holds the mace.

Krishna preferred the *chakra* or discus. He had an unerring eye for accuracy in throwing a noose round the neck of an obstinate bull and he easily mastered the art of whirling the discus. He would whirl it around his forefinger with such energy that, when he aimed it, the *chakra* would slice the target into two and return to him. He was also taught different elements of military science with treatises on the use of arms and directions for mystic incantations meant to secure supernatural weapons.

The boys read through the Dhanur Veda, which deals with military matters such as the *rahasya*—the mystical parts, and the *astra prayoga sangraha*—the collection or compendium on the deployment of weapons.

Every year, Sandipani made two pilgrimages, one to Kurukshetra where the august Veda Vyasa had his ashram, and the other to the holy Prabhasa Tirtha on the shores of the western ocean. On full moon day, a bath at this Tirtha, where three rivers met the sea, was considered most sacred. Sandipani told the boys that they would soon be going to Prabhasa Tirtha from Bhrigukachhapa—modern-day Bharuch, by boat. Their education would come to an end here, after worshipping the Sun God and Lord Shiva at Prabhasa.

Krishna was pleased to hear this and said:

> I thought we were worshipping the Sun as the giver of life when we saluted

him with our palm full of water and chanted the glorious Gayatri. Sir, I am very fond of the Gayatri Mantra and Sama Veda. I heard you saying that the author of the Gayatri Mantra was the great Rishi Vishwamitra, the preceptor of the Ikshwaku prince, Ramachandra. Whenever I chant Gayatri, my body resonates in spiritual ecstasy, revered Gurudeva. I would be privileged to go on this pilgrimage.

Acharya Sandipani, his wife and the thirty boys left Bhrigukachhapa for Prabhasa Tirtha in six boats. They had skirted the coast leisurely. Due to his annual visits, Sandipani was known and respected throughout the coastal area and wherever the boats touched, the locals were spontaneous in their hospitality.

When the school reached Prabhasa, they were heartily welcomed by the king, Bhimdev, who always looked forward to Sandipani's visit. During his stay, the Acharya set up a temporary school headed by Shvetaketu to educate the locals about the Aryan way of learning.

Prabhasa was a large settlement. Besides the Aryan colonies, the bulk of the population belonged to a different race of people who were dark and short in stature, very adventurous, friendly and hospitable. They lived in houses made of baked clay, neatly arranged in streets. They had public baths attached to the shrines where they worshipped Shiva, not in the form of a *linga,* as in Mathura, but as the clay image of a naked human being, seated in a resolute yogic pose. The people of Prabhasa had their own ships and traded with Bhrigukachhapa and other local ports. They spoke a language difficult to understand, but having to travel for trade, many learnt to speak in Aryan language.

Sandipani's school settled down near the temple of the Sun God on the seashore. Its presiding preceptor was Ghora Angirasa, belonging to the Angirasa clan of rishis who worshipped light and luminous bodies such as the Sun. They were followers of the Atharva Veda. In fact, the hymns of the Atharva Veda are called Angirasa. A protector of sacrifices practised in accordance with the Atharva Veda, the clan was supposed to have descended from Rishi Atharvan. On the second day of their arrival at Prabhasa, Sandipani told the sons of Vasudeva:

I have taught you everything I know. Now you may leave for your father's place. Your studies are over; however, there is no end to studies in one's life. Genuine studies are those that help you inculcate virtues in your life. The real learning begins after one takes on the struggles of life. The test of life is in its struggle. After leaving the ashram, you may spread your goodwill and the sweet aroma of your life throughout the world.

He concluded by saying:

Remember the great truths. Honour your parents, teachers and guests. Marry and see that your line is not broken. Do not neglect the truth and dharma. Do not neglect your own welfare and the daily recitation and teaching of the Vedas, or the rites to the gods and your ancestors. Perform only those acts, which are above reproach and nothing else; honour holy and learned men; give willingly and according to your means, to all who need. Whenever you are in doubt, act as the wise men of sober judgement and holy living do or advise. This is the inner teaching of the Vedas and their core message, my sons. May Mahadeva bless you both.

'Sir, what shall we offer as *gurudakshina*?' asked Krishna. 'Nothing,' replied Sandipani. 'It is enough that you have been my pupils. Future ages will remember me because of you.' When the boys insisted on giving him something in return for what he had taught them, the guru said, 'There is only one thing that I can accept as *gurudakshina* from you, but it is not a thing you can give. Leave it for now.' Sandipani looked sad.

Krishna was puzzled to see his guru unusually distressed. That night, Krishna saw Sandipani staring pensively at the sea, lost in the far-off horizon. A deep sorrow was writ on his face as he gazed at the moonlit sea. Krishna approached him. 'Master, I know what you want as *gurudakshina*. It is your son. I owe it to you to bring back your son, Purnadatta.'

Krishna had learnt from Sudama how sea demons had kidnapped Sandipani's son. The cruel Punyajana sailors who came from the western seas, beyond which some cruel Mlechha tribes resided, had abducted him. This arid land that lay beyond the Kushasthali and Raivataka (Girnar), was extremely hot and uninhabitable, yet some non-matrilineal tribes resided there. It was called the land of Yama—the place of no return.

Sandipani was overwhelmed.

Krishna continued:

Gurudeva, it has been our privilege to be the pupils of such an enlightened sage.

> What we mean by *gurudakshina* is not in terms of material wealth, but our sense of deep gratitude. Even if everything which one possesses is given to the preceptor who turns a monkey-like young boy into a human being, or a *pashu*—brute, into Pashupati—Lord Shiva, the obligation towards the teacher cannot be repaid. I am merely expressing the sentiments of my heart so that I can have the satisfaction of having given something in return.

Krishna bowed, Sandipani hugged him and said, 'I am beholden in your presence, Krishna—you are Narayana in our midst.'

PUNYAJANA TRIBES

Cruel and known generally as Semitic tribes, a wild group of desperadoes colonised the region from the Indus basin, near the present-day port of Gadwar in Pakistan, to the Iranian desert on the west. Krishna looked at his brother with an impish smile and said, 'I have a great assignment for you when you return to Mathura.'

'What do you mean by that?' asked Balarama. 'Are you not coming with me?'

'No, you are going back alone and I request you to organise and reclaim the moat around the Mathura fort, strengthen the breached walls and, along with our cousin Satyaki, rebuild our cavalry and war chariots. Organise the mace regiment, archers and foot soldiers for the impending attack by Jarasandha. The Magadha Naresh would strike exactly a year after the anniversary of Kamsa's death. I know you will like this assignment,' said Krishna.

'Krishna, where are you going alone?'

'I will not be alone; Uddhava is going to keep me company,' Krishna said. Balarama refused to be separated from his brother, but Krishna insisted that he was needed in Mathura.

The next morning, Krishna noticed Acharya Sandipani gazing intensely at the horizon. He showed Krishna a dark spot on the distant western horizon and said that it was Panchajana's ship. The chief of the Punyajana tribe had captured Kushasthali—modern Dwaraka, a few years ago, from King Kukudmin, who had fled into the wilderness and had since been missing.

Panchajana would visit Prabhasa Tirtha every year on the Kartik full moon day—the day most sacred to Lord Shiva. Many young boys from the Aryan tribes would be present on this day, giving Panchajana ample choice to abduct handsome youths.

Sandipani revealed:

> I hear that there are two or three coastal towns near the basin of that great river Sindhu. These cities are called Samyamani, Vaivasvatapuri and Shonitapuri. Most of the times, I have come to know, Panchajana's boats call at the port of Vaivasvatapuri, also known as the Sun City. Located at the edge of an arid desert with salt lakes all around, this town is lit so bright by the reflection of the sun on the vast white beds of *lavana*—salt—that it is difficult to survive in this harsh terrain. A tribe of Nagas live there and it is a matriarchal society. The queen is said to have occult powers, and the king is only for namesake, often chosen from a stock of handsome Aryan youths. His main purpose is to share the bed of the queen and often acts as her bodyguard.

He continued:

> These Naga tribes are wild. Their women are said to have originated from a distant tribe in the west called Hittites and they call themselves Nagas, after the hooded black cobra. All Naga Kanyas owe allegiance only to the queen mother. She is very powerful and, when in a trance after worshipping the Mother Goddess, possesses fierce occult powers. It is said that no Aryan youth can hope to escape if she looks at him. They get possessed and surrender before her hypnotic powers.
>
> After Purnadatta was kidnapped a couple of years ago by Panchajana, I had enquired from the local sailors who often trade with these coastal towns. One of them even said that they had seen a handsome youth recently, standing behind the queen in an occult festival, when their trading boat anchored near Vaivasvatapuri. Therefore, I cannot let you go to a place from where you might not return.

But Krishna insisted, 'Sir, have faith in me and be assured that I will rescue your son.'

With that, Krishna took his leave. Uddhava joined Krishna in the adventure. After anchoring the ship in deep waters for four days, Captain Panchajana returned in a small boat. He was one-eyed, burly and fierce-looking, with dark skin and a bloodshot eye. As soon as he boarded the ship, Panchajana yelled at the crew and whirled his leather whip in the air to catch the attention of his mates. He screamed at the navigator, 'Kaivat

Bhikru, where were you when I was on the shore?' Bhikru was old and the harsh sea life had taken its toll on him. He had a white beard, dark skin and would stoop a little. 'I was on board, my captain, guarding it like a hawk.'

'Fine, let us take the waters at first tide. We will be heading westwards, and keep near the coast.'

Meanwhile, Krishna and Uddhava swam to the ship and clambered up its side, stealthily. Hearing some movement behind him, the wily pilot, Bhikru, whipped out a short knife and called out, 'Who is it?'

Krishna replied, 'Uncle, we want to go with you. You took our brother Purnadatta last year and we cannot live without him. Please take us to him.'

Old Bhikru was shocked to find two youths volunteering to go with the Punyajana chief. 'Such audacity! Who are you? I will wring your necks and throw you to the sharks, you fools! Do you know you have come to a wolf's lair? Get out before I kill you both,' warned Bhikru.

When they did not leave, Bhikru grew suspicious. Taking them to be thieves who had come to steal the supplies, he tied their hands and forced them to sit.

On hearing a shout, the pilot lifted the anchor and raised the main sail. High tide and good wind propelled the ship westwards, towards the dark red glow on the horizon. The brig had an ensign of a black shark, indicating that it was a dangerous predator of the seas. Krishna chatted up Bhikru to try and get him on his side. He enquired about the ship and their captain. Bhikru told them that he was afraid of Panchajana and that they should be too.

Panchajana was prowling around the vessel and when he came near Bhikru, he stood fiercely with his hands on his hips. A beautiful pink conch dangled from his waist on the right.

'What are you grumbling at?' he asked. 'You have become old and are talking to yourself. Would you like me to send you to your forefathers?' The captain, flanked by two goons who were his nephews, blew his conch. Krishna liked the conch and its shrill musical notes. The observant Krishna noticed that the conch was *Dakshinavrita*—right handed, a rare species that is found deep on the ocean bed.

'Master!' said Bhikru, 'I want to have a word with you in private. I caught two stowaways. They look very handsome and can fetch you a good price in Vaivasvatapuri. They claim to be the brothers of the fair one we kidnapped last year.' He took him to the two captives.

Krishna addressed the captain. 'Noble sir, we want to travel in your ship to see our brother whom you took last year. We know the risks involved, but miss him dearly.'

'Very well; Bhikru, give them water and let them sleep in the hold, I shall see them tomorrow morning.'

Next morning, Krishna heard somebody yelling and found Panchajana lashing the back of a young crew member with his leather whip. The youth was bleeding and crying piteously, but was left on the harsh sunny deck, unattended. When the chief retired to his cabin, Krishna walked up to the youth and stroked the lad's wounds with his gentle palms. When Krishna asked him what his offence was, the youth replied, 'I wanted an extra pail of water, which I took forcefully when they refused to give me some. These are wicked and heartless people.'

Suddenly, Panchajana was on the deck shouting at Krishna, 'How dare you touch that scoundrel! He is a thief who disobeyed my orders.'

'How did he disobey? He only wanted some water to drink as he was thirsty,' countered Krishna.

Incensed by this rejoinder, Panchajana took out his whip to lash Krishna. But Krishna grasped it quickly and jerked it with such force that the chief who was standing near the deck wall, tripped and fell overboard. Everyone was left stunned. When the two bodyguards came out of their shock and turned to attack Krishna, they were thrown overboard as well—like two sacks of sand.

The crew rejoiced. Krishna saw that the conch had fallen on the deck and grabbed it for his own and named it Panchajanya. He wanted to paint it yellow as soon as he got a chance. Krishna then proclaimed that after worshipping the Sun, Ocean and the Wind—the three main element gods—he will be known by this conch shell, it will become his symbol. Bhikru promptly changed the insignia of the mast flag to a yellow conch, discarding the black shark. Krishna then informed the crew that he would like to get back his brother. The crew warned him against such a terrible folly, but Krishna was adamant. He said:

> Bhikru, we want to get our friend who you said was sold off to the queen at Vaivasvatapuri. Please do not be afraid. Anchor your ship nearby. I shall bring my friend; it may take a few days, but you should not leave the ship. On our return, I promise, we shall sail to Bhrigukachhapa, safe waters for you. All of you will be free to go wherever you want.

'As you wish,' said Bhikru. 'When you land at Vaivasvatapuri, take my nephew Raddu with you. He knows their tongue and might be of some help to you. May Varuna, the Sea God, be with you!'

'Make friends at the port of call. Do not misbehave with women—I am cautioning one and all. Be prepared to leave the port at short notice,' warned Krishna. There was jubilation and the crew volunteered to clean the deck holds and fumigate the whole ship by burning dry cowdung.

THE CITY OF LIGHT—NOORPURA

The ship, rechristened Sankhu after the conch Panchajanya, sailed on as the sea swallowed the former master and his two cohorts. The star-studded sky looked down in all its splendour as Krishna stood in command at the ship's bow.

The Punyajana ship took on a different character, for Krishna, its new master, was benign and friendly, informal and jovial. His electric presence motivated the crew to complete their chores enthusiastically.

Krishna inspected the ship along with Uddhava and Bhikru. They discovered a hidden stock of arms and Uddhava took charge of this armoury. The weapons were distributed among the crew.

Krishna and Uddhava selected clothes, ornaments and two copper swords for their own defence. Bhikru briefed them about Vaivasvatapuri, also called Noorpura by the locals. The city was situated in Nagaloka near Patala and was ruled by a family of Naga Kanyas who could fight like men. They would hypnotise men with their sensuous charms and force them to do their bidding like pet dogs. In this matriarchal state, the men were needed only for procreation and to perform menial tasks around the city.

Houses were built of mud and walls were washed with lime. The reflection of the sun on these mud brick walls and roofs could be seen from far out into the sea. Located on the fringe of a desert, with only arid mountains beyond, the locale was bleak and desolate.

The cult worked on prophecies made by an oracle and there was an altar with a sacrificial fire. Occasionally, to please the Mother Goddess, human sacrifices were performed. To find a suitor for the princesses, a festival of choice would be held, which was a sort of blood sport. The fair and handsome man, Purnadatta, was bought by the queen at a high price last year, possibly to marry one of the princesses, most likely her successor.

After about seven days of journeying, Bhikru sailed into the creek on which stood the city. Krishna noticed a freshwater stream joining the sea and deduced that this would be the water source for the populace, with a check dam to store water. In the rays of the setting sun, the city, encircled by a stone wall, glowed as if made of burnished gold. There was a small jetty tied to hewn rock pillars by ropes. This seemed to be the landing point from the sea and steps led to the city gates.

When the ship came in sight of the fort, they saw a crowd gather on the steps. Krishna asked Raddu and another deck boy to go ashore in a small boat with some gifts and seek the permission of the queen to enter. The boys were received by armed Naga women guards and taken to the queen.

Bhikru lowered the anchor and waited through the night.

The next morning, Uddhava, Raddu and one of the Punyajana boys were dispatched with a request for an audience with the divine queen.

As soon as Uddhava reached the harbour, a beautiful and scantily-clad Naga Kanya started fondling his fine limbs with great admiration. The young girl asked with authority, 'Where is your friend?'

Uddhava was taken aback by this question. Sensing his surprise, she laughed and said, 'The Divine Mother knows all about you. She welcomes you and your friend. Enjoy our hospitality and pleasures forever. You now belong to us. Forget about your world.'

Uddhava was taken in a royal boat to the main ship. Bhikru brought down Krishna and then Uddhava repeated to him his conversation with the Naga attendant.

Krishna smiled and said, 'Do not worry. We will have to succeed. Do not fear, my friend; have self-confidence and self-control, the latter is most essential for us.' In the palace, Krishna met two strikingly beautiful princesses, who seemed to be in their twenties. He then presented them with gifts he had got from the ship. He noticed there was a handsome young man, about twenty and prince-like; he was armed with a short sword that hung from a golden shoulder strap.

Krishna saluted them in the Aryan way and the prince stepped forward to greet Krishna. He welcomed Krishna and Uddhava in the language spoken in Mathura. Krishna guessed that they had reached the right place and said to the princess, 'Divine princess, I, son of Vasudeva, the lord of the Shooras and the disciple of the best of gurus, Sandipani, salute you.'

At the mention of Sandipani, the young man grew pale and the shadow of fear crept into his eyes. He paused, hesitated, and then interpreted what Krishna had said to the princess. Krishna then presented a golden necklace, from the loot in the ship's hold, to the princess and a bracelet to the prince. The prince blushed as he was familiar with its origin.

The princesses welcomed the two boys. One of them issued a command in their tongue and the party started moving into the royal palace. The younger princess seemed to be enamoured with Krishna as she kept looking at him and blushing.

They reached the palace of the queen, a large stone structure standing in the middle of the fort. Krishna was led to an apartment where his men from the ship, aided by two officers, stood ready to guard him. The princesses then left the room. As Krishna stood by the window, gazing at the sea and the fishing boats, the young prince was ushered into his room accompanied by the same Naga Kanya who had brought Krishna from the boat.

Krishna addressed him:

> Purnadatta, I am glad to have finally found you. Gurudeva has sent his blessings. He has not forgotten you even for a moment. He says that a son is one's own self, projected into the future. In life he is your staff, in death he saves you from hell. He can never be replaced and can never be forgotten.

Purnadatta was in tears. 'I am sorry you had to come here. Please do not forget that though this woman does not understand our language, she is watching every glance and gesture we exchange.'

'Are you a prisoner?' enquired Krishna. 'I thought that you were the consort of the princess and would be king someday.'

'Yes, only if I survive long enough! You do not know this place; the women are enchantresses and they will never let you go. After enjoying the pleasures, which these Naga Kanyas give, no one would like to leave. This is *maya*—illusion, which my father used to caution his pupils against. At that time, I could not comprehend it, now I know, I am in *maya*'s vicious circle and my end will be here and soon. Krishna, please leave this place before it is too late. The queen wants to replace me with you...the elder princess is Larika, and the younger one is Asika...she is a better person. Please escape; I shall try to help you. The only alternative is that someday we will have to fight each other to death.'

Krishna could understand the gravity of the situation they were in and said, 'Purnadatta, we will take you from here at any cost. I must keep the promise made to my preceptor, your father. Please try to understand and cooperate. Let us disperse, but be ready to escape at very short notice. Come what may, I am going to take you to Prabhasa.'

Pausing then, Krishna looked at the prince, his eyes filled with pity. Then he resumed in slow, affectionate tones. 'Purnadatta, I am glad I was sent here to rescue you from this demonic life. You live in fear of losing your position, power, luxury and your life itself. You have fallen, my brother, and hesitate to return to Gurudeva and lead the life of our sages.'

'You are right. I was forced into a life of sin and ruin and was afraid I would never be able to return to the stern life of the ashram. But, with your help, I will try to atone for my unintended sinful life,' Purnadatta promised.

Purnadatta then narrated what happened when he first came here.

> I was cordially received by the Divine Mother and the Festival of Choice was held. It is the greatest and the most exciting event in the city; a blood sport, a most tragic game. The Queen invokes the Oracle and, if she ordains, we have to fight each other to the finish. If we don't kill each other, the king will slay us.
>
> I had to fight the former husband of the Divine Princess. Poor chap had no chance against me and I had to kill him, lest I should be killed.

'I thought only men are cruel tyrants, but this kingdom of women is no less! I have destroyed Panchajana; hereafter, this slave trade in Aryan youth will stop,' said Krishna. His mind was frantically working out ways and means of escape. He asked Purnadatta if the king, who is of Aryan descent, would like to escape as well. Purnadatta felt it was unlikely because it is very difficult to forego the pleasures of a Naga Kanya.

HALL OF THE SACRED FIRE

In the afternoon, Krishna and Uddhava were led to the Sacred Presence. They laid aside their arms and followed their escort with the presents they had brought from the ship.

Armed, fierce-looking and voluptuous female soldiers guarded the corridors through which they passed. They entered a dark hall, the Hall of the

Sacred Fire. The altar there was a platform with a square pit, in the middle of which a sacred fire had been lit. Its flames threw fitful gleams of light on those present, lending the place an eerie and fearsome look. Behind the sacrificial fire, was an image of the Mother of the World—big-bellied and heavy-breasted!

Krishna was amused that the Mother of the World should be so fearsome. Krishna and Uddhava were led to the steps of the platform, where the two princesses stood with the prince behind them. The king, the only person who had the privilege of staying armed in the Sacred Presence, stood on the platform. He was a well-built man of about fifty, with benign looks, a large forehead and handsome face. Krishna smiled at the Divine Father and felt that he responded in kind.

The Divine Mother stood behind the sacrificial pit. She was a strikingly beautiful, middle-aged woman. She was wearing a large girdle around her waist, necklaces and a diadem in the shape of a hooded cobra. A live cobra coiled around the neck. Her jewels glittered in the flames. Everyone prostrated before her and rose at her command. Then, at a sign from her, the king asked the prince to invite Krishna to deliver his message.

'Divine Mother, I, Krishna, son of Vasudeva, the lord of the Shooras, bring you a message of friendship from King Ugrasena of Mathura. I humbly request you to accept these gifts.'

The mother spoke in her resonant voice:

> Son of Vasudeva, we welcome you. We learnt some days before that you were coming to us. At the command of Ma, the Mother of the World, we welcome you. We accept the presents and assure you of our hospitality. We command you to the care of our august consort, the Divine Father. The command of Ma is that you shall live with us forever as one of us.

The king stepped down from the platform and led him through a private corridor into a chamber behind the hall where, on a stone couch lay the mother, exhausted after the trance-like ritual at the altar.

The king spoke in his language and enquired about Parashurama, the ancient warrior who had now retired to the mountain hermitage near Sowparnika river in the Sahyadri Hills on the west coast of the country.

'Krishna, I once belonged, like you, to Aryawartha and I had, by an accident of fate, a shipwreck which ended in this strange hell. I am a regal prisoner here.'

Meanwhile, Asika brought him something to eat. Krishna took some fruits, which tasted strange to him and drank some milk. Like a snake, Asika tried to coil around Krishna, but he resisted her advances and stood up, requesting her to leave with folded hands. She blushed and, with tears in her eyes, left.

In no time, Krishna was escorted to the king's chambers where Krishna was told that he was in grave danger and had to leave immediately. Both the princesses had taken a liking to Krishna and the queen wanted him to fight with the prince to win the hand of Larika.

Purnadatta came, weeping, to Krishna's chamber later that night and said he would not fight him. He would rather be killed by Krishna. But Krishna assured him that he will plan out their escape much before that happens.

The next day, Krishna asked Uddhava to instruct Raddu to keep the boat ready for departure. The Festival of Choice commenced in the afternoon. The royal family was seated on a platform and the citizens had all gathered to witness their favourite sport. Purnadatta was brought into the arena, armed with a short copper sword. 'Purnadatta,' whispered Krishna, 'we will indulge in a mock fight where we will pretend to lose our swords. We will then wrestle and get to the wharf and our waiting boat.'

The young men fought, going round and round the arena, inching nearer to the wharf. Suddenly, Krishna delivered a quick blow with his sword and Purnadatta lost his weapon. There were great cheers from the crowd. Krishna then dropped his weapon and invited the prince to wrestle.

As they rolled on the ground, they wedged nearer to the water. The crowd however, understood their intention and demanded that both boys be killed. As the king descended on to the platform with his sword raised to kill, Asika came running and fell on both the boys. She begged her father not to kill them or take all three lives. In that confusion, Krishna asked Purnadatta to jump into Raddu's boat, which he did.

In a swift move, Krishna grabbed the king's raised sword and asked Asika to get into the boat as well. Krishna followed and rowed swiftly towards the ship. When the queen demanded that Asika should return, she wriggled out of the boat, jumped into the sea and swam back.

Purnadatta said to Krishna, 'A Naga Kanya belongs to her mother, never to her lover and husband.'

Bhikru took advantage of westerly winds and the square sails responded beautifully as the ship cruised in the south-east direction, towards Prabhasa. It was almost ten days before the ship was seen by the people of Prabhasa. Guru Sandipani, who, for several months, had been anxiously waiting for Krishna and Uddhava at Prabhasa, informed King Bhimdev of Veraval about the arrival of a new ship. The ship was anchored in deep waters and Raddu was told to go ahead and announce their arrival.

When Sandipani heard the thundering sound of a conch emanate from the incoming ship, he looked up at the sky and worshipped the setting sun. The blowing of the conch signalled to him that he should stay prepared, as something significant was about to occur. It was also at the same time, a call to the whole of humanity, announcing the unfolding of momentous events.

When they came ashore, the guru, Sandipani's family was reunited and the joy that prevailed showed that Krishna's debt had been repaid in the most befitting manner.

Before dawn, everyone awoke, bathed in the sea and worshipped Somnatheswar. After the morning prayers, Krishna asked Sandipani, 'Gurudeva, you said that there was a Sun temple nearby, where an ardent, if not a fanatic Atharvana, known as Angirasa, lives. Can I seek your permission to visit his ashram?'

'Of course, I am sure you would enjoy the sage's company. He is known as Ghora Angirasa because of his uncompromising stance on sun worship and his rigid notions on Vedic knowledge. Please go, my son, and convey my regards to him.'

GHORA ANGIRASA

Towards the east of Prabhasa Tirtha, near the confluence of the three rivers—Hiranya, Kapila and Prak Saraswati, there was a beautiful temple of Sun God and the ashram of Ghora Angirasa. Angirasa welcomed the handsome boy. Krishna prostrated before the sage and, with great humility, requested him to accept him as a pupil. 'I am eager to learn the Saura philosophy—Shaurayan—from you, O great Angirasa.'

Ghora Angirasa replied:

> Of course, I accept you as my pupil. People have wrong notions about my form of worship. They call me *ghora*—the terrible. There is nothing terrible about me, except that I am an uncompromising worshipper of the

Sun God—the giver of life, the Supreme Being and *timira samhara*—the destroyer of darkness.

Long before the crack of dawn, Krishna was ready and all set to take the oath of allegiance to the teachings of Atharvana Angirasa. The sage was waiting for dawn, when he signalled Krishna to join him with folded palms, filled with water from the ocean. They then started chanting the famous Gayatri Mantra:

Om Bhuh, Om Bhuvah, Om Suvah,
Om Mahah, Om Janah, Om Tapah,
Om Satyam, Tat Savitur varenyam
Bhargo Devasya Dheemahi,
Dhiyo Yonah Prachodayat.

Angirasa was thrilled and felt as if the Sun God himself had come down to accept the oblations from the handsome boy. 'There were two primeval verses from the Rig Veda on the Sun God,' said Angirasa.

Proceeding from Primeval seed,
The early morning light they see,
That gleameth higher than the heaven,
From hour of darkness all around,
We gazing on the higher light
Yes, gazing on the higher light,
To Surya, god among the gods,
We have attained—the highest light!
Yes, the highest light!

After a few months, Angirasa told Krishna that he had learnt all that the sage could teach him. 'My son, I am not *ghora* anymore. Let me be known simply as Atharvana Angirasa. I have learnt from you what humility is, my son.'

'O, great guru! I am nothing before your knowledge. Please sir, I would like you to teach me the purpose of human life,' said Krishna.

Angirasa then explained:

> Krishna, remember that the whole life is a sacrifice. When one hungers and thirsts and does not enjoy himself, it is the *diksha* or preparatory consecration ceremony. When one eats and drinks and enjoys himself, then he joins in

the *upasana* ceremonies. When one laughs and eats and practices sexual intercourse, then he joins in the chant and recitation ceremonies. Austerity, alms-giving, uprightness, non-violence and truth, these are one's gifts to the priests. Death is an ablution after the sacrificial ceremony. In the final hour, one should take refuge in these three thoughts.

You are Akshita—the indestructible
You are Achyuta—the unshakeable
You are the very essence of Prana—life.

Verily, O Gargi, at the command of that Imperishable, the Sun and the Moon stand apart.

Verily, O Gargi, at the command of that Imperishable, the Earth and the Sky stand apart.

Verily, O Gargi, at the command of that Imperishable, the Moments, the Hours, the Days, the Nights, the Fortnights, the Months, the Seasons and the Years stand apart.

Verily, O Gargi, at the command of that Imperishable; some rivers flow from the snowy mountains to the east, others to the west, in whatever direction each flows.

Krishna returned to Prabhasa, prayed at the Somnatheswar shrine, offered his homage to the great Mahadeva and requested him for guidance to fulfil his mission. As he was leaving, he saw Bhikru and asked him why he had not left for his village.

'No, my good master, I belong to this place now. Raddu married a local girl and he wants me to stay with him. Did you know that the city of lights was destroyed? I heard it from some sailors. I was told that the king was killed by the queen and Asika was tortured by her elder sister. Then, on a full moon night, there was a big fire and the earth shook. The whole place collapsed and the great sea had swallowed the land of Yama. The God of Gods has acted at last.'

The next morning, Krishna left for Mathura with two attendants, on a chariot yoked to two handsome white steeds. Before leaving for his native land, Krishna bowed to the king and blew his conch. Thus began the Krishnayana, the saga of Krishna.

Vasudevasutam Devam Kamsa Chaanura Mardanam
Devaki Paramaanandam Krishnam Vande Jagatgurum

Krishna the Divinity Himself, son of Vasudeva, pride and pleasure of Devaki.

Slayer of terrible Kamsa and Chanura, the World Teacher, I salute thee, O God.

*****

Episode 2

Krishna: The Man

Tava hritasmi puraina gunairaham
Harati maam kila chedinrupo adhuna,
Ayi krupalaya palaya mamiti
Prajagadey Jagadekapatey taya

I am indeed already stolen (captivated) by Thy virtues. Now it is said that the lord of Chedi is to take me away,

O the receptacle of mercy! Mayst Thou save me. Thus, O sole lord of the world, has she sent word.

—Narayaneeyam

KRISHNA'S MISSION BEGINS

The king of Magadha, Brihadratha, had two wives, who, after being childless for long, gave birth to two halves of a male child. These aberrations were regarded with horror and discarded on the outskirts of the city. They were found by a Rakshasi named Jara, who picked them up and put the two halves together. On their coming in contact with each other, the halves became a whole and took the shape of a baby boy. The Rakshasi returned the baby to the king and retired to the deep Kirataka forest in the northern Gangetic region.

Brihadratha named his son Jarasandha, as he had been put together by Jara. The royal astrologers predicted a great future for the baby. As he grew older, Jarasandha became an ardent devotee of Rudra. Blessed by the grace of Mahadeva, he prevailed over many kings. Jarasandha opposed a republican form of government such as in the confederation of Mathura. Being highly ambitious, he conducted the famous Ashwamedha Yagna, conquered eighty-six kingdoms and imprisoned their kings in Aryawartha Madhyadesa. His marital alliance with Kamsa was based on convenience and opportunity. The rule of Kamsa over Mathura whetted Jarasandha's ambition to ultimately conquer Panchala and Hastinapura and become the supreme monarch of Aryawartha.

Jarasandha was an incongruous combination of spirituality and materialism; he represented the ancient practices and beliefs as he would perform Vedic yagnas and sacrifices, he also supported brahmanas—the practice of traditional priesthood. But Jarasandha also held rituals and tantric festivals, at times, involving *nara-medha,* or human sacrifice, to propitiate Vedic gods, especially

Rudra and Shakti, in order to obtain occult powers for domination. This was contrary to Krishna's approach. He believed in the equality of all men and women in the eyes of God. Krishna was opposed to archaic Vedic rituals that involved animal sacrifice.

Jarasandha's dreams of becoming the supreme ruler were shattered when he heard of Kamsa's assassination. This incident made him doubt his own invincibility. It was said that for several days after Kamsa's death, despite being a great devotee of Lord Shiva, Jarasandha did not attend the daily worship of the lord. He even refused to meet the head priest.

Consumed with feelings of revenge, he sent for his trusted commanders from the Magadhan Army—Dimbhak and Hansa, to plan out a military strategy. Jarasandha sought to raze Mathura to dust and get the heads of Vasudeva's sons.

In the meantime, Rukmi, the impertinent prince of Vidarbha, left Mathura in a hurry to meet the emperor. Rukmi reached Girivraja and gave a first-hand account of the events at Mathura. To the consternation of Jarasandha, Rukmi said, 'Your majesty, Kamsa was fearful when he came face to face with Krishna. In fact, when Krishna was advancing, Kamsa started retracing, thereby tripping over his throne, dropping his sword and losing his crown. I had a feeling that Kamsa died more out of fright than Krishna hurting him.'

Jarasandha summoned his minister, Kanika, and asked him to send word to the Chedi Raj, Damaghosha, to come urgently to Girivraja. He then asked his minister if he knew what had happened to Kamsa. Kanika replied that he had heard the same story from travellers passing through the city.

'What am I to do Kanika? You have been very wise in your counsel so far,' asked the emperor.

'My lord, at the risk of being insolent, I must say that Kamsa was not as wise a ruler as you are,' said Kanika respectfully, with folded palms. 'The people of Mathura did not appreciate him for killing six newborn sons of Vasudeva.'

Jarasandha was a great diplomat who wanted to assess the pros and cons of the situation before the arrival of Damaghosha. 'What is your honest opinion on the events in Mathura and how should we proceed?' he asked. 'The prestige of Magadha is at stake.'

Kanika humbly addressed Jarasandha:

> Oh Magadha Naresh! As an old servant of the house of Brihadratha, I advise patience and request you not to take any hasty action. Before the might of

> Magadha, the confederation of Mathura is nothing. You can reduce Mathura to ashes in no time with your invincible army. But the people of Mathura never had any animosity towards you or Magadha. This calamity occurred due to Kamsa's fear and misjudgement. For that, the sons of Vasudeva should be punished, not the innocent people of Mathura.

'I like your wise analysis of the situation, Kanika; and what did you think of the prince of Vidarbha, Rukmi?'

'I believe that he has his own axe to grind in the predicament of Magadha. He is keen on rash action. Your majesty, it may not be in our interest in the long run to be associated with him,' replied Kanika.

'I agree with you. Prince Rukmi has always been insolent and highly temperamental. A king needs patience and firmness. He should not rush into mindless action, only to regret it later. Let me retire for the day; Kanika, you may leave now. Please let me know when the Chedi Raj arrives,' concluded Jarasandha.

Damaghosha arrived and was welcomed with open arms. Damaghosha was a shrewd ruler and did not want to be on the wrong side of Magadha Naresh, so he chose his words carefully. With great reverence, Damaghosha offered his condolences on the death of Kamsa and said:

> Magadha Naresh, I was shocked at the assassination of my cousin, Kamsa and refused to attend the Upanayanam ceremony of Vasudeva's sons. I could not, however, prevent my wife and son from attending the ceremonies. After all, Shrutashrava is Krishna's paternal aunt. But she came back in a great hurry, almost panicking at the state of affairs in Mathura.

'I see!' said Jarasandha. 'What about my young friend, Shishupala? I came to know that he has become very handsome after meeting that cowherd son of Vasudeva.' Damaghosha was surprised at the extent of the king's knowledge.

Jarasandha continued:

> With the murder of my son-in-law, the interests of Magadha are compromised. Mathura was my outpost on the west. I wished to annex Panchala, ruled by that impudent Drupada. I am also waiting for the demise of Bhishma, the invincible warrior and patriarch of Hastinapura. Do you understand the gravity of the situation, my friend? Two cowherds had the temerity to take on the mighty Magadha!

Damaghosha grew very cautious and asked, 'What would you want me to do? I am ready for any service to the mighty emperor.'

Jarasandha calmed down. 'I heard that the cowherd, Krishna, is revered as a god in Mathura. Is it true?'

Damaghosha said warily, 'I believe it is so because the black mark on Shishupala's cheek vanished when Krishna touched him.' He also told him about the transformation of Trivakra.

'I hear he has a brother—a giant and a great wrestler, fair unlike Krishna.'

'My lord, I am yet to meet the sons of Vasudeva. If Your Majesty permits, I can make a trip to Mathura.'

'You may have to wait for it. It seems they will join Sandipani's *gurukul*...I want their heads. Can you get them for me?' Jarasandha growled. Damaghosha was stunned at the request, but remained composed. 'Mighty emperor! Your wisdom has no bounds. As soon as the boys return, I shall try to bring them to you,' Damaghosha said rather meekly.

The next day, a faithful soldier of the Magadhan regiment rushed to have an audience with the emperor. 'Hail Magadha Naresh,' greeted the soldier, named Kasya. 'I have news, my lord. The sons of Vasudeva have departed for Avanti along with guru Sandipani. They are now *brahmachari*s and will return to Mathura only after one or two years. Things are getting back to normal at Mathura; the old King Ugrasena wears the crown,' said the soldier.

'What? Krishna refused kingship of Mathura? Then why did he kill his uncle?' asked Jarasandha.

Jarasandha sent feelers to several kings in the neighbourhood and tried to win them over with persuasion. Many rulers joined Jarasandha's campaign either out of helplessness, or out of fear of Krishna—a mere boy who was able to kill Kamsa with such ease. Before another similar contingency arose, the Magadha Naresh invited these kings to his palace to discuss the strategy to suppress Krishna.

The emperor addressed the group of kings who had gathered in the council room. 'My friends, is it not better to create a feeling of terror in the psyche of Mathura? We want them to surrender the sons of Vasudeva if they want peace with Magadha.' After a few more consultations, the group agreed that they should disrupt the peace and stability in Mathura through frequent border clashes and incursions. They must create panic and keep reminding them to hand over Krishna as soon as he returns.

Harivamsa mentions that there were several such incursions before Krishna and Balarama returned, after three years of absence.

DRAMA AT MATHURA

Despite the jubilation at Mathura on the return of their beloved Krishna, the people were scared. Krishna advised his father to call for the Yadava assembly to take stock of the situation. Ugrasena presided over the assembly. Krishna and Balarama were welcomed and then briefed about Jarasandha's terror attacks, his plundering of the crops, threats to innocent citizens and his demand that Krishna and Balarama surrender themselves. Krishna, very calmly, listened to the discussion and then asked the people what they felt.

Vikardu, a member of the assembly, spoke:

> Krishna, we have immense love for you and feel grateful for the things you have done for us. But the people of Mathura are suffering. The civic life of our city has been completely destroyed. Commerce and trade are ruined. We cannot attend to our farming. We are hungry, but do not complain, out of love for you. We could never dream of handing you over to the emperor. Under these circumstances, would it not be prudent for you to leave for some far off place till Jarasandha relents?

Krishna, ever smiling and unperturbed, stood and thanked Vikardu for telling the truth. 'Let Mathura have many more Vikardus to put things in proper perspective. My brother and I will leave the city. Please do not worry about our safety; our dharma will protect us.'

Krishna folded his hands and, with due humility, interrupted his father to first address the assembly. 'Lord of Shooras, I move among the people and know all about them. War is fought not with arms, but with hearts. And few men in Mathura have the heart to die in defence of their home. Am I not correct?' asked Krishna. He was met with silence.

'My elders!' Krishna raised his voice and spoke:

> The people of Mathura are in no mood to suffer any more than what they had been going through all these twenty-five years; there are no warriors left to face the might of Magadha. We do not have any *rathi*s and *maharathi*s to keep the Magadhan army at bay, even for a day. In the event of an

invasion, I will not be surprised if there were to be an exodus of the people to the neighbouring kingdoms. I would not like to witness the humiliation of Mathura at our expense. We shall now depart and come back to fight another day. Prudence is the best part of statesmanship. The welfare of the people should be the prime goal of a ruler at all times and our immediate departure is a small price.

There were loud cheers at this statement.

'Krishna, we have implicit faith in you, your foresight and your wisdom. Suggest to us the best course to adopt; we are too weak to resist the enemy at present,' said Vikardu.

'Jarasandha only wants the two of us and will therefore not invade Mathura if we are not here. He will instead try to find us,' said Krishna.

'But where will you go? His domain is vast, and his allies are all spread out as far as the Sahya Mountains and Paschima Samudra—west coast,' said Akrura.

Krishna smiled confidently. 'Do not worry about us. Jarasandha has become mighty by *adharma*; unaided by dharma, his might dies,' said Krishna.

THE GREAT ADVENTURE

Krishna asked Vikardu, a well-travelled noble warrior seasoned by many battles, to suggest a place where it would be difficult for Jarasandha to reach them.

> Far beyond the domain of Jarasandha, lie the Sahya Mountains in the south-west, that touch the high heavens. Beyond them, there is Karavirapura on the banks of river Venya. It was founded by Padmavarma, the step-brother of a Yadava ancestor called Madhava. It is now being ruled by his descendant, King Shrigalava, who is likely to welcome you.

Balarama was curious to know more about the Yadava ancestry.

Vikardu narrated the following story:

> King Haryashva, a descendant of Emperor Yayati, married Madhumati, the daughter of demon Madhu and received the cities of Anarta and Saurashtra as a gift. He founded Girinagar—modern Girnar. By five princesses, who were the daughters of Naga king, Dhumravarna, he begot five sons. They were—Muchkunda, who founded Mahishmati and Purika in the Vindhyas; Padmavarma, who established Karavirapura on the Venya; Sarasa who set up Kraunchapura; Harita, who inherited the island in the sea,

> known for pearl fisheries, from his maternal grandfather; and Madhava, your ancestor who begot Satvata, who in turn gave birth to Bhima. This line of Yadavas was called Satvatas.
>
> In his time, the Madhuvana region, then ruled by the sons of the demon Madhu, was destroyed by Shatrughna, the younger brother of Ramachandra. He founded Mathura in its place. Later on, the valiant Bhima regained Mathura from the descendants of Shatrughna and the city became the home of Yadavas.
>
> Bhima's son Andhaka begot Revata who ruled over Girinagar in Saurashtra, which, in the course of time, became Raivataka. Revata's son was the great king Riksha, whose son was Vishvagarbha. Your immediate ancestors, Shoora and Bhabhru, descended from him.

Vikardu said in conclusion:

> Vaasudeva, you are most powerfully connected. You have clansmen in Anartha and Saurashtra in the Vindhyas and in the Sahya Mountains. Sons of your father's sister Pritha, are the claimants to the empire of Bharatas and the throne of Hastinapura, whereas his other sister, Shrutashrava, is the queen of Chedi. Just as the Yadavas, the kings of Vidarbha are Bhojas.

'Vikardu, these connections do not address the present problem of where they can stay,' Vasudeva said. 'I heard that Shrigalava is an ally of Jarasandha and to curry the emperor's favour, he could betray my sons to the Magadha ruler.'

'We could seek the help of the immortal Bhargava Rama, the son of the revered Jamadagni,' pitched in Gargacharya. 'Though he lives in Shurparaka, which he reclaimed from the sea, he often visits the tribal settlements of the Sahyadri Mountains—his main abode is Mahendragiri. I will go personally and beg him to look after you both.'

Balarama interjected, 'How can the esteemed Bhargava be of any help? Has he not renounced the use of arms?'

'True, yet his ancient wisdom is mightier than the terrible *parashu*, the double-headed battleaxe, with which he once destroyed wicked kings,' Garga said.

Finally, Krishna spoke:

> Let us not spend much time in talk. Time is the essence of life and much has to be done. Jarasandha should not reach us and, at the same time, we must ensure he does not harm the people of Mathura. Long before the dawn breaks, we shall be on our way to the west.

Krishna then addressed Ugrasena:

> After we have been gone for a day and a night, please send Gada, my brother, to Jarasandha with a message that he will not find us in Mathura, and he should seek us elsewhere. Tell him we fled out of fear, inciting his vanity. That could avert his attack on Mathura for the present.

Krishna took leave of his mother, assuring her that they would come back victorious. Before dawn broke, Krishna, Balarama and Uddhava rode out on the best horses, speeding westwards. They had to pass through Vidarbha to reach the Sahyadri Hills for safe passage.

Meanwhile, Jarasandha had sent for Rukmi to come to Rajgir in Magadha. Jarasandha knew that Rukmi was ambitious and had been a pupil of Bhargava Rama. He was therefore an able warrior, well versed in the art of warfare; the army of Vidarbha was formidable.

Jarasandha felt that in his imperialistic plan to annex as many kingdoms as possible, Rukmi was the right person to fill the gap left by Kamsa. Rukmi chose to be in the good books of the ruthless Magadha Naresh as he aimed to eventually succeed him. This suited Jarasandha and he decided to prop up Vidarbha as a staunch ally in his scheme of things.

The only person in Vidarbha concerned about Krishna's well-being was Rukmini. But she was powerless and could only share her anxiety with Kaishika, who was her grandfather. Kaishika, after his son Bhishmaka dethroned him at the instance of Jarasandha, lived outside the city of Kundinapura. Kaishika was a pious man who, with his brother Kratha, had retired from the affairs of the state after Jarasandha shattered the autonomy of Vidarbha and converted it into a vassal kingdom.

Kaishika said he knew about Rukmi's schemes, but could do nothing as he had lost all power. Rukmini learnt that Jarasandha had advised Rukmi that he should give her hand in marriage to Shishupala and, in return, Rukmi should marry his granddaughter Viplavi. This way they could forge a grand alliance to march against Mathura. In fact, with a single stroke, Jarasandha endeavoured to be as powerful as the Bharatas of Hastinapura.

Rukmini was disturbed about her imminent nuptials. One day, she received a message from Trivakra that sent her aflutter. Uddhava was the messenger and he insisted on delivering the message in person. Rukmini met Uddhava and took him to her grandfather. He enquired about the welfare of Mathura and Ugrasena.

Uddhava said:

> I have come from Mathura with a message from its lord and from my mother Devaki. The army of Jarasandha is marching into Mathura to capture Krishna and Balarama. As Mathura is not strong enough to fend off this attack, Krishna and Balarama have decided to leave town. They would like to go to the Mahendra Mountains where the revered Bhargava Rama is likely to meet them. They will be passing through Vidarbha on foot in a few days' time. I came on horseback in advance to convey a message to princess Rukmini from mother Devaki. She wanted me to enquire if the princess could arrange a safe passage for Krishna and Balarama through Vidarbha.

This was a dangerous situation for Rukmini and Kaishika to be in. If Rukmi found out, there would be hell to pay.

Turning to Uddhava, he said, 'Young man, change your clothes and come to stay with me as a brahmana. You may bring Vasudeva's sons in the guise of brahmanas when they arrive at Kundinapura. I will see that all of you get a safe passage through the city.'

In a few days' time, two ascetics in black clothes and matted locks, accompanied by a brahmana boy, came to the palace of Kaishika and were cordially received by him. 'I have already made arrangements for a few brahmanas from Kundinapura to join a caravan that is going to Karavirapura on a pilgrimage to Gokarna Kshetra on the west coast. You may join them and make your way,' assured Kaishika. Rukmini told the maids that she would attend the holy persons herself.

Rukmini looked into Krishna's beautiful eyes and, with a smile, served food to all three.

BHARGAVA RAMA OF THE BATTLEAXE—PARASHURAMA

Krishna and Balarama parted from the caravan when they saw the Sahya Mountains and travelled towards Mount Mahendra. Uddhava remained at Kundinapura along with Acharya Shvetaketu, the principal disciple of Sandipani.

The mountain air and tribal hospitality were refreshing. 'Krishna,' asked Balarama, 'how could you leave your comfortable life and make this journey? Could we not have stayed at Mathura and faced the challenge of Jarasandha? Do you not feel our lives have changed beyond the ordinary?'

'I would have liked to continue our lives as it was,' replied Krishna. 'However, we are not ordinary beings; we meet challenges head-on and we choose to fight injustice. At the same time, we enjoy life and have enriching experiences. In my opinion, leaving Mathura was the right strategy to protect innocent citizens from paying with their lives on our behalf.'

As they journeyed further along the slopes of Mount Mahendra, the brothers saw a large hermitage. They were told that the great sage Bhargava Rama had recently stayed there. Acharya Sandipani had mentioned that Parashurama, as he was widely known, was vigorous despite his advanced age. It was said that he was the embodiment of ancestral greatness—Lord Shiva Himself, who walks amongst us in flesh and blood! He was also known to have fought a host of rulers whose barbarian defiance of the Aryan code had threatened to overwhelm dharma in its very home. He had killed, with his bare hands, the invincible Haihaya king, Kartavirya, who, it was said, possessed the strength of a thousand arms. He had conquered the world, from the snow clad Himalayas to the rolling rivers of Narmada. He then settled in the west coast, renouncing his Kshatra Dharma and now lived as a kindred soul on the Sahayadri mountain range. When the boys neared the ashram, they were overtaken by the peace and harmony surrounding the place. They found the great Bhargava sitting under a giant tree, firm and straight before a sacrificial fire, chanting sacred verses. The sage was tall and sinewy, with a long white beard and a beautiful head with a silver mane. A tigerskin was wrapped around his loins. A long battleaxe reposed by his side along with a *kamandalu* filled with water.

Krishna and Balarama prostrated before the great man and were greeted by Parashurama. 'Welcome my sons,' said the sage. 'I was informed of your arrival and have been looking forward to meet you.' When Krishna and Balarama told him how they had to leave Mathura and travel this far, he was impressed. 'My dear sons, what you did was right. Death should not be courted, unless dharma demands it. Else, it is either vanity or cowardice, a flight from dharma!' He continued, 'What the world thinks is not always correct. Often, action is heroic. But at times, retreat from action requires greater heroism. You have done well my sons; prudence is the better part of valour.'

Krishna felt blissful in the sage's presence. 'Lord!' spoke Krishna, 'Our elders at Mathura suggested that we can seek refuge at Karavirapura, ruled by Shrigalava.'

Parashurama frowned and said:

> Shrigalava will never help you. He is selfish and cunning like a fox, as his name suggests; he considers himself a god and has been persecuting all men of learning who do not recognise him as one. Shrigalava would hand you over to Jarasandha for his benefit. What do you think Jarasandha would do now? Do you believe that he will leave Mathura in peace?

After a pause, Parashurama continued:

> I have a plan for you; do as I say and it will be almost impossible for Jarasandha to find you. Gomantak Hill, on the seashore, would be a suitable place for you, as it is a steep, inaccessible hill. When you reach the summit, you will see a gentle plateau sloping towards the sea. A very picturesque place and the people there are harmless and hospitable. They are called Garudas because they march into a battle with eagle faces. The Garudas are devoted to me because I once saved them from destruction. They have a very fine chief, and I believe you will be happy in their company. They will never betray you.

Led by the mighty son of Jamadagni, the three of them then started for Gomantak Hill, in the present-day region of Goa. They had to pass through dense jungle and Balarama was surprised at the agility of this veteran. He asked him, 'Lord, having conquered all the kings, why did you give away the earth? If you had not done so, all these aggressive kings would not have raised their heads.'
The great sage replied:

> That is a very pertinent query! You are aware of the Aryan culture that preaches renunciation after attaining the order—dharma, which is protecting *rita*, the discipline of Vedas. The Aryan way of life exudes *brahmatejas*—pursuit of spiritual enquiry and not temporal power. That is why I gave up my rule.

Krishna then asked, 'Oh mighty one, would you not tell us all about *kshatratej* and *brahmatejas*?'
Parashurama then said:

> Well, my sons, listen to me attentively. Long ago, around the time of the Ikshvakus, there lived a king of the Haihayas, who had descended from the Yayati–Yadu clan. He was known as Kartavirya Arjuna, the son of Kritavirya, and was a great devotee of Dattatreya, who came from the race of Atri, the celestial sage. Dattatreya granted Arjuna great boons such as the might of thousand arms, a golden chariot that moved at his will, the power of

restraining wrong by justice, the conquest of the earth and the disposition to rule it righteously, and finally, death only at the hands of a man more renowned than him in the world. But the very boons Arjuna had sought, led to his downfall.

His fall came when Arjuna began oppressing and harassing good people and defying the eternal *rita*; he derided the gods and mocked our ancient ways; nothing was sacred to him, except abject subjugation to his power and might. He thought he was above all things and his will was the law for all. He burnt the ashram of the greatest of rishis, Vasishta. He visited the hermitage of my father, the noble Jamadagni and was received by my mother, Renuka, with all respect due to a mighty king. However, he repaid her hospitality by forcefully carrying off the calf of the milch cow meant for the sacred oblation, destroyed our ashram and killed my father.

The earth was calling for his destruction since times immemorial. He had burnt all ashrams along the great river Ganga and when the noble sage Parashara confronted him, he whipped him and drove his chariot over the legs of the sage. Life is *tapas*—self-discipline, which conquers our weaknesses and makes us men, else we turn into contemptible worms, which was what Kartavirya had become. What a pity!

When such demonic power establishes its sway, it listens to nothing; it then has to be destroyed. The combined forces of Haihayas turned against me and attacked. I had to cast aside my *brahmatejas* and vanquish them. I had to cut off the head of Kartavirya with my battleaxe, a gift from the great Mahadeva. I wanted to make the world safe for those who want to pursue *rita*, *satya* and *tapas*, but I had never loved power and never wanted to rule. My mission was to re-establish dharma, which I thought, at that time, I had achieved. Therefore, I gave up everything.

They finally reached Gomantak. On the top of the hill was a fairly large plateau with running streams, groves of shady trees, floating misty clouds and a cool breeze—an all-encompassing serenity! The villagers welcomed the sage with great enthusiasm.

Parashurama told the two brothers:

These hill tribes are called Garudas for their acute perception, swift flight through the mountain passes, sure-footedness and keen sight. They never fail in hunting their prey; they are like falcons. Great guides of the forest paths,

> honey hunters, very transparent, friendly and fun-loving people. You will be welcome to stay as long as you like. Also, most of them visit Karavirapura, so they can get you first-hand information of the outside world.

Just before leaving, Parashurama reminded Krishna of his mission to establish dharma. He then looked at Balarama and said that his presence would help establish dharma and his weapon would be a *hal*, which would earn him the name, Haldhar. Together they would be a formidable force to reckon with. 'My blessings are with you and if you ever need me, send one of the Garudas.' Saying that, Parashurama left for his abode.

JARASANDHA PREPARES TO INVADE MATHURA

Jarasandha flew into a rage when he heard about Krishna and Balarama's escape. He ordered Hansa and Dimbhak to regroup all the Magadhan troops and allies. The preparations for an immediate march to seize Mathura began in earnest.

The combined armies moved westwards towards Mathura and camped on the banks of the Yamuna, which was about two days' march from the city. The force consisted of 200 war chariots, 50 elephants, 500 cavalry, over two thousand bowmen and several thousand foot soldiers and other support staff.

A royal tent with Jarasandha's insignia—an elephant flying on the mast, was laid out. Drupada, the King of Panchala, had declined to give his army safe passage through his kingdom and this had infuriated Jarasandha. But for his urgency to invade Mathura, he would have trampled Kampilya, the Panchala capital in no time. During the afternoon meal that day, he noticed that the ever-punctual Chedi Raj—Damaghosha, was not present. Jarasandha was also told that messengers of peace had arrived from Mathura, but Damaghosha had refused to meet them. When Chedi Raj did return, Jarasandha enquired about the messengers. Jarasandha doubted Damaghosha's intentions; after all he was a relative of Krishna and Balarama. Damaghosha told him that the boys had fled Mathura. Jarasandha feigned surprise at the news.

'Akrura has come along with Brihadbala and Vasudeva's other son, Gada, to make a submission to you, my lord!' Damaghosha said. Jarasandha agreed to meet them.

When Akrura, Gada and Brihadbala, the son of Devabhaga, offered their greetings, Jarasandha suddenly got up and shouted: 'What is this silly story I hear about the two rogues running away, Akrura?'

'It is true, my lord. They left Mathura seven days ago without informing anyone and we are not aware of their destination.'

'I do not believe you. You must have concealed them somewhere,' yelled Jarasandha.

'They are not cowards. They did not want the Yadavas of Mathura to die. They knew that you were after their heads and if they stayed at Mathura, the people who love them would have laid down their lives for the cowherd boys,' replied Akrura.

'I am going to punish you all the same for sending them away,' thundered Jarasandha.

Akrura reminded him that it was against Raja Dharma to destroy Mathura when the two boys at fault had left. He also reminded Jarasandha of the fate that befell Kamsa when he did not follow the path of dharma, but Jarasandha was adamant.

'Many Yadavas have already fled Mathura and, after our return, the others will run away as well. The noble Bhishma of Hastinapura and Drupada of Panchala have promised to grant us asylum in their kingdoms,' said Akrura. 'We have come here to beg you to spare the innocent citizens of Mathura,' concluded Akrura with folded arms.

Jarasandha then tried to learn the location of the boys, but Akrura assured him that none in Mathura knew where they were. The emperor then dismissed him, but ordered Brihadbala to stay there.

Jarasandha analysed the situation and concluded that it was futile to attack Mathura at this point of time, realising that he would permanently alienate the Yadavas if he persisted. He thought of winning Mathura as an ally. He turned his attention to Brihadbala, who was scared and much in awe of the emperor, having heard about the might of Jarasandha.

Brihadbala was the second son of Kamsa and Devabhaga, Ugrasena's favourite daughter. Brihadbala was taken by surprise when the Magadha Naresh spoke to him affectionately, 'Come, my son, do not be afraid. I am like a grandfather to you. One day, I want to see you become a great king—Brihadbala could be Brihadrajah! How are your grandfather and his favourite daughter?'

'Very well, Your Majesty,' replied Brihadbala.

'Do you call your grandfather Your Majesty? Please call me Tatasri. It sounds more informal!' Jarasandha said.

Brihadbala was moved by the affection showered on him by the mighty emperor. Jarasandha continued to make the prince feel as if he was his favourite. Brihadbala was smitten by this sweet talk as he had never been treated with such favour at his own place. Such treatment was reserved only for Krishna. A sudden flash of jealousy seared through him. He believed that, now, even he had a chance to become king like Jarasandha was saying, as Krishna was out of the way!

Jarasandha realised that his plan was working and he could now use the boy as a pawn. 'Well...son, what do you know about these cowherds, Krishna and Balarama?' asked the emperor.

Brihadbala was quick to react, 'Tatasri, I was shocked to see uncle Kamsa killed by Krishna. When Balarama cracked the skull of Mushtika, I could hear the sound and almost fainted when blood began splattering on the ground. They were cruel, but they ran away in fear when they heard of your anger. Krishna refused the crown of Mathura; if he was afraid to be king, then why did he murder uncle Kamsa?'

Jarasandha knew that Krishna was not afraid, but said, 'The coward ran away, but what is done is in the past. Now that Krishna is no longer around, what about you becoming the king of Mathura? I hope your grandfather Ugrasena will not object.'

Brihadbala could not believe his ears. 'Tatasri, suppose Krishna returns and claims the throne of Mathura? I am afraid he might kill me as he killed my uncle.'

'Son, leave that to me. Krishna will not come back. Do you know where he has gone?' asked the emperor.

'South I am told, near some mountains...to Venya...Karavirapura where some of our Yadavas have a kingdom, but I cannot say so for sure,' Jarasandha assured him that no harm would come to Mathura and he would see to it that Krishna and Balarama do not return.

Brihadbala was elated as he left the room. Jarasandha was happy at the turn of events and bid goodbye to Brihadbala, promising to meet him the next morning.

Jarasandha made peace with Mathura and sent his spies to Karavirapura, in the forests of the Sahyadri Mountains. Shrigalava would not dare challenge Magadha.

However, in return for peace, Jarasandha demanded that Mathura pay him a tribute of twenty-five young elephants with mahouts, a hundred chariots and two mounds of gold by the next full moon day.

Jarasandha then called Chedi Raj and revealed his plan.

> The boys have gone to Shrigalava. Hansa knows Shrigalava personally, and he tells me that the king of Karavirapura is a megalomaniac and most of his people live in terror of him. As we cannot move this big army to those forestlands infested with mosquitoes and wild animals, I have decided to take only horsemen and bowmen; the chariots and elephants will be waiting in Vidarbha where our friend Rukmi will help our army. I think twenty *atiratha*s, twenty *maharathi*s and about a hundred bowmen would be sufficient to capture the boys. Meanwhile, I shall ask Dimbhak to keep the army ready on the western Vidarbha, near the riverbank of Venya.

Damaghosha's mind was in overdrive; after Kamsa's death he had been keen to check Jarasandha's absolute rule with an alternate power base. And Krishna, he thought, was his best bet. But now, with the emperor having information on his whereabouts, Krishna did not stand a strong chance of survival. Damaghosha made up his mind to somehow reach Krishna and warn him, but did not know how to do so without enraging Jarasandha. One way would be to gain the emperor's trust and hunt for a suitable messenger to go to Karavirapura, one who would be loyal to him as well as Krishna. As soon as he made this plan, he knew who he would send—Uddhava, his nephew.

UDDHAVA—THE CHARIOTEER OF DAMAGHOSHA

Uddhava had been Krishna's inseparable companion ever since Devabhaga sent him to Vrindavan, away from the palace of Kamsa, which was full of conspiracies. Devabhaga, unlike his wife Kamsa, was gentle and god-fearing and wanted at least one of his sons to be like him.

Uddhava continued to live as a brahmana priest in Kaishika's household. He could see that princess Rukmini was worried about Krishna's safety. Both of them took Kaishika into confidence and kept open a line of communication with the hill tribes of Sahyadri Mountains. Kaishika had promised to keep a tab on the boys' movements through his network of tribal informers.

Then one day, Prince Rukmi's soldiers arrived in the fort of Kundinapura, announcing that the armies of Jarasandha and his allies will be transiting shortly and expected the hospitality of King Bhishmaka. When Uddhava heard that Damaghosha would be arriving soon, he arranged for an audience with him as he was certain that Chedi Raj would not harm Krishna. Uddhava went to the Chedi camp in his disguise and presented himself before Damaghosha.

Damaghosha patiently heard Uddhava express concern for his friend's safety. He found here the perfect opportunity to further his own intention to prop up Krishna as a check against the emperor's hegemony. He thought, if Vasudeva's sons were as valiant as reported, this was the best time to checkmate Jarasandha's supremacy. He, therefore, asked Uddhava to accompany the Chedi army contingent in the guise of a charioteer. Uddhava was elated at the prospect of meeting Krishna again. Damaghosha was equally happy to put his strategy into action.

KRISHNA AND BALARAMA IN GOMANTAK

The Garuda tribal chief, Arteya, derived his name from his mother Arta. He was said to possess miraculous powers. The people believed that the god of fire was his friend, because fire would change stones into streams of dark red metal whenever he worshipped fire while chanting the appropriate hymns. This metal was used to make arrowheads, exclusively for his use, while other Garudas would use flint. Arteya had secured the prime position amongst the Garuda tribe due to his skill of producing *tamra*, or copper, which was a material of great strength for use during warfare till *loha*, or iron, was discovered.

Krishna soon established a good rapport with the chief, who took a great liking to the charming young man from Aryawartha. Krishna trained the Garuda youth in making better bows and arrows with flintheads and showed them how to slingshot high-flying birds. He taught them wrestling and sword-wielding techniques. Krishna also tended to the sick and wounded with herbal preparations.

The Garudas were an open society—innocent, affectionate and loving. Their huts were tidy, simple and hospitable. The walls of the huts were washed with red clay and cow dung, and painted with flower and animal motifs native to the mountains. The older women welcomed the dawn and sunset by blowing on a conch. It was believed that at these hours, the negative forces of nature try to inculcate fear in the minds of humans. In order to ward off these energies and foster positive thoughts, a conch was blown in all directions, as a mark of salute to the Lord of Creation.

At the behest of his wife, Arteya approached Krishna with a request on a moonlit night. He told him about his invalid eldest son, Vainateya. Though born normal, Vainateya had been struck by a strange fever when he was ten years old and had become a cripple. He could only crawl helplessly; his mother was the one person who could attend to his needs. The boy stayed confined to a small hut and no one else cared for him.

As it was a full moon night, the youngsters of the tribe were enjoying themselves with a group dance and were high on *madira*, a sweet alcoholic drink. Hearing a moan, Krishna turned back to check and saw a boy badly bruised, clasping his feet. The boy was looking up at him with great expectation and complete surrender. Moved by the boy's plight, Krishna held him by his arms and, smiling, stared deep into his eyes.

Bowing down, Krishna caught hold of the boy's hands and said, 'Vainateya, stand up.' Hearing the command, Vainateya hesitantly moved his limp legs and found that they did not collapse under him. Gaining confidence, he then went up till the tree and came back to Krishna, who hugged him with much love. Krishna then took the boy to his parents who stared in disbelief.

This was the first acknowledged miracle performed by Krishna, which was lauded by Vyasa in verse:

Mookam karoti vachalam, Pangum langhayate girim
Yatkrupatamaham vande paramanandamadhavam

(Krishna, your grace made a deaf-mute speak, and a cripple run and climb a mountain; you are the epitome of joy and happiness. I salute you.)

Krishna then addressed Arteya:

Please take your son to your medicine man and ask him to treat him with suitable herbal juices; rub his legs with anointed herbal oils to make them strong. The boy has not had proper nourishment and he needs good food, especially the cooked flesh of monitor lizards, which I find in plenty on this hill. In about two full moons' time, he should be ready to dance with the girls.

Hearing this, Vainateya clasped Krishna's feet again and said, 'I want to stay with you, you are my God.'

Krishna looked into the boy's eyes and found them pleading. He, therefore, could not help but permit Vainateya to stay with him.

Vainateya's mother fell at Krishna's feet, sobbing. Krishna lifted her up and said, 'Vainateya will always be with me; in fact, he will precede me wherever I go; when I am not there, he shall hold my standard to represent me. My standard will be an eagle with wide open wings and hooked beak, standing erect on strong legs.'

The once emaciated Garuda turned out to be a handsome bronze-skinned youth with shining white teeth and a long aquiline nose. The boy's walk became normal and sure-footed and, with time, turned into a leap. From hillock to next rock, he now moved like an eagle and swooped down like a falcon, as sudden as the bird of prey. Krishna was amused and soon Vainateya became his inseparable guide, companion and friend on the Sahyadri Hills.

Krishna prevailed on the chief that, in order to strengthen his tribe, he should permit every Garuda warrior to have arrows and hatchets made with the red metal. At the outset, Arteya was reticent as he feared he would lose his status of technological superiority. But Krishna convinced him by showing how much stronger the tribal youth would be when armed with such formidable weapons. Krishna then commanded the young men to collect the red blocks of earth and commissioned a number of fire pits fuelled by coconut oil and dry wood, abundantly available on the plateau of the hill.

After a few weeks, they had smelted enough copper to replace hundreds of arrow and hatchet heads for the Garuda army. Arteya was beaming with confidence as he had acquired a veritable arsenal of copper implements to defend against any enemy.

While Krishna was engaged in equipping the Garudas with weapons of formidable power, Balarama was busy frolicking with the Garuda girls. He stayed intoxicated most of the days and would make fun of Krishna's diligent efforts. Krishna knew that soon he would have to face Jarasandha's army and, with singular devotion, prepared for the event.

One day, as he was supervising the formation of copper in the sacred fire, Krishna saw that a rock, which had not melted with the others, began to glow. It was a strange sight. As Krishna continued to pour more offerings into the fire, the flames leapt up from the altar and the glowing ball emitted steam. When diverted into a channel of water, the ball sizzled loudly and gave out more steam. As soon as the molten liquid cooled down, Krishna flung it at the copper blade. The blade broke into two.

Krishna was elated and, looking up at the sky, exclaimed, 'Hail Indra!

You have sent a piece of your thunderbolt, heavy and unbreakable.' He called this, black metal or *loha*. The Iron Age thus arrived and, with it, dawned the age of Kali.

Krishna and Vainateya forged a large number of short daggers, swords, and hundreds of arrowheads, which were sharpened and fastened to beautifully crafted bamboo arrows, their tips bound with fine vines. The balance of each arrow, with its fastened iron head, was achieved by suitably fixing the beautiful feather plumes of hill birds. A veritable armoury of weapons was piled in a small room, adjoining Krishna's hut.

Krishna crafted a beautiful *chakra,* with twenty-four sharp teeth, from the black metal. He mastered the art of spinning it with the help of the Garudas who, though unfamiliar with a *chakra*, were expert at using a crescent-shaped weapon made out of a light wood—a boomerang.

One day, Balarama saw a farmer ploughing his field with a pair of brown bullocks yoked to a plough. He approached the farmer and unyoked the bulls, lifted the plough on to his left shoulder and returned to where Krishna was busy shaping a sword. 'This is the mace I will use to break Jarasandha's head,' proclaimed Balarama, swinging the heavy plough all around him as if it were a mere bamboo stick and then placing it on the ground. Next, Balarama went out and pulled up a medium-sized tree trunk. He axed the fringe branches and the roots, dressed up the ends with the axe and sculpted a four cubit long, half cubit round, pestle-like weapon. He threw it before Krishna. 'This is my other weapon to beat all the charioteers of Jarasandha. With just one hit, the chariot will break.' Thus, he proved to Krishna that though he had been taking it easy, he would still be able to go into battle and be mightier than most!

After sunset, the brothers met to name their personal weapons. Balarama named his plough, Samvartaka and the redwood pestle, Saunanda. Krishna named his bow, Saranga and his discus, Sudarshana. At the end of this meeting, the Garudas danced with joy, blew conchs and the warriors played their war drums.

Krishna had a feeling that the emperor was in the vicinity of the Sahyadri Hills. The peace and prosperity of the mountain air and the hospitality of the Garudas was only an interlude before the threat of Jarasandha descended on them. Krishna did not want to be caught unawares and bring untold suffering to these beautiful people. He, therefore, cautioned Arteya and asked him to send his trusted men to Karavirapura and gather information on any unusual activities in and around the kingdom.

After a few days had passed, the chief informed Krishna, 'The king of Karavirapura is expecting a mighty monarch with his army, welcome arches are being built to greet the great king. They say he is coming from a faraway land as the guest of Shrigalava Vasudeva, and is called Magadha Naresh.'

Krishna asked Arteya to assemble all the able-bodied Garudas before noon so that he could train them to use the new weapons. He also asked for men to help gather the red rocks so that he could forge more daggers, swords, maces and hundreds of sharp arrowheads and long lances with the great metal.

Aided by the young Vainateya, Krishna surveyed Gomantak Hill. He traced every path and explored the unscalable slopes to check if it could be approached in any other way. Krishna was assessing whether the Gomantak was indeed impregnable, as the venerable Parashurama had said. It had land on three sides, sloping down with steep rock overhangs and on the western side was the ocean with waters pounding incessantly. They had also dug up a moat as an additional security measure, which, on Krishna's orders, was cleaned up for operations again.

His plan was to loosen the earth and the boulders so that, at short notice, they could cut the dyke, let the sea water into the moat and take their enemy by surprise. Krishna also warned Arteya that the hill could be burnt down by their enemies during the dry months, leaving the Garudas with no escape route, but the sea.

JARASANDHA AT GOMANTAK

Jarasandha's juggernaut moved towards Gomantak. Shrigalava Vasudeva assured him of not only safe passage for the army, but also hospitality. Jarasandha commanded Hansa to go ahead in advance and discuss, with the king of Karavirapura, their intention to capture the sons of Vasudeva when they reached in a few days' time. Hansa sent a message that the boys had been sighted on a solitary hill in Gomantak region and could be captured with ease. Jarasandha had left the bulk of his army in Vidarbha under the command of the trustworthy Dimbhak as they had to pass very difficult terrain ahead.

The journey from Vidarbha through jungle tracks and over high mountains proved to be a tiring one. Stocks of food and drinking water were getting depleted and there appeared to be no easy source of replenishment in that mountainous terrain. The nights were terrible, with insects attacking the men and beasts. The morale of the army was waning and the patience of the allied princes was wearing thin. It was a futile effort in their opinion and they asked the prince of Darada to convey this message to the emperor, but to no avail.

They finally arrived at the foothills of the great mountain range, which were rife with pasture lands and fresh water, and set up camp. From here, it was only a day's march downhill. Jarasandha realised that he needed a few chariots and sent Hansa to Karavirapura to secure them. Looking at the hill and its environs, he found it too steep, with a few overhangs. While the soldiers were surveying the foothills, they noticed men pushing boulders from the top, which hit those climbing up and plunged them into the ravine below.

Jarasandha saw that seizing the hill could be an indefinitely long battle as two men could defy a whole army for days together from their vantage point. The princes were all tense, except Damaghosha. He would see to it that Krishna and Balarama came to no harm so that they could counter the emperor's power.

Damaghosha addressed his allies:

> Noble kings, let us not give up our resolve to make the emperor successful in his mission of capturing Vasudeva's sons. If we give up at this stage, we will be exposed to ridicule. The reputation of Magadha Naresh will be tarnished. Let us all think of a way out of this awkward situation. It appears that our soldiers cannot climb the steep rock faces of the hill and even if they do so, there will be heavy casualties. We need tact and strategy to flush out the two boys, if they have not already escaped.

Everyone was stunned at the prospect that their targets might have escaped, and their journey would have been in vain.

Damaghosha continued, 'This is late summer. Have you not noticed dry grass on the slopes of the hill, right up to the top? Let us set fire to it tonight on all sides. By tomorrow, the forest atop would have caught fire, destroying everyone there.'

Jarasandha considered the suggestion for a while and agreed.

Krishna was awakened when a Garuda screeched to warn him of the impending doom. The chief sounded the alarm with the beating of the drum and everyone rushed out. Krishna addressed them, 'Do not panic. We have to act fast and save ourselves. We will try to quench the fire and Vainateya will lead us to the path through which we can reach the sea.'

Krishna led them to what looked like two ridges, which had been loosened up a few days ago, at his insistence. He asked Arteya to command his men to push the loosened boulders into the sea and wait for a tidal wave to do the rest. As the boulders rolled down, a wave splashed water into the channel. The gap became a breach as huge waves rushed water into the moat.

Down below, Jarasandha, the kings of his entourage and the soldiers jubilantly watched the fire reach the top of the hill. The allies were very happy for they believed that by next morning their mission would be over and they could start their victorious march back to Vidarbha and finally reach home.

It was past midnight when the rushing waters woke the guards on night vigil. They rubbed their eyes and looked on helplessly as the base of the hill was girdled from both sides by gushing seawater that put out the fire. Jarasandha suggested they moved their camp to a higher ground.

Suddenly a giant form descended upon them, followed by screeching men who held torches and rushed towards the camp. In panic, Jarasandha looked for his chariot. Everyone ran for their lives. Chariots crashed under the heavy blows of the giant's plough; horses, neighing in fright, broke loose and galloped away into the forest. Before Jarasandha and his friends could collect their arms, the blows of a mace, deftly wielded by an expert, had crushed the skulls of many.

When the eastern horizon was lit by the golden sunrise, the dazed kings found the giant Balarama amidst them, spreading terror and destruction with his plough. On a rock, on the other side, stood Krishna, stringing his mighty bow. Every arrow sped from it with unerring precision and claimed its victim.

Anuvinda, the prince of Avanti, took up his bow and arrow and came forward to face Krishna. Krishna handed his bow to Vainateya, took the Sudarshana Chakra in his hand and whirling it, beheaded the prince of Kashmir, Gonard. A deathly silence and panic gripped Jarasandha's camp, for they had never seen such a precise instrument of death. A shocked Anuvinda withheld his stringed bow with passing regret as he and Krishna had studied together at Sandipani's school.

At that moment, a conch sounded just a few paces from where Krishna stood. He heard the rich notes of Panchajanya and guessed that Uddhava had arrived in a chariot.

Damaghosha was very happy to see Vasudeva's sons. He saw Balarama wielding the mighty Samvartaka and calling out to Jarasandha. On sighting him, Balarama dropped his plough, picked up his mace and attacked the emperor. Jarasandha, an expert in fighting with the mace, was astounded when Balarama's blow broke his grip and his mace fell. Balarama was about to shatter his head, but Krishna held his brother's arm and said, 'His time is yet to come, leave him. The Magadha Naresh is not well, we shall deal with him another day. Let him go!' Krishna looked at Anuvinda and requested, 'Avantiputra, take the emperor in your chariot and leave him in Magadha.'

A smiling Krishna then addressed the emperor, 'Mend your ways, for now I am releasing you; next time, you may not be lucky, Jarasandha. You have just met your match in my brother Balarama, but my brother is a standard of dharma, which is the opposite of yours!'

Damaghosha saw Hansa's dead body and told Krishna that Jarasandha drew his power from his two brave faithful commanders, Hansa and Dimbhak, who were also his great friends.

Damaghosha said:

> So long as these two are in command, it is not possible to defeat Jarasandha. If Dimbhak comes to know that Hansa is dead, he will most likely commit suicide. Jarasandha will never attempt another invasion on Mathura with these two no longer by his side. Dimbhak is at Kundinapura. You should send a message there about the emperor's defeat and Hansa's death. As per the shastras, we must root out the enemy.

When the special dispatch reached Dimbhak, he was aghast at the turn of events. As Damaghosha had observed, the shocked warrior jumped into a lake and drowned himself, unable to bear the loss of his friend. Rukmi arrived at the gates of Kundinapura, wounded and humiliated. When Rukmini learnt of her brother's sorry state, she taunted him, 'Brother, this is the second time Krishna has got the better of you—be wise and befriend him.'

KRISHNA AT KARAVIRAPURA

Damaghosha's strategy to check Magadha's supremacy was working so far. He advised Krishna's brother to join him in Mathura and assure the Yadava council and the citizens that Jarasandha had been vanquished by Balarama who, at the insistence of Krishna, had spared the emperor's life. Finally, Balarama agreed and both of them left for Mathura immediately.

In the meantime, Krishna asked Uddhava to go to Karavirapura and inform King Shrigalava Vasudeva that he would like to pay his respect to the Yadava elder. Uddhava reached the fort and, after much waiting, was permitted to enter alone. The atmosphere was festive as everyone was waiting to welcome the Magadha Naresh.

The next morning, the king sent for him. Uddhava found him seated on the throne, as immovable as a statue, bedecked with gold ornaments. Beside him stood Queen Padmavati—emaciated and frightened by the pomp of Shrigalava. The queen was supported by a young and very beautiful woman, who stared adoringly at Shrigalava. Next to her stood a boy, who he assumed was prince Shakradeva. 'I am Uddhava, son of noble Devabhaga, the valiant Shoora of Mathura, and I have come on behalf of my cousin, Krishna Vaasudeva, noble king,' he said.

Shrigalava raised his voice and said, 'Krishna of Mathura? That cowherd who murdered his uncle? He is no Vasudeva; I am the only lord here.' With folded hands, Uddhava said, 'Forgive me, O king! I am ignorant of the ways of Karavirapura, but there might be two Vasudevas.'

'Yadava!' shouted Shrigalava. 'You have committed a sacrilege and I must punish you till you rectify your mistake.'

Heavily ornamented guards then led Uddhava into a dark tunnel. Here, he saw some old acharyas, emaciated yet pious-looking, who were offering oblations to the Sun God near a running stream in the valley. Suddenly, Uddhava saw Purnadatta leading a very old acharya to the stream. Purnadatta recognised Uddhava and called out to him. He introduced the respected acharya as his maternal grandfather, Rudracharya, whom Shrigalava had imprisoned in this 'hell' till the time the old man agreed to recognise him as Vasudeva—the God of Gods.

Rudracharya was one of the foremost acharyas dedicated to the *rita* way of life and was a worshipper of the Sun God. The vain Shrigalava had not only banned the Vedic way of life, but also imprisoned those who refused to worship him as Vasudeva. The acharyas were starved to death. Purnadatta said that he had volunteered to serve his grandfather during his suffering. Uddhava was curious and enquired about this cult of Vasudeva. Purnadatta narrated this story:

> Some ancient sects in these parts of the country worshipped Vasudeva as the Supreme Being. Years ago, a rishi named Galava came to Karavirapura

with the conquering armies of Yadavas. He had great influence on the ruling family. When a son was born to the Yadava king of Karavirapura, the infant was named Shrigalava. The young prince was brought up in the sect of Vasudeva worshippers. When Rishi Galav died, the king of Karavirapura disbanded the ashram and declared himself as the head of the sect. In the course of time, pride and cries of sycophants raised the vain king to the status of Vasudeva and the king started believing that he was supreme. He became a despot and ruled the kingdom like a demon. He not only persecuted the non-believers of this cult, but also terrorised his queen, Padmavati, into submission. He did not spare his own son Shakradeva, who was reduced to being a recluse as the boy submitted meekly to his egoistic father. Shrigalava's niece advocated Vasudeva worship as well.

Uddhava was much concerned that Krishna was unaware of the happenings in Karavirapura, but was at a loss as he knew not how to reach him.

On the third day of Uddhava's imprisonment, two men from Shrigalava's army arrived with some food for the prisoners. They reminded the non-believing acharyas that they would be pardoned if they accept Shrigalava as Vasudeva. One of the men seemed to be a high ranking officer in the army.

He pushed Uddhava to the ground, but Uddhava retaliated and, after some fist fighting, the two were engaged in a fierce wrestling match, aiming at each other's throat. Surprised by the young boy's skills, the officer asked him if he was a disciple of Sandipani. Uddhava then looked closely at the officer and asked, 'Are you not Shvetaketu, the favourite disciple of our guru?'

Shvetaketu then said, 'Uddhava, I am a sinner and do not deserve any mercy. I was trapped, seduced and enticed by that witch of a girl, Saibhya, and my story is a tale of disgrace.' Uddhava consoled Shvetaketu, saying he should not feel guilty because it could happen to the best of men. Right now, their priority was to inform Krishna of the happenings in this city. To secure that end, the two together overpowered the second soldier and Uddhava now wore his clothes.

When they reached the assembly hall, they saw the keeper of the fortress inform the king, 'A Yadava from Mathura, calling himself Krishna Vaasudeva, wants to pay his respects to you and enter the fort.' Shrigalava roared, 'We shall not meet such men,' and summoned Shvetaketu. 'You are familiar with his language. Ask him what the visitor wants from us.'

Shortly after his meeting with Krishna, Shvetaketu rode back to the palace and, with folded hands, informed the king:

> The visitor claims he has come alone to inform you that Jarasandha has retreated to Magadha after suffering defeat at the hands of the visitor's brother, Balarama. He said that he has come to befriend the lord of Karavirapura and also requested you to release the acharyas and his friend Uddhava, whom you had imprisoned. He wants to take them back to Mathura.

Shrigalava laughed loudly in contempt and asked sternly, 'Is he armed?'

'He rides a chariot driven by a charioteer and is attended by a man with an eagle face who holds his banner of a Garuda. He is armed with a mace, a bow, a *chakra* and I saw a conch hanging from his waistband. He also warned me that he will wait at the gates quietly only for a short while and if Uddhava and the acharyas are not released, he will force open the gates and free them himself,' replied Shvetaketu.

Uddhava slowly slipped out and, reaching the gates, ordered them to allow Krishna to enter. Meanwhile, Shrigalava mounted his unwieldy golden chariot drawn by four horses and saw Krishna entering the fort in a light combat chariot driven by a horse and an attendant.

Krishna wanted to avoid a fight and hence addressed Shrigalava as the lord of Karavirapura. But Shrigalava replied with an arrow that brushed Krishna's left shoulder. Krishna then blew his conch and, the next moment, hurled a discus at the king that cut his head and returned to Krishna's finger. As Shrigalava's head rolled on the ground, there was utter confusion in the fort.

Krishna asked Shvetaketu to take him to the queen who now looked relieved. Krishna paid his respects to her and enquired about her son. Krishna told Padmavati that he would like Shakradeva to succeed to the throne of Karavirapura. 'After that, I would request you to release all the acharyas and disband the cult of Vasudeva.' Suddenly, Saibhya, the doting niece of Shrigalava, rushed at Krishna with a dagger to stab him, but Shvetaketu wrenched it from her fist. An enraged Shvetaketu asked Krishna to behead her also.

Krishna smiled and spoke with lot of compassion, 'Shvetaketu, she is a woman, a pretty and foolish person who seduced you into this mess. She is like a sister to me, I cannot harm her. If she is willing to marry you, I would be most happy to witness the wedding.' Krishna requested Shvetaketu to arrange for the royal coronation and after the solemn ceremonies were over, all the captive acharyas were released and Padmavati distributed the royal gold and jewels to the citizens.

Krishna asked Shvetaketu about his future plans. Shvetaketu replied that he would like to go to Vidarbha and train their forces and continue to teach Vedas to the pupils there. Krishna was happy to see Shvetaketu on the right path—the chosen path of his guru. He turned to Saibhya, 'Sister, my mother Devaki wants you at Mathura; she has no daughters and you will be happy in her house. Of course, if you wish you would be better off as the wife of Acharya Shvetaketu, you can marry him.' Saibhya refused to marry a traitor, so Krishna entrusted Uddhava with the responsibility of taking her to Mathura. In his presence, she softened and was gentler towards Krishna.

Krishna then ordered the Garuda to drive him to the Gomantak foothills and sent for Arteya. He wanted to rest and recoup for a few days and plan the future course of action. Krishna was no more the pastoral playboy; he was now a mature man and a warrior too. He reflected that the world around him was very complex and ruthless. Kings treated people like cattle. While waiting for the Garuda's return, Krishna was alerted by the sound of an approaching chariot. It was Shakradeva. He was grateful to Krishna for releasing him from the constant terror of his father. Shakradeva invited Krishna to stay in one of the royal palaces, but he refused, saying he wanted to be alone. The king then insisted that he accept a decent tent and Krishna relented.

Meanwhile, Vainateya arrived with Arteya. Krishna introduced Shakradeva as the king of Karavirapura and requested the chief to be an ally and guard the young king. Shakradeva took leave of Krishna, now confident and sure.

The next morning, a horseman brought a message from Damaghosha informing Krishna that Jarasandha was camping outside Kundinapura, and would soon leave for Magadha. He also said that a Magadhan commander had drowned himself in a lake and after that the army had become one of stragglers. By the time the emperor had reached Vidarbha, most of the soldiers had either died of starvation, disease or wild beast attacks. Krishna told Vainateya that he was needed by his people and so could no longer accompany him. 'I shall call you when needed; you are my guide and inseparable witness to my mission to establish dharma.'

The following morning, another messenger arrived from Chedi and handed over a scroll to Krishna. He moved into his quarters—a tent—and opened the scroll. He found a letter with the seal of Chedi Raj—the wild boar insignia, and read it:

Glory to my nephew, Krishna Vaasudeva!

The grace of Mahadeva is always with you. I have an important development to report to you. When we reached Vidarbha, we were told that Jarasandha and his allies had arrived at Kundinapura. They were the guests of Rukmi and Bhishmaka. I learnt that Jarasandha did not enter Kundinapura, but camped outside. The emperor weaved a story saying that he had let off the cowherd boys after capturing them because, as an emperor, he should fight his equals and not an inconsequent cowherd. The foolish allies believed him.

He was trying to recoup and we must admire his capacity to turn a defeat into a success. A very crafty leader, he was suspicious of my role. Also, Rukmi feels that I was responsible for this debacle.

Balarama and I met the old man Kaishika outside Kundinapura. He told me that the emperor has proposed that Rukmini should marry my son, Shishupala. I know that this is a trap laid for me by the wily Jarasandha. Krishna, I am told by Kaishika that Rukmini is deeply in love with you and she has confided in her grandfather that she would commit suicide if she were forced to marry Shishupala. I will be very happy if you marry this girl some day.

The crafty emperor has also proposed that prince Rukmi marry his granddaughter, Aplavi, in return. King Bhishmaka was apparently not happy about this marriage of convenience. He reminded the emperor that, as per the traditions of Vidarbha, a *swayamvara* has to be held to choose a groom for Rukmini. Jarasandha has agreed to arrange it, assuring him that the women of Magadha will be allowed to choose their groom. My dear Krishna, I thought I should keep you informed of these events so that you can be on your guard when you reach Mathura. Balarama and I propose to wait outside near Kaishika's palace, till the emperor leaves, which we were told, would not be before the full moon that is three days hence. By the time my personal guard reaches you, the emperor would have moved out. The wily emperor has not given up Mathura yet, therefore you have to be cautious. We hope to reach Mathura soon, it is about a week-long ride from Kundinapura. Balarama is enjoying his stay with his grandfather Kaishika.

May you be blessed by the god of gods!

Krishna read and reread the letter. Calling for the rider, Krishna asked him to return to the Chedi ruler at once. He had requested Damaghosha to wait for him to join the Chedi contingent. Krishna wished to inform Damaghosha that he was held up due to the coronation ceremony of Shakradeva as the Regent of Karavirapura.

Upon receiving the message, Chedi Raj reflected upon how Krishna was transforming into a man, a warrior and a statesman. His aim, to nurture Krishna as the alternate power centre in Aryawartha to checkmate Jarasandha, could well be fulfilled in the near future. He realised that his days as a ruler would also be numbered as he had earned the wrath of Magadha Naresh just like Krishna had. As the future events of the story unfold, it proves how right Damaghosha had been in estimating Jarasandha's vengeance.

KRISHNA—THE DARLING OF MASSES

After the assassination attempt by Saibhya on Krishna, Shvetaketu took over the command of the fort and Krishna's security was his primary concern. Krishna, Uddhava, Rudracharya and Purnadatta were taken to the king's chambers and loyal guards were posted by the door.

Jarasandha had lost his western outpost with the loss of Shrigalava. Now his armies could never reach the western seas without facing two adversaries—the Garudas of Gomantak and an unfriendly Shakradeva at Karavirapura.

The next morning, Shakradeva and Padmavati called on Krishna in his tent. After a brief meal, the queen presented Krishna with gold ornaments and chests of jewels and precious stones, which he humbly refused. The queen said, 'You may please distribute this gold among the people of Mathura!'

He then accepted the generous gifts and, along with Saibhya, the caravan prepared to leave for Mathura. Krishna's caravan joined Damaghosha's entourage on the outskirts of the kingdom. Balarama hugged his younger brother when they met and briefed him on the events that had occurred after they had parted. The caravan started moving towards Kundinapura and then on to Mathura.

Damaghosha had sent messengers in advance, to share great news with the people—the rout of the formidable Jarasandha and death of the wicked Shrigalava; the devotion of the eagle faces of Gomantak towards Krishna; the release of the acharyas from Shrigalava's hell; and the coronation of Shakradeva as the king of Karavirapura.

The news spread like wildfire, assuming titanic proportions, wherein each retelling, Krishna's achievements were heralded as miracles that could only be performed by the God of Gods. With time, this legend became a myth and over time Krishna was identified with Vishnu—the all-pervading spirit.

People came from far off places for a glimpse of the caravan. Supervised by Uddhava, the caravan reached Avanti. Acharya Sandipani and King Jayasena with his twin princes, Vinda and Anuvinda, received the party and welcomed the brothers with great pomp and pleasure. Anuvinda had outgrown his regard for Jarasandha, having been a witness to the emperor's defeat at the hands of Balarama. Krishna then expressed his wish to spend a couple of days at Acharya Sandipani's ashram. Balarama and Uddhava joined him as well. Balarama was in great spirits as he touched the feet of his guru and began narrating how he had overpowered the emperor.

While Balarama was talking, two young women came to serve them water. One of the girls was tall, gold-complexioned, broad-shouldered and muscular, yet very graceful looking. She had large eyes, which were full of mischief. Sandipani watched the way Balarama was looking at her and smiled. Sandipani said:

> My son, her name is Revati and she is a child of tragedy. You must have heard of a place called Kushasthali, near Prabhasa Tirtha. It is a port that, years ago, had a flourishing maritime commerce. The Punyajanas arrived in Kushasthali in their ships, attacked it, put the citizens to the sword and burnt the place to ashes. The king of Kushasthali, Revata Kukudmin, who was the father of Revati, escaped.
>
> King Kukudmin's lot was pitiable; his thirty brothers and seven sons had died fighting. He had seen his womenfolk dishonoured and brutally murdered. He escaped miraculously with infant Revati and some trusted retainers, and hid in the hills.
>
> Kukudmin was a man of fiery determination. He vowed before Brahma, his guardian deity, that he would recapture Kushasthali. Then he wandered from place to place seeking assistance, but did not get any. He lost all his kinsmen; his retainers grew old with no hope, as his resources dried up. Kukudmin was baffled by this state, but was certain that one day he would regain his

kingdom with the help of his daughter Revati. He had made her enduring and strong and put her through severe training.

With such a singular mind, he went to Sowparnika and begged the esteemed Parashurama to train his daughter as if she were a boy. The master agreed and shaped her into a warrior princess and then, to attain finesse, recommended my ashram to her.

Involuntarily, Balarama said, 'I will help her in achieving her goal to get back her father's kingdom.' Balarama was smitten by Revati. He had finally met a young woman who matched him in stature and strength, yet was an embodiment of beauty and grace.

Krishna and Acharya laughed and clapped their hands in great joy. 'A great match for our Rama,' said Sandipani.

THE ADVENTURES OF BALARAMA

King Kukudmin was a tall, wiry man and looked weather-beaten, having lived long under extreme hardship. Krishna and Balarama arrived at the cave where he lived and found him sitting erect, his gnarled arms folded firmly. He looked like an ageless tree dominating a stretch of desert, a tree that had weathered many storms through the ages, in solitary grandeur. He sat motionless while Sandipani introduced his two disciples. He appeared cold and indifferent as though he had lost all interest in mankind.

Krishna said to him, 'Noble king, tomorrow we want to stage a mock fight with maces among the expert disciples of our guru. I hope your daughter, who is already proficient, will join us.'

Revati frowned, thinking that he was mocking her, but Krishna was quick to grasp the situation and spoke to her, 'Acharya says you are an expert, O daughter of noble Kukudmin. My brother is a master in mace-wielding and would have cracked the skull of emperor Jarasandha, if I had not stopped him.'

The old king spoke at last, 'Revati, my child, you may join them; you might learn some new tricks.'

Krishna and Balarama then took leave of the king. Krishna said to his brother, 'How I wish we could help them regain Kushasthali. From what I have heard from Acharya Sandipani, this Punyajana tribe is a menace to mankind. We must destroy them and, as a bonus, you can take Revati as your wife and settle down and be its king ultimately. We can call the place Raivatak.'

'Krishna, you are a dreamer and, at times, you go too far, although I agree that what you say sounds good to my ears,' said Balarama.

When Sandipani heard of the boys' plans, he said, 'My sons, I am sure you will establish dharma; you have my blessings to restore Kushasthali to Kukudmin and save Mathura from that Magadhan tyrant.' It was decided that, while Krishna was needed at Mathura, Balarama would follow this quest on his own.

Krishna's shrewd mind was looking for contingency plans in the event of the Yadavas losing Mathura to Jarasandha. Kushasthali, near Prabhasa in the Saurashtra region of Agarta country, would be an ideal place as a fallback area for the Yadavas. Therefore, it was imperative for Balarama to win it for Kukudmin and Revati. Since Uddhava was familiar with Prabhasa and Bhikru, their loyal friend, was also living there, he was keen that Uddhava should join Balarama's expedition.

The next day, Sandipani's pupils gathered to stage a mock fight with Krishna and Balarama, which was more a trial of skill than of strength. After the first round, Krishna retired from the contest.

Balarama was excited to see Revati, in her tigerskin dress, enter the field with her mace. She had a dogged spirit, great muscular power and was itching for a real match of skill. Balarama was restrained and lost a few rounds to her, yet instinct forced him to use a technique, which made Revati's mace fly from her hand. There was loud applause, laughter and clapping that made Revati blush. She burst into tears and, hiding her face in her hands, ran away. Balarama felt miserable not knowing what to do.

He found her in the cave weeping on the lap of her father. King Kukudmin looked at Balarama in obvious annoyance. Balarama said, 'O king, your daughter is a fine warrior, my compliments to you; now we can, together, win back Kushasthali once again for you.'

Both father and daughter were amazed at this confident young man. Kukudmin was more confident than ever that his promise to himself would, at last, be fulfilled.

BALARAMA'S ADVENTURES AT SEA

When Chedi Raj learnt of Balarama's decision to help Kukudmin, he thought of meeting his nephews. Damaghosha had no doubt about the skills and prowess of both Balarama and Uddhava, but was worried about their safety; after all, the Punyajana were a demonic and bloodthirsty tribe. Before Balarama and

Uddhava could begin their journey, Damaghosha took them aside and said, 'I suggest you take along a few of my crack soldiers and bowmen, you should never overestimate your strength vis-à-vis the enemy's.'

Sandipani also offered a few of his best pupils to assist Balarama. Jayasena sent advance messengers to Bhimdev, the king of Prabhasa, that the Yadava vanquisher of Jarasandha would be visiting Prabhasa Tirtha to pay homage to Lord Somnath. Bhimdev was eager to do his utmost to help Balarama. Balarama's party arrived on a ship from Bhrigukachhapa and was given a rousing reception at the Prabhasa port. Balarama offered his homage to Lord Somnath.

Bhimdev held a feast for his guests and they discussed the strategy and perils involved in capturing Kushasthali. He requested Balarama to restore him the town of Girinagar after he defeated the Punyajanas. Balarama agreed.

Bhimdev then said:

> Son of Vasudeva, the Punyajanas' forts are impregnable from land as they are surrounded by water on three sides. They carry out heavy patrolling on boats as a security measure. The best way to attack them is from the sea when their fleet is away for trade. They trade with desert lands where people are far more ferocious, but their lands are endowed with the finest breed of horses. Due to their horse-trade, the Punyajanas are much sought after by the kings of Mahishmati, Sowparnika and even Saurashtra. They trade foodgrains and precious stones in exchange for the horses.

Reconnaissance parties confirmed Bhimdev's assessment that Kushasthali was almost impenetrable, as the Punyajanas had built three rings of fortresses to bar all access from the land. Being seafaring people, they were not good fighters on land and, therefore, built heavy fortifications. After careful planning, the party decided to attack Kushasthali by sea.

Bhikru was overjoyed to see Uddhava. He was now the master of Panchajanya, the ship and Kukuru, his grandson, was the second in command. But when Bhikru heard of their plans to capture Kushasthali, he withdrew. 'The Punyajanas are wild beasts. They attempted to massacre us on this ship, but we managed to escape. Their fleet is formidable and you would be certain to meet your end if you continue with your plan.'

Balarama, ever-resilient, said, 'We are going with or without you. We have five small ships and we wanted a man like you who knows the sea to guide us to Kushasthali.'

At last, Bhikru agreed reluctantly. In the days that followed, he took command of the fleet, comprising six ships. After storing water and food in sufficient quantities, the small fleet left the port.

That night, Bhikru sighted Punyajana ships and informed Balarama that they were being surrounded by the enemy fleet. Balarama walked to the bow, looked up at the sky and affirmed, 'If I am Anantha, the timeless serpent, I command the Marutas, the all-pervading winds, to blow away the Punyajana ships to the high seas.' Suddenly, dark clouds gathered with winds blowing wildly, that scattered the Punyajana fleet. Most of the fleet capsized before they could raise their masts. Balarama then commanded, 'At daybreak, we reach land; right now, Bhikru, let us ram into the Punyajana ships guarding the mouth of the harbour. It is dark and would confuse them.'

Bhikru was terrified for the crew, but did as he was told. With a deadly aim, Balarama hurled a grappling iron at the ship, which was defending the mouth of the port. It fastened itself to the stern and the ship came to a standstill. The timber creaked and the ship broke. The crew struggled to save their lives as they were plunged into the deep sea. The second ship was sunk when the bowmen set it afire with their fiery arrows.

Balarama and others then swept the city, killing anyone who resisted. Kushasthali was completely taken by surprise as most of the Punyajana ships were out at sea. It was an easy and quick victory for Kukudmin and Balarama. They stormed the temple where human sacrifices were held and Balarama swept his mace to smash the skulls of the priests. Balarama ensured that no trace of the Punyajana race was left in Kushasthali.

Ceremoniously, Kukudmin was reinstated as king and all his loyal followers, who had gone into exile, now returned.

The Nagas, who held authority over Girinagar, surrendered after a brief fight in which Balarama killed the Naga king. Girinagar was restored to Prabhasa as promised. Having done what he had set out for, Balarama requested Kukudmin to permit him to leave for Mathura. Kukudmin offered him his daughter's hand. Balarama blushed and told him that he would love to marry the beautiful princess, but right now he was needed at Mathura. He would, however, return for her soon.

MATHURA

While Krishna and Balarama had been away, Mathura's political scene had grown murky and increasingly intriguing. The meek Ugrasena's palace had become a nest of ambitious political manoeuvres for succession as people assumed that Krishna would never return. Kamsa, the ambitious daughter of the king, was grooming her son, Brihadbala, to succeed Ugrasena; Brihadbala had spread the false notion that he was the one who influenced Jarasandha not to attack Mathura and pursue the sons of Vasudeva elsewhere. Brihadbala's principal ally was Yuyudhana Satyaki, son of Satyaka—a competent Yadava warrior, ambitious and hasty, but dependable.

Devabhaga was against his wife's ambitions for their son, Brihadbala. With no news of the brothers for more than a year, everyone was led to believe that the two were dead.

Ugrasena, though hesitant, consulted Gargacharya regarding the succession plans. Gargacharya was reluctant to meet the king's request as he was certain that Krishna would come back, so he suggested Ugrasena to wait awhile, saying the timing was inauspicious. His confidence regained, Ugrasena got up and said, 'Acharya, I am not abdicating Mathura to anyone in the absence of Krishna, be assured. I am only worried about Jarasandha's plans.'

Meanwhile, a royal attendant announced the arrival of chief Vasudeva.

'Admit him and close the doors behind; no one is to be allowed into my chambers till I am through with the Shoora chief,' ordered the king.

Vasudeva was all smiles as he greeted Ugrasena and Gargacharya: 'Greetings my lord! I am glad to share this with you…our Krishna is on his way to Mathura…Damaghosha sent a messenger from Avanti. Krishna is in Sandipani's ashram. They have vanquished Jarasandha at Gomantak and the emperor is on the run, heading back to Magadha….' Gargacharya intervened and said, 'Let us keep this to ourselves till Krishna enters Vrajabhoomi. We must welcome him as a Chakravarti.'

This news, however, reached Satyaki through his sources in the palace. He went to Brihadbala to warn him of the arrival of his nemesis. He was distraught to hear this. Satyaki distanced himself from Brihadbala, lest he must bear the brunt of his actions.

When Vasudeva reached home, a messenger from Hastinapura informed him that Akrura would like to meet him. Vasudeva suddenly remembered Kunti sending a distressed message, seeking his help, soon after Krishna had left for Gomantak. He had then sent Akrura to her for comfort and support.

Akrura informed Vasudeva about the grave situation in Hastinapura. He conveyed that, though the elders treated the Pandavas with affection, Duryodhana and his coterie were persecuting the brothers in diverse ways. Yudhisthira was made the crown prince, but only in name. 'Vyasa has assured me that no harm will come to the Pandavas. But the situation at Hastinapura is unstable.'

The topic then shifted to that of Mathura's security and Vasudeva said:

> Akrura, the Magadha Naresh will not spare Mathura and we are too weak to face another invasion. Our youth have become lazy and there is no one worthy of being called a Yadava warrior. The city walls are weak and in need of heavy fortifications. The moat is to be deepened and the gates must be strengthened and spiked if they are to withstand the charge of Magadha's war elephants. Our situation too is grave. A small force is sufficient to bring us to our knees. We need money and people; I had, therefore, sent a special request to Acharya Sandipani to come and train our men to make them battle-worthy. I will also request my brother-in-law, Damaghosha, to help us.

Mathura had to gear up to face Jarasandha's wrath or perish.

KRISHNA ARRIVES AT MATHURA

Rains had impeded the journey of Krishna and Damaghosha to Mathura. When they finally reached, Ugrasena and Vasudeva gave them a tumultuous welcome. It was a triumphant march into town and Damaghosha was amazed at the affection that the people of Mathura had for Krishna.

When Krishna met Ugrasena, Vasudeva, Gargacharya, Akrura and the other elders, he prostrated himself before them with deep respect. He also informed them about Balarama's mission. Krishna then presented princess Saibhya before Devaki, who was thrilled that her son was back. She was extremely happy to accept Saibhya as her daughter.

The next day, Krishna went to meet Kamsa and Brihadbala. To his surprise, both returned his affection with coldness. They were actually frightened that Krishna would come to know of their treachery and banish them from the kingdom. Satyaki, on the other hand, went out of his way to be pleasant to Krishna and assure him of his loyalty.

Krishna's priority, at the moment, was to secure the city. He prevailed on Ugrasena to issue an ordinance informing citizens that Acharya Sandipani would train Yadava youths in martial arts and that all Yadava chieftains needed to equip themselves with a war chariot. The ordinance also stated that a chariot race would be held in the month of Kartik on the full moon day. Orders were issued to train and breed horses; the money for this purpose came from the gold gifted by Queen Padmavati. Satrajit and his cohorts opposed the chariot race out of spite; these men had gone into exile during Kamsa's reign and they now felt left out of the new regime. The dissenters were counting on Brihadbala to stake his claim as Ugrasena's successor.

Krishna's presence in the Yadava assembly uplifted the mood of the people, who had been, otherwise, deliberating listlessly. Balarama and Uddhava soon arrived and were received with delight. Mathura was again in a festive mood.

Krishna then apprised Balarama of his plans, 'I want you to personally supervise the build-up of martial forces and war chariots of Mathura.' In the next few days, it was planned to send craftsmen from Mathura to rebuild Kushasthali.

When Uddhava went to meet his mother, Kamsa blurted out, 'My son, will you let Krishna ruin your brother's future? Will you not help him?' Uddhava was stunned and said, 'Mother, Krishna will never hurt a right-minded person. If my brother is worthy, then Krishna himself will install him as the crown prince and see that he becomes a great king.'

YAMUNA CHANGES COURSE

Nanda and Yashoda sent a message that they would like to meet Krishna and Balarama at Vrindavan. Yamuna had changed its course and left Vrajbhoomi high and dry. Krishna had to refuse because he was needed at Mathura. 'If I go, they will be happy for the time being; but their hearts will break for a second time when I leave again,' said Krishna.

Instead, Krishna told Balarama, 'Take your plough, mobilise the men and cut the course of Yamuna back to Vrindavan. You were born to tame the Yamuna and bring succour to the people living by the river.' Balarama left for Vrindavan with a retinue of able-bodied Yadavas to assist him in taming the river.

After Balarama left, Shvetaketu arrived in Mathura to share with Krishna, the latest developments in Kundinapura. He was honing the military skills of Vidarbha's army and giving lessons to the youth on Vedas. Thus, he had first-hand knowledge of the situation there. Jarasandha and his allies now had thought of a new plan. 'Krishna, in order to prevent Damaghosha from walking out of Jarasandha's alliance, do you know what the shrewd emperor has suggested? A marital alliance. Preparations are on for the wedding of Rukmini with Shishupala and that of...'

Krishna stopped Shvetaketu. He told him that he was aware of these plans; Damaghosha had already informed him about them.

'Okay...but do keep in mind that all this is happening to fill the place of Kamsa, once Rukmi marries Jarasandha's granddaughter Aplavi, he would become the principal lieutenant of the Chakravarti and work to consolidate his empire.'

Krishna was lost in thought, he was trying to understand the thought process behind Rukmini's marriage, meanwhile Shvetaketu continued:

> Following the custom of the royal house of Vidarbha, it had been decided to hold a *swayamvara* from an assembly of princes, and Rukmini is to choose her bridegroom. But Bhishmaka will manipulate the ceremony in such a way that Rukmini will only be able to choose Shishupala as her husband. The *swayamvara* would be held on the fifth day of the bright half of the month of Magha, on the day of the spring festival. Invitations have already been sent...have you received it?

Krishna replied, 'No...er...not to my knowledge...let me check with my grandfather...'

'Krishna, I have a feeling that no prince from Mathura has been invited; it is a clear attempt to provoke Mathura and, of course, you,' concluded Shvetaketu.

Krishna was unsure what to do. He was not a prince and therefore not eligible for a formal invitation. Moreover, he had no time to think about marriage. 'Let us elect a prince of Mathura to represent us from among the many who are eligible to succeed the throne,' suggested Krishna. He was reminded of the contents of the letter Damaghosha had written to him. He did not want Rukmini to suffer for her brother's ambitions.

THE ASSEMBLY OF YADAVAS

When the Yadava chiefs met Ugrasena at the palace, Shvetaketu apprised everybody about Jarasandha's new strategy to consolidate his position. Shvetaketu also told them that Jarasandha had befriended Brihadbala when they had met, before the debacle at Gomantak.

Ugrasena looked at Krishna and said, 'You, Krishna, are more than a crown prince. I am willing to offer you the throne itself, if only you agree!'

'O best of kings! You have always been very kind to me, but I am content to be what I am—a *gopala*,' said Krishna. 'If you so agree, I have a suggestion. Brihadbala should be named your successor. After that, inform Bhishmaka that an invitation should be sent to Brihadbala for the *swayamvara*. If Bhishmaka refuses, it will be an affront and that gives us a reason to avenge the insult.'

Brihadbala's face turned pale and he was nervous at the turn of events. 'If Brihadbala loses?' asked the minister, Vikadru.

'If we all support him with our lives, he cannot lose. Uddhava will accompany him,' replied Krishna. 'In the meantime, brother Brihadbala and all our young chiefs will have to undergo intense training under Acharya Sandipani. The chariot race will also give our warriors the perfect opportunity to prepare for war.'

Brihadbala was already married to Vishakha, the daughter of Pradyota who commanded Kamsa's army, and was not keen to have another wife. Moreover, he did not want to clash with Jarasandha's ego.

The assembly was then adjourned by Ugrasena. On their way home, Shvetaketu turned to Krishna and said, 'My dear Krishna, princess Rukmini will not marry any victor in *swayamvara*, except you.'

'Not if she is abducted. Over time, the princess will be reconciled. This has been the usual practice, dear Shvetaketu,' replied the composed Krishna.

A distressed Brihadbala approached his mother first and then went to his wife for sympathy. Vishakha had martial blood in her veins. When she heard of her husband's dilemma, she said, 'My lord, you have the opportunity to vindicate the honour of the Yadavas. Please attend the *swayamvara* and marry the princess. I will be honoured to have the princess of Vidarbha as my co-wife. Please…do not be afraid, you are a kshatriya.'

Brihadbala then turned to his friends Satyaki, Virata, Satrajit and Bhadraka for advice, but even they could not find a fault in Krishna's plan. Brihadbala had no choice but to go to his grandfather and renounce his claim to the throne. 'Krishna alone can bring back our ancient glory. I will always remain loyal to him,' he told Ugrasena.

THE LOVE TRIANGLE

Saibhya, with her frequent tantrums, had become a problem for Devaki. Trivakra told Krishna that the behaviour of the princess had changed due to her unrequited love for him. She requested Krishna to intervene. Krishna smiled and then went in search of Uddhava. He found his brother absorbed in conversation with Shvetaketu and guessed that Saibhya was the subject of their discussion.

'Krishna,' Shvetaketu called out. 'This young brother of yours is lovesick.'

Just then Saibhya walked in with Trivakra. She was smiling when she touched Krishna's feet, but then began sobbing, uncontrollably. 'Forgive me, Krishna. Love, hatred, vengeance have been driving me crazy all this time. I never realised that I was in the presence of divinity; you are the real Vaasudeva, the one that dwells in every heart. Let me join you in your mission to establish dharma.'

'That is very gratifying to hear, my sister. It would be wonderful if you were to marry one of these young men, Shvetaketu or Uddhava, both of whom are deeply in love with you.'

'No, Krishna, forgive me. I cannot marry either of them till dharma is established by you.'

'Saibhya, Shvetaketu is leaving for Kundinapura,' said Krishna.

'If I can be of any help to Shvetaketu, I am prepared to accompany him.'

THE PRINCESS OF VIDARBHA

Princess Rukmini was in a foul mood. Brisk preparations were going on for her *swayamvara* and Kaishika had confessed his inability to prevent it. The arrival of Shvetaketu and Saibhya gave Rukmini some hope. She confided in Saibhya, 'If Krishna does not come to my rescue, the only escape left for me would be to drown myself in the river.'

'Everyone who comes across Krishna, falls in love with him—he is so charming. But he does not belong to anyone; rather, everyone belongs to him. If you marry him, you will have to deal with everyone else who vies for his attention. He is like the sun and you cannot monopolise the sun's warmth...If you wish to be his partner, you have to help him in his mission to establish dharma. At present, you are in the presence of *adharma* and being forced into a *swayamvara*.

Rukmini was agitated. 'I know Rukmi is walking on the path of *adharma*. He wants to succeed Jarasandha by bartering me to Shishupala and then marrying Aplavi. I am not going to marry Shishupala at any cost...'

Saibhya then left for Karavirapura to atone for the unfairness shown to Padmavati, during her uncle's foolish rule. Rukmini went to meet her father who was discussing the preparations with Rukmi. She wanted him to stop the proceedings, but he didn't pay heed to her request. Rukmini was furious.

She told both of them, 'I would rather kill myself than go through with this sham.' Saying this, she stormed out of the room.

Bhishmaka and Rukmi were both alarmed by Rukmini's serious declaration and looked at each other with grave concern.

SHVETAKETU NULLS THE SWAYAMVARA

Shvetaketu had ushered in a great change in the confidence of the armed forces of Vidarbha. Although he was an employee of the royal house, he strongly felt that Rukmini would be a good wife for his dear friend, Krishna. He thought the only way by which he could help Krishna was to relieve himself from the royal responsibilities. Thus, he decided to meet the ruler immediately.

With a staff in one hand and holding a begging bowl in the other, and only a deerskin wrapped around his body, Shvetaketu walked gracefully towards Bhishmaka's palace. He entered the palace and sent a request for an audience with Bhishmaka. When Shvetaketu entered the royal chambers he saw that Bhishmaka and Jarasandha were jointly presiding over the assembled kings. Bhishmaka rose from his seat and greeted the august teacher, 'Acharya, you are most welcome. What brings you here?'

Shvetaketu blessed the assembly and said, 'O noble king of Vidarbha, I am grateful for the courtesy extended to me, but now I must leave.'

Bhishmaka was taken aback and asked, 'Why now? Has anybody offended you? Where are you going? You have been with us only for one year and we are honoured by your presence; we would like you to continue your stay...you have instilled great confidence in my army...'

'...I am not leaving Kundinapura for any disrespect shown to me, but because I believe an act of *adharma* is going to take place and you are allowing it. I have been praying to the great god of gods to show me a way out to prevent this *adharma*, but my prayers have not been heard,' replied Shvetaketu. 'Pardon my words, but this *swayamvara* is being held against the wishes of your daughter and only for political gains.'

Hearing this, Jarasandha got up from his chair and thundered, 'I will ensure that the ceremony goes ahead as planned.' Bhishmaka could not stand up to the emperor and nervously requested Shvetaketu to leave, if he must. Jarasandha was furious at the turn of events and left the assembly in a huff.

THE CHARIOT RACE

Meanwhile, at Mathura, preparations for the chariot race were in full swing.

Balarama arrived from Vrindavan in an upbeat mood, having tamed the Yamuna by digging a number of interconnecting canals and, thus, bringing the river back to its original course. Krishna and Balarama then summoned Satyaki and his friend Virata to discuss the ongoing preparations. Other Yadava youths too were requested to join the meeting.

Krishna asked Satyaki how many chariots had been built for the festivities. Satyaki replied, 'One thousand.'

'Brother Satyaki, very soon, you will become an *atiratha* and lead a thousand war chariots,' said an elated Balarama. Everybody was surprised to hear such talk of war.

Satrajit screamed, 'War with whom? We do not want any war.'

Balarama shouted back, 'Satrajit, you are a coward; during Kamsa's time, you were the leader of all those who ran away, fearing for their lives. We will go to war against Jarasandha.'

Finally, the appointed day arrived and the race began on the banks of Yamuna. The thundering chariots infused a new confidence in the Yadava youths, who felt increasingly equipped to face any eventuality.

Krishna called Satyaki aside and told him to take a hundred *atirathi*s with archers and leave for Kundinapura immediately to reach in time for the *swayamvara*. A rumour began to spread in Kundinapura that an uninvited king was arriving with a large army. Rukmi's spies informed him that Krishna and the Yadavas were busy with a chariot race as part of the spring festival in Mathura. They could never imagine that Krishna's chariots, headed by Satyaki, had already reached the outskirts of Kundinapura!

Krishna, along with Uddhava and Satyaki, left for Kaishika's palace outside the city walls. The Yadava commander, Virata, was instructed to halt their chariots in the nearby forest and be ready to reach Kundinapura at short notice.

When Kaishika heard that Krishna was waiting at the gates to pay respect to the grand old man, he went to receive him. Krishna said, 'Grandfather, I have come to pay my regards to you. Please help me to prevent this fraudulent *swayamvara*. I request you to make an announcement in the city that the Yadavas have come with their battalion to stop the ceremonies.' Kaishika did as he was asked.

When the people of Kundinapura heard that Krishna had arrived, they rushed towards the old man's palace. There was chaos all around. When Bhishmaka heard this news he collapsed, and Jarasandha, along with Shalva, the ruler of Saubha, retired to their tents. Shishupala panicked and declared that he was no longer interested in the marriage. Vinda and Anuvinda, along with Damaghosha, went to meet Krishna.

Krishna had brought along fifty Garuda archers in his retinue. Jarasandha was informed about Krishna's chariot force and the Garudas. The Magadha Naresh remained calm and told Shishupala that the shrewd Yadava had once again defeated him, but advised Shishupala to be patient. He said that he would also ensure that Shishupala got to marry Rukmini within a year. Crestfallen and humiliated, Shishupala decided to leave for his kingdom.

Jarasandha confided in Shalva that he was no longer interested in forming a confederacy of allies against Mathura. However, Shalva told him that a terrible Mlechha, called Kalayavana, who ruled the marshlands west of River Sindhu, beyond the great desert, could prove to be a great ally.

> Kalayavana and his hordes are barbarians and are dead against the kings of Aryawartha. Kalayavana especially hates Yadavas because he is an illegitimate son of a Yadava called Yavana. My lord, I can incite him to attack Mathura from the south-west along with my forces and you can attack from the east. Unlike the last time, now we can also expect the right of passage for your army from Drupada of Panchala. But for the moment, let us leave Kundinapura.

Within hours, Jarasandha's contingent left Kundinapura.

Rukmini was thrilled beyond words at the sudden turn in her fortunes, but her brother was fuming and threatened his father that he would kill Krishna. Bhishmaka then lost his patience and screamed at his son. 'You obstinate fool, what will you kill him with and for what reason? He has not abducted your sister. I am going to meet him; you may join me if you wish.'

Krishna touched Bhishmaka's feet when they met and assured him that he had no intention of abducting his daughter. He was there only to vindicate the honour of the Yadavas of Mathura and stop the false *swayamvara*. He requested Bhishmaka to conduct a *swayamvara* as per the Aryan code and allow the princess to choose her partner.

The next morning, Krishna and his chariots left for Mathura.

CRISIS OF CONFIDENCE—KALAYAVANA

The Yadavas were jubilant as, once again, Krishna had triumphed over Jarasandha. Krishna, however, was pensive. He shared his observations with Ugrasena:

> O noble king, I expect serious repercussions of our actions as Jarasandha will not spare Mathura any longer. Now, Jarasandha is not only against me, but the entire Yadava clan, and we are not yet strong enough to repulse a determined attack by him. We have to keep our armed forces alert and battle-ready. To this end, I am going to request Acharya Sandipani, along with Shvetaketu, to impart intense training in war games to our men.

A few months had passed and it was almost the end of summer. One day, Bhima arrived from Hastinapura to meet Krishna.

Krishna enquired about the well-being of the Pandavas and his aunt Kunti. A frustrated Bhima revealed:

> Yudhishthira is in more trouble, now that he is the crown prince. My mother lives in perpetual fear that Duryodhana would harm her sons. I would have killed Duryodhana if it was up to me, but my elders always talk of dharma and I cannot take any action...well...I have a message for you from Uncle Vidura. He says that after what you have done to Jarasandha at Gomantak and Kundinapura, the emperor has decided to kill you at any cost and obliterate Mathura from the face of the earth. Jarasandha has realised that he cannot depend on his allies from Aryawartha any longer as they have become your admirers. Uncle Vidura reveals that at the instance of Shalva, Kalayavana, the barbarian king from the marshlands of Sindh, has been asked to attack Mathura from the south-west while Jarasandha will march into Mathura from the east. They will attack after the rains, possibly after the month of Kartik.

For the first time, Krishna felt that things had gone too far and he would have to find a solution soon to avert the impending catastrophe. While leaving, Bhima made it very clear that the Yadavas should not expect any help from Hastinapura as long as Duryodhana was there. Krishna told no one about the impending attack and took the burden of finding a solution on his own shoulders.

Meanwhile, Shrutashrava was on her annual visit to her parental home, Mathura. She too warned him of Jarasandha's plan against Mathura. It seemed that the time had come for him to take some decisive action. Krishna finally confided his worries in Uddhava.

> I have not told anyone except you about Jarasandha's plan, and before I go to the assembly, I wonder whether we can take Uncle Damaghosha into confidence and seek his help. You have been very close to Chedi Raj, therefore, right after I inform King Ugrasena about Kalayavana, I want you to talk to your father and accompany him to Chedi to meet Damaghosha.

Krishna then passed on the grim information to Vasudeva and requested him to ask Ugrasena to summon the assembly of elders. The chiefs were stunned into silence, but once they recovered, they blamed Krishna for having brought this doom upon them. Krishna responded, 'Noble chiefs and clansmen, I assure you today that no harm will come to any Yadava while I am alive.'

The news spread like wildfire in Mathura and the whole city was tense and terrified.

That night, Krishna was more thoughtful than ever. He thought to himself: People have lost faith in me; it is as good as losing faith in yourself. Faith can move mountains; blind faith in me transformed Kubja into Trivakra and Vainateya into an able-bodied man. I could not believe in the miracle myself. Now I wonder how I will regain everyone's confidence.

Soon after the assembly, Uddhava had left for Chedi. In the meantime, Krishna had sent a message for Vainateya. He had requested him to keep a watch on the south-west edge of the desert for any unusual movement, like that of a large army.

One day, Krishna met Vasudeva and said, 'Father, I understand Gargacharya was at the court of Kalayavana… I would like to talk to the Acharya alone. Could you please arrange for a meeting?'

Later, Krishna told Balarama, 'You have to protect Mathura because, when Kalayavana and his army attack, there is going to be rape and murder of innocent citizens. I have been thinking that we should shift our people to a safer location such as Kushasthali. There we can build a new society free from *adharma*.' But Balarama countered him, saying that the women and children might not be able to make the arduous journey.

> It will take a minimum of thirty sunrises for the population to reach the port of Bhrighukachhapa. From there, we can transport the seaworthy population

> by boats to Prabhasa Kshetra. Others have to take the land route, which will involve another thirty days of transit. I think only half the population can make it to Raivataka, the old and the sick may not last the journey.

Krishna took a deep breath. '...we cannot help it. Instead of certain death in Mathura, there is hope of living in freedom at the end of the journey. I already have plans to build a beautiful city for the Yadavas, which will be the envy of the world. Brother, what is needed is faith and that will procure a great future for the Yadavas.'

GARGA'S STORY

Gargacharya was a descendant of the ancient clan of Garga, the kshatriyas. Because of their knowledge of Vedic lore, they were also considered as brahmana. Vasudeva had great regard for him. When he was imprisoned, Vasudeva had requested Gargacharya to name his sons as per their astrological charts. His choice of the name 'Krishna' was attributed to two considerations: Krishna means dark, as was the baby's complexion; and secondly, when the baby was placed in his lap, the beauty of the lotus-eyed child influenced Gargacharya to name him so.

Finally, the day arrived when Gargacharya came to meet Krishna. He reverently touched Gargacharya's feet and said, 'Acharya, please accept my apologies for asking you to come here. These days, the people of Mathura seem to have lost faith in me and I did not want to further perturb them by visiting your ashram.'

'Yes my son, I understand...how can this old man help you?'

'Respectable Acharya, I have heard that you spent your younger days in the court of Kalayavana. I would like to know about him and his tactics, you must have heard...Kalayavana has joined forces with Jarasandha against us...I am a little anxious.'

Garga replied:

> Yes, I understand, it is a very serious situation...Kalayavana is a cruel barbarian. His kingdom is far beyond the desert in the marshlands of the River Sindhu. To reach him, you have to pass through another wild country called the Rann, where the western ocean meets the River Sindhu. This kingdom is known as Saubha and is ruled by another brute called Shalva. Kalayavana presides over a number of wild tribes living in the wilderness

of the western desert and the rugged mountains of southern Gandhara. He maintains a huge army of horses and camels. In a way, I am his stepbrother and was also his preceptor, before I escaped to Madhyadesha.

Gargas have been the teachers of the Yadavas from ancient times. Yadavas are known to be powerful and arrogant. My father, a *balabrahmachari*, was once the preceptor of the Yadavas of Andhaka clan. In one of the Yadava assemblies, when they were in an inebriated state, they made fun of my father saying that he became a *brahmachari* because he was impotent. This enraged him and he left the Yadava court in deep anguish. He reached the forests in the western mountains and did intense penance, worshipping Lord Mahadeva. All through this period of twelve years, he lived on wild fruits and slept over dark brown earth; the great God of Gods favoured him at last and asked him to seek a boon. My father could not forgive the Yadavas even after twelve years of penance and out of spite, he foolishly asked for a son who would be dark and strong and, one day, would punish the Yadavas.

My father wandered for a while and moved to the west, to the kingdom of Yavanas. The Yavana kingdom was a loose confederacy with unruly tribes from the mountains, bordering Kashmir in the north and stretching to the ocean in the south. The Yavanas were known, by Aryawarthans, as Mlechhas and Dasyus, so called because they did not belong to any of the Aryan clans. For almost twenty-two years, there was war between the Aryans of Aryawartha and the Dasyus. In the end, the highly organised Aryans had driven away these Mlechha tribes, beyond the desert. My father became the high priest of the Yavana chief, who was a just ruler.

The Yavana chief had no issue as he was impotent. He consulted my father regarding a successor and asked him about the ancient Aryan practice of *niyoga*—surrogate fatherhood. The chief requested my father to conduct *niyoga* with his wife. Accordingly, the Mlechha queen had a union with my father in his ashram and gave birth to a boy. The boy grew up into a physically strong but cruel prince. He was named Kalayavana and he took over the throne when the chief died.

Sometime after this event, I was born. After my father's demise, I assumed priesthood. I had served at Kalayavana's court with great anxiety and fear for my life till my mother's death. I then left Kalayavana's service when he was away from his kingdom and reached the court of Bhojas.

Garga then became grave and warned Krishna. 'Kalayavana is not aware of the word mercy. He has a huge army comprising foot soldiers with spears and a good cavalry of horses and camels. They are beasts. Their raids result in death and total destruction. Even if you were to surrender, he would kill you and destroy Mathura.'

With a heavy heart, Krishna took leave of Garga. He started for his father's palace and found that Uddhava had returned with Damaghosha. Damaghosha hugged him. 'My dear son, we will all find a way out of this menace. I am no more on speaking terms with my son Shishupala as he has chosen to follow the path of *adharma*. Allow me to be a part of your mission to establish dharma.'

One day, Krishna received a message from Vainateya. One of his scouts had seen a large army moving in single file, like ants. They were coming from the west.

Krishna said, 'Undoubtedly, it is Kalayavana. It will take two full moons for the army to reach Mathura.'

'Krishna, give me a swift Garuda runner and I will send a message of warning to Kalayavana,' requested Damaghosha.

Damaghosha's attendant then brought a black pot. Its mouth was covered by a thick cloth. Damaghosha said, 'It is a normal practice for kings to test the power and determination of their enemy. There is a black cobra in the pot that represents Mathura. It conveys the clear message that death is certain to the one who tries to attack Mathura.'

In a few days' time, the Garuda returned with the black pot. Upon opening the cover, they found the cobra's skeleton; a pot full of black ants was feasting on its flesh. The message was loud and clear.

KRISHNA LEAVES TOWN

Krishna decided it was time for him to leave Mathura for a while. He felt that the people were getting too dependent on him to establish dharma. They would rather live with *adharma* than rise up and challenge it. 'They wanted me to be the king of Mathura and thought dharma would be established automatically. The naive people did not know that they also need to be equal partners in establishing the virtuous order,' Krishna told Uddhava. 'I would like to leave alone before dawn to seek my own answers on dharma. I will return as soon as the people of Mathura regain their faith in me. Meanwhile, I need to rejuvenate my own faith in myself.'

As Krishna left the gates of Mathura, he was joined by Vainateya and a few of his clansmen. 'Last night, the Garudas saw campfires lit up, far away.

During the day, we should seek the safety of the thick jungle on the west of the Yamuna,' Vainateya told him. Four Garudas carried Krishna and virtually ran through the thick forest.

As the night progressed, Krishna too could see the western sky lit by campfires, indicating that Kalayavana's army was indeed a huge one. That night, Krishna walked to the nearby stream, refreshed himself and sat in solitude, meditating. The next morning, the party was once again moving through the forest track.

When people heard about Krishna's departure, they panicked. There were some like Satrajit who felt Krishna had fled out of fear, but they were silenced by others who still believed him to be their saviour. When Brihadbala was approached to take over the reins of the kingdom, he refused and asked people to save themselves in the best possible way they could.

A large crowd had gathered outside Balarama's house, reaffirming their faith in Krishna and requesting him to bring back his brother.

Gargacharya had told them how curious Krishna was about Kalayavana, 'He must have gone to surrender himself to that Mlechha, sacrificing himself for the safety of Yadavas,' the Acharya said.

Balarama was aghast. 'Uddhava, let us go in search of Krishna. The people of Mathura do not deserve a saviour.' So they left in search of their brother, Krishna.

By evening, following the shrieks of the Garudas, Balarama and Uddhava had found their brother. Uddhava narrated to Krishna, the state of panic back home. Krishna then said:

> We must return to Mathura and evacuate the city. There is not much time left. Kalayavana's army is just two full moons away. I am aware that the path to Kushasthali is not easy, but for the sake of freedom, we have to face this peril. We have to ensure that no one is left behind; not even the Nagas, Nishadas or other weaker sections of our society. Our enemy should be welcomed by a deserted city!

Back at Mathura, it was decided that Balarama would address the people about the evacuation plan and in a week's time, they would begin their journey to build a new world for the Yadavas.

THE EXODUS

Damaghosha told Krishna that he would return to his capital with his wife, lest she learn about their plan and divulge it to someone. He also offered to send some gold and a score of choice steeds. Soon, the people of Mathura set off on their journey, crawling like a giant centipede through forest swamps and deserts to seek safety and freedom on distant shores.

Being familiar with the terrain, Balarama and Uddhava led the march. Krishna, along with some able-bodied Yadava youth on horseback, made up the rear guard. These horses were supplied by Damaghosha. Krishna chose a beautiful white steed from this lot and Satyaki took a chocolate brown one for himself.

It was an arduous journey and, as was inevitable, some died on the way, including cattle, horses and elephants that perished due to the heat of the desert and strain of the journey.

Ultimately they reached the River Lavanika. Though usually shallow, late monsoon showers had made the river turbulent. Most of the caravan negotiated the river successfully; however, another four days were needed to complete the journey.

When night fell, Krishna called Satyaki aside and confided in him that he would have to leave the group. Krishna said:

> The tailenders are in grave danger. Last night I saw the western sky faintly lit up, but today the lights are brighter. The enemy is much nearer. There is a danger that they will overtake us in a day or two, much before we make it to safety. I need to create a diversion to delay them further. I shall go and meet Kalayavana himself in his camp. I do not know after how long I will return but when I do, this world would have been rid of Kalayavana, the devil itself.

Before he left, Krishna requested Satyaki to give a message to his brother:

> Tell him to start preparations for building a new city on the western sea shore; I want to name it Dwaravati—the gateway to virtuous living. Also, ask him to plan a large hall in the midst of the fortifications and name it Sudharma. We must establish dharma in this new world of ours and let Dwaravati be its gateway.

Krishna disappeared into the night on his horse, with his guide walking beside him. Arriving at Kalayavana's camp by daylight, Krishna sent him a message that a disciple of Gargacharya had come to surrender Mathura. Stunned by the message, Kalayavana rushed out to meet the stranger.

Krishna introduced himself: 'I am Krishna Vaasudeva, son of the Shoora chief Vasudeva and disciple of Gargacharya, who was once your preceptor.'

Kalayavana recognised him as the cowherd who killed Kamsa. 'Jarasandha wants your head,' snarled Kalayavana.

'O Yavana King, I only spoke the truth. Here I am in person, offering to surrender Mathura to you…I could have escaped along with the other Yadavas, but I wanted you to take over Mathura before Jarasandha does. Jarasandha failed to conquer Mathura even after several attempts. The Yadavas of Mathura are very proud and powerful, but they have had enough of Jarasandha.'

Meanwhile, a few armed soldiers came to see their king and fell at his feet, trembling. They reported that the villagers living near the Lavanika river saw a large number of people crossing the river to the west, a month back. They were being led by Vaasudeva Krishna.

An infuriated Kalayavana turned to Krishna, 'You tried to deceive me; I am not Jarasandha, who will fall for your tricks.'

'I knew it!' replied Krishna. 'That is why I came here to show you a path, which would take you straight to Mathura, before Jarasandha,' replied Krishna with a charming smile.

'The southern route through the valley will delay you by over a fortnight, whereas the alternative path, which is slightly north of where we are, would take you to Mathura, before Jarasandha. Mathura is a prosperous city and you could claim a good booty for yourself,' said Krishna.

Kalayavana consulted his generals and returned to ask Krishna, 'When will you lead me by the northern route?'

'Chief, the sun is very hot during the days in these wastelands; hence we shall start after the midday heat. You better follow me with a few crack soldiers on horseback and once we reach the crossroads, which is near a stream, you can pitch your tent and call for your army to join you,' replied Krishna.

The northern route was a hilly track and one could only walk in a single file. The column began negotiating the gradient. After a while, the mountain terrain grew more rugged and stony. The horsemen found it difficult to keep their balance every time their horses tripped over stones.

Suddenly, a landslide occurred, causing stones and boulders to roll down, hitting both men and horses. The first horse tripped on a stone and tumbled down along with its rider into the thorny bushes below, dying of a broken neck. The second guard followed, meeting a similar fate. Amidst this chaos, Krishna planned his escape. Manoeuvring his white steed skilfully, Krishna climbed on to the ridge and reached a clearing on the small plateau. Thereon, the path descended rather steeply. Krishna, with great care, negotiated his horse to another clearing below where a small stream was flowing. He took the horse there and allowed it to graze in the green patches. Krishna assumed it would take the Yavanas at least an hour to catch up with him. He then remounted his horse and rode into the forest path, ahead of the Yavanas.

This path was also strewn with boulders and well-rounded pebbles and, much to his dismay, the animal fell headlong and broke its front leg. The horse lay there in pain, staring at its master for help and comfort. Krishna was filled with compassion; he patted its head and whispered something into its ears. 'You did your dharma; it is time you get the rest you deserve. Bless you, noble animal.' The horse appeared to have got the message and closed its eyes.

Krishna heard the army getting nearer. It was getting dark and a steeper gradient lay ahead, yet to be negotiated. On his way down, he found four cave-like openings and smoke was coming out of one of them. Krishna deduced that someone lived within and, therefore, headed towards it.

Krishna could hear Kalayavana cursing and dropping all his heavy armour. Unlike the sprightly Yadava, the Yavana chief was heavy and found it very difficult to climb.

Inside the cave, Krishna found a scantily clothed ascetic sleeping beside a fire pit. The embers were still hot, and the ashes in the pit were scorching. Krishna covered the sleeping body with his yellow waistband and hid himself in a dark recess of the cave.

RISHI MUCHKUNDA

After an arduous climb, Kalayavana reached the cave where Krishna had entered. He saw the sleeping figure clad in the familiar yellow cloth and, in the faint light of the dusk, mistook it to be his prey. He kicked on the figure. The ascetic woke up with bloodshot eyes and hit the unwary Mlechha so hard that he fell into the hot ash pit and badly burnt his back. The sage called out to his disciples in anger, 'Bhadra, kill this animal who woke me up.'

Three men suddenly appeared in the cave and pierced the Mlechha with their tridents and that was the end of Kalayavana. The sage sensed the presence of another and asked him to come out into the open. Krishna came out of the recess and, falling at the feet of the old sage, introduced himself.

The sage said to Krishna:

> I have wanted to meet you for a long time. I do not remember when I came to these Muchkunda caves. They got their name from King Muchkunda, of Mahishmati, who meditated here aeons ago; I am a descendant of that great sage. After ruling for a long time as the King of Mahishmati and having enjoyed all the earthly comforts, I reached these caves of my ancestor to find the purpose of life. Having met you today, my son, that wish is fulfilled.

The sage then asked his disciples to cremate Kalayavana's body as laid down in the scriptures.

Krishna participated in the ascetic's ritual worship of Mahadeva. They applied ashes to their naked bodies as part of tantric rites. Bhadra soon reported that the Yavana soldiers were searching for their leader. Due to the heat of the desert and lack of food and water, the men and their animals were dying. Krishna had to wait for some more time before attempting a safe passage. The sage and his disciples were supposed to leave for Prabhasa Tirtha, for the Uttarayana, and he decided to join them. During his stay with the ascetics, Krishna learnt their ways and gained tantric knowledge.

After a fortnight, in the latter half of December, the ascetics, five of them, including Krishna, smeared with ashes and holding tridents, left for Prabhasa Kshetra. On the sixteenth day, they reached the coast. In the company of the Tejasvi, Krishna saw a new divinity in the Somnath temple at Prabhasa. Streams of holy men from all over Aryawartha had gathered on the auspicious occasion of Makara Sankranti, when the sun traverses into the northern ascendant. It was an ancient Vedic festival, very popular in all the riverine *tirtha*s across Aryawartha. Prabhasa Kshetra, already famous for sun worship, owing to the Bhrigus, was equally known for worshipping Shiva, who was known here as Somnath.

In the auspicious moment, when the Sun entered Makararasi (sankranti in January), there was a magnificent chanting of the Vedas with special *abhishek* of the sacred Shiva linga of meteoric origin, which had a sign of Soma, or the moon, at Prabhasa Kshetra.

Krishna now felt that he was ready to return to his people. The sage understood his circumstances and said, 'Vaasudeva, the time has come for me to depart to the land of Manes. I have lived too long and it was worth it, as I met you; there is nothing more I want.' He then stood up and, with folded hands, walked into the setting sun. As he walked, the sea seemed to consume him and Krishna witnessed a radiant beam of light passing into the elements. Krishna offered oblations to the great sage.

When Krishna set foot on Kushasthali, he heard the jubilant screeching of the Garudas. Vainateya greeted him, saying he knew the fastest path to reach Raivataka, and offered to carry Krishna.

After three nights of travel, they reached a clearing from where the coastline of the western ocean was visible. From a distance, Krishna could sight a wooden palisaded wall with several watch towers. These were the temporary fortifications improvised by Balarama and Satyaki. There was a three-cubit-wide trench outside the wall, with sharp wooden spikes planted at an angle, to thwart any invading enemy, either on foot or mounted. A wide gate, also made out of wooden posts, was guarded by two armed soldiers.

Krishna, still dressed in his ascetic attire with a trident, approached the gate and asked the guards for Vasudeva. The Yadava guards enquired who he was and Krishna replied that he was a devotee of Mahadeva from Prabhasa. The guards opened the gate and let him in. A wide but unpaved street welcomed him. He noticed the houses were made out of bamboo or wild wood and fastened with twisted vines. The township looked clean; he thought his elder brother had done a good job in the short span of six to eight months.

As Krishna reached Vasudeva's house, built on low stilts made out of stout wooden poles, Uddhava ran out to meet him, instantly recognising who he was. Krishna met the others and all of them shared their tales. Balarama had married Revati, as he had promised Kukudmin. Balarama was now the chief of Raivataka. Overjoyed to have her son back, Devaki left no stone unturned to pamper him.

It was heard that out of vengeance, Jarasandha's army had burnt down Mathura completely. Krishna swore he would behead Jarasandha, if he ever dared to come near Kushasthali.

RUKMINI—PRINCESS OF VIDARBHA

For the next few days, Krishna surveyed Raivataka. Kukudmin had retired to the Himalayas after the wedding of his dear daughter. His dream fulfilled, he had decided to leave the arena for the new generation of Yadavas who had inherited the land.

Once Krishna had settled down in Raivataka, Balarama broached the subject of Rukmini and Jarasandha's vow to get her married to Shishupala.

Krishna replied:

> I remember it, and have been thinking what I can do about it. I feel it will not be wise for me to marry right now. Dwaraka is to be built as a bastion of dharma and we need to gather resources for that. If I get married and have a family, what will happen to the Yadavas who have immigrated to your kingdom at my instance? It is my *prathama dharma (*primary duty) to rehabilitate them.
>
> The Saurashtra coast is to be developed into trading posts. Yadavas must become seafaring people if they are to be prosperous. We have a vast coast along the Sahayadri Hills. Sowparnika, Tamaraparini and Simhala islands are great trading posts. We should establish commerce with these civilisations and make Kushasthali a thriving kingdom. We need gold to build Kushasthali, with Dwaraka as its principal city. We have to build impregnable fortresses to ward off not only Jarasandha, but also Shalva of Saubha and Sambara, and many other kings who follow the path of *adharma*. What is the hurry for my wedding at this point in time?

Balarama clasped Krishna's hand very affectionately and said, 'My dear Krishna, you have been living all these years for others. Mother desires that you also should start a family of your own. Please do not say no to her.'

'Give me some time to think about it.'

While the two brothers were busy discussing Rukmini, Uddhava arrived with a message. Balarama had been in touch with Kaishika to stay informed about the princess and now was told that the *swayamvara* had been fixed on the day of Akshaya Thrithiya. 'We must rescue her,' said Balarama. 'She has taken a vow to either become your bride or drown herself in the palace well. It is now up to you to speed up our rescue mission. She can be the right partner in your mission to establish dharma.'

Krishna was, at last, convinced by his brother's arguments. He prepared to leave for Kundinapura with his troops.

Meanwhile, as the day of reckoning neared, Rukmini grew desperate. She did not even know if Krishna was alive or not. She spoke to her family priest Agni Jyotana and requested him to go to Krishna and reaffirm her resolve to wed only Krishna. Agni Jyotana arrived in the city with a message from the princess and handed over the Bhoja Patra to its intended recipient, Krishna:

Srutva Gunaam Bhuwana Sundara! Shrunvataam Tey! Achyuta...

> Krishna, you are the most enchanting person in the entire world and I address you as Bhuwana Sundara. I had the good fortune of seeing you on two occasions and these were enough to make me fall in love with you. I have heard about your many noble qualities from the learned and the lofty. My ears have been drinking in these words and my mind is lost in you.
>
> Please do not ridicule me for this indiscreet expression of my feelings for you. Mukunda, how can anything else be possible for me, except loving you? I shall try my best to become a deserving wife to you.
>
> Here, my elders, in order to attain their own selfish desires, are forcing me to marry Shishupala, who has no better culture than that of an animal. I want to marry a man before whom I can bow my head in respect and not out of fear. That person, for me, is you. I would be happy to run away from my father's house and come to you, but this would not be fitting for a brave man like you. Please come in person and take me away in the presence of everyone. This is known in our shastras as *rakshasa vivaha*!
>
> According to our tradition, I am to visit the temple of Katyayini, the mother goddess Parvati, before the wedding. It is my desire that you should abduct me there, in the presence of all the gathered princes.

Krishna was highly amused by the letter. He asked Agni Jyotana what he should do.

'My lord…the kings and princes, under the leadership of Jarasandha, have already arrived with their forces. You have barely three days left and I beg you to leave for Kundinapura immediately. It takes two days of continuous journey by horse to reach our kingdom. Please rescue the princess.'

Krishna called for his charioteer, Daruka, and instructed him that, on the day of Akshaya Thrithiya, by the first *ghatika* (twenty four minutes) after sunrise, they should be in Kundinapura. Agni Jyotana would accompany him.

Damaghosha arrived with Shishupala for the *swayamvara* in Kundinapura. The king had lost his confidence after the burning of Mathura and also because he was not aware of Krishna's whereabouts; any hope of restoring the balance of power seemed over and, with his morale low, Shishupala had emerged as the ruler of Chedi. Slowly, he had wrested control from his father, who had been the ruling authority of the kingdom. Shishupala was scheming to become the fulcrum of power in Vidarbha and Rukmi was aiming to be the first among all the allies. Shishupala and Rukmi, through their marriages, would become arch-rivals for the throne of Mathura, after Jarasandha.

The ceremonies had started in right earnest, with entertainment, feasts and processions. The priests of Vidarbha inaugurated the *mandapa* with great religious fervour. The time of the *swayamvara* was fixed for midday. It was called Abhijin Muhurata, when Shishupala would shoot an arrow at a fixed target, and the bride would choose him as the bridegroom.

As per custom, on the morning of Akshaya Thrithiya, the bride was taken, in a palanquin, to the shrine of Annapoorna to offer prayers to Katyayani. All the women of the palace accompanied her. The temple was located one-and-a-half *yojana*s from the wedding *mandapa*. The surroundings, at the confluence of Poorna and Tapti rivers, were gorgeous with flowering trees and steps leading to the riverfront.

Though Rukmini was being adorned with the finest jewels of the Bhoja kings, she remained distressed and listless. At that moment, a maid announced the arrival of the royal priest and Rukmini rushed out to meet him. 'He has come and is waiting near the mango grove of the temple,' the priest whispered to her. 'He will abduct you, stay prepared.' Rukmini blushed in ecstasy, her golden cheeks flushed into a lotus pink colour. Suvrata, Rukmi's wife, was surprised at the sudden change in Rukmini's mood. When she asked her about it, Rukmini just said that the priest gave her a sacred mantra to chant, which will ensure that whosoever she chooses today will be a great warrior.

As the procession reached the temple, all the ladies alighted from their chariots and surrounded the bride, who was heavily veiled with flowers. Almost all of them were dressed in red saris and, out of modesty, had covered their bejewelled necks and heads with veils. The only way to distinguish the bride from the other women was the floral adornment. No soldier was allowed near the precincts of the temple.

The temple was square shaped and the sanctum sanctorum was surrounded by a dark passage with three low doors facing the mango grove. The head priest, Rudracharya, led the bride to Katyayini, through the narrow dark passage meant for *pradakshina*—circumambulation of the sanctum. Rukmini saw Shvetaketu, with a faint smile on his face, standing near the beautifully decorated idol of Parvati.

The bridal party followed in single file; Rudracharya, followed by Rukmini and Shvetaketu, were negotiating the last segment of the square, when a swift hand pulled Rukmini out of the low door. Krishna lifted Rukmini into his chariot and swiftly rode to a shallow part of the river where he blew his conch, announcing his arrival. This alerted the guards and the assembly of princes who had followed the bridal procession. Krishna spurred his horses; they flew at their master's command and, in no time, had crossed the river.

Balarama, Satyaki and the crack regiment of the Yadava army were waiting to ambush their pursuers, if any. There was chaos and pandemonium in the assembly of kings and princes. No one, including the priest, was aware of what had happened.

The kings of Saubha, Paundaraka and Karusha rushed their contingent of mounted bowmen to the riverfront. They faced a volley of arrows from Balarama's army, stationed on the other side of the riverbank. Fearing heavy causalities, all of them retreated and joined Jarasandha's contingent. However, Rukmi, who was alert, started chasing Krishna, along with a few mounted bowmen of Vidarbha. Krishna, moving like the wind on his chariot, with Daruka navigating, garlanded Rukmini with the garland he always wore on his neck—poets called this garland Vyjayanti.

Jarasandha was nonplussed and tried to console the crestfallen Shishupala. 'That cowherd, who I thought was killed by Yavana, has resurfaced. Not all is lost though; a prince like you deserves a willing bride and not a wayward and arrogant maiden like Rukmini.' The Magadhan emperor then commanded his entourage to leave.

Meanwhile, Rukmi was in hot pursuit of Krishna. Arrows flew from the pursuing chariot in quick succession and one of them hit Krishna's shoulder pads. Krishna lifted his bow and released a series of arrows at Rukmi. Rukmi was a good marksman as well and put up a good fight. Krishna then shot an arrow at the flagstaff and another at Rukmi's chariot wheel at such a speed that the chariot fell apart, and the yoked horses ran away in terror. The wounded charioteer fell on the ground, along with Rukmi.

Krishna was about to unleash his discus when Rukmini fell at his feet, crying, 'Lord spare my brother's life!' Krishna relented. Daruka stopped the chariot and Krishna, with eyes red in anger, caught hold of Rukmi's long locks and shouted, 'Stupid Prince, what harm have I ever done to you to deserve this hatred? I spared your life at my bride's request. Now, I will punish you by clipping your locks and shaving your moustache.' Krishna cut Rukmi's long locks and clipped just one side of his moustache.

At this moment, Balarama arrived and cried out, 'Krishna! The prince is your brother-in-law and you should not treat him such.' Then, facing Rukmi, he said to him, 'You should be happy that your sister married Krishna. Get up, take one of our chariots and go back to Kundinapura.'

Rukmi, his ego badly hurt, shouted, 'I had taken a vow not to return to Kundinapura without the head of Krishna and a kshatriya's pledge is his honour. Therefore I shall never go back.' Balarama said he was welcome to come with them to Kushasthali, but Rukmi said he would never accept such an offer. Later, Rukmi built a township called Bhojakota and raised his own army to avenge Krishna.

Krishna and his bride were received by eager Yadava women. Revati greeted them and helped Rukmini alight from the chariot, almost lifting the delicate girl. She took her to Devaki who hugged and kissed Rukmini and said, 'My Govinda won an *atilokasundari*—most stunning beauty. You are blessed, my daughter, to be married to Krishna.' Addressing Revati, Devaki then said, 'Revati, I now have two daughters; I leave this princess in your care till she weds Govinda. She is the princess of Vidarbha, from a high lineage of Bhojas. Her comforts are to be looked after to the best of our means.'

Rukmini was quick to say, 'Mother, I ceased to be a princess the moment Govinda took me in his chariot. You said that I am your daughter and so I am in my home. Please treat me as one amongst you,' she requested.

It was decided to celebrate the wedding on Vaisakha Paurnami—full moon day, at Abhijin Muhuruta—the apex of the sun at noon. Invitations were sent out across Aryawartha. Uddhava personally went with an invitation to Vidarbha to invite Kaishika and King Bhishmaka.

Upon receiving the invite, Kaishika said:

> After I place Rukmini's hand in Krishna's, I shall retire to Badarika as my mission in life is fulfilled. We shall travel by ship from Bhrigukachhapa to Prabhasa and from there on, you should come and take us to Kushasthali. At Prabhasa, please arrange for bullock carts and camels to carry the royal dowry from the house of Bhojas to the house of Vrishnis.

When Balarama told Krishna that he would go to Hastinapura, Kampilya and Matysadesa to invite the royalty, Krishna smiled and said, 'I am a cowherd; my wedding should be simple like those of *gopa*s in Vrindavan. Please also invite father Nanda and mother Yashoda and our friends from Vrindavan.'

'Krishna, what about the *gopi*s?' asked Balarama. Krishna's eyes reflected deep compassion and love for the *gopi*s and he understood what Balarama meant.

'The gopis are my immortal lovers, they have a special place in my heart. Let us leave them for the moment,' Krishna replied.

Uddhava was assigned the task of inviting Nanda and Yashoda.

BALARAMA AT HASTINAPURA

Duryodhana, at the insistence of his maternal uncle Shakuni—the prince of Gandhara—was keen to accord a grand welcome to Balarama.

As Balarama entered the Kuru Sabha—the court of King Dhritarashtra, Duryodhana and his brothers hailed him loudly as the hero and saviour of Yadavas, the vanquisher of Jarasandha, a god who tamed the Yamuna and the king of Kushasthali. The Pandava princes, on the other hand, welcomed him silently and with great respect.

Balarama then read out the formal invitation, addressing each of the Kuru elders by name and in the order of their seniority, requesting them to attend the wedding of his younger brother, Krishna. His announcement was greeted with loud applause in the assembly.

After the assembly, Balarama met Bhishma Pitamah and King Dhritarashtra individually to offer his respects. Both were pleased at the news and promised to attend the auspicious occasion. Balarama also met the Kaurava princes, lest he offend them. The next morning, he received an urgent message from Kunti. She wanted to meet him immediately. Balarama rushed to her quarters. He assured her that he was aware of the plight of her sons. 'Aunt, I am fully aware of your present state. Krishna has asked me to escort you and my five brothers to Kushasthali; I shall do so on my return from Kampilya and Matsyadesa.'

Kunti then said:

> Balabhadra, I shall convey this to Yudhishtira, but keep your plan a secret as this place is overrun with spies of the Gandhara prince. He has turned our life into hell; even Pitamah has not been able to check our problems. Since King Pandu's demise, we have become orphans. Bhima is seething with anger and full of anguish, only restrained by Yudhishtira. Son, please do

not invite Bhima for any of your skill demonstrations that involve wielding the mace, lest he lose control.

Balarama took leave of Kunti and moved his chariot towards Kampilya, the capital of Panchala. Drupada Yagnasena, Drishtadyumna Yagnasena and Krishnaa Yagnaseni welcomed him with open hearts. Drupada told him that he had heard of Balarama and Krishna from Sandipani. 'Like you, my son and daughter are also the disciples of the great Acharya,' said the king. Drupada was overwhelmed by the invitation to attend Krishna's wedding and remarked, 'Nothing accords me greater pleasure than a chance to meet Krishna Vaasudeva at his wedding.'

After a day's rest, Balarama left for Matsyadesa, which was ruled by King Virata. The kingdom was a small principality, green and prosperous. Virata was fun-loving and the kingdom was controlled by his brother-in-law, Keechaka, who was a master wrestler and a womaniser. His rule was the law, the king being a mere figurehead. Balarama had been briefed about this situation by Vidura at Hastiṇapura.

After a brief stay there, Balarama returned to Hastinapura. The next morning, he had three visitors: the prince of Gandhara, Duryodhana and his younger brother Dushassana. The Kuru princes were muscular and athletic. The wily Shakuni requested Balarama to teach his nephews the martial art techniques he knew. Balarama reluctantly agreed to teach a few tricks to Duryodhana the following morning.

At the appointed hour, Duryodhana took Balarama to the arena and asked him if he would agree to be his guru. Balarama was flattered and said promptly, '*Tathastu*—let it be.' During the exercises, Duryodhana impressed Balarama far beyond his expectations. The concentration of the prince amazed Balarama. Praising him, Balarama said:

> Well done! To beat you, will be a formidable job for your enemy. Be a good king to your people. I am leaving for Kushasthali this afternoon and my noble father has asked me to bring his sister Pritha and her sons along with me. We have the permission of the Pitamah and your father.

Shakuni was surprised at this move and said, 'So soon? The wedding is in Vaisakha and this is the month of Phalguna. We do not have problems with the decision, though.'

'Why would there be any problem, uncle?' asked Balarama.

Balarama requested for a separate chariot from Hastinapura to transport his aunt Kunti and the Pandavas. His brothers and aunt were welcomed very affectionately by Vasudeva, Devaki and Krishna; Revati greeted the party with brightly lit wick lamps in true Aryan tradition.

When Krishna met the Pandavas, he pleasantly addressed Arjuna as Partha—the son of Pritha.

Krishna requested Vasudeva to build wooden cottages for Bhishma, Dhritarashtra, Drupada and Virata. He felt that Duryodhana will not be allowed by his wily uncle to visit them when the Pandavas are around. Bhishma's cottage was built on a high ground facing the western sea.

Preparations went on under the supervision of Balarama. The month of Vaisakha is generally hot; the western seas are windy and rough. Bhishma Pitamah and Dhritarashtra, along with his foster son, Sanjaya, arrived a few days ahead of the full moon. King Drupada and Virata reached a couple of days later. Shakradeva, Padmavati and Saibhya arrived, with carts loaded with gold and jewels as gifts from Karavirapura to their Krishna Vaasudeva.

A few days after their arrival from Hastinapura, a large caravan unloaded huge quantities of gifts from the Kurus of Hastinapura, the grand royal house of Aryawartha. The prince of Gandhara sent a special gift—a large blue sapphire for the bridegroom.

King Bhishmaka and Kaishika were the last to arrive, two days before the full moon. As was the custom in those days, a caravan of elephants carrying huge boxes of gold and caskets of rare gems, as part of the bridal dowry, accompanied them.

Krishna felt rather uncomfortable at this bounty of magnificent gifts. However, Balarama assured him that they would use it all for the welfare of the Yadavas.

When Krishna shared his dream with Bhishma Pitamah, of building the city of Dwaraka as the gateway to dharma, Pitamah said:

> Vaasudeva, I know some great architects, called Visvakarmas, who are proficient in Vastushashtra and Sthapatya Vidya as sanctified in the Atharvan lore. They are great carvers of wood and stone, and live in the Himalayas. Their ancestors were renowned for having built the capital of Trivishtapapitha and the city of Amaravati for Indra. I shall depute the best

among them to design the city. As I scrutinise the landscape, I see a strip of land protruding into the sea, like an outstretched tongue. Strengthen this tongue, reclaim the sea with rock and rubble and make that your fortress. I know some Gandharva tribes from the Himalayas who could help you reclaim the sea; they have long been reclaiming land from the Himalayan rivers during colder months when water becomes a frozen mass. I will offer my prayers to Lord Somnath; I would like to worship him before I return to Hastinapura. I also give you my blessings; I understand your bride is as beautiful and bountiful as Sri Mahalakshmi.

Krishna was humbled and said, 'Grandfather, you are a role model as the keeper of dharma and doer of karma. This is your last birth!'

Krishna then called on Drupada, where he also met Acharya Sandipani. Krishna said:

> Yagnasena Panchala Naresh, my affectionate greetings and respects to you! Acharya has briefed me about the injustice suffered by you due to Dronacharya's vengeful behaviour. What he did was against the normal code of dharma, especially brahmana dharma. Please do not blame the Pandava princes. The young warriors were carried away by the traditional *gurudakshina* ceremony; Arjuna used his prowess, rather wrongly, to slight your honour and Bhima compounded it; that was a disgrace to the kshatriyas as well! Hatred consumes the mind like fire consumes fuel. Hatred and jealousy are the worst enemies of man.

Drupada relented and replied, 'Vaasudeva, if you say so, I shall forgive. The Vedas preach that forgiveness is the greatest sacrifice one does, equivalent to the highest yagnas as scripted by our sages.'

Krishna then summoned Arjuna and was briefed about the event at Drupada's camp. Krishna insisted that Arjuna must ask for forgiveness, to which he replied, 'As you wish, my brother. I am ready to seek pardon for my actions as I seek harmonious relations with the house of Panchala.'

Krishna's meeting with King Dhritarashtra also reiterated the hapless situation at Hastinapura; the king was unable to ensure peace between his sons and the Pandavas. Learning about the situation at Hastinapura, Krishna thought that he had a long battle ahead before he could establish dharma. Suddenly, Uddhava called him for the ceremonial *mangala snana* and shook him out of his reverie.

As they were going towards Vasudeva's apartments, Uddhava heard some commotion at the main gate of the palisade fence around the city. 'Krishna, please get going, I shall join you soon; let me find out what is happening,' saying this, Uddhava headed towards the gates.

Satyaki was already at the entrance. The armed guards were arguing with some naked sadhus. 'They are Naga sadhus from the Himalayan region and they want to bless Krishna Vaasudeva and these Garudas were not allowing them to enter,' said Satyaki, shaking his head in despair. Vainateya explained that the sadhus contend they came at the behest of their chief, Aryaka, from the far off north, beyond the Ganga.

The name Aryaka rang a bell for Uddhava. He immediately rushed to call Vasudeva. He had heard that the Shoora chief's maternal grandfather was called Aryaka. Vasudeva arranged a separate enclave for the guests and reminded everyone that his mother, Marisha, was the Naga chief's daughter. The Nagas were happy to see the great grandson of their chief marrying a royal princess. When Krishna came to pay his respects, their severity melted into warm blessings.

KRISHNA WEDS RUKMINI

On the auspicious day, the bride reached the wedding *mandapa* beautifully attired in a golden yellow sari and bedecked with flowers. Krishna was seated to her right and was also wearing a veil made of feather-light white pith. The priests recited Vedic chants and the couple had to go round the sacred fire seven times—*sapta padi*, taking a vow of eternal friendship. The Bhagavata Purana says that the recital of Rukmini Kalyana will bring peace and prosperity to the household.

After the wedding feast, Rukmini was waiting in the nuptial chamber. She was nervous, excited and also in a state of ecstasy as the events had far overtaken her wildest imagination. When Krishna entered the room, a whiff of sandal and fragrant lotus enveloped Rukmini. Rukmini then broached the subject of Radha:

> Govinda, is it true that you left your love in Vrindavan? I had met her sister, Anuradha, who told me about it. It seems Radha wanders around the gardens and forests of Vrindavan, calling out to you, carrying a flute with her, everywhere she goes. Her sister feels that you have been cruel to her.

Krishna replied gently:

> Vaidarbhi, I had no choice, as Mathura needs me. Vrindavan was a fantasy world, whereas Mathura was the reality—the living world of men, intrigue, greed, jealousy, anger, ambition and lust, a world of *adharma*. I live by the moment; I cannot afford to be fond of any one person, because I am not sure of my next moment. Therefore, I cannot belong to anyone. Is it not strange that everyone thinks that I belong to them? I get so much love even from strangers and this makes me concerned about them, and their problems. Vaidarbhi, I am not destined to have a life of my own.

'I often wonder, what would your lot be, with me?' Krishna continued, almost in a soliloquy.

'Govinda, Saibhya told me all this, and how life would be when married to you. I wanted to be your wife and I am prepared to be a partner in your mission. You know, I am a strong-willed person, I shall not fail you,' saying this, Rukmini bowed to touch his feet.

'Vaidarbhi, with you by my side, my mission becomes an enjoyable one. Wherever you are, wealth precedes you. You are the Sri and, from now on, your Govinda will be known as Sri Krishna!'

Rukmini was a longing fulfilled, and Radha, a longing that will be eternal like the wind, thought Krishna.

Just before the break of dawn, Krishna left the bridal chamber, leaving the blissful princess in her fulfilled dreams. Uddhava had informed him that two large boats carrying Yadavas to Bhrigukachhapa had capsized in the high seas due to a storm. Krishna and Uddhava left in boats to rescue the survivors.

Rukmini heard about the accident when she woke up from her blissful sleep. She had understood the purpose of Krishna's life, right at the outset. 'Govinda belongs to all. I am a flower in the garland, and my Krishna is the invisible thread,' she thought to herself.

Krishnaya Yadavendraya Gnaana Mudraya Yogine
Nathaaya Rukmineeshaya Namo Vedanta Vedine

Krishna! Epitome of eternal wisdom, lord of the Yadavas, Rukmini's spouse,

I salute thee, O world teacher.

*****

EPISODE 3

KRISHNA: THE STATESMAN

Rajaadhi Raajaya Vishnave namo
Vai brahma nidhaye namo namah
Krishnavey Bharatvarsha vidhyaake
Haree Jagatbhandhave

—A traditional prayer

KRISHNA AND DRUPADA

The Panchala land was green and fertile throughout the year and their capital was situated at Kampilya—near present-day Uttar Pradesh. It was a powerful kingdom and Yagnasena Drupada was known to be a just and stern ruler. Acharya Sandipani was the preceptor of Panchala.

Sandipani spent two months every year at Kampilya and, under his guidance, the Panchala army became a formidable war machine, thwarting even the ambition of Jarasandha to dominate Aryawartha. The Kurus of Hastinapura were also aware of the power wielded by Panchala and, therefore, maintained friendly ties, overlooking Acharya Drona Bharadwaja's great enmity with Drupada.

Yagnasena Drupada was an austere and unforgiving man who had, for years, brooded over the humiliation he suffered at the hands of Acharya Drona. His sole purpose in life was to avenge Drona's indiscretion in subjecting him to a humiliating defeat by Arjuna, Drona's favourite pupil.

In his younger days, as a student in the ashram of his guru, prince Drupad and Drona had been devoted friends. The schoolmates took a pledge that each would share the other's fortune in life. At the end of their studies, both went their own way to make their destinies. In course of time, Drupada ascended the throne of Panchala, a flourishing kingdom along the River Ganga, prosperous and militarily powerful in Aryawartha.

Drona had great intellectual prowess and superior knowledge in martial arts and the art of warfare. He was a descendant of the Bharadwaja clan of brahmanas. He was proficient in Vedic lore and Aryan code and was highly respected even in his youth. Despite his knowledge, Drona remained poor. He married Kripi, the sister of Guru Kripacharya. When such a learned acharya lived in poverty, it showed that the state had failed to attend to the welfare of its brahmanas. Drona was unable to even provide milk for his infant son Ashwathama.

In such dire straits, Drona approached his school friend Drupada and reminded him about the pledge they had taken in their school days. However, being young and intoxicated with power, Drupada simply laughed out and said, 'Look, noble brahmana, kingship and wealth do not go well with an acharya. You are supposed to lead an austere life and propagate Vedic knowledge. I can look after you as a state guest for a few days, but no further.'

Drona was offended when repulsed by his royal friend. His impoverished state and childhood friend's betrayal turned him bitter. Drona took the insult to heart; he neither forgot nor forgave his old friend. Determined to avenge the insult, he underwent intensive training under the great Parashurama and acquired mastery in arms, including the Brahmastra, a weapon of mass destruction.

His brother-in-law, Kripacharya, was in the service of the Kurus. Bhishma, meanwhile, was in search of learned acharyas to train the Kuru and Pandava princes. When he came to know of Dronacharya's outstanding scholarship and military prowess, Bhishma entrusted the princes to Drona's care.

By the time his pupils completed their training, Drona had earned the reputation of being the leading teacher in Aryawartha. At the end of the studies, it was customary for students to offer their teacher a gift as an act of gratitude. When the Pandava brothers conveyed their wish to present him a gift of his choice, Drona replied that he would accept the humiliation of Drupada as a gift from them. Drona urged his pupils, Bhima and Arjuna, to avenge the insult he had suffered at the hands of Drupada, years ago.

At Dronacharya's bidding, Arjuna attacked the Panchala king and captured Drupada in an unguarded moment. The king was bound in ropes by Bhima and made to fall at the feet of Drona. The vengeful brahmana warrior extracted an apology from the king and, as ransom for his release, demanded a part of the most fertile lands in the kingdom, which lay north of the Ganga. Under duress, Drupada conceded, but could never forget and forgive Drona and Arjuna for this dishonour.

After conducting a yagna to beget children, Drupada was blessed with two sons whom he named Drishtadyumna and Satyajit, and a daughter Krishnaa, also called Draupadi. All three were trained to be fine young warriors, their sole mission being to avenge the humiliation suffered by their father at the hands of Dronacharya.

Draupadi resolved to marry the most formidable warrior in Aryawartha to help fulfil her father's sole aim in life. While everyone was busy plotting revenge, the king's third son, Shikhandin, was overlooked. Shikhandin was a boy in a woman's body. Everyone shunned his presence as he was considered to be abnormal, which finally led him to take his own life.

Dronacharya and Kripacharya became famous as the preceptors of the House of Kurus at Hastinapura. Drupada observed these developments at Hastinapura with concern and felt threatened. He was also wary of Jarasandha's ambition to conquer and subjugate the kings of Aryawartha for absolute control. In order to encircle Mathura, Jarasandha was trying to consolidate his powers by allying with a number of smaller kingdoms like Chedi, Karusha, Kashi and Paundara, the underbelly of the Kuru and Panchala kingdoms.

Drupada was growing old and his sons were no match for the Kuru and Pandava princes. The obsessed Panchala king was desperate that his daughter marries the best warrior in Aryawartha, who would eventually defeat Drona. When he learnt of Krishna, Drupada felt that he had found the ideal match for his daughter. Drupada was very eager to meet this Yadava hero as he had heard that Krishna was the only person in Aryawartha who could string his bow and shoot with deadly accuracy from a fast moving chariot. He wanted to know more about this boy wonder, from Sandipani.

Sandipani was a regular visitor to the court of Panchala as he had great regard for its king. In fact, Drupada was known as Yagnasena for supporting the spread of the Vedas in Aryawartha. The king, despite his passion for revenge, which dominated his life, was just and benevolent and ruled over Panchala in the best tradition of dharma.

King Drupada unburdened his heart to the Acharya and requested him to convince Krishna to marry Draupadi.

Acharya Sandipani said:

> Noble king, Krishna will not accept your alliance and might consider this as a marriage of convenience. Krishna will not accept a bride who wants him

not for what he is, but for what she wants him to be. I shall request Krishna to meet you in person; his wisdom is beyond his years and he can help you find a solution to your problem.

Noble king, this young man releases streams of faith and has become the source of inspiration to the Yadavas; they are no longer what they were—turbulent and irrepressible. The trials they have endured and the leadership of Krishna, has imbibed in them a wonderful sense of discipline. That is why the Yadavas could subdue the neighbouring principalities and checkmate the ambitions of Shalva. Tell the princess that she should meet Krishna when he visits Kampilya because I foresee a lasting friendship between Draupadi and my charming pupil. Dharma itself would be your friend, I assure you.

SANDIPANI AT PRABHASA TIRTHA

Acharya Sandipani and his pupils were expected to reach Prabhasa from Bhrigu Tirtha, by sea, by midday. They were travelling in the royal yacht of Avanti. Krishna looked forward to meeting his guru. Brahmanas kept the common consciousness flowing throughout the Aryan world by going on pilgrimages, attending rituals, visiting schools of learning, reciting the exploits of ancient kings, imparting the teachings of great sages and ascetics and seeking the patronage of kings, warriors and the rich members of the merchant community.

Krishna and Balarama, along with Satyaki, went to receive the contingent at the beach. Yuyudhana Satyaki, or Satyaki as he was popularly known, was a fiery young man, lithe and sinewy, skilled in arms, an able athlete and an expert chariot warrior.

As part of infusing a sense of discipline, Krishna insisted that the Yadava youth should meet at the beach by the crack of dawn to acquire greater skill in weaponry and to keep themselves fit. These exercises formed a daily training programme for collective action and had stood the Yadavas in good stead in their swift rise to power. They had come to look upon physical endurance as the key requirement in the life of a kshatriya. This basic training in martial arts added to their strength and vigour and had helped them inflict a crushing blow to the King of Saubha. Shalva was a cunning jackal who despised Krishna and was thus dealt with severely by the Yadavas, within three years of their colonising the Kushasthali region of Saurashtra. Shalva then became a reluctant ally of the Yadavas, waiting for a chance to harm Krishna.

With a staff in his hand and dressed in deerskin, Sandipani stepped out of the last boat, his face radiant like the morning sun. His heart overflowed with love and affection for his exceptional pupils. Sandipani enquired about Uddhava and was told that he was in Hastinapura. Sandipani was well aware of the peril in the court of the Kurus.

The guru informed Krishna that Jarasandha was threatening to annexe Kashi which, being the underbelly of Panchala, would make the kingdom vulnerable. Drupada was therefore keen to enter into an alliance with the Yadavas of Saurashtra by offering his beautiful daughter to the best among the Yadavas. Sandipani looked at Krishna as he said this, and Krishna understood what his guru meant. 'Gurudeva, how can I take another wife while I am married to Rukmini? Will it not be *adharma*?'

'Krishna, you are a kshatriya and the shastras have sanctioned up to four wives to kings.'

'Acharya, I am not a king, nor I would like to be one.'

Guru Sandipani then said:

> I know it, Krishna, but your mission is to establish dharma in our known world. The Panchala king is very particular that you become his son-in-law because he considers you the greatest warrior in Aryawartha. By marrying off his daughter to you, he can ward off the threat of Jarasandha and also become a counterweight to the Kurus of Hastinapura. You are also aware that Drupada wants to avenge the insult he had suffered at the hands of Dronacharya. The king is obsessed with revenge.

Krishna had a hearty laugh and said, 'The Panchala King wants me to enter into a marriage of convenience and one that would make me a player in the politics of these kings. This is the worst of scenarios; revenge, anger and jealousy will destroy the human spirit. How can I pursue my mission if I agree to this, revered sir?'

The guru replied:

> I was sure that you would reject this proposal outright and I had told him so plainly, but the king is confused and insecure. He even contemplated giving his daughter's hand to Jarasandha's grandson, Meghasandhi, and get Magadha's support to avenge Drona! Krishna, you have to find a way out and help the king and save Aryawartha from Magadha.

Krishna touched his guru's feet and said:

> I am planning a trip to Hastinapura to see my cousins, the Pandava brothers. Please inform Drupada that I shall pay my respect to him too and would also like to talk to his daughter. The Panchala princess holds the key to the riddle. Convey to her that Krishna Vaasudeva would be like a brother to her and it is a brother's duty to marry off his sister to the most worthy man! I resolve to find Draupadi a husband who is an invincible warrior; please ask the king to rest assured.

'I do not know when I will see you again. From now on, your canvas will be the world, my son. Dharma will not allow you to rest. My blessings are always with you. Many a time, you may feel lonely on your path, but I am afraid only the god of gods would be capable of being your guide.' Sandipani knew of the burden that his young pupil was to carry on his own, but was also convinced of his divinity and ability to do so.

Krishna knew that the final victory of dharma largely depended upon the attitude of the Kurus of Hastinapura and Panchalas of Kampilya—the two premier kingdoms of Aryawartha. These kingdoms, along the banks of the Ganga, formed the heart of Aryawartha, including Kurukshetra and Brahmarishi Desha.

Krishna had come to know that Yudhisthira had recently been appointed as the crown prince of Hastinapura with the blessings of the mighty Bhishma Pitamah. Yudhisthira had earned the love of his people and a reputation for being a just and benevolent ruler.

Arjuna had helped secure the frontiers of the Kuru Empire, making it strong and stable. He was often referred to as 'the invincible'. His fame as a warrior with miraculous prowess, had spread all over the Aryawartha.

When Yudhisthira became the crown prince, Duryodhana came to Saurashtra on the pretext of perfecting the art of mace combat under Balarama. He then wormed himself into Balarama's good books and made overt efforts to get closer to Krishna. Krishna diplomatically encouraged Duryodhana to reveal his real character. Spiteful and malicious by temperament, Duryodhana seethed in anger and jealousy as Yudhisthira was given the coveted responsibility. In fact, the main mission of his trip to Dwaraka was to influence the Yadavas and poison their minds against the Pandavas. This political strategy was the brainchild of Shakuni who was disliked by all the Kuru elders, including Dronacharya.

During his year-long stay, Krishna maintained a diplomatic distance in his relationship with Duryodhana. He was not fond of Duryodhana. When the time came for him to leave, Balarama gave him a warm farewell, enveloping the prince into an affectionate embrace. With Duryodhana's departure, Krishna could see that life would now be full of intrigue for the Pandava brothers.

The time, therefore, had come for him to go north and assure them of his support for establishing dharma in Aryawartha. An opportunity presented itself soon after Duryodhana reached Hastinapura. Yudhisthira sent him a pressing invitation to come to the Kuru capital. Krishna asked Uddhava to go in advance to Hastinapura and announce that he would be there as soon as he finishes his job at Dwaraka. Meanwhile, he went to Sandipani's camp to inform him about his forthcoming trip.

'You are going to Hastinapura!' exclaimed Sandipani. 'You need not go there for now. Yudhisthira is no longer the crown prince.' Krishna was taken aback. Sandipani continued, 'Shvetaketu was at Hastinapura when the five brothers were banished by Dhritarashtra. He has just arrived from Bhrigu Tirtha and could tell you more about it.' Sandipani then sent for his principal disciple.

Shvetaketu collected his thoughts and narrated the events at the Kuru court.

> Vaasudeva, when I went to Hastinapura to escort a few cadets who were to join our school, I met Uddhava, who was preparing to accompany the five brothers to Varanavata—exile into the forest. Yudhisthira, being a noble soul, readily agreed to proceed to Varanavata with his brothers and mother. The blind king was happy as he could satisfy his beloved son Duryodhana at last, by making him the crown prince of Hastinapur.
>
> Yudhisthira was loved by his people and was known as Dharma Raja by them. Gloom has enveloped Hastinapura. During my brief stay there, I happened to meet Dronacharya, who was not too pleased with Yudhishthira as the crown prince. The ambitious and greedy acharya could not tolerate the staid and honest prince, who would not yield, bend or even be influenced by the high and mighty. The self-centred acharya had indirectly engineered the drama of banishment. Bhishma Pitamah was not too vociferous in his disapproval of the banishment either. Only the wise minister, Vidura, pointed

out to the king, the injustice that was being meted out to his brother's sons. Dhritarashtra was reminded that he was sitting on the throne of Pandu, his late brother. This is my review on the recent development.

Krishna turned pensive and stared into the distant future. 'Gurudeva, I am going to Hastinapura in a few days and would like to take Shvetaketu with me,' said Krishna.

'Acharya, please visit the royal households in Aryawartha; I wish to know all about the persons who control the Kuru's destiny at Hastinapura. I hear that Minister Vidura, the half brother of King Dhritarashtra, is very wise, pious and devoted to religion and dharma.'

'Krishna,' replied Sandipani. 'As you do not have much time to lose, I will try my best to consolidate everything I know of them. However, my assessment of personalities and situations could be subjective, as I never had the occasion to visit Hastinapura. Shall I start with Dronacharya? Krishna, please listen to the story of the great Acharya.'

DRONA AND HASTINAPURA

Drona was a son of the renowned sage Bharadwaja—a very learned brahmana who pledged himself to austere poverty and took the traditional vow of not keeping more food in his house than was needed by his family for three days. Since his childhood, therefore, Drona had smarted under the hardships which his father's self-imposed vow had entailed.

When Drona joined his guru's ashram to pursue education, he also had to accept self-imposed poverty. As it was the duty of a *brahmachari* to provide for himself, Drona would collect his daily food from generous neighbours, sleep on a deerskin, collect fuel from the forest and perform other domestic tasks in the guru's household.

Other pupils who stayed in the guru's ashram took pride in such spartan living, but not Drona. He envied those who came from princely families. Drona was the most competent pupil in the school, both intellectually as well as in martial arts. Intrinsically, he had a strong character, yet poverty shook his self-confidence from time to time. He was full of scorn for Brahmanical self-discipline, which entailed giving up worldly comforts in the pursuit of higher learning. He felt that one need not be austere to acquire higher knowledge. This was the main reason he became a bosom friend of Drupada, pledging eternal friendship with him. The keen intellect of Drona grasped that the future weapon of war and glory would be the bow and arrow. Archery and mastery in the art of bowmanship became his forte; he had the required accuracy and intense concentration.

Drupada was a very impressionable prince. His friendship for Drona soon turned to worshipful devotion in the face of the brahmana's superior intellect. Carried away thus, Drupada then took the sacred waters of the Ganga in his palms and solemnly vowed that when he ascended the throne of Panchala, he would share his royal authority and riches with his friend.

Some years went by; Drona married Kripi, the daughter of his guru, Saraswata Gautama, and fathered a son who was named Aswathama. Drupada succeeded his father to the kingship of Panchala. Drona was happy that his days of poverty would soon be over, now that Drupada would definitely honour his childhood pledge. But the young king had forgotten all about the vow taken in a moment of boyish enthusiasm.

In his quest to become the greatest archer of his time, Drona went to the school of the great Bhargava Rama at Shoorparaka in the Sahayadri mountain range and became his student.

Showing great diligence, Drona acquired mastery over all the *astra*s, including the Brahmastra. Bhargava Rama had taught about this terrible weapon only to the choicest few, on the promise that it would be used against the enemy only in the rarest of rare occasions. The application of the weapon also could be taught only to the most worthy pupils. The sage advised Drona to be discreet before imparting the secret of this weapon. Thus, Drona spent a few years with the great sage and learnt the intricacies of the fabrication of arms, different army formations and also the counter-formations to break these formations. These were called *vyuha*s and *prati vyuha*s—strategic formation of infantry, cavalry, archers and other arms of military. His guru was pleased with Drona's skill and determination.

At the time of parting, the great sage addressed him, 'Son, may the god of gods give you the wisdom to impart all the knowledge you have acquired in my school, only to the worthy. I have found in you a person of great intellectual calibre with matching physical prowess, although you are a brahmana.'

Drona bowed with folded arms and said, 'I shall try to tread the path of my glorious ancestor, Rishi Bharadwaja.'

Cautioning Drona, Bhargava Rama said:

> My son, when you first came to my ashram, you were a *grihastha* and father of a son and yet, I accepted you, having seen in you a thirst and will to know more of all the ancient *vidyas*. Just remember that a brahmana's wealth is his *vidya*. Impart this *viveka* for the welfare of society at large. A brahmana's knowledge has no bounds as he is eternally in search of truth. I hope I have done my best to mould you, among other things, into a seeker of truth and keeper of the dharma and *rita* of Vedic rishis. I have found in you, a strong craving for acquiring wealth, material comforts and control of temporal powers; a strange quality for a brahmana of great lineage! The intensity with which you pursue these would thwart your moral progress. Instead, you should try to be a partner in propagating righteousness like my exceptional student, Gangeya, now known as Bhishma. Farewell my son, you may go to the court of the Kurus of Hastinapura. Gangeya would be useful in achieving your ends.

The sage again reinforced the fact that desires cause attachment, attachments lead to affection, and affection tends one to be indiscreet and selfish. Ultimately, it leads to toleration for adharma. Along with his family and brother-in-law, Kripacharya, Drona returned to Aryawartha.

Drona, with rare self-assurance, presented himself to no less a person than the Kuru patriarch, Bhishma, at Hastinapura. Gangeya, himself a pupil of Parashurama, recognised the worth of this expert in military affairs and immediately engaged him and Kripacharya. All the Kuru princes were entrusted to Drona's care for lessons in Vedic lore and art of war.

Drona was appointed head of the Yuddhashala of the Kurus. Bursting with energy and enthusiasm, Dronacharya began training his pupils, transforming the military machine of the Kurus into a disciplined and organised army, which was to become a formidable force in Aryawartha, almost equal to that of Panchala.

Drona reorganised the corps of swordsmen, archers, experts in mace combat, masters of elephants and chariot warriors. Being a brilliant strategist, he became an advisor on the affairs of the state to Bhishma, who was impressed by his insightful intelligence.

The Kuru princes and other cadets proved worthy of their master. Bhima and Duryodhana excelled in the art of mace combat. But it was Arjuna, with his intense concentration and diligence for excellence in action, who became his favourite pupil. Aswathama, too, was reputed to be a fine warrior, though he was known to be temperamental. Drona later humbled the Panchala King Drupada, drawing on the great valour of his pupil, Arjuna. Power turned Drupada haughty after he assumed the reins of his kingdom. The king need not have been so arrogant and unreasonable to his old schoolmate, who happened to be a brahmana in distress. It was a tactless act by the young king, one that invited the wrath of the brahmana.

In a sudden and unexpected attack, Drupada was captured by Arjuna and laid at his guru's feet. The helpless king of Panchala had to apologise for breaking his vow and, by way of ransom, part with a slice of his kingdom to the north of River Ganga. Dronacharya thus earned the fair city of Ahichhatra as his *gurudakshina* from Arjuna.

This was only the beginning of Drona's rise. He was not content being the master of Ahichhatra. He despised the pomp and ceremony associated with the birth of royalty and scorned the rule of inheritance, which glorified royalty into little divinities, most of the time unworthy. Drona's aim was to control the Kuru Empire and manipulate the fortunes of kings who were supplicant to Hastinapura. The scheming acharya grasped the situation in the Kuru court, which was very fluid owing to the perceptible division among the sons of King Dhritarashtra and the Pandavas.

The great patriarch, Bhishma, despite the supreme power he wielded, was getting old, having held the reins of the empire for over seventy years. King Dhritarashtra lacked character, conviction and vigour, besides being blind. Drona's pupils were a divided lot—the sons of Dhritarashtra being jealous of the Pandavas. Duryodhana once poisoned and tried to drown Bhima in the Ganga. The hostility provided Drona the necessary opportunity to manipulate the affairs of the state to his liking. The shrewd Drona was aware that Dhritarashtra's sons, though loyal to him, were intrinsically unreliable. Duryodhana, although a formidable warrior with outstanding skills in mace combat and archery, was fiery and unpredictable. Duryodhana's hatred towards his cousins made him paranoid to a fault. That would be his bane; jealousy destroys and plunges one's life into chaos and conflict.

Drona was aware that only the five brothers could expand the Kuru Empire to the ends of the earth. Yudhisthira would be an ideal emperor—righteous and noble—and Bhima and Arjuna would keep the empire. Being aware that swiftness and surprise are essential for success in any conflict, Drona specialised in cavalry and chariotry in his scheme of training the princes. He found, in Nakula, an expert in breeding and training horses, no one could match him. Sahadeva had great foresight, a must for an advisor. So, when the time came, Drona heartily approved of Bhishma's suggestion that Yudhisthira should be appointed the crown prince of Hastinapura.

Duryodhana's council of advisors consisted of his maternal uncle, Shakuni; his younger brother, Dushassana and the *sutaputra*—charioteer's son, Radheya, who had been recently crowned as the king of Anga Desa by the eldest son of Dhritarashtra. The people of Hastinapura called them the Dushta Chathustayam—the fearsome four. The Anga Raja was known as Karna, because of his beautiful gold earrings. He was a master bowman, an expert archer and a true match for Arjuna. When Karna joined him, Duryodhana turned aggressive. Karna had been trained by the great sage Parashurama and had acquired an arsenal of *astra*s.

Shakuni was the mind of malice in the Kuru house. When the princess of Gandhara was married off to the blind Dhritarashtra, the Gandhara King Subala had insisted that her brother should be a part of the dowry too.

Right after becoming the crown prince, Yudhisthira, in his very conscientious way, took upon himself all the responsibilities of the office. He earned the total confidence of Bhishma, his ministers and the general public in all affairs of the state. Vidura become his best advisor.

Drona felt that he had now become all powerful, in many ways more than even Bhishma himself, with the appointment of his student in such a high position. Unlike the self-centred Drona, Bhishma was stern, steadfast, and equitable in dispensing justice without favour or prejudice. Within a short time, Drona realised that Yudhisthira, too, was like the Kuru patriarch. The great acharya was annoyed at Yudhisthira's attitude. Now that he was a crown prince, Yudhisthira no longer behaved like his docile pupil.

Drona observed that Yudhisthira was preparing himself to be a monarch, with the self-confidence of one who knew his business and with an honesty of purpose, which could not be deflected by personal loyalties. Only in matters of military and security affairs of the state, Drona's counsel was asked for. This came as a shock to the crafty brahmana. Drona had not only planned to push his agenda, but also wanted his son Aswathama to be inducted into the affairs of the state.

Hard as he tried, Dronacharya could not dominate over Yudhisthira. At all times, the young prince was fair, just and cordial, but firm in his determination to fulfil his royal duties conscientiously; intrigues did not affect him. He sought advice from many, but accepted guidance from none, except his grandfather, Bhishma. He governed the empire to the satisfaction of all concerned. Above all, he earned the love and affection of his people.

To the consternation of Drona, Aswathama was on the best terms with Duryodhana and secretly nursed a dislike for Yudhisthira and his father's anxiety to curry favours from the crown prince. Aswathama kept himself aloof from his father on all matters and instead preferred the company of Duryodhana and Karna.

The brahmana felt threatened when people started talking about Krishna's exploits and his rise in the political arena of Aryawartha. It was said that Drona sat scheming while feeding gram to the fish and tortoise that he reared in a pond near his cottage. He planned his moves on his mental chessboard as he fed his aquatic friends. To make Hastinapura the centre of the empire, he wanted to checkmate Yudhisthira's plan that gave importance to Krishna.

Drona had earned notoriety for his selfishness. In the past, a Nishada boy named Eklavya once fell at his feet, begging to be trained in archery. The acharya refused him as the boy was of no consequence in his plans of advancing his own interests. Eklavya was disappointed, but was also blindly devoted to the acharya and strongly determined to excel in archery. He, therefore, returned to his forest home, carved an image of his 'guru' and practised archery all by himself. After some time, the boy achieved mastery and gained perfection in bowmanship. In a moment of intense devotion to his guru, he displayed his prowess before the acharya and requested him to teach him the advanced techniques and skills. The guru, at heart, was immensely pleased and admired the Nishada's perseverance. Shrewd as he was, he sensed the danger that lay in Eklavya's raising a generation of Nishadas to practice advanced archery, of which he was the master. Drona asked Eklavya for a *gurudakshina* as he had practised under the guidance of his guru's idol. Feeling intensely grateful to the acharya, Eklavya agreed. The heartless brahmana asked the boy to gift him his right thumb, knowing that would prevent Eklavya from being a superior archer, therefore ensuring that Arjuna remained his most qualified pupil.

Thus was the story of Drona and the lives intertwined with his. Krishna was astounded at the degree of political scheming and was now more concerned than ever for the situation at Hastinapura.

Sandipani told Krishna that the time had come for Krishna to leave for Hastinapura. 'Dharma is in peril; rush now, son, my blessings are with you.'

KRISHNA IN ARYAWARTHA

On an auspicious day, Krishna, who had attained a divine stature amongst the people, proceeded to Aryawartha to redeem his destiny. Daruka yoked four beautiful steeds to his chariot. As Krishna arrived in his gossamer folds of yellow silk, the horses* became excited as if they had met a long lost friend. Krishna, too, responded affectionately, calling each horse by its name and whispering an endearing personal greeting in its ear. Satyaki was in charge of the party travelling with Krishna to Hastinapura. He commanded a contingent of chariot warriors well-armed with sharpshooting archers.

Each chariot was provided with relay horses, in addition to the harness and two riders meant to protect the rear in the event of battle. Each horse had a dedicated groom. There were several retainers who travelled on bullock carts, carrying provisions, tents and cooking equipment in advance. After crossing the mountain passes of the Paaripatra range—Satpura, the party reached Pushkar lake, near present-day Ajmer. The area was under the control of a Yadava chieftain called Chekitana. Their camp was like a miniature township around the lake. Krishna's chariot was parked on high grounds. It was conspicuous with the Garuda banner flying against the backdrop of the glorious setting sun.

Krishna dismounted and climbed up to a vantage point and surveyed the route through which the Yadava exodus had migrated to Kushasthali. He reflected upon how his life had changed drastically in just three short years. He was now married to a beautiful princess and had a son by her, Pradyumna. The Yadavas were carving a prominent kingdom out of Kushasthali, with Dwarakavati as capital. Blessed with an excellent port, the Yadavas, within a short time, had become prosperous by virtue of their trade with lands beyond the western ocean.

**His horses were: Saibhya, who had a rare greenish-tinged mane; Sugriva, who was grey like ice; Meghpushpa, who was the colour of a new cloud; and Balaahalka, who was ashen in colour. (Source: Padma Purana).

Krishna was pleased to see that the route had, by now, become a well-defined one for the caravans. He wondered if this coincidence was linked to his life's mission.

'Lord,' he heard Satyaki addressing him and found a few local chiefs prostrating at his feet in great reverence. 'Welcome, my friends,' Krishna greeted them and introduced himself. 'I hope our party will be welcomed in your land for a few days' stay.'

'Lord, we are privileged to have you as our guest. You are our saviour. Welcome to our humble hearths and grace our homes with your visit,' replied the chiefs. Krishna was moved by the love and affection of these simple folk who reminded him of his happy days in Vrindavan. Suddenly, he heard someone shouting, 'The Raja is on his way. Make way, clear the path.'

Krishna saw a royal chariot approaching and his one-time foe, Shalva, descending from his chariot. Shalva bowed reverently and greeted Krishna. 'Vaasudeva, I am pleased to welcome you to our land. Hope your camp is well looked after. When I heard that you would be passing through our territory, I instructed my feudatories to offer your troop all the hospitality.' Krishna thanked him for his generosity, following which, Shalva left for his capital.

After the party had rested, there was a commotion as King Chekitana, the ruler of Pushkar, arrived in his chariot to welcome Krishna. Chekitana bowed to touch Krishna's feet. Lifting him up, Krishna gave him a hug and enquired about his welfare. 'Chekitana, my friend, how is your neighbour behaving?' asked Krishna.

'So far so good,' he replied.

Chekitana continued:

> Shalva is lying low for the moment but I do not trust him, my lord. The skirmish at Gomantak seems to have chastened him as he has conveyed that your journey be uninterrupted through his territories that fall on the way to Hastinapura. However, I have taken necessary precautions just in case he has some tricks up his sleeve.

Krishna had dispatched advance riders to Hastinapura and asked Uddhava to meet him at Pushkar. One evening he arrived, looking tired and wan after his long and non-stop journey through the dusty Gangetic plains. Distress and despair was writ on Uddhava's face. The horses of his chariot were foaming at the mouth and their bodies were wet with sweat. Uddhava's retinue was following and would reach in a day. Satyaki and Shvetaketu exchanged glances, both guessed that something sinister must have happened. Satyaki released the horses from the harness and ordered that they should be looked after. The exhausted charioteer was entrusted to the care of a retainer.

Krishna embraced Uddhava and put him at ease with a drink of cool water. He washed his cousin's face. 'Krishna…,' broke down Uddhava, 'A calamity has overtaken us. The Pandavas, along with their mother, were burnt to death in their mansion at Varanavata.' Krishna was aghast. Uddhava flung himself under the shade of a tree. Kunti was like a mother to Krishna and her sons were his brothers.

Uddhava narrated:

> When I went to Hastinapura, I met Bhima and Arjuna at the city gates, who then took me to their mansion. I met Aunt Kunti, Yudhisthira and the twins, all clustered and talking in whispers. Unexpectedly, Vidura came to call Yudhisthira for an immediate audience with the king. Later, I heard from Bhima and Arjuna that Yudhisthira agreed to vacate the seat of crown prince to buy peace from Duryodhana. Dhritarashtra had warned him of an impending civil war, saying the five brothers were plotting a coup against him. The king then told Yudhisthira that they should all go to Varanavata for a year as a festival was being held there in honour of Lord Mahadeva.

'Why did Yudhisthira agree?' asked Krishna in surprise.

'Bhima was fuming, saying that he had known for a while that Duryodhana and Karna, abetted by Shakuni, were plotting to murder them in cold blood. But Yudhisthira advised Bhima to be patient and kept saying that dharma will win in the end.'

Krishna was silent, trying to take in the tragic news. 'There is something more,' said Uddhava. 'The king informed Yudhisthira that a palace had been specially built for them to stay in comfort at Varanavata. Vidura later called him aside and whispered something in confidence and Yudhisthira grew solemn.'

'Uddhava, something sinister was planned for the Pandavas,' said Krishna, 'I think they were murdered. But why were you not with them in their hour of such crisis?'

Uddhava replied:

> I accompanied them to Varanavata and lived with them for a few days.

> When the brothers were leaving, the people of Hastinapura were sad. In fact, wherever the Pandavas went, people honoured them with shouts of victory, but the air was fraught with portents of an impending calamity. The new palace built for them was reportedly made out of a light and inflammable wood. The walls were plastered with some strange-smelling substance. I learnt that the oil of this wood is used as a solvent for painting in royal households. It could have been a type of resinous oil used to burn down towns during a siege. I was told that Purochana, the Mlechha officer, was in charge of the welfare of the Pandavas. I believe he supervised the construction of this mansion and he was also burnt. I was saved because I went to Utkochaka to see our great grandfather, Aryaka.

'Purochana belonged to the school of Sthoonakarna Maya. They were architects native to Rakshasavarta,' said Krishna. 'They are master builders and employ hideous techniques at the behest of their clients. In fact, Maya was the architect who designed Dwaraka as recommended by grandfather. Shakuni would have chosen Purochana to spy on our brothers.'

Krishna became pensive and said:

> With the five brothers gone, the Kurus will be in the grip of Duryodhana. With Duryodhana's uncle Shakuni in power, the venerable Bhishma will no longer be able to retain control, and the Kurus will drift away into an abyss of *adharma*. I now see clearly what our duty is. I must pay a condolence visit to Hastinapura and meet the esteemed Bhishma. There, I will untangle the mystery which surrounds the death of our beloved cousins.

'I received your message at Utkochaka,' said Uddhava. 'I was given an escort through the territory of the venerable Aryaka. I crossed the Yamuna near Mathura, which now has a few scattered settlements of Nagas and Nishadas.'

'Someday, Uddhava, we shall restore Mathura to its ancient glory,' said Krishna.

Krishna then looked at Shvetaketu and told him, 'You must go to Kampilya and pay our humble regards to King Drupada and inform him that I will be visiting him in person after I complete my work at Hastinapura. Tell the noble king that he would be part of my mission.'

SHAKUNI'S ADVICE

Having got rid of the Pandavas, the new crown prince, Duryodhana, Shakuni and Anga Raja Karna were relaxed, and went on a hunting trip into the forests along the Ganga.

The people of Hastinapura disliked the foursome for their arrogance and irreverence for just governance. No love was lost between the ruler and the ruled; the group was feared and despised. Duryodhana, just to spite Arjuna, it was said, planted Karna to the kingship of Angadesa.

The hunting party, on the way back, halted near a shallow bank of the river to freshen up and have a sip of wine. Duryodhana voiced his displeasure at Krishna's visit. Karna pitched in, 'I am very eager to meet Krishna, having heard much about him.' Shakuni noticed his nephew's discomfort at Karna's statement and said, 'I am not looking forward to Krishna's visit either, at this or any other time. I have also never met him, but royalty does not overtly exhibit their feelings in public. Your calling Krishna a cowherd is not wise. Duryodhana, it is in your own interest that you should cultivate poise and, as a future king, weigh every word, before you blurt it out. This is politics.'

The foursome were worried that Krishna would figure out their sinister plan, which brought about the end of the Pandavas and they might lose an important ally.

Duryodhana said, 'The guilt is haunting me, Uncle. Aunt Kunti is the sister of Krishna's father and she was also affectionate towards me. Now, she is burnt with her sons. How could I do this to her?'

He then looked at Karna and said, 'Angaraj, Aunt Kunti was very beautiful and gentle and I occasionally see her reflection in your face.'

Karna felt a strange feeling pass down his spine and tears welled up in his eyes. 'I am a *sutaputra* and not entitled to have the delicate features of nobility.' Karna then collected himself and said, 'The Pandavas are dead and you have already performed the ceremonial rites for your aunt's departed soul; that ends the matter. You are a kshatriya and kshatriya dharma commands that you should have no sentiment and no remorse!' This finally put the prince at ease.

Shakuni reminded him that even if Krishna is a god, he cannot bring the Pandavas back to life. 'Remember, gods are only pleased when you flatter them with praise. Vidura has been a great admirer of this Yadava and has influenced your grandfather to develop a liking for him as well. You cannot get rid of him, but you cannot trust him either.'

Duryodhana then asked, 'I am wondering...why should Krishna come along with so many Yadava warriors, if his trip is only a condolence visit? There is a wicked purpose behind his visit, of that I am certain.'

Shakuni replied, 'It is because the Yadavas of Dwaraka have grown confident under the leadership of Balarama and Krishna; they are a power to reckon with and want to make their presence felt among the kings of Aryawartha. Krishna is no more a cowherd; he is the uncrowned king of the Yadavas and he is now trying to reach out with his charm to the rest of Aryawartha.'

'Boys, you will never learn how to deal with the affairs of the state,' continued Shakuni. 'You are hasty and impulsive. Never underestimate your adversary, dear nephew. Welcome him, flatter him and make him an ally. Win him over and the empire shall be yours.'

KRISHNA REACHES HASTINAPURA

Courtesy demanded a ceremonial welcome for the guest, before the city gates of Hastinapura, and this welcome party was headed by Prince Duryodhana. He was accompanied by Dushassana and other important officials.

Krishna, Satyaki and Uddhava left their chariots, had a quick wash in the river and changed into formal clothing. Leaving their weapons and ornaments, they now emerged in simple white dhotis and scarves. Krishna wore a yellow headband with peacock feathers. As the mourning party walked towards the royal apartments, a crowd assembled to see the famous guest.

Krishna's heart was weighed down with sorrow not only at the death of his aunt and cousins, but also at the genuine grief of the people who appeared to have cherished a deep affection for the Pandu princes. He was aware that Duryodhana was just pretending to be overwhelmed by grief. Krishna was amused to see Shakuni looking desolate, his eyes swollen, as he suppressed an occasional sob.

Krishna was escorted to meet Dhritarashtra. Vidura led him to a throne placed in front of the king. Krishna noticed that the king was prematurely hunched, sat on the throne with piteously blind eyes, his mouth sagging. Almost a recluse of a king, sitting on the throne of the ancient Kurus! Duryodhana stood beside him, along with Sanjaya.

Krishna addressed King Dhritarashtra:

> Noble sovereign, please accept my heartfelt condolences at the loss of your brother's sons. My father was inconsolable with grief when he heard that

> his sister, Pritha, also was burnt. Out of shock, he could not accompany me. I am saddened that my saintly aunt should have met a terrible end at Varanavata. Noble king, you could have sent her to Dwaraka instead.

The king was apologetic.

> Vaasudeva, I now feel sorry for having agreed to Yudhisthira's request to attend the festival of Mahadeva at Varanavata, which lies in the desolate north-east corner of the empire. People liked him and called him Dharma Raja. Krishna, I have lost such a son! Queen Gandhari and I were speechless when we heard about the horrendous palace fire at Varanavata.

Krishna then went to meet Bhishma, leaving behind Duryodhana in an obvious state of discomfort. The veteran statesman and ancient warrior sat on a gold encrusted seat while Vidura stood nearby. Bhishma said to Krishna:

> Vaasudeva, let me breathe the fresh air that has entered this room with you, my son; I guess it is the scent of dharma. Son, you are my only hope in this hour of darkness, I have no shoulder worthy of sharing my burden. I have kept the Kuru throne intact for over seventy years as promised to my father. I thought I could pass on the baton to Yudhisthira, the epitome of dharma. Yet, fate has cheated me once again, Vaasudeva.

'You are also blaming fate for this tragedy, grandfather? Please forgive my insolence, Pitamah, but this was engineered by man. I suspect foul play in the whole episode.'

'I know Vaasudeva; I had become powerless for a moment.'

'Respected sir, I understand your grief,' replied Krishna, folding his palms. 'You hoped that Yudhisthira would revive the glory of the Kurus and now he is no more. God never gives up on dharma and that is why he has created this world; we must have the courage to restore dharma.'

Bhishma spoke up again:

> Vaasudeva, the Pandavas were not banished, but went of their own accord. Yudhisthira saw the difficult situation in which we were all placed, as he always did. Had he not voluntarily stepped down, there would have been a civil war. Duryodhana and Shakuni had spread their net very wide and there would have been bloodshed. We were told that they were plotting to murder

> the five brothers. Bhima would have retaliated and rivers of blood would have flowed and, possibly, they would have been killed, either way. Duryodhana, Shakuni, Karna and Aswathama are bold warriors. A new generation has sprung up and they have no values; they consider us to be ancient fossils. It is time I leave for the Himalayas as I am no longer of any value here.

Krishna looked at Vidura and asked, 'Uncle, are you sure they were burnt alive?'

'Their bodies were charred beyond recognition. Even their keeper, Purochana, was burnt,' replied Vidura.

'Uncle, grandfather thinks the Pandavas are alive,' said Krishna, peering intensely into the eyes of Bhishma. 'Dharma never dies, sir.'

Krishna then requested permission to withdraw. Bhishma asked Krishna if he would return to Dwaraka after his stay at Hastinapura. 'No, grandfather, I am invited by King Drupada to go to Kampilya,' replied Krishna. There was a flash in the eyes of the old man and he said, 'Drupada is our enemy. What makes you go there?' Krishna told him that he wanted to find out whether the king of Panchala stands firm in the quest for dharma. 'Pitamah, I heard that you do not have any direct enmity with Panchala.'

Bhishma's eyes seethed in rage, 'Vaasudeva, if our Dronacharya was insulted, we consider it a personal affront.'

'Pitamah, please forgive me, I did not mean to hurt your feelings,' said Krishna. 'I would never hurt the interests of the Kurus, unless Duryodhana takes to *adharma*.'

Krishna then withdrew, retracing his steps backward, as a mark of great regard for the Pitamah. The patriarch of Aryawartha, an ancient Vata Vriksha—*Ficus Indicus*—was the embodiment of righteousness; a man of stoic discipline, imperious, all encompassed in a magnificent frame, and Krishna was pleased to have met him.

Krishna returned to his friends and voiced his concerns.

> Bhishma would have had his reasons for agreeing to the banishment. Perhaps the empire would have been shaken up, thus vulnerable to attacks from Panchala and Magadha. In a way, he had averted such a catastrophe and, I am sure, he was aware of Drupada's move to get closer to Jarasandha, in order to avenge Drona. This would have given the Magadhan emperor

the opportunity to dominate Aryawartha. Therefore, Yudhisthira had to be moved out of Hastinapura for a while. But things went out of control with their unexpected deaths. Uddhava, my instinct tells me that our cousins managed to escape. They could be hiding in the Rakshasavata, the impenetrable forests adjoining the Kiratavata. I am certain they are alive, but how can we reach them?

'Krishna, I will go in search of them,' replied Uddhava.

DURYODHANA—THE HOST

For the next few days, Krishna was busy meeting people who had come to pay him their respects. Duryodhana accompanied Krishna to a number of shrines and was going out of his way to be friendly. Krishna kept a diplomatic distance in all his dealings with the crown prince. At the end of the ninety-day mourning period, Krishna accompanied Duryodhana and his brothers for a ceremonial dip in the Ganga. He partook of the ceremonial feast where many brahmanas were treated with royal delicacies and gifts were given in the name of departed souls.

Duryodhana invited Krishna, Uddhava and Satyaki to dine with his family. Krishna met Queen Gandhari, who had taken a vow to remain blindfolded all her life as her husband was blind. She was a shrewd and powerful woman who, as Krishna found, doted on her sons and encouraged them in their ambitions.

Duryodhana introduced Krishna to the other ladies of the royal household, including his beautiful wife, Bhanumati, the princess of Kashi. Duryodhana also invited Krishna to join them the next evening for the Gowri Puja of Devi Bhanumati, where the damsels of Hastinapura would dance before the Mother Goddess.

Bhanumati did her best to charm Krishna. She told him how she had heard of his Raas Leela with the *gopi*s of Vrindavan and hoped he would dance and play his flute again for her. The next day, she insisted he join them for the festival. As soon as he entered the royal grounds, which were garishly decorated and lighted with several lamps, Krishna could sense Duryodhana's crude attempts to win him over as he presented his charming wife. 'The easy method of a dastardly husband,' Krishna thought. 'Bhanumati is the honour of the Kuru house. For Bhishma's sake, she must be protected from her vicarious husband in order to safeguard the honour of the Kurus.'

A sumptuous feast was served and light wine to go with it. As they were dining, beautiful dancers started gyrating to the rhythm of soft music. Bhanumati was charming beyond description. She often lisped like a little child and was always bubbling with laughter, very often without any provocation. She was just tipsy enough to blabber about Krishna and his *gopi*s, as if she had known him earlier.

She monopolised the conversation and was clinging to Krishna, who tried to keep his distance. Meanwhile, the music reached a crescendo and everyone was heavily intoxicated. Debauchery was the theme of the evening. He found Bhanumati unconscious and bared of her modesty. He collected himself, lifted the princess in his arms and started for the mansion of Queen Gandhari. When he reached the gates, the keepers were stupefied to see their princess in such a state.

Krishna asked them to go and fetch the queen. Gandhari was woken up and informed that princess Bhanumati was drunk and needed to be taken to her chambers. She was shocked beyond belief. 'I had to rescue Princess Bhanumati, your daughter-in-law. Please put her on your bed and save her, mother. The child is innocent; please do not be harsh with her when she wakes up,' said Krishna.

The queen broke down, 'My son, you saved our honour. You are indeed the saviour of dharma as everyone says. May Mahadeva always guide you.'

THE DOWAGER EMPRESS

The evening before Krishna was to leave Hastinapura, Vidura came to invite him for an interview with the empress, the most venerable mother. It was a rare honour because she rarely granted an audience to any visitor who came to Hastinapura. She spent her time chanting Mahadeva's name, spinning her rosary.

She was the daughter of Dasa Raja, who was the chief of a fishing community on the banks of the Yamuna. Her maiden name was Matsyagandhi—infatuating fish aroma. She had borne a son to no less a person than the great sage Parashara, who was the grandson of the most famous Vedic rishi, Vasishta. In a moment of passion, the sage had fallen under the spell of her dark eyes, her petite form and her vivacious charm. She was fifteen years old and used to help her father transport people across the banks of the Yamuna.

Her son was called Krishna Dwaipayana; Krishna for he took her dark colour, and Dwaipayana because he was born on an island, Kalpi—near present-day Kanpur. When the boy was seven years of age, Parashara had taken him away to his ashram in Kurukshetra where the learned rishis dwelt. Inheriting the mighty traditions of Vasishta, one of the founding pillars of Aryan society, Krishna Dwaipayana became Veda Vyasa.

Emperor Shantanu of the Kurus, while on a hunt, fell in love with Matsyagandhi, who was barely in her late teens and, beautiful as a wild flower. The king could not resist her charm and the very smell of the woman drove him crazy with desire. The emperor asked her father for her hand. The latter was a shrewd chief who refused to give her in marriage unless assured that her son, and not the crown prince, Gangeya—later known as Bhishma—would succeed to the throne of Hastinapura after him. Gangeya, having come to know of his father's desire and being a worthy descendant of the great race of Bharata, took the terrible vow of lifelong celibacy and renounced his claim to the throne for good. Shantanu married the fishergirl who, thereafter, came to be known as Satyavati.

The simple fishergirl emerged as a shrewd and just empress, upholding the best traditions of the imperial house of Chakravarti Bharata. She bore two sons to Shantanu—Chitrangada and Vichitraveerya. Chitrangada died very young, fighting a Gandharva raja. Vichitraveerya was a weakling from birth. He abused his manhood with indiscrete excesses with all and sundry and, therefore, acquired an incurable sexual disease that made him unfit to procreate. No king in Aryawartha was willing to give his daughter in marriage to this Kuru prince.

In order to ensure that his father's line continued, Bhishma abducted Amba, Ambikaa and Ambalikaa, the three daughters of the king of Kashi, and had Ambikaa and Ambalikaa married off to Vichitraveerya. However, luck was against the house of Kurus. Vichitraveerya died childless as a result of his disease. Princess Amba, in protest and desperation, after she was rejected by Shalva and Bhishma, retired for penance in the forest and perished in a forest fire. Her story became a legend.

The empress begged Bhishma to give up his vow, ascend to the throne and marry. But Bhishma was firm; he would not give up his vow. She then invited her son, Veda Vyasa, to beget children by the childless widows of the deceased king as per the ancient tradition of *niyoga*.

But fate was relentless in its torture of the royal line of Kurus. Ambikaa gave birth to the blind Dhritarashtra, and Ambalikaa to Pandu, who was born with many congenital defects. Thus, Satyavati failed to provide a healthy successor to the line of Bharatas.

As per the ancient law, a blind man could not be a king; hence the elder child could not succeed Shantanu. Pandu succeeded him, he ruled well and wisely. However, his reign was short. His congenital disease took its toll and Pandu passed away, childless, while he was on a retreat in Himalayas. Pandu was succeeded by his two wives, Kunti and Madri, who gave birth to five boys by *niyoga*.

Dhritarashtra begot numerous sons and the burden fell on the ageing empress to ensure that these princes were brought up with care and affection. And now, crisis had again struck the royal house with the deaths of the Pandavas and Kunti.

When Krishna met her, she was sitting in her usual place, in front of a small shrine of Mahadeva. Satyavati smiled sweetly and asked Krishna to a take a seat before her. Krishna prostrated himself before her and sat down. She asked Vidura to be seated too.

'So, you are Krishna Vaasudeva, I have heard so much about you,' she said. 'I understand, Vaasudeva, that you are going to Kampilya tomorrow morning. I am glad you came to Hastinapura, though I wish the occasion was auspicious and pleasant. We are faced with a great crisis and what a calamity!' she exclaimed. 'Krishna, meeting you, I recollect the great Parashara Muni narrating a remarkable incident of his life.'

Satyavati then narrated the story:

> Muni Parashara did great penance and *tapas* to please Lord Mahadeva and his divine consort, Ma Bhavani, at the lord's abode, Mount Kailash. The lord appeared along with the Divine Mother and blessed him with a son who would be the repository of eternal knowledge—Sanatana Dharma—and would spread the word. Before the *muni* (sage) could comprehend, he was enveloped by a haunting melody, resonating with Omkara. Amazed by the vibrations of the word AUM, Parashara, the celibate sage, wondered how he could father a son.
>
> As he was descending from the mountain top, Parashara saw a brilliant flash of light near a cave that seemed to beckon him. He heard a voice, 'O *muni*, your son will be blessed by Me, with divine intellect, and he will live to

> be immortal, spreading the message of Sanatana Dharma amid mankind. Parashara, my Amsa will be born soon thereafter, and the son of yours will know of Him and sing His praise, He would be the saviour of mankind and eternal repository of my dharma.' That moment seems to have come with your visit, Krishna; I feel you are that Amsa of the Divine Mother. A great life is ahead of you.

The empress enquired about his wife and son. 'Do you know what your son's name, Pradyumna, means? It means Manmatha—the God of Love. Your son must be beautiful as you.'

Satyavati then thanked Krishna for saving Bhanumati's honour.

Krishna told her:

> Venerable mother, Bhanumati is innocent; she is a child and it is her husband Duryodhana who was behind this. He wanted to please me and enticed me to covet his wife; it was a terrible situation. The worship of Devi, the Mother Goddess, was converted into an orgy. The poor princess was forced to get drunk and so was I, but I threw the wine away and the honour of the house of Kurus was thus saved.

'Krishna, you are the favourite of the Great God, the one I worship. You will accomplish that which no one has done so far,' said Satyavati. 'I do not know what conflict Gangeya is in for the past several decades. At the moment, he suffers from *adharma*. Why is it so?'

Krishna replied:

> My noble guru Sandipani taught us that the Vedas describe dharma as that action by which human beings derive both worldly and spiritual welfare. Today, people do not lead a holistic life as they think worldly life is different from the spiritual. The Vedas do not advocate such a division. Man's material and spiritual well-being are intertwined and every action of his has a bearing on both, so all actions must be god-centric.
>
> In my opinion, this integration is dharma; Ishwara dwells in dharma. Hastinapura is drifting away from dharma despite the presence of Bhishma, a pillar of dharma. I am too young to advise my esteemed elders. But I beseech you to correct the course and re-establish righteousness. The banishment of Yudhisthira was unjust and the price that Hastinapura pays is heavy.

> If grandfather has lost control, he should abdicate and let the pot of *adharma* boil and overflow, earlier than later.

Satyavati's face assumed a solemn look. She glanced at Vidura, lowered her voice to almost an inaudible whisper and said, 'Will you stand by the five brothers as you stand by dharma?'

'What do you mean? Are they alive?' Krishna asked. 'Of course, I stand by them. That is why I came to Hastinapura.' Satyavati smiled gently and then revealed that the brothers had escaped from the burning palace by a tunnel dug by Vidura's man. The dead bodies found were not of Kunti or her sons. Vidura had kept a boat ready for them to cross the Ganga and then they disappeared into the forest.

Satyavati had a request:

> Govinda, I urge you to find out where they are and whether they are safe. No one will suspect you of trying to do so. All we know is that the forest they entered is ruled by Nagas and your paternal grandmother, Marisha, was a Naga. Her father, the old Aryaka, is their king. When you find them, please take them to Dwaraka without anyone knowing about it.

Krishna was more than happy to do as he was told. 'May your path be victorious, my son,' said the empress. Krishna then took her leave by prostrating at her feet.

'Dharma always triumphs,' mused Krishna.

KRISHNA AND VEDA VYASA

At the insistence of Queen Gandhari, Vidura informed Bhishma about the fiasco in Gowri puja. The grand sire was furious and ordered the gardens to be, henceforth, a forbidden place and a temple for the Mother Goddess be built there as a mark of respect. Shakuni severely reprimanded Duryodhana. Even Karna showed his extreme displeasure and admired Krishna's actions. He had been unable to meet Krishna and hoped to speak with him soon.

Krishna and a few leading members of his party departed for Kampilya by river. The other Yadava chiefs were left behind. They would follow in chariots, horses and carts, by the land route, to Nagakoota, which was the headquarters of King Aryaka. The king was Vasudeva's maternal grandfather and Krishna was keen to visit him before leaving for Dwaraka.

The Ganga was a wide and swift river in these parts of the country. For safety, the river traffic always cruised along its banks, avoiding the rapids; none dared to cross to the other side, fearing certain capsize.

Krishna belonged to Yamuna, the river of beauty and splendour, whereas Ganga was a river of fury and glory. A nature lover, Krishna saw birds of various hues wheeling over the water, swooping down and, in a moment, rising out of the water with their beaks full of juicy fish. The green treetops, the dense woods and the swinging vines reminded Krishna of his days in Vrindavan.

The Ganga, along its banks, had virgin forests and some of these places were impenetrable. There were clearances though, of narrow footpaths, leading to interior villages, often inhabited by Nagas. These tribes were Nature's creatures and continuously plied their canoes along the river. They articulated themselves very well with gestures. At some places, Krishna found large tracks of forests cleared for settlements, farming and cattle-rearing. These settlements resembled classic Aryan habitats.

As soon as they saw the procession of boats, the residents of these settlements came to the bank of the river and welcomed the guests with flower garlands, fruit baskets and honey pots. As they coasted along, the Yadavas came across the ashram of some ascetics and stopped to pay their respects to the presiding rishis, also joining them in their worship of the sacred fire.

So far, Krishna was not keen to share the information about the brothers with Satyaki. Satyaki, though extremely loyal to him, was too outspoken. He, however, confided in Uddhava. 'How do we go about the search?' asked Krishna. 'I am too prominent to pursue the search myself and I want you to come with me to Panchala. I want to propose your name for the hand of Draupadi,' mentioned Krishna casually.

'Oh brother, you must be joking. I cannot marry the fiery princess. If the Pandavas are alive as you say, propose Arjuna's hand in marriage, for he is the most formidable Pandava hero,' said Uddhava.

As they were sailing on the river, they reached a large opening in the forest with well laid out pathways. They heard melodious chants and found smoke, having an exotic aroma, rising into the sky. Krishna signalled to the boats to moor along the banks near the ashram.

They came ashore and found a large settlement surrounded by wild lantana hedges. At the centre was a fire burning in a sacrificial pit and a large company of anchorites of both sexes were chanting and offering oblations. About two hundred Nagas and dark skinned Nishadas, along with their chiefs, in feathered headdresses were also sitting there. There were a number of ailing women, men and children among them.

The ashram belonged to Rishi Dhaumya. Dhaumya blessed Krishna and his companions and led them to *homa*—the sacrificial fire before which a venerable figure sat, offering oblations. Veda Vyasa also happened to be present.

Krishna prostrated before the *muni* when Rishi Dhaumya introduced him. The large eyes in the swarthy face widened in surprise for a moment, then grew soft with the light of recognition. 'Vaasudeva,' said Vyasa, in the rich voice of a fond father, 'I have been waiting to meet you. I met your father, Anakabandhu, before you were born.'

Meanwhile, Dhaumya and Vyasa's principal disciple, Jaimini, distributed milk and honey to the assembly. The ailing were taken to Vyasa, who put a leaf into their cups and blessed them by applying *vibhuti*, or sacred ash, from the *homa* pit. After he made sure that every man, woman and child were fed, Vyasa ate. Krishna, Uddhava and Satyaki joined him as well.

'What brought you to Hastinapura?' asked the sage. Krishna told him of the sad circumstances and his meeting with Satyavati. Vyasa asked, 'Are you going to Kampilya?'

Krishna replied:

> Yes, master. Bhishma was disturbed when he heard this; but I assured the grand sire and empress that my mission to Drupada was only to bring Panchalas, Kurus and Yadavas together to face the powerful Magadha. When Yudhisthira was the crown prince at Hastinapura, I wanted to attempt a reconciliation between Drupada and Dronacharya, but now my plans are in disarray; *adharma* has taken over Hastinapura and I am at a loss as to what should be done next.

'Vaasudeva, teach Raja Dharma to the kings of Aryawartha. Teach them the ways of Manu, Vivasvata and Janaka. Drupada should shed his hatred for Drona; Drona should not covet too much wealth and power, it is against his lineage. Check Jarasandha once and for all—Aryawartha is not safe while he lives,' said Vyasa.

Krishna then asked, 'Should I have allowed my brother to smash Jarasandha's head at Gomantak? Was it a mistake that I stopped him from doing so?'

'No, his time is yet to come. *Adharma* has to ripen before it is routed. Vaasudeva, you were wise,' said Vyasa.

'Respected master, are the Pandu brothers and Aunt Kunti alive?' asked Krishna, almost gasping to hear the news from Vyasa's mouth.

Vyasa looked at Krishna with a smile. 'We have to find out where they are and I am on that mission myself! Vaasudeva, dharma never dies. My father prophesied that you are the Amsa of Mother Nature; if so, then my life's mission is fulfilled in having met you.'

Thus saying, Vyasa got up and raised both his hands in blessing, 'Mahadeva is with you! You will be victorious always.'

Krishna retired to his hut, but could not sleep. His immediate job was to find his cousins. He remembered Vyasa mentioning that Aryaka had grown very old and lived in Nagakoota. 'You can trust him; he will help you find your Aunt Kunti, who is also his granddaughter.' Krishna decided to send Uddhava in search of the Pandava princes.

Krishna was told the next morning that Uddhava had left with the sage to meet Aryaka. Uddhava left behind a message that he would join Krishna at Uttkocha on their way back from Kampilya.

'Satyaki, must say our Uddhava is a clever fellow! He wanted to avoid coming to Kampilya because he was scared that I would propose his name to marry the princess of Panchala.' Satyaki said that he knew they were on a mission, much like Krishna was, to find the Pandavas. Krishna was surprised at his astuteness and said:

> Not that I wanted to keep the secret from you, my brother, but we were afraid that the chances of the information leaking out would increase if more people knew the secret. Duryodhana's spies are all around and he does not trust me. Now that Uddhava has gone with the master, I know he will succeed in finding them. Let us go to Kampilya and then return to Dwaraka.

KRISHNA AND DRUPADA YAGNASENA

Krishna's party resumed their journey by the river, cruising along the beautiful Ganga—serene and yet, swirling. Krishna and a few leading members of his party were headed for Kampilya by river. The other Yadava chiefs were left behind. Shvetaketu had already reached Kampilya to receive Krishna.

Krishna was received by Drishtadyumna at Ekachakra Tirtha, just before Kampilya. This was a mark of great respect and protocol, reserved only for reigning monarchs. The prime minister of Panchala, Acharya Udbodhana, garlanded Krishna and requested him to board the royal yacht. With the beating of trumpets, the prince led Krishna to a flower-bedecked seat. Krishna saw his old friend, Acharya Shvetaketu, in the reception party.

Krishna was happy to meet the fine young prince of Panchala. At the request of Krishna, the royal yacht halted at some of the well known ashrams along the banks where he paid his respects to the rishis and received their blessings. He was glad to learn from the holy men that they were being well looked after by the Panchala Naresh. At last, the yacht was moored at Kampilya and King Drupada himself received Krishna with an affectionate embrace. 'Panchala is very happy to welcome you to Kampilya, Vaasudeva,' he said loudly. 'The good fortune is mine, my noble lord,' replied Krishna.

Drishtadyumna and his brother Satyajit then led Krishna on to an elephant that had been elegantly painted and adorned with golden trappings. As the royal elephant marched majestically, the bells tied to its legs tinkled and an overwhelmed Krishna said, 'Noble lord, I am not royalty, to deserve this privilege.'

'Vaasudeva...you are more than a king. Is it true that you rarely sleep and look fresh always?' Krishna smiled and said, 'Noble lord, I am always awake.'

Krishna was also impressed by the two princes, Drishtadyumna and Satyajit. They looked like expert warriors, and he felt that Panchala was safe, for the moment, with both of them at the helm.

When they arrived at the palace, Drupada, with evident reluctance, introduced Krishna to his third son, Shikhandin. He was a shrinking and undersized, but very good-looking boy, almost girlish in his behaviour. The boy looked frightened and apprehensive. Krishna smiled and said to him, 'You are such a handsome prince,' and placed his palm for a minute on the head of the bewildered boy. To the surprise of everyone, Shikhandin replied with great dignity, 'I am pleased to meet you as well Krishna Vaasudeva,' and touched Krishna's feet with great reverence. Everyone was astonished at the transformation that Krishna brought in the boy by his mere touch!

The ceremonial banquet was attended by the leading chiefs of Panchala. Krishna noticed that the king, as well as the princes, abstained from alcohol; none of them drank, though the other guests had their fill. Shvetaketu whispered in Krishna's ear, 'The king and his sons have forsaken alcohol till the family vow is redeemed.' Krishna, too, politely kept the golden cup away and asked for water instead.

Princess Draupadi had been observing Krishna with a keen eye and developed a deep admiration for him.

The next day, Drupada invited Krishna to the mango grove behind the palace. Krishna said to the king, 'The people of Panchala seem to be happy being ruled by a benevolent king and a loving father. I see dharma reigning well in your kingdom, noble lord! I am very happy to have met you.'

Drupada raised his greying head and looked Krishna in the face with a wry smile. 'Vaasudeva, I have invited you here to make a very strange offer, Acharya Sandipani must have told you about it. Will you take my daughter to be your wife?'

Krishna replied:

> Noble lord, I realise your feelings and am aware of the background. May I humbly remind you that I am already married. However, I do not reject the offer either, which is so generously made. It is just that I do not feel that I would be in a position to fulfil the expectation of such a noble king as yourself.

'Are you afraid of Drona?' asked the king, knitting his brows. 'No, lord, but at the same time I would not like to be the cause for more enmity between the Panchalas and the Kurus. Dharma can flourish only if both the Kurus and Panchalas defend it. If they fight against each other in a bitter war, what will happen to Aryawartha?' asked Krishna. He continued:

> Dronacharya should have forgiven the personal wrong done to him. Perhaps, being trained in arms, he has forgotten that a brahmana's first duty is to overcome anger. I am also sure that Arjuna would never have treated you the way he did, had he not been commanded by his guru. Arjuna sought your pardon at Dwaraka. That young man was ignorant of the ways of his guru and only obeyed him innocently.

'Vaasudeva,' Drupada said brusquely. 'If you do not accept my offer, I will have to seek alliance elsewhere.'

Krishna kept his cool and said, 'Noble lord, of what use can an alliance with the Yadavas be to you? If you help us relocate to Mathura, you will draw the wrath of Emperor Jarasandha.'

Drupada shook his head and said, 'We can meet Jarasandha's challenge; we are fairly strong and, with you as my son-in-law, I can defy the Kurus. Jarasandha is afraid of you and Bhishma and Drona would not like to be your adversaries.'

'I can try to bring about an understanding with Bhishma Pitamah. Drona is not my concern, noble lord.' Drupada was fuming and said, 'You are mistaken, Vaasudeva, in thinking so. You do not know how powerful Drona is in Hastinapura. He will have no settlement with me, nor I with him.'

'If only the Pandavas had been alive!' suggested Krishna.

King Drupada then said:

> It would have made no difference, Vaasudeva. The Pandavas were very loyal to Drona; yet, I understand he instigated Duryodhana through his son, Ashwathama, to negate the authority of the crown prince, Yudhisthira. The wily brahmana did not support Yudhisthira and stayed neutral when Bhishma was forced to banish them and prevent civil war among the cousins. Vaasudeva, I can understand the intrigues of Drona. This looks like a hopeless situation to me.

Continuing his tirade, the king said, 'If you reject my offer, I will offer my daughter to Meghasandhi, Jarasandha's grandson. I am left with no other choice.'

'Noble lord, you are a righteous king. You are a protector of dharma, and you want to hand over Aryawartha on a platter to Jarasandha, the symbol of *adharma*?' asked Krishna.

Drupada flared up, 'Vaasudeva, I have never been unjust. I have stood for dharma all my life. If you come to my aid, we will be able to consolidate Aryawartha in the ways of our ancestors.'

'Noble sir, I still fail to see your logic. We Yadavas are so far away from Panchala. Logistically, there would not be any advantage in doing that,' replied Krishna.

'Vaasudeva, together we can be a bulwark against *adharma*. It would prod Bhishma to get rid of Drona, who will have to then return to his original home in the Shivaliks.' The king was carried away by his own argument. 'Noble sir, you mean to say that Drona cannot be changed?' asked Krishna.

Drupada laughed bitterly. 'I have known him for a lifetime. Even as a boy, he was conceited, unforgiving and implacable. He would set fire to the whole world if it suited him.' Drupada was dejected that Krishna had spurned his offer. To counter Krishna's argument about marrying his daughter to Meghasandhi, he said that once Duryodhana takes charge, the Kuru kingdom would also fall into *adharma*. Krishna then asked if the princess would be happy to go to Magadha. The king asked him to speak to her himself.

Krishna said, 'I want to do everything to help you, but I do not want bitterness to take away the happiness of your daughter. She does not deserve to be the wife of the cruel old emperor's grandson!'

'We have no loves and hates, Vaasudeva. We have only one aim in life and that is, to avenge Drona. I shall make arrangements for a meeting with my daughter.'

GOVINDA AND DRAUPADI

The next morning, Drishtadyumna came to invite Krishna to the mango grove to meet Draupadi. The princess and her two brothers took a seat opposite Krishna, having first saluted him respectfully. She looked down modestly.

Krishna enquired about the third brother, Shikhandin, who was absent. 'Vaasudeva, he has been missing since last evening,' said Draupadi. 'I told my father to let me meet you, though it was rather immodest for a well-born maiden to do so.'

'Noble princess, both you and your father are very gracious,' said Krishna. 'How can I help? The Yadavas being far away and not that strong yet, I am not sure how I can help. I cannot fight Drona, for I will not war with the Kurus till they give me a reason to do so.'

The princess said in a firm voice, 'They say that you live to uphold dharma. Do you know how unjust Drona was to my father? We just want to vindicate the insult and seek your help in that regard.'

Draupadi then narrated:

> My father was celebrating a festival at Ahichhatrapura. He had just come out of the shrine of Mahadeva, surrounded by priests. Drona and his pupils encircled the royal party inside the precincts of the temple. Was it not *adharma*, Vaasudeva? Arjuna then took aim from a distant tree and, with one arrow, brought my father's crown to the ground, with another he cut his right earring into two and then shamelessly wounded the right leg of the king. My father collapsed in pain and shock. Then Bhima and Arjuna bound my father and dragged him to Drona.

We would not do such a dastardly act. The descendants of Bharata seem to have cast away the basic decency of civilised behaviour. Drona, the great acharya in the court of Kurus, presided over by Bhishma, did not even have the basic dignity to settle his scores in a face-to-face battle. My father would have loved to go down fighting and Drona could have annexed the whole of Panchala. He did not dare to do that, instead he forced my father to sign off the fertile lands of Panchala. On top of it, Drona insisted that my father should offer an apology for having broken his childhood promise. Drona took possession of our lands, robbed our men of whatever they had and drove them out, starving and helpless.

Draupadi's voice quivered with anger.

Krishna tried to calm down the princess.

I have not rejected you; I love your candour, your determination and admire your temerity to indirectly upbraid the grand sire of Kurus as a doer of *adharma*. Drona deserves to be condemned and he shall pay for this someday, very dearly. I only wonder, how could you accept to be the wife of Jarasandha's grandson, Meghasandhi, only to avenge Drona.

Before Krishna could complete his sentence, the princess flared up, 'Vaasudeva, who are you to prevent me from marrying anyone my father likes, after you have rejected me?'

Krishna said to the princess:

I am your friend, well-wisher and brother; you can depend on me. Draupadi, you need not go to the house of Jarasandha—it is a temple of doom. I promise to find you the foremost warrior in Aryawartha as your husband, have faith in your Sakha. You want to marry me only to defeat Drona. What happens to us after that? Marriage is not a matter of commerce. You are free to choose whom you like, regardless of your father's pledge.

There is one more request I have to make, through you, to the noble king. I would like to talk to your little brother, Shikhandin. Let him be my ward. I have watched him, I know who he is and what he is meant for.

The next day Drupada asked Krishna what he had decided to do after his meeting with the princess.

Krishna explained:

> Noble lord, I have promised her that if you are willing, I am ready to help you as best as I can. May I suggest that you to hold a *swayamvara* for her? Let the Panchala Naresh set up a test that the princess will marry the warrior who proves to be the best archer in Aryawartha. If you permit me, noble king, I will ask Acharya Shvetaketu to arrange the *swayamvara* for you. When Guru Sandipani comes here, he will decide upon the nature of the archery test. No one should know about the competition till the last minute. You will acquire more allies, and it will not alienate anyone as the *swayamvara* will be a genuine test of the victor's valour. In the end, you will emerge stronger, I assure you.

Drupada thought for a while and wondered what were to happen if no one was able to stand up to the test? Krishna said that, then the princess is free to choose her groom. Drupada was finally convinced and agreed to Krishna's plan. The *swayamvara* was to be held the following year in the month of Chaitra.

KRISHNA AND ACHARYA DRONA

Dronacharya was upset when his son, Aswathama, presented Duryodhana and Karna before him. They had come to narrate to their teacher, the great victory they had won over Chekitana. A frowning Drona said in a raised voice:

> Duryodhana, you are adept at increasing your enemies. The future emperor lacks the basic requirement needed in a ruler—diplomacy, tact and the art of winning people's hearts. I told you to make a friend of Chekitana and bring his son here to be educated. You say you won! Indeed, you have run over a small fly and that fly of a king has escaped into the Naga territory, north of the Yamuna. You disturbed the hornet's nest and we have added one more hostile neighbour. The Yadavas and the Nagas, in addition to the formidable Panchala, could be a threat to Hastinapura. Anga Raja, how can you destroy your enemies without any friends?

His plan had failed and his mind was spinning. He had wanted to strengthen the frontier against the Shalvas and Yadavas by making Chekitana an ally of the Kurus. For a moment, Drona looked remorseful and felt he had blundered in ousting Yudhisthira and replacing him with the foolish Duryodhana. Now that the brothers were dead, guilt haunted him. The acharya decided to remedy the situation; he looked at Duryodhana with consternation and said,

'I intend to correct the wrong done to Chekitana. Pushkar must be restored to him and I am going to ask Pitamah to do it.' With these words, he dismissed his pupils.

After they left, one of his senior pupils, Shankha, awaited him with new cadets. Shankha was a middle-aged disciple, in charge of recruiting new pupils to the Yuddhashala. He informed the guru that there were four new entrants, and that one of them looked more like a girl than a boy.

'He says he will not go unless he meets you. He even refuses to eat,' said Shankha. The Acharya examined the other three boys and observed that they looked older than the age prescribed by him for admission to the school. He addressed them sternly, 'Boys, I am afraid that you do not meet my requirements, you may leave.' 'Noble sir,' one of them pleaded, 'We come from the remote land of Uttara Kuru and we all pledge to work hard and keep your reputation intact. Please try us for two full moons and decide thereafter.'

Drona relented and then asked Shankha to bring the last boy. Shankha introduced him to the guru and withdrew into the dormitory. This boy was dressed as an anchorite; he was handsome and had feminine grace. He fell at the feet of the acharya, sobbing.

'What is your *gotra*? Are you a *brahmachari*?' asked the guru. 'I am not a brahmana, but a kshatriya of Kaushika *gotra*. I have been initiated into the study of the Vedas and archery. I want to learn the elements of body combat from you.'

'Who sent you here?'

'Krishna Vaasudeva,' replied the boy. 'I am Shikhandin, the unfortunate son of King Drupada Yagnasena. My father has no knowledge of this. He thinks that I have drowned myself in the Ganga out of shame.'

Drona softened considerably towards Shikhandin and asked the boy to have some milk and honey. 'No lord, I will not touch even water till you accept me as a pupil.'

'What if I refuse your request?'

'I shall drown myself in the Ganga right before your eyes.'

'Tell me Shikhandin, is Vaasudeva marrying your sister?'

'No sir, he declined to marry her, but promised to get a worthy husband for her.'

Drona then asked him about his life.

Lord, I was married, as a child, to the princess of Kambhoja. My mother was

> alive then. Recently, the king of Kambhoja sent a message to my father that his daughter has come of age and I should visit to take my bride. This threw my father into utter confusion as the moment of truth had finally arrived. I could not take the humiliation due to the status of my gender anymore and, therefore, decided to put an end to my wretched life by drowning in the Ganga. I reached the banks of the river, but was afraid to commit suicide. I, therefore, sat on the steps, reflecting on my life. Just then, I heard a sweet voice telling me that death is not the answer to my problems. When I looked behind me, I found Vaasudeva lifting me up and caressing me as a mother would do. He said that he had promised my father and sister that he would take care of me and he asked me to come to you.

The boy's determination astounded Drona. 'Hmmm...how were you so sure that I would accept you?'

Shikhandin replied in all honesty:

> You are a great teacher and, as a true brahmana, you will never say no to a deserving aspirant who wants to learn. Vaasudeva cautioned me that I should expunge from my heart, all the hatred for you; as you are aware, the House of Panchala is consumed by it. He asked me to be frank and honest with you. He advised me to serve as a loyal son.

The acharya was at ease and said, 'Shikhandin, I shall transform you into a man and a warrior. I know a yaksha, Sthoonakarna. He has knowledge of the science, which can change a woman into a man. But you will have to go through fearful torture for months. Are you ready to go to him?'

'I will obey the master in everything. In the name of Vaasudeva, you can do with me as you wish.'

Dronacharya explained:

> Shikhandin, in a few days' time, a person from the mighty Himalayas will come and take you to his land. You will have to climb snow-clad, lofty mountains to get there. You will meet medicine people there...that is what they are called. They are known for their miraculous cure of ailments that none can heal. Meanwhile, you may rest in my Yuddhashala.

As promised, in a few days' time, Shikhandin was introduced to a stranger with a weather-beaten face. 'Meet Sthoonakarna, the yaksha from a far off land, who has come to take you. Do as you are told and have faith in yourself.

God bless you! He will bring you back to me when you may return to Panchala,' said Drona. Shikhandin prostrated himself at the feet of his guru and left with the yaksha.

They travelled first by horse and as they reached the Himalayan region, Shikhandin was made to mount a yak. This animal carried Shikhandin to great heights where there were no trees; only white snow and bitter cold greeted him. In the nights, they would take shelter in some caves. His clothes were made out of thick animal skins. His food was a foul-smelling liquid, some strange-smelling cheese and tough, salted meat. Shikhandin endured the ordeal. Finally, they reached a settlement, nestled in a valley surrounded by lofty snow-clad mountains. It was called Kinnara—present-day Kinnaur.

Sthoonakarna spoke in Sanskrit and led him to a dark cave, 'This is your lodging till my treatment is over; it may take many full moons before you become a man.'

Shikhandin was to survive the next four months on just herbs and water. A bitter concoction was given to him every morning. His body was pounded with oils and the pain was so severe that, many a time, he fell unconscious while he bled. At times, he felt that he was being cut to pieces. Whenever he could, he prayed to Krishna. After the first hundred days, he was given a cup of warm milk by a kind old lady who talked in an unfamiliar tongue and rubbed the soles of his sore feet. Sthoonakarna appeared once and asked him how he was feeling. The prince feebly answered, 'Better.'

Shikhandin was gradually allowed to come out of the cave and would sometimes take a stroll in the cool air and watch the golden sunset and the beauty of the Himalayan spring.

One day, he noticed a few strands of hair dangling from his chin. He touched his upper lip and felt the beginnings of a moustache. For the first time in his life, he felt like a man. After some time, his genitals developed as well.

Seeing this improvement, Sthoonakarna brought with him an archer, with his bow and flint-tipped arrows, and asked Shikhandin to accompany the hunter for a hunt. Both of them walked through the rugged plateau and hunted a few birds and rabbit. For the first time, the prince was given some hot, roasted meat and gruel.

The treatment became lighter over time and soon Sthoonakarna informed him that his mission was complete and he could go back to where he had come from. Till then, Shikhandin had been fed meat stew every day. Upon enquiry, he was told that the stew was made out of the testes of wild goats. Shikhandin thought he had lived for over 180 days in that cave. When the time came for him to leave, Sthoonakarna travelled with him to the riverbank of the Ganga.

After a few days of travel, they could see the plains and the mighty Ganga, flowing like a placid lake. As they climbed down, they passed through a forest of beautiful, lofty trees. They were like divine sentinels and an ethereal wind blew amidst them. They were swinging like dancing damsels and Shikhandin heard melodious music coming from the forest. Sthoonakarna smiled and said, 'This is the chanting of the Sama Veda by the rishis on these hills. This mountain range is known as Rishyamooka. They chant the sacred hymns while propitiating the gods before the sacred fire, which was lit many years ago.'

Shikhandin noticed fair people with broad foreheads and fearsome moustaches and asked who they were. 'Prince, these mountain people are called Gandharvas. They sing very well, a gift from the rishis,' replied the yaksha. They soon reached a small port on the Ganga and commissioned a boat to sail to Hastinapura. On the third day, they reached the wharf near Drona's cottage.

When Sthoonakarna presented Shikhandin before the acharya, the great teacher could not believe his eyes. Shikhandin prostrated before Dronacharya and said, 'Lord, I am a man now and would like to be taught martial arts by you.'

Drona then informed the prince of his sister's *swayamvara*, scheduled to be held in two months. 'O noble acharya, please teach me as much as you can during this period. I am a kshatriya and I must prove that to Hiranyavarma, my father-in-law.'

'Very well, we shall start tomorrow.'

Under Drona's guidance, Shikhandin became a good marksman, an expert archer and a skilful horse rider. He also learnt a few lessons on personal combat. The exercises and gymnastics turned him into a fine athlete. At the end of his training, Shikhandin had changed drastically.

The prince then took leave of the great acharya. He was overwhelmed with tears of gratitude, 'Lord, I will be indebted to you all my life. I shall never disappoint you.' He prostrated before his master and boarded the sailboat leaving for Kampilya.

THE SEARCH FOR THE BROTHERS

There was conflict among the native tribes like the Nagas and the Aryans, because the latter had imposed their strict Aryan code on the tribes who encroached upon their settlements. Veda Vyasa played a crucial role in allaying their fears and ending the hostilities. This was achieved by constantly maintaining friendly contacts with the Naga elders, learning their language and customs, curing the ailing and maimed and teaching them the path to dharma. Over a period of sustained interaction with the Naga and Nishada tribes, the sage had gained great affection and respect of the people. Veda Vyasa often prayed to their god, Pashupati; they did it with flowers and he with melodious hymns and sacred fire.

The sage took Uddhava to meet Aryaka, who was over hundred years old. Revealing the true purpose of Uddhava's visit, Vyasa requested the chief to do the needful. Uddhava was hopeful that the grand old man would be able to send a search party to comb the dense forests for the Pandavas and Kunti. His wish was granted and, soon, this responsibility was given to a group. The sage assured Uddhava that they would soon be able to locate the missing relatives.

Meanwhile, Krishna had stayed away from Dwaraka and his family for almost a year. As planned, Krishna, on his return journey, was to visit Nagakoota, to pay his respects to Aryaka. He had sent an advance party, headed by Kritavarma, (an important Yadava *atirathi*) to Nagakoota, to inform them of his arrival.

Upon arrival, Krishna prostrated himself before his great-grandfather. He also met the twin granddaughters of Aryaka, Pingala and Kapila. Maniman, Aryaka's grandson, was curious about the gold-tipped conch that hung from Krishna's waist. He also noticed a shining disc strapped to his left shoulder. Krishna smiled and patted Maniman on his back, assuring him that they were harmless trappings. They went to the shrine of Lord Pashupati to pay their respects and then, to the residence of the royal family.

When Krishna could not spot Uddhava, he asked Aryaka about his whereabouts. 'He has left us,' said Aryaka, his voice diffident. 'He has gone to Rakshasavarta, the land of the demons, ruled by Vrikodara. One of our chiefs had captured a Rakshasa boy at a frontier village; he mentioned seeing a woman and five men deep in the forest. One of them was like a huge elephant, carrying a woman on his shoulders.'

Uddhava's devotion to the mission pleased Krishna. Suddenly, he heard someone sobbing and looked around. Prince Karkota's wife, Ravika, intervened, saying, 'Krishna, my twin daughters have fallen in love with Uddhava and want to marry him. But now they fear that Uddhava will not survive the rakshasas.' Krishna assured them that they had no cause to worry, for Uddhava was a great warrior; moreover, he intended to go into the forests and bring Uddhava back alive.

Krishna left the royal dwelling, followed by Satyaki and Shvetaketu. The search party was headed by Satyaki, a few stalwart Naga warriors and Garudas.

As they reached the craggy heights of barren Rakshasavarta, Krishna began to sing the war song of the Yadavas to the beats of a couple of drummers. Krishna blew a victorious note on his conch, Panchajanya, till the forest echoed with its sound. As if obeying his command, Uddhava emerged from the densely wooded valley with a joyous shout, a limping Rakshasa boy running by his side. Krishna hugged Uddhava and, looking into his eyes, asked, 'Are they alright?'

'Yes…,' smiled Uddhava. 'Krishna, I am coming from the land of Vrikodara. He is a friend of the Nagas now. Our great-grandfather need not be afraid of the rakshasas anymore…Bhima has married, a Rakshasi. Very soon he will become a proud father…'

'How are Arjuna and Aunt Kunti? When do you think they can come to Dwaraka?'

'Not until Bhima's child is born and that could take a while,' said Uddhava. 'I want them to remain where they are till the month of Margasirsha, as Draupadi's *swayamvara* will take place at Kampilya in Chaitra month…I want Arjuna to participate in this ceremony, which is why I wish that they should come to Kampilya only in Paush month which will give them sufficient time.' Uddhava then briefed Krishna about the Pandavas:

> O Vaasudeva, they are leading a very harsh life in the rainforest; they get sparse sunlight in their clearing and, that too, only at noon; the monsoons are very severe. Vrikodara is very happy to rule over the weirdest creatures on earth. He keeps himself busy by carrying Aunt Kunti to the river. No Rakshasa dares to come near the clearance because of him. Arjuna is always frowning; he keeps sharpening his bamboo arrows and shoots at the birds and small game. Nakula raises rabbits and wild cats. Sahadeva is always in his mother's cottage and their big brother gives them company.

> Once a day, they all meet in Aunt Kunti's cottage to have their meal, which comprises wild fruit, roasted meat of wild fowls and edible birds. King Vrikodara gets some rock salt and narrates to Aunt Kunti, interesting stories of his queen and her people, evoking laughter in an otherwise gloomy world. Arjuna rarely speaks a word, unless spoken to. He has mastered the skill of releasing multiple arrows in one attempt, all of equal power and strength.

When the party reached Lahuria—the frontier post—a messenger from King Aryaka was awaiting them. 'The king requests you to come immediately as the Nagas have been invaded by a neighbouring king from across the Yamuna.' Krishna looked at Uddhava: 'Neighbouring king could only mean Chekitana; I cannot imagine a Yadava doing this.'

They reached Nagakoota by nightfall. The next day, the messengers brought the details of the invasion. Chekitana had been attacked by Duryodhana. Instead of surrendering, the Yadava chief, with his people, had crossed the Yamuna and, in turn, had evicted the Nagas out of their settlements—appropriating their possessions. In the skirmishes that followed, many Nagas were killed and the rest fled into the forest.

The Nagas were jubilant at Uddhava's safe return. The twins brought marigold garlands for Uddhava and Krishna took the opportunity to ask for two more so that Uddhava may also garland Pingala and Kapila. Thus, the twins were married to Uddhava as per the Naga custom. Uddhava looked highly embarrassed, but Krishna had fun. King Aryaka joined them as well and told them how his people had been killed and Naga settlements run over and their women molested by the invading army.

Krishna tried to pacify his great grandfather:

> Grandfather, I sense something sinister behind Duryodhana's move. Chekitana stands guard over the highway between Saurashtra and Hastinapura. Duryodhana may have captured Pushkar to prevent us from going north. Chekitana is a noble chief and would have crossed the Yamuna, just to survive. In warlike situations, it is always women and children who suffer the most. I will meet Chekitana and stop this aggression forthwith. But please extend your hospitality to Chekitana till the end of the rainy season. I shall see that he vacates your territory after that.

Krishna then tried to explain to the grand old man that great changes were on the anvil in the near future.

> Venerable king, the Aryans have carved out a new civilisation with their code and introduced new techniques in farming, cattle rearing, horse breeding and building chariots for rapid communication. Our land is at the crossroads of change, a change for our own benefit...we should evolve and you must definitely address its importance to the Nagas while you are around. For instance, your beautiful women must emulate the dress code of the Aryan woman. A woman is a thing of beauty created by Pashupati. Her beauty has to be concealed, adding grace to the creator.

'Show me the way, my son…I am too old to be the king, but I do not want my people to sink into slavery.'

Krishna said:

> Grandfather, this is possible if you invite a learned rishi to establish an ashram here. It would be a home of learning and love, where your people could learn the ways of dharma. I shall request Dhaumya to help you. Shake your people from the easy-going life they are used to, because, in reality, this world of ours is not peace loving and they need to learn to defend themselves when required. I am aware of the role great Veda Vyasa has played in trying to bring the Aryans and Nagas together…but we need more concrete steps in order to boost the morale of the people.
>
> Dhaumya's school will train Nagas in Vedic lore, impart stern *tapas* and a life of dharma. Acharya Shvetaketu, my good friend, will train your men in the Aryan ways of life. I will place at your disposal, a few horses and mares, which King Drupada had presented to me. I shall arrange, through Drupada, a few hundred cows to be attached to the ashram. Cows give you milk; their dung enriches your land; their butter becomes the offering to the gods, who are invoked by the rishis, by the sacred fire.
>
> Nagas shall be a fighting force soon. I will ask Satyaki to invite Chekitana to Nagakoota. I assure you that, by the time I return to attend Draupadi's *swayamvara*, I shall bring a contingent of the Yadava army. I would like prince Maniman to accompany me to this event, where he, too, shall be invited to participate in the contest.

Hearing these words of assurance, Aryaka knew his people were in safe hands, so he closed his eyes and departed the world of the living, peacefully.

Krishna saluted the grand old Naga king and stayed to complete the funeral ceremonies. At the end of the three-day-long mourning period, Krishna called Satyaki and Kritavarma; he asked Kritavarma to take prince Karkotaka and assure Chekitana of Naga hospitality. He asked Uddhava to remain at Nagakoota. Saying this, Krishna left for Dwaraka. Over time, Karkotaka was made king of Nagas.

DHARMA CONFRONTS KRISHNA

When Krishna returned to Dwaraka, he was disturbed by the situation prevailing there. During his long absence, the Yadavas had become indolent and pleasure-loving. Peace and prosperity had brought indiscipline, and a sense of false security enveloped the whole community.

Krishna believed he was partly to blame for this state of decadence; by going north, he had removed from their midst, Satyaki and Uddhava, who, together, maintained the Yadava power structure. The other *atirathi*s whom he had left at Saurashtra were brave men, good and loyal warriors, but they could not function as centres of self-generating strength as they did not have a clear grasp of Krishna's mission. In his absence, they were easily carried away by the general atmosphere prevailing in Dwaraka. Their prosperity had made the Yadavas complacent. Their cattle wealth had increased manifold; the earth had been yielding bountiful corn and barley; the groundnut crop supplied enough edible oil and fat for the men and the cattle; cotton was used for weaving fine muslin cloth. The talented Yadava weavers were also expert dyers and colourful textiles, along with white muslins, were in great demand. Overseas trade prospered manyfold. The ports of Dwaraka, Prabhasapattana and Sabar Kaccha had become the centres of trade and commerce for ivory, diamonds, sandalwood, spices and shell cowries. Prosperity ushered in luxury and ostentatious lifestyles that included heavy drinking, gambling and associated pleasures.

The leader of this indulgent society was Satrajit. In a short time, the Yadavas, who had so painstakingly built Dwaraka, lost their heroic spirit. Their diligent nature was replaced by idle dereliction. They started neglecting their skills in martial arts that had kept them fighting fit. The Yadavas were no longer interested in regular exercises, wrestling practices, horse riding, fencing and chariot racing, which Krishna and Satyaki had introduced in their daily routine. Balarama, too, had become a heavy drinker.

Krishna was greatly disappointed at the state of affairs in Dwaraka and requested that the council of Yadavas be summoned. He explained to the chiefs, the situation in Aryawartha, how Duryodhana had driven the Yadava, Chekitana, from Pushkar. He stressed on the fact that Pushkar is a vital outpost for the free passage of Yadavas to their ancestral hinterland along the Yamuna. He rebuked the elders for tolerating rogue elements in Dwaraka. Pushkar must be secured at any cost, he insisted.

He warned them that if the princess of Panchala married Meghasandhi, the latter, in alliance with Drupada, was sure to overwhelm the kings of Aryawartha. With Mathura in ruins and Pushkar in the hands of Kurus, the Yadava king of Agravana, present-day Ajmer, Charudeshna, would be isolated and Shalva could easily force a war on them, once again. He was forceful when he said that frontiers were to be defended by unflagging readiness, not by complacent self-confidence. He looked around for Balarama, who was conspicuous by his absence.

Krishna was highly disappointed and indirectly censured his brother in absentia:

> The days of basking in the glory of past heroic deeds of the Yadavas are over; the present is uncertain and the future is bleak. Let us wake up to the realities. Saurashtra cannot isolate itself from Aryawartha, to where we once belonged. We are not an island but a part of the whole civilisation on which Arya Dharma has been built.

At the end of his forceful briefing, silence descended on the assembly. Vasudeva and Akrura, despite their great confidence in Krishna, discouraged the idea of the Yadavas undertaking an active role in the politics of Aryawartha. They were in no mood to unsettle their hard-earned peace, prosperity and security in the absence of Balarama.

Meanwhile, a disappointed Krishna wanted to talk to his brother. As he reached the portals of the palace, Balarama rushed out to greet him.

> Govinda, I have missed you. You took up the task of repairing the whole world with your dharma! Look how happy and contented I am; no one dare touch the Yadavas again. Be contented. Your wife, Vaidarbhi, and your beautiful son, Pradyumna, were longing for your company. Spare some time for them. Look at my daughter, Sashi, who was born in your absence. She has yet to meet her *kaka*.

Krishna took the baby in his arms and kissed her with a solemn blessing. 'Krishna, Duryodhana is my favourite disciple, a much misunderstood man. So what if he occupied Pushkar? Duryodhana would never be unfriendly with us and intercept the safe passage of Yadavas. As for Chekitana, let him return to Dwaraka as one of the Yadava chiefs, I welcome him with all my heart,' said Balarama.

'But the matter is not that simple,' reprimanded Krishna. 'If Jarasandha enters into a matrimonial alliance with Drupada, it could mean the end of Panchala as a great power. The independent Arya kings would be turned into vassals of Magadha. Homes of learning, now flourishing in Aryawartha, would be destroyed or left to wither away for want of support.'

Balarama's face turned purple. 'Krishna, why didn't you allow me to break his skull at Gomantak? May I suggest that Duryodhana weds the Panchala princess?'

'Draupadi will refuse to marry the pupil of Dronacharya. There were rumours afloat that Duryodhana, at the behest of Shakuni, had engineered the murder of our cousins.' Balarama was shocked to hear this. Krishna continued, 'We should attend the *swayamvara* and checkmate Jarasandha. No Yadava warrior is to participate in the ceremony, yet we should lead a huge contingent of Yadava *atirathi*s under your leadership, and be present. Acharya Sandipani has instructed Shvetaketu to prepare a tough archery contest for winning the bride.'

Balarama thought deeply and, after a pause, said, 'Krishna, I am prepared to lead the Yadavas to the ceremony, as long as you and I do not participate.'

Krishna replied hesitantly, 'Most of the Yadava men are no longer interested in the affairs of Aryawartha and are following Satrajit's path of indulgence.' Balarama grew furious when he heard the name of Satrajit.

> That fellow is the cause of the decline in Yadava morals. His wealth has spoiled our best warriors. His wealth and the rare jewel, Syamantaka, which he claims is a gift from the Sun God himself, lure the people away from their duties. That greedy Satrajit and his wealth will lead to the fall of the Yadavas!

Krishna told him that Satrajit believes the Yadavas are not the guardians of Arya Dharma. Krishna was disappointed that, instead of defending Pushkar against Duryodhana's forces, Chekitana ran for his life and disrupted peace in the northern jungles. He also related to Balarama, the vices of Duryodhana as he had seen at Hastinapura.

Balarama stood up and roared, 'Krishna, please proceed to the north and restore Pushkar to Chekitana. I shall follow you with the best of the Yadava *yodha*s.'

Krishna did not divulge anything about the escape of the Pandavas, so as to keep them safe. He was distraught that not even one Yadava chief had felt the need to restore to Chekitana, his principality of Pushkar. For the first time in many years, Krishna faced a crisis of confidence, and he did not know how to proceed. His only counsel was Uddhava, but he was at Nagakoota.

The monsoon showers, too, added to his anxiety. He knew he would have to wait for the rains to subside and flood waters of the great northern rivers to settle sown so as to have a smooth passage. So, it was decided that post-monsoon, the Yadava contingent, under the overall command of Satyaki, would leave for Pushkar. An advance team would precede the contingent to erect tents at predesignated sites, where a running stream or a good waterbody was available.

The month of Asvayuja, dear to the Goddess Amba, put all the Yadava damsels in a festive mood. On the full moon night of Sharad Ritu, when the sky was clear and caressed by a soft breeze from the sea, Krishna asked Rukmini to invite all the Yadava beauties for a moonlit dance.

'Vaidarbhi, my flute and music were left in Vrindavan. I can no longer play the Rasa. Please ask Satyaki to arrange for bamboo sticks of an arm's length, some clay diyas and bells. I will teach you how to play Rasa. We shall call this dance Garbha, or Dandiya.' He then showed her the steps. 'After you light the diyas, form two circles; the damsels carrying the lighted diyas will form the outer circle, the ladies in the inner circle will have the sticks and they should move, clapping the sticks against one other, while the ladies in the outer circle will move in the opposite direction.'

Rukmini led the first circle with diyas, and Satrajiti, Satrajit's daughter, led the second circle with sticks. To the rhythm of drums and the play of the sticks, the circles moved in opposite directions with the swaying hips and lilting anklets of the Dwaraka damsels. Satyaki was leading the drums and Krishna was standing with hands on his hips, enjoying the festive mood.

Satyaki mentioned to Krishna that he had turned down the proposal to marry Satrajiti. 'She is too smart for me, Govinda. Satrajit's wealth has spoilt her. Satrajit seemed more upset at my rejection than this silly girl. Her real name is Satyabhama.' Krishna spent the rest of the night enjoying the celebrations.

KRISHNA LEAVES DWARAKA

The monsoons ended and the month of Kartik came with crisp winds from the north and calm seas at home. The weather was salubrious. The shipping trade between Saurashtra and the west coast, and with Simhala Dvipa down south, picked up. The Yadava sailboats were plying not only to coastal India, but were also visiting the present-day Arabian countries known as the Mlechha *desas* or barbarian lands. The main imports from these foreign lands were pearls, ivory, thoroughbred horses and *khajur*—dates.

Once a year, their tribal chiefs would visit Dwaraka to trade, with the Yadavas, their finest stallions in exchange for fine cottons, oil nuts and other millets, spices and silk. While strolling on the beach sands one evening, Krishna heard a resounding prayer as he passed a large tent in the traders' colony. Getting curious, he asked Satyaki if he could meet these foreigners.

Krishna was taken into a large tent, carpeted with soft sheepskin. The chief, Ishmael Ben, from the house of David and Abraham, was tall and fair with a handsome beard. Greeting Krishna, he said, '*Abshalom,* Vaasudeva. Our Yahova told me in a dream that I would meet, in the east, a great person; I think I see that person in you.' Krishna greeted him in the traditional way, with his palms folded.

'Ishmael, welcome to Dwaraka. Your horses are the best I have ever ridden and your prayers are very musical. Who do you pray to?'

'Only one god—the god of Abraham, Yahova,' he said and raised his arms to the sky and touched the earth with his head.

Krishna clasped his arms with great affection, kissed his palms and said, 'Ishwara, the one god, Brahman. Ishmael comes from Ishwara—the servant of god.'

The stranger was immensely pleased at this unique encounter with the dark young man. He felt a divine presence and said, '*Aloy Shalom Khusham deedh.* Your eyes are the most beautiful I have ever seen. My god has no form, but if he did, his eyes would be like that of yours.'

'Ishmael, my friend, Ishwara or God is within us. He dwells in our heart.'

The next morning, a delegation from Kampilya brought Drupada's invitation to the Yadava king, Ugrasena. It requested all the *athirathi*s to attend the *swayamvara* on the eleventh day of the bright half of the month of Chaitra. The council chiefs were happy to accept the invitation and deputed Krishna, Satyaki and Kritavarma, the best of the Yadava *atirathi*s, to attend the ceremony. However, they were not to participate in the contest.

Krishna told Satyaki and Kritavarma that he would be the first to start for Agravana, leaving at the earliest, because he had received an urgent message from Uddhava. 'I think Chekitana is restless as no help was coming from the Yadavas. As soon as the priests fix the departure date, I will leave,' said Krishna. 'You can join me with the bulk of the chariots at Agravana. Kritavarma, you accompany Balarama.' The three dispersed to meet at Agravana and, from there, to march on to Pushkar for their mission.

The next morning, Krishna kept waiting for Satyaki and his contingent to join him at the appointed hour, but there was no sign of him. 'This must be the work of Satrajit, who was opposed to our going to Pushkar in support of Chekitana,' said Gada, who had been appointed by Krishna to help build Dwaraka. Krishna looked at Gada and said, 'I will take Satyaki's contingent too. Gather all our forces meant for Pushkar and catch up with me by tomorrow night.'

Fully armed, Krishna blew his conch. He saluted the sun, which had just risen. Climbing on the chariot, he took the reins in his own hands, commanding Daruka to sit in the rear part of the vehicle. He asked Gada to inform Rukmini about Satyaki's disappearance. 'Tell her, also, to inform Balarama that if Yadavas betray their dharma, I must find others who will stand by it.'

When Rukmini heard about this, she was upset and immediately left for the mansion of Balarama and Revati. Balarama had just woken up and had a hangover from the previous night, which made him irritable.

'Krishna sent word that dharma called him and his mission has just begun,' said a solemn Rukmini and conveyed the remainder of the message. 'I am afraid, he may not come back to us. You have abandoned him in this hour of trial.'

Balarama's face flushed with rage. 'That scoundrel, Satrajit! I shall break his head if he has killed Satyaki. I am joining Krishna, and together we shall bring dharma into our lives.'

Balarama got up from his bed, tightened his dhoti, picked up his huge conch and, going to his terrace, blew it loudly. The sound echoed all over

Dwaraka—a call to all the Yadavas that he meant business. In the assembly of the chiefs, Balarama confronted Satrajit on the disappearance of Satyaki, but Satrajit was shocked and replied, 'Noble Balarama, I have no clue of Satyaki. I never met him after he returned from Hastinapura.' Balarama roared:

> I do not trust you. You are a conceited crook. You were a moneylender in Mathura, who made you a merchant in Dwaraka? You want us to believe that Syamantaka, the pink stone, was given to you by the Sun God? You found it on the beach, washed ashore when you were giving *arghya* to the Sun God. I can take it away from you by force as it belongs to the state—the people of Dwaraka. You claim that it gives you twelve mounds of gold every day. Tomorrow morning, I will come to your house to buy the gold. Citizens of Dwaraka, come with me tomorrow morning for I shall distribute the gold amongst you.

Balarama continued to bellow:

> Satrajit, do not fool us with your concocted stories. I know how you have hoarded so much gold. Your ships brought gold from the western Mlechha countries. You also trade in ivory and pearls in exchange for gold. Krishna made all this wealth possible for you. I am pardoning you for the present, but you must part with most of your chariots, horses and some gold for raising a powerful Yadava contingent, that will be used to restore Pushkar to Chekitana.

A crestfallen and deeply anguished Satrajit returned to his mansion. He called for his daughter and asked where she had been. 'I saved Satyaki's life from his assassins—Jayasena and his goons, through whom you settle your many scores. He is now on his way to Balarama's mansion,' she replied.

Satrajit was worn out. He said, 'I did not commission that wretched Jayasena to kill Satyaki. I only told him to delay Satyaki from accompanying Krishna. To atone for that sin, I am now pledging one hundred war chariots and as many horses and twelve mounds of gold for Balarama's campaign expenses.'

Krishna led Satyaki's chariots at breakneck speed. A relay, dispatched from Dwaraka, informed him that within a fortnight, Balarama and Satyaki would be joining him at Agravana with a large Yadava force. Krishna's route skirted Shalva's territory. Once a bitter enemy, this crafty king had not yet recovered from the stunning defeat that Krishna had inflicted upon him. He sent his courtiers to extend an ostentatious welcome. Krishna was anxious to reach Pushkar as fast as the contingent could make it.

Krishna had dispatched a courier to Uddhava at Nagakoota, directing him to go to the court of Hastinapura and meet Vidura. With his help, Uddhava should request Bhishma to intervene and have the principality of Pushkar returned to Chekitana. Krishna had a hunch that Drona had not approved of Duryodhana's capture of Pushkar. He also came to know that in the event of Duryodhana or any Kuru prince winning the hand of Draupadi, the acharya had made up his mind to leave the court of Kurus for good.

Krishna and his contingent camped at a clearing from where Pushkar was just two days away. Soon, Charuadeshna of Agravana, the Naga prince, Maniman, along with his primitive bowmen, and Chekitana, joined Krishna's forces.

The news of Balarama's forces being on the move emboldened Krishna. He decided to take a calculated risk and march to the gates of Pushkar. Krishna was waiting for the right moment to move, and it came when his informers reported that Dronacharya had arrived at the Pushkar fort.

At dawn, on the third day, they could see the Pushkar fort, which was built near a vast lake, hamlets lining its *margi*. The Yadavas camped outside the fort, about a *yojana** away.

Krishna spoke to Chekitana. 'I had promised you that I shall restore Pushkar to you by the end of the rainy season. Here I am and I shall not fail you.' Krishna left the camp on his chariot, followed only by his personal escort. If Dronacharya or Duryodhana wanted to fight him, he would accept the challenge as an individual, as expected by the Aryan code of conduct.

When Krishna reached the gates of the fort, an extraordinary sight met his eyes. There were no war cries or archers positioned on the walls. On the contrary, gaily dressed men and women stood on the walls, showering flower petals in welcome. The gates opened, trumpets blew and three chariots issued forth.

As Krishna stood on his chariot, holding the rein in both hands, his eyes caught sight of the flag on top of the chariot which appeared before him. The flag bore the sign of a water pot, embroidered in gold. That was the insignia

*Yojana: Between 6 to 15 kilometres, scholars are in dispute as to the exact number.

of the redoubtable teacher, Dronacharya. The next to follow was a Yadava chariot carrying a smiling Uddhava. Shakuni was following Uddhava in his chariot.

Krishna turned to Gada and said, 'Gada, put down your bow. Pushkar is delivered to us. Go and ask Chekitana and the others to join us.'

Decked in expensive golden silks, Acharya Drona addressed Krishna, 'Noble Vaasudeva, you have taken Pushkar without even stringing your bow. You alone could have done it. King Dhritarashtra and Pitamah have sent me to welcome you and Chekitana.'

'Vaasudeva, Duryodhana sends his blessings,' Shakuni said and smiled ingratiatingly. 'What the noble Kuru won by the force of arms, he is happy to hand over to you as a tribute to the wisdom which you embody.' Drona's hospitality was excellent and gracious. He was not only well versed in the art and science of war, but also in statecraft and diplomacy. Drona was also contemplating how he could win the confidence and loyalty of this young man, a rising power on the horizon of Aryawartha. Krishna, then, enquired about Shikhandin. Drona told him that he was still recovering at his ashram. Krishna insisted that Shikhandin join him for his sister's wedding, after which he would be put in Uddhava's care. 'Why are you so interested in Drupada and the *swayamvara*? I understand that you refused the hand of his daughter,' asked Drona.

'Yes, noble acharya, one of the reasons I refused was that I did not want to fight with you…I did not want to annoy you.'

Drona was stunned at the transparent honesty of this formidable young man. Krishna continued, 'Acharya, Drupada is a noble king. If he overcomes his bitterness for you, he will be a pillar of dharma!'

The Acharya laughed and replied, 'If I overcome my hostility, I would also become another, would I not? I was against Duryodhana attending the *swayamvara*. He has disgraced himself by deciding to attend it. If the princess comes to Hastinapura, I will have nothing to do with the Kurus any more.'

'Acharya, how can you be so vengeful? It is unbecoming of a brahmana of your lineage.'

The acharya said:

> Yes, Vaasudeva, I agree with you and I regret my anger. Drupada's arrogance provoked me to teach him a lesson, that kings need to be compassionate and offer succour to the needy and poor. You may announce to Drupada that he

can take back his lands, which I had occupied. I have now reached a stage in my life where I no longer crave for material wealth.

The next day, Bhanumati came to Krishna's tent, accompanied by Shakuni and his wife. She was pale, hesitant and apprehensive of her companions. Bending lightly, as she was carrying Duryodhana's child, she touched Krishna's feet with her right hand, as a younger sister does, and received his blessing.

Krishna asked her, 'How is our noble Duryodhana?' The princess replied meekly, 'Aryaputra is doing well.' With tears welling in her eyes and a tremor in her voice, Bhanumati said hesitantly, 'Aryaputra would like you to help him win Draupadi in the *swayamvara*.'

Krishna turned to Shakuni and said, 'Noble prince of Gandhara, what can I do in such matters? The Panchala princess will obey her own instincts and I have no say, whatsoever, in this.'

Krishna pitied her state; the poor girl must have been forced by that arrogant brute to play this role. 'Alright, my sister, I will help you.' He then turned to Shakuni. 'Please do not misunderstand me, prince of Gandhara. I cannot promise to secure the princess of Panchala for Duryodhana. All that I can do is to help you press Duryodhana's suit. But the groom has to pass a test before he can win the hand of the princess.'

When they had gone a few steps, Krishna rose from his seat and called Bhanumati: 'Little sister, I am forgetting my obligations. Come near, I must give you a present.'

Bhanumati rushed back; Krishna unclasped a bracelet, came a step nearer, and lifted her hand to fasten it on. He then whispered to her, 'Do not worry; I will keep my promise. Duryodhana will never have Draupadi.' Bhanumati's face was flushed with joy and she lowered her eyes in mute gratitude.

Two days before the full moon day, Balarama arrived with a mighty force of Yadava warriors, accompanied by Naga chiefs. Chekitana welcomed them at the gates of Pushkar fort.

The Yadava army camped outside the city gates. Two days later, the Yadava *atirathi*s, led by Balarama, Krishna and the Naga warriors, started their journey to Kampilya to attend the *swayamvara*. As Dronacharya watched them depart, he felt certain that Krishna held the future of Aryawartha in his hands.

THE SWAYAMVARA

The principal players present at the *swayamvara* were Drupada, Draupadi, Shikhandin, Duryodhana, Shakuni, Aswathama, Jarasandha and Arjuna, with Krishna as the *sutradhar*, the string of connection. Vyasa calls Krishna: *Soothrena manigana iva*—the invisible thread that holds a string of beads in the necklace.

The city of Kampilya, the seat of power for the Panchalas, was on the banks of the Ganga. It was transformed for the occasion; tents were allotted to guests as per the standing of the kings, paved roads were constructed for easy movement, roads were kept wet constantly to prevent dust from rising, kitchens provided free food for brahmanas and the poor and the *sreni*s or guilds were given improvised premises to sell their wares.

Duryodhana's mind was restless and impatient. No one in Kampilya had expected the Kurus to respond to the invitation, but Duryodhana's party had been one of the largest and the most imposing. He was accompanied by several of his brothers, Shakuni, Karna and Aswathama.

He was well aware that, to become a Chakravarti, he had to worm his way into the powerful Panchala kingdom. The easiest way was to seek the hand of Draupadi in marriage. When Shakuni entered Duryodhana's quarters, the latter was anxious to learn Krishna's response to his request. 'Krishna thinks that it will be difficult to persuade Draupadi to choose you because she might not be accepted by Guru Dronacharya, but he has promised to try his luck,' replied Shakuni. 'She is likely to demand a pledge that the acharya would welcome her at the gates of Hastinapura.'

Duryodhana jumped from his chair and said, 'Uncle, you should have told him straight away that I have made up my mind. Go and tell him, I will always ally with Drupada regardless of Acharya Drona.'

'My son, the princess of Panchala appears to be a difficult young woman. She may not be prepared to take your word,' replied Shakuni. 'Vaasudeva thinks that Aswathama should take a vow that, even at the cost of his life, he would prevent his father from leaving the Kurus if she comes to Hastinapura.'

'Is that all? I will get him to agree to it,' said Duryodhana, greatly relieved.

THE MAGADHAN CAMP

The camp of Jarasandha was perhaps the largest at Panchala. Jarasandha, despite his years, was still vigorous and was seated on a couch, surrounded by his principal feudatories. He was an expert bowman, mace wielder and a wrestler of great repute. His son, Sahadeva, and his grandson, Meghasandhi, who would compete in the *swayamvara*, were seated on either side of him.

He was informed, to his annoyance, that Krishna had also arrived in the city and that Balarama would soon join him with a large contingent of Yadava forces. The emperor began doubting his invincibility at the mere mention of Krishna; a nameless fear suddenly overtook him. He had a vision of a naked ascetic, with a garland of skulls, leaving Mathura in flames. These gory sadhus were called Kapalikas, the keepers of the God of Death and Destruction—Rudra, which is Shiva in his fearsome form. The ascetic's words rang in his ears, 'You will never conquer Aryawartha till you offer to sacrifice the heads of a hundred kings.'* He shuddered, but was reassured when he remembered that he had already imprisoned over ninety Aryan kings. Just then, an attendant informed him that an archery contest would decide who marries the princess.

Meghasandhi was not a good bowman and was likely to fail the test. He was also informed that Drupada had suggested that Jarasandha could himself take part in the contest and win his daughter's hand.

'Sahadeva, alert our commanders. Tomorrow we shall decide how to win the princess. At a moment's notice, our horses and chariots should be ready to leave for Rajagriha, once we have abducted Draupadi,' ordered Jarasandha.

THE DILEMMA OF DRUPADA

The priests had advised a sixteen-day ceremony to precede the *swayamvara*, which would be held on the eleventh day of the bright half of Chaitra. Drupada and the rest of the royal family were on tenterhooks as they waited for the main event. They had met Duryodhana's contingent at Krishna's behest and Jarasandha had threatened to kidnap the princess if his grandson was not chosen. Drupada did not know what to do and whom to trust.

'Father, let us trust Krishna Vaasudeva. I will meet him and inform him about Jarasandha's threat,' said Drishtadyumna.

After taking leave of the king, Drishtadyumna reached Krishna's tent. Krishna was visibly annoyed about what he heard and said, 'Jarasandha is up to no good once again. When will he learn the civilities of an Aryan *swayamvara*?

---

*When Mathura was burning, Rudra appeared as a fearsome Kapali—mendicant—and Jarasandha, being a staunch devotee, prostrated before him and asked for the boon of immortality. He said he would do anything. At first, Shiva refused, but later agreed on the condition that he sacrifice the heads of a hundred kings.

Drishtadyumna, I shall never allow a *rakshasa vivaha* for Princess Draupadi. Assure your father of this.'

As a yogi, Krishna was used to taking short, deep naps called Yoga Nidra. He took one after Drishtadyumna had left. It was midnight. The placid waters of the Ganga were lit up by the majestic moon. In the camps, the royal guests had settled down to rest after the hectic activities of the day.

In the Magadhan camp, the emperor's trusted retainers stood guard outside Jarasandha's tent as he had retired for the night. Asking Uddhava to wait outside, slowly and fearlessly, Krishna walked into the camp. He was stopped by the leader of the guards. 'Stop there!' he commanded. 'Who are you and what do you want?'

'I want to see the Chakravarti.'

'At this time of the night! We cannot allow it. Please come back tomorrow morning,' exclaimed the leader.

Krishna laughed in good humour and asked, 'Who is the prince in charge of the night vigil?'

'Vidanda,' replied the guard.

'Then call him here; I must see him,' said Krishna and fixed his compelling eyes on the leader. Prince Vidanda of Magadha was shocked to see Krishna, who he had heard so much about, standing in their camp. Vidanda was as terrified as the guard and did not want to wake up the emperor. Krishna suggested that he ask prince Sahadeva to convey the message.

'Tell him that at Gomantak, I saved his life and want to save it again. Tell your crown prince that I shall meet the emperor, unarmed. I am on a mission of peace.'

Sahadeva reluctantly woke up the emperor and told him about the visitor. Jarasandha agreed to meet him, so Krishna was led into the tent by Sahadeva. Jarasandha sat on a huge bed covered with soft bearskin, his stalwart and heavy body, unbent and unwrinkled. Jarasandha was flabbergasted by Krishna's temerity. Despite being his most bitter enemy, he dared to come into his tent, in the dead of night and was seated before him, relaxed and smiling. 'Why are you here, Yadava?' asked the emperor.

'Emperor, I am unarmed. I have not come to harm you, but to save you. My advice is that you give up your plans to kidnap Draupadi,' said Krishna, with a disarming smile.

Jarasandha sprang like a tiger, clenching his fist. 'How dare you accuse me of this? You are an impertinent fool! We have come here to win her in a *swayamvara*.'

'Then promise me that the Magadhans will not attempt to kidnap her. The Yadava army, at the gates of Kampilya, can take the combined might of all the kings present here. They are led by my formidable brother, Balarama.'

Jarasandha gritted his teeth and sneered, 'You are a conceited young man! Who told you that we wanted to kidnap her and who are you to threaten me? You are in my camp and I could do anything to you right now.' Krishna warned the emperor:

> If you do what you say, then, as per the sacred code of *swayamvara*, the scores of kings assembled here will take your life. The code says that if a visitor to the *swayamvara* is killed, he who kills forfeits his life. The mighty Balarama will not only break your skull, but would invade Magadha and burn Rajagriha, like you did Mathura years ago. Jarasandha, do you not remember the naked ascetic with the necklace of skulls?

A startled Jarasandha asked, 'How do you know about the ascetic?'

'I know all about you, mighty emperor. Your days are numbered and you will never succeed in conquering Aryawartha; your grandson cannot win the contest. If you win, your own people will ridicule you for trying at your age and if you lose you will have to go back to Magadha as an ordinary king—no more the invincible Naresh.' Saying this, Krishna left the tent.

Jarasandha could not sleep the rest of the night. He called for his son. 'Sahadeva, do you have any idea what the test would be?'

'Father, I have heard it will be a tough archery test. I hear some *yantra* is being prepared by Acharya Sandipani. Meghasandhi will fail, I am certain. How shall we proceed? Father, you must enter the contest; it is our only option,' said a timid Sahadeva.

Jarasandha laughed aloud, 'Son, at my age, take the bride, meant for my grandson, as my wife? Never! I have decided to return to Rajagriha. Please make preparations for our return journey. No one should come to know of our departure.'

As Krishna and Uddhava reached their camp, Satyaki was waiting for them. 'Uddhava, you have a visitor. He says, he is your relation, Prince Maniman,' said Satyaki. 'Krishna, a young lad was asking for you. I found him weak and unsteady; he was dropped in a chariot.'

Krishna rushed to see the lad. 'Prince Shikhandin, I am happy to see you, young man,' said Krishna warmly. 'I am astonished to see the transformation brought in you by Acharya Drona.' At Krishna's orders, food was served to Shikhandin and the prince was provided an accommodation to rest. Krishna's gamble on Shikhandin had worked—Acharya Drona has become his friend.

Uddhava came to meet Krishna before he retired for the night. 'Siguri Naga, who was sent as a scout for the search, has sighted the brothers among a group of brahmanas and ascetics on the outskirts of Kampilya. But there is no way to make contact with them; they have disappeared near the potters' colony, close to the slippery banks of the Ganga.'

THE PENULTIMATE DAY

Drupada's minister, Udbodhana, came to him with good news. 'My spies have reported that the Magadhan camp was dismantled last night and Jarasandha has left for Girivraja.' But Draupadi was not too amused. 'Krishna seems to be clearing the way for Duryodhana to win; I am not going to marry him.' Drishtadyumna prevailed upon her to put her trust in Krishna.

Just then, the chamberlain came hurriedly and unceremoniously announced the arrival of prince Shikhandin. Drupada and his children were startled at this news. Young Shikhandin walked in, almost a ghost of his former self—frail and lean, grown perceptibly taller, walking with tottering steps, with a fuzzy growth of hair above his lips and on his chin. Everybody stood speechless. Shikhandin fell at his father's feet who took him in his arms. Draupadi, Drishtadyumna and Satyajit were overwhelmed.

Shikhandin addressed his father, 'I am sorry for leaving you abruptly. I wanted to remove the blot on our family and I have succeeded. I am no longer a woman,' he added in a whisper. Everyone gaped.

'Yes, the great God has blessed me with manhood,' continued Shikhandin. 'Father, you can now send a message to King Hiranyavarma to send his daughter to Kampilya to live with her husband.'

A grateful Drupada drew Shikhandin into his arms and said, 'My son, I am indebted to the person who helped you become a man.'

'Yes, father, with the blessings of my guru, I have been transformed in body and mind. My guru was none other than Dronacharya,' said a smiling Shikhandin.

Drupada's face transformed into a raging volcano and he roared, 'The acharya of the Kurus! You have received the gift of life from my most bitter enemy?' Draupadi instantly scolded Drupada, 'Enough of this vengeance, father; it has already consumed our family. You have become unreasonable and irrational.'

Shikhandin was escorted to the inner chambers, quivering. When he regained some strength, he told Draupadi about the sequence of events that had brought him here. He waxed eloquent about Krishna and his foresight. This annoyed Draupadi, who asked him to choose between his family and the cowherd and stormed out of the room.

SHAKUNI AND ASWATHAMA

When Shakuni, Karna and Aswathama had met Drupada to endorse Duryodhana as the most deserving man for Draupadi, the Panchala Naresh told them that the selection was not in his hands. Only the winner of the archery contest would claim his daughter. He also mentioned that Duryodhana was most likely to win, given his skill in the art.

Aswathama tried to reassure the forlorn king, 'Noble king, I understand your predicament. Your enmity is with my father, noble Dronacharya. I have come here to promise you that if the noble princess marries a Kuru prince, my father will not leave Hastinapura. I will back the promise with my life.' Shakuni intervened, 'Acharya loves Aswathama more than his life. He will never let a solemn promise given by his son be broken, oh lord, King Drupada.'

After they left, Shikhandin sat with his family and pointed out to them, how Krishna's interferences had worked in their favour, from him becoming a man to the sudden departure of Jarasandha. 'Father, Aswathama's pledge was a bluff. Bhanumati is like a daughter to the Acharya, therefore, he would never allow Duryodhana to get a second wife. Duryodhana is the epitome of *adharma*. Please never let Draupadi marry him,' pleaded Shikhandin.

He also divulged what yaksha Sthoonakarna had told him about the Kuru's plot against the Pandavas. Shikhandin introduced the tall and lean yaksha, who carried a trident, to his father and said, 'Noble father, the yaksha speaks only twenty words in a day. He has only five more words to speak before tomorrow's sunrise. You may put any question you like. He will give the appropriate reply.'

'You treated Shikhandin?' asked Drupada. Sthoonakarna nodded his assent. 'Did you construct the palace of lac and sulphur at Varanavata for the Pandavas?' Sthoonakarna nodded again.

'Who asked you to do it?'

'Duryodhana.'

'Do you know who set the fire to the palace?'

'Purochana.'

'On whose orders?'

'Duryodhana's.'

'How do you know?'

'Heard.'

'Did you hear the orders yourself?' Sthoonakarna nodded assent.

Shikhandin took the yaksha out of the room and asked one of the waiting attendants to take him back to the chariot. Drupada was in a quandary

Shikhandin said:

> If Duryodhana wins the test, I want to intervene and expose his heinous crime in the presence of kings. I shall charge him with the crime of patricide, for burning his cousins to death, and call upon the rishis to pronounce whether a criminal can take advantage of marrying my sister.

They all knew that it would mean war—a war of righteousness. Drupada thought for a while. 'Yes, I have made up my mind. Shikhandin is right; Duryodhana must be denounced. I prefer leading a war for the protection of dharma.'

KRISHNAA, SHARE MY BURDEN

Krishna sought an audience with the king. Satyajit welcomed Krishna and led him to the chamber where his sister was waiting, unable to decide whether Vaasudeva is her friend or adversary.

'Noble Vaasudeva, father has sent word that I should see you as he is not well,' said Draupadi.

Krishna said with a sigh:

> None of you have faith left in me. Is it not a pity? Princess, can we not vanquish Drona without going to war? The hatred you all have for him should be converted into dharma. Hatred and revenge are negative forces; life is positive. I cannot see dharma as the instrument of pride and hatred.

Draupadi continued to look at him, amazed. She saw his face surrounded by a dazzling halo. 'I am your brother who wants to share his burden with you,' said Krishna.

'What is the burden you carry, Krishna?'

'Sister, my burden is to purge the world of *adharma*.'

'Princess, I want to see dharma crowned in Panchala and Hastinapura and in all the kingdoms of Aryawartha—that is why I never rest.'

'Show me my dharma, Govinda.'

'Your dharma is to go through the *swayamvara* with faith in your heart. Select the best archer of Aryawartha; follow his footsteps wherever he goes, and by your devotion to him, create an empire of dharma,' said Krishna with brevity.

'What about my father?'

'If you follow your dharma, your father will triumph. Drona will suffer defeat—not in battle which only ends life, but in dharma which ends pride, wrath and hate. I will teach Dronacharya a lesson which he will never forget—make him conscious that he fell from the highest state of brahmanahood when he humiliated your father. People change with time; Drona will regret and relent one day that he erred your father. But sister, you need two hands to clap.'

Just then, Drupada walked in. He was glad to see Krishna and had overheard their conversation. Drupada said to Vaasudeva, in all humility:

> Fate has been playing with me. I now agree with you; my family and I were living with feelings of hatred and revenge! Life is not worth living that way. Looking back, I reflect that I could have erred when a penniless brahmana approached me for succour. It appears that I failed in my Kshatra Dharma. Vaasudeva, can you forgive me?

'Of course, that is why I am here. Noble lord, today dharma worships you. Tomorrow, the princess will wed dharma. I am relieved and feel redeemed,' assured Krishna.

THE SWAYAMVARA

The Pandavas arrived in Kampilya disguised as anchorites and travelled with many such ascetics; they stayed in the house of a potter. Their daily food was still the alms they collected. In the course of their daily wanderings within the city, they heard about the approaching *swayamvara*.

Guru Sandipani and his principal pupil, Shvetaketu, had placed a mighty bow in the *swayamvara* hall. On their commands a *yantra* was fixed on the hall's ceiling. The *yantra* was a rotating fish and the task set was to hit this target's eye with five arrows, just by looking at its reflection in a pool of water kept directly below the ceiling.

Kings from all over Bharatvarsha had assembled in the great city. Draupadi, led by priests and accompanied by fifty maidens singing auspicious songs, proceeded along a path strewn with flowers, on her way to the *mandapa*. As she entered the hall, all eyes turned towards the radiant bride.

Drishtadyumna led his lovely sister into the hall. She was dressed in a beautiful rich golden silk sari. The ornaments added beauty to her graceful figure. She carried a garland of flowers in her hand. Drishtadyumna led her to the stage* that was built in the centre of the hall.

Sacred mantras were chanted and oblations were poured into the sacred fire. Absolute silence now prevailed in the hall as Drishtadyumna ascended the stage. In a voice resembling the low rumbling of a thundercloud, he addressed the assembly.

> Please give me your attention, noble kings and princes! Here is the bow and here are the five arrows with which the target has to be hit and brought down to the ground. The person who is able to perform this difficult feat will win my sister, Draupadi's, hand. This is my solemn promise on behalf of Drupada Naresh.

Drishtadyumna then approached his sister and recounted the names of those present at the assembly. They were both surprised to see Jarasandha and his son Sahadeva sitting along with Salya and Bhagadatta. Jarasandha gave the Panchala prince a friendly smile. The suitors went near the bow, one by one. The bow was divine and was called Kindhura. Its string was made of specially twined cat's gut—tough as modern steel. It was a very hard task to bend the bow and string it. The bow was made by many thin layers of bamboo, cross-linked with reed fibres and laced with special resins—in modern parlance, the staff of the bow was laminated and cross-linked, hence tough to bend, unless one was

---

*The use of the word stage, or mandapa, here, is singularly apt. With Draupadi on the stage, the first act of the Greek tragedy was to be enacted. She takes the lead all the time. Several acts would pass before curtains are drawn on the last one. She was the chosen one and would fulfil the Kaaran Janmi—purpose for which she was born—the destruction of all kshatriyas who had become a symbol of adharma... Krishna was the sutradhar, the puppeteer.

adept at it. No one was able to tackle it and they all returned crestfallen. Krishna's eyes roved around the hall and came to rest on the forms of the Pandavas who sat scattered in the enclosure for brahmanas.

The contest went on. Kings and princes tried and failed. Shishupala missed the mark by the width of a sesame seed; the bow flung him down, such was the reflex of the laminations of the staff. Duryodhana rose from his seat and walked majestically towards the bow. He lifted the heavy shaft and tried to bend it by holding the lower end with his big toe. As he was about to string it to the other end, his toe slipped and the taut shaft threw him to the ground. The audience jeered as the Kuru prince returned to his seat in humiliation.

Jarasandha was next. Uddhava informed Krishna that there were no Magadhan troops, except for his bodyguards. Jarasandha greeted Drupada and said:

> I showed up this morning to thank you for the invitation. I thought you would give your beautiful daughter to my grandson, Meghasandhi. The test you have prescribed is only fit for the best archer and my grandson is not one. I am too old to participate, for the bride is like my granddaughter. I wish her well and congratulate the young man who would get her. I will now leave for Rajagriha. Farewell, my friend.

Jarasandha thus converted a faux pas into his personal advantage and left.

Next in line was Salya, Nakula and Sahadeva's maternal uncle, who missed the target by the width of a bean seed. The assembled kings despaired. All reputed archers had failed so far. Karna rose and walked towards the stage—handsome, princely and graceful as he bent the bow to string it. There were rumblings amongst the kings as he was not a kshatriya. He released the five arrows, but they missed the target by the breadth of a hair. Krishna sighed in relief.

Like a sudden flame leaping up from a heap of ashes, Arjuna stood up. It was a startling sight. All eyes were turned towards this young brahmana, handsome, with unusually graceful limbs and the gait of a king! Arjuna ascended the stage and addressed Drishtadyumna. 'Is a brahmana allowed to try and hit the target? It appears that no kshatriya is able to tackle this *matsya yantra*.'

Drishtadyumna replied, 'Certainly! Anyone is at liberty to try; whoever he may be.' Arjuna turned to the king and saluted him. The Pandava approached the great bow and went around the stand on which it was placed as a mark of respect—the act is called *pradkshina*. Then, with a confident smile, he looked at Krishna, seeking his blessing and took the bow in his left hand.

Arjuna strung the bow and sent the five arrows in quick succession towards the target. The target was hit by the first arrow itself. The *matsya*, fish, which had baffled all of them for so long, fell to the ground.

There was a terrific uproar in the hall. With the gait of a swan, Draupadi walked up to Arjuna and placed the garland around his neck. The hall resounded with the blare of conchs and Drishtadyumna handed a fresh garland to the brahmana who then garlanded the bride. Arjuna took her hand and descended from the stage. Some kings stood up in the royal gallery, their arms upraised. 'This is an insult,' shouted one. 'The princess cannot be given to a brahmana. The *swayamvara* is only for the kshatriyas,' shouted another.

Duryodhana was stunned, but soon realised that this was none other than Arjuna. 'This is the time to dispose of this young man, let us rush,' said the sly Shakuni.

King Bhurisravas, who was sitting next to them, heard the whispered advice. He stood up and placed his hands heavily on Duryodhana's shoulders, 'Yuvaraja, we shall not do anything of the kind. Do you not see that the Yadavas, who are the cousins of Arjuna, are here? They will not spare any disruption of the solemn function.'

Seeing some princes move towards Drupada aggressively, Bhima pushed forward, parting the crowd of enthusiastic brahmanas with irresistible strength. With a frightening roar, he uprooted a tree which stood nearby and, placing it on his shoulders like a mace, stepped forward to arrest the rush of the angry princes.

Bhima stood by Arjuna's side and, with a broad smile, took the wedded couple to the king. The newly-weds prostrated before Drupada and the crowd cheered in appreciation of the winner's miraculous deed. Balarama and Krishna, with the Yadava *atirathis*, made their way through the crowd, accompanied by Virata and other allies.

When Arjuna saw Krishna's smiling eyes, he held Draupadi by the hand and swiftly made her kneel as he himself fell at Krishna's feet. He lifted them both and embraced Arjuna. Then to everyone's shock, Krishna touched the feet of the giant who stood protectively near Arjuna and Draupadi. Krishna looked at Draupadi, who said shyly, 'Vaasudeva, I have always trusted you.

Forgive my discourtesies and foul moods. I am relieved to be the bride of this noble brahmana.'

Arjuna and Bhima led the bride out of the chaotic enclosure and they quietly departed for the potter's house. 'Who are these brahmanas, Vaasudeva? They fight like kshatriya warriors?' asked Drupada, turning to Krishna.

> Noble lord, Bhargava Rama was a brahmana, Dronacharya is a brahmana. Our Gurudeva, the great teacher of the art of war and science of warfare, is a brahmana. The valiant Shvetaketu, the author of the *matsya yantra,* is a noble brahmana. You are most fortunate that a noble brahmana won your daughter's hand! Have faith and all will be well. Your son-in-law seems to be a mighty warrior—just what you wanted.

Krishna and Balarama started for the Yadava camp, leaving King Drupada in utter confusion!

THE FIVE BROTHERS AND DRAUPADI

Panchala was buzzing with excitement. Some of Kunti's neighbours rushed home and related to her the events of the day. She was naturally proud and happy, but also concerned that her sons could be harmed by Duryodhana if he came to know that they were alive. What bothered her most was whether the close unity among the brothers could be maintained after Arjuna's marriage to the princess of Panchala. Her other sons, barring Bhima, were unmarried, including the eldest—Yudhisthira.

Melancholy descended on her as she reflected on her past. She had been adopted by King Kunti Bhoja and, in her teens, she served Rishi Durvasa during a visit to her father's kingdom. While in his service, she gave birth to a beautiful baby, as brilliant as the sun. The young unmarried girl had to abandon her infant to avoid the stigma that would follow; this incident haunted her till date.

When she married King Pandu, who was sickly and had conjugal dysfunctional deficiencies, she had to go through *niyoga* three times in order to continue the dynastic lineage. In addition to the three sons she gave birth to, she also looked after the two sons of Madri after the untimely death of King Pandu. After their exile, she had suffered with her sons.

By the sheer grace of God, they had been saved, at the last minute, from getting roasted alive in the palace fire. Their life of recluse in Rakshasavarta, the land of cannibals, became endurable because Bhima married a Rakshasi, Hidimba. She bore him a son, named Ghatotkacha, who was declared to be the successor to King Vrikodara of Rakshasavarta. After sage Vyasa found them in Rakshasavarta, the brothers reached Kampilya in disguise. Now that Arjuna was reported to have won the princess, would this marriage signal the end of the bonding and unity of purpose and spirit among the five brothers? Kunti was tense when she heard her sons were returning. With great anticipation, she walked to the entrance of their hut. She blessed Draupadi with an affectionate hug and said, 'I am lucky and blessed that you chose my Arjuna!'

Draupadi was surprised and looked at Krishna who had now joined them. Krishna smiled and said, 'Princess, I promised you the best warrior and I think I succeeded.' Draupadi lowered her eyes, tears of joy rolling down her cheeks. It was a happy reunion for the brothers.

Draupadi was immensely pleased to be in the company of such an affectionate family. Krishna knew what troubled Kunti. He addressed her, 'There is need for continuing the unity among the five brothers. As long as you stay together as one, you shall remain invincible.' Draupadi grasped the meaning of what Krishna had said and turned towards Kunti:

> Have no fear, mother. I shall accord to each one of your sons, the treatment and respect due to a husband, without any partiality. No disagreement, however small, shall ever arise among them because of me. I shall be the consort of the Pandavas and shall be the unifying force for their rightful action.

Krishna smiled in contentment and Kunti was overwhelmed with joy.

Meanwhile, Drupada could not come to terms with what had transpired. Drishtadyumna promised to unearth the mystery. He had followed his sister at a discreet distance to trace the mystery of this unknown youth who had accomplished the impossible and also withstood the wrath of kings with the help of his giant brother. From a recess in the mud wall, he could see the happenings inside the hut. He saw Draupadi sitting happily on the mud floor surrounded by five brahmanas and a woman who was obviously their mother. Then he could hear their voices and he heard someone addressing the young man as Arjuna.

Drishtadyumna could not believe his ears. Could they possibly be the Pandavas? He started placing the events of the morning in perspective. He rushed back to the palace and confided his suspicion in Drupada. The next day, the king sent *purohit*s to the hut with expensive dresses and gifts. Drupada also sent an invitation, through Satyajit, that arrangements for the wedding had to be made and that it would be better if they all came to the palace with their mother and the bride.

When Yudhisthira revealed their identity to the king, Drupada and his queen, Sautramani, were stunned. Drupada was overwhelmed that Arjuna was his son-in-law. Yudhisthira then told him about the decision that Draupadi would wed all five brothers. 'But that would be *adharma*,' said the bewildered king. 'What will the society say?' Draupadi remained firm and replied, 'Nothing which is in the interest of righteousness for all could be perceived as *adharma*, noble father!' The king announced the commencement of the wedding ceremony. Veda Vyasa came to Drupada's court to bless Draupadi and said, '*Jaya ho Dharmameva Jayate.*' The rishi reassured the king, saying, 'Truth shall always prevail.' He continued:

> Rejoice in the knowledge that your daughter is following the path of dharma. Do not get confused at the prospect of Draupadi being married to five brothers. Even if a man has only one father, he often treats his uncles as his father. Draupadi's mind is pure and her motives are unimpeachable. Hers is a *kaarana janma.* I have no doubt that she is destined to play a pivotal role in ensuring the unity of purpose and action among the sons of Kunti in their endeavour to establish dharma. History will remember her as long as the sun shines.

The king and the queen were convinced after the intervention of the venerable sage. The five brothers were seated around the sacred fire and Draupadi's marriage was solemnised with each one of them.

In due course, she went to Hastinapura. Later, as the consort of the Pandavas, she wielded authority over Indraprastha. Here, she also acted as the official hostess during Yudhisthira's Rajasuya Yagna.

PANIC IN THE KURU CAMP

It was not long before the Kauravas came to know that the brahmana was none other than Arjuna. Duryodhana was furious. 'I could make out in the assembly that day; the brahmana's gait, mannerisms reminded me of Arjuna…it is the work of that cowherd.' Shakuni intervened to say:

> What has Krishna to do with the lac house built in Varanavata? Your friend

> Purochana failed, which is, in a way, your carelessness; you could have involved one more person to make the plan foolproof. A spy cannot be trusted—one should put another person to spy over a spy. Now let us get back to Hastinapura and, for once, let some maturity come to your intemperate friend, Karna. He is too jealous of Arjuna and that emotion hinders his skills.

When Vidura heard of the glad tidings, he went to Dhritarashtra and informed him suggestively that there had not been any depletion in the Kuru dynasty. Blinded by his attachment to his son, Dhritarashtra was happy, thinking that Duryodhana had finally married Draupadi. Vidura, being an astute minister, was diplomatic enough to gauge Dhritarashtra's reaction and hence, his culpable guilt. 'It is indeed very fortunate that the children of the Kuru house are flourishing. The eldest son has now married the daughter of the king of Panchalas.' The king fell into the trap. Pleased at the news he asked, 'Then why have you not brought her before me?'

Vidura corrected Dhritarashtra saying that it was one of the Pandavas who won Draupadi in the *swayamvara*. Dhritarashtra's expression changed, but he shrewdly concealed his emotions and said, 'It is…it is equally fortunate. Pandu's sons are dearer to me than my own. I am so…happy to hear that the Pandavas are…alive.' The king's mouth, however, sagged and he looked crestfallen. Vidura won on his suspicion that the blind king was also a part of the conspiracy to do away with the five brothers at Varanavata.

Duryodhana entered the palace of the king and overheard the latter part of the conversation between his father and the minister. Once Vidura left, Duryodhana confronted Dhritarashtra, who sheepishly told his son that he spoke good things about the Pandavas because Vidura was present at that time, otherwise he was not at all happy at the turn of things.

'Son, our apple cart seems to have tripped. Destiny is playing with your luck,' he said. Duryodhana was fuming and shouted, 'Fate and destiny are only for weaklings, father. It is not fate, but one of the tricks of that cowherd.'

Undeterred by the events, Duryodhana, Karna, Shakuni and Dushassana began to plan another conspiracy. The first course of action was to wean away Drupada from the Pandavas and, if that failed, to instil seeds of doubt in Draupadi's mind as to her marriage being immoral. They felt that Draupadi would then definitely opt out of the match. They even thought of trying to cause dissent among the brothers by making Draupadi prefer one over the other.

One day, while they were discussing the plot, Dushassana suggested what if Bhima was killed, it would break the backbone of the Pandavas. Karna countered it, 'All your suggestions are unwise and intemperate; as a proud kshatriya, one should opt for a fight and overpower them before they become powerful with Panchala. Fight them and claim your right to the throne of Hastinapura, and not by your outlandish ideas.'

Shakuni tried to intervene but was stopped when a chamberlain announced that Bhishma Pitamah and the king had invited them to the assembly hall for a council.

THE ASSEMBLY HALL

As the quartet entered the hall, there was a hush in the assembly of Kurus, which consisted of Bhishma, Drona, Kripacharya and the priests, Baahlika and Somadatta, who were the allies from the north-west and important for the Kurus. Bhishma spoke first; although he was addressing Duryodhana, the Pitamah looked at the assembly of kings:

> It is not proper to nurse anger against the Pandavas any longer. It is not Raja Dharma. Noble Dhritarashtra and late Pandu are both my nephews and their sons are equally dear to me, I do not differentiate between them. Duryodhana is as dear to me as Yudhisthira. Of late, the affairs of the state have taken ominous turns due to jealousy, envy and treachery. I feel, it is my duty as the custodian of the Kuru Empire to set things right. I mean to be fair to the sons of Pandu. They are fatherless children and I have seen them being humiliated many a time in this court.
>
> Duryodhana, my child, they have as much right as you over this kingdom. Do you not think, being the crown prince, that it is your Raja Dharma to invite them to Hastinapura and share this big kingdom with them? This kingdom of Bharata is vast and has enough place for more than one king. Please think this over, my son.

Bhishma paused, and then continued:

> The Kurus have never been warmongers. This has been our strength, which has kept even the mighty Jarasandha at bay. This course of action, that I suggest, will win for you everlasting fame. Any other route you take will only end in unhappiness and infamy for you. Once you lose your good name, your

life will be a waste. You live only as long as your good name lives, and perish when you lose it in the eyes of men. Do what befits a noble prince like you.

Looking at Shakuni and Karna, Bhishma said, 'A king should be afraid of flatterers, sweet-talkers and impetuous and self-opinionated persons; it looks as though fate has given you a second chance. Do not miss this unique opportunity. Give half the kingdom to the Pandavas and rule in peace.'

Drona reminded Dhritarashtra that he became king by default. Karna was furious at this suggestion and advised Duryodhana to settle the scores on the battlefield.

Bhishma roared, 'Anga Raja, do not forget who got you to this status. It is the munificence of the royal house of the Kurus! Who are you to advise us? You are permitted to leave the assembly.' Vidura then got up and spoke to Dhritarashtra:

> We are all your well-wishers and want to save your reputation and that of your son. What infamy has been brought on you and the house of the Kurus by the burning of the house of lac! The people of Hastinapura have stamped your name with the seal of ignominy. You have now been given a chance to cleanse your soul of all evil thoughts and rise above trivialities. Welcome the Pandavas and give them half the kingdom. They are now strong. Drupada and Drishtadyumna will stand by their sons-in-law. Krishna and Balarama are on their side.

Dhritarashtra looked pitiable and said:

> I agree to all that you have said and, notwithstanding my son, the Pandavas will be treated justly. They shall be looked after by me equally well as my own sons. This kingdom is also their birthright. Let them share equitably. Vidura, please carry my message to Panchala and welcome them to Hastinapura.

Vidura departed for Panchala the next day by river and landed at Kampilya. He paid his respects to King Drupada and congratulated him about the wedding of his daughter. He offered gifts for the bride on behalf of the kingdom of the Kurus.

'King Dhritarashtra is very pleased that the five brothers are alive and has sent with me an invitation to welcome them and their bride to Hastinapura.' The Pandavas did not know what to make of it. 'Of course,' replied Drupada.

'Inform Dhritarashtra that I am also immensely pleased and honoured by this alliance with the noble house of the Kurus. As for their going to Hastinapura, I leave Yudhisthira and his brothers to decide.'

Krishna intervened and said, 'It is but proper that they should go to Hastinapura.'

Drishtadyumna made preparations for the departure of the Pandavas and Draupadi. Krishna would accompany them as well.

DRAUPADI'S BRIDAL NIGHT

In one of the palaces in Kampilya, Draupadi was anxiously waiting for her husband in the bridal chamber. She was richly dressed, as a bride meeting her husband on the first night should be!

She heard the sound of footsteps. Her heart was bursting with excitement when Yudhisthira came in with his kindly smile, eyes beaming with affection, and closed the door. He lovingly addressed her, 'Noble Princess Draupadi, are you happy?'

She looked up. His eyes expressed tenderness and her confidence in herself was restored. Draupadi replied, 'Why lord? Do I give an impression that I am unhappy?' Yudhisthira was put at ease by her reply. She continued:

> I had dreamt yesterday that a divine sage affirmed I am doing a sacred duty, to restore dharma, by being the wife of five husbands. I know the path I am choosing is very arduous for a woman, but I have always been told by my father that I am special. I shall accept my destiny as a kshatriya and Arya. Lord, I can only achieve the building of an empire based on dharma if I am the wife of each one of you. If you have no objections, I would like to be with each of you for one year in turn. At the end of each year, I will perform the Chandrayana Vrata and then live with the next brother.

Yudhisthira smiled and said, 'Princess, come nearer, sit down and feel at ease. You know, your coming to us has been very auspicious. Uncle Vidura has arrived, from Hastinapura, with an invitation from King Dhritarashtra and Bhishma Pitamah. They have requested us to come to Hastinapura and stake our claim for the kingdom,' said Yudhisthira.

'Duryodhana would accept that?' asked Draupadi. Yudhisthira was taken aback by Draupadi's impression of his cousin. 'You are a very shrewd observer, Panchali, and a proud princess. He appears to have reconciled to the events.'

'Are you sure that he has reconciled, Aryaputra? His appalling look after he failed the contest still haunts me.'

'Panchali, you must forgive his weakness. He is a victim of his destiny; we may have to ignore his reactions.'

'And your guru, Dronacharya? Will he accept me? I am his enemy's daughter.'

Yudhisthira laughed heartily, 'There is no difficulty on that score; your *sakha*, Govinda, overcame that difficulty when he sent your brother to him. Krishna also got Aswathama to make sure his father does not leave the kingdom.'

Then, looking around the room, he remarked, 'How did you know I like the game of dice? I see a chequered piece of game board and pieces of ivory dice. Do you know how to play?'

'I know a little...'

'Shall we play a game then? I am fond of dice. Perhaps, I have a weakness for it.'

The next morning, Arjuna went to meet Krishna. 'Vaasudeva, I am sure you would have come to know of the decision of our eldest brother? I feel miserable; I should not have gone to that *swayamvara*. I could have carved out my own life, all by myself, however bleak it may have been.'

'Partha, you are a kshatriya of the finest descent and a hero—the best in Aryawartha. I can understand your feelings. But can you see Draupadi's situation? Can she suffer the intimate attentions of five husbands at the same time?'

'I see your point,' Arjuna replied. Krishna placed his hand affectionately on Arjuna's shoulder and said, 'Partha, in your place, I would feel stifled too.'

Krishna thought of speaking with Yudhisthira. He was perplexed at the invitation from Dhritarashtra. During their meeting, Yudhisthira said, 'Krishna, I am so glad you are here. I am not too eager to accept this proposal. I want your advice and shall abide by it irrespective of what my brothers think.'

Krishna replied with brevity:

> Dharmaputra, Hastinapura is a place of intrigues. *Adharma* is reigning in the kingdom. It has come to my knowledge that there was a palace revolt in Hastinapura with Duryodhana threatening to commit suicide, Dushassana and Shakuni leaving for Gandhara and Anga Raja, Karna, leaving the kingdom to renounce the world. The old king is now a nervous wreck and has secretly promised many things to Duryodhana to prevent him from

committing suicide. They might trick you again and create new difficulties and plots to finish you off, once and for all.

'Vaasudeva, I do not want to be a king. I can renounce this world and live like a hermit in the Himalayas,' replied Yudhisthira in exasperation.

Then Krishna said:

> Dharmaputra, do not forget that you are a married man. What will happen to the noble Draupadi, who has sacrificed her entire happiness for the welfare and unity of you and your brothers? I want you to be a king and create your empire of dharma. Build a new kingdom away from Hastinapura, far from the court intrigues of the Kurus. Such a kingdom is worthy even if it is made of scrubland and dense forest. I know of such a place; it is a scrub jungle where wolves and other wild beasts rule the roost. It has, in its neighbourhood, dense forests inhabited by wild tribes where no Aryan king has dared to go. It is called Khandavaprastha.

An enthused Krishna assured Yudhisthira:

> Do you know, Aryaputra, that it was the ancient capital of your forefathers, Pururavas, Nahusha and Yayati? You can build a city more beautiful than Amaravati—the city of Devendra. Noble prince, have no concern. The Yadavas will help you in building a wonderful city as the capital of your kingdom; we shall name it Indraprastha!

Yudhisthira was speechless. 'Krishna, my mentor, I shall follow your advice. My brothers would also be excited at the idea of Indraprastha,' he said. 'Now, let us go and invite Balarama to lead our entourage to Hastinapura.'

Before their departure, Drupada formally announced their decision to leave Panchala in front of the assembly and officially bid farewell to his daughter and her husbands. 'Oh, sons of Pandu, you have my blessings always. I am so happy that my Krishnaa married you. I will give you part of my kingdom if you decide to stay with us.'

'No, no!' exclaimed Bhima. 'Lord, we have already deprived you of your daughter, we cannot take your kingdom as well. But I am sure the noble lord would not like us to arrive at Hastinapura empty-handed.'

'Why do you say so, Bhima? The kingdom of Panchala is very prosperous. We are only too happy to give you whatever your eldest desires,' said Drupada.

'That is the problem lord,' blurted out Bhima. 'Our eldest is a saint and would like to go to Hastinapura on foot, in the dress he is now wearing! He has directed me not to ask you for anything. Left to himself, he would be satisfied with five coconuts, one for each one of us.' The whole court rang with laughter and the king generously said, 'Along with five coconuts, I intend to give, among other things, one hundred elephants—would that be alright?' asked Drupada.

'My cousin Duryodhana will die of envy when he sees me trooping with the army of elephants,' said Bhima.

When Bhima went to Yudhisthira's apartment, Krishna was waiting for him along with the prince and princess of Kashi, Susharma and Jalandhara, who were Bhanumati's siblings. Krishna introduced them to Bhima.

> Bhima, meet prince Susharma and his sister, Princess Jalandhara, from Kashi. They were on their way to Hastinapura by boat, which almost capsized near Kampilya when it hit a sandbar. They are waiting for a relief boat and are in a great hurry to reach Hastinapura, as Duryodhana's wife needs help during childbirth.

Bhima promptly fell for the girl whereas Susharma showed an instant dislike for Bhima. Krishna invited the prince to join their entourage as they would be leaving for Hastinapura in a day or two. But the prince said that it may not be possible, for Jalandhara had to reach at the earliest to assist Bhanumati in childbirth.

Krishna instructed Satyaki and Uddhava to arrange for another suitable river transport, which they did and Susharma left along with Jalandhara. While taking leave of Krishna, as Jalandhara bowed to touch his feet, Krishna whispered into her ear, 'Princess, do you like King Vrikodara?' She blushed. Krishna blessed her and they went on their way.

Krishna turned to Bhima who was smiling at the prospect of marrying the princess. 'In good time, Jalandhara shall be your wife,' said Krishna. 'Please do not do anything hasty, let Princess Bhanumati's confinement end.'

DURYODHANA RECEIVES THE BRIDAL PROCESSION

The weather in Hastinapura was pleasant as though the triumphant return of the Pandavas would bring happy days back for the people. Perched on the lead elephant, Bhima led the procession into town.

The royals from the house of Kurus were sitting on an elevated platform. As Bhima approached the royal platform, he waved to Uddhava, Satyaki and

Maniman who had accompanied Jalandhara and the Kashi prince, Susharma, in a specially commissioned boat. Bhima scanned the welcome party and noted the absence of Karna, Dushassana and Aswathama. He saw Guru Dronacharya and ceremonially saluted him. He glanced towards the enclosure meant for the royal ladies and found Jalandhara sitting there, next to Bhanumati.

Attired in ceremonial garments and a diamond diadem presented by his father-in-law, Yudhisthira got down from his chariot. Somadatta, the preceptor of the Kurus, greeted Dhaumya, the preceptor of the Pandavas. Duryodhana and the others stepped down from the platform to greet Yudhisthira and Balarama. Duryodhana embraced Yudhisthira with a reserved smile and prostrated before Balarama. Accompanied by Arjuna and Krishna, with the twins behind them, Bhima approached Duryodhana with his mischievous, boyish smile.

Duryodhana was not too comfortable in Krishna's presence. Krishna noticed this and he bowed and touched the feet of Duryodhana, his elder. Duryodhana placed a garland around his neck.

At the end of the ceremonies, Bhima and Nakula sought the eldest's permission to approach Duryodhana's brother, Vikarna, for arranging accommodation for the camp attendants and the horses, camels, cattle and the elephants that were part of their entourage. While the menfolk, the hosts and the guests were exchanging greetings, Draupadi was being received by Bhanumati and Jalandhara with utmost cordiality. Draupadi noticed that Bhanumati had fear and concern writ large on her face, not a good sign for a woman in advanced pregnancy.

RAJYA SABHA—THE GRAND COUNCIL

Bhishma had summoned a meeting of the Rajya Sabha to be convened in the Throne Hall. Three weeks before this, Princess Bhanumati had died in childbirth, having given birth to a stillborn son. Even while breathing her last, she made Krishna promise that he would not deny Duryodhana the throne of Hastinapura. Krishna felt sorry that such a wonderful soul had to leave the world so early due to the cruelty of her husband.

The seating arrangements in the hall were as per royal protocol. The hall was a large square built with three arms; the fourth side was kept open for a *vedi* in which the holy fire was enshrined. Vaishampayana and Paila, the principal disciples of master Vyasa; Somadatta, the preceptor of the Kurus;

and Dhaumya, the preceptor of the Pandavas, sat around it, invoking Agni in the rite known as Vaishwadeva. This was an exclusive Vedic rite involving a sacrificial session to invoke Agni, the guardian deity of the sacrificial sessions. The priests were known as Agnihotri, a class of brahmanas who took the vow to keep the sacred fire burning throughout their lives.

A raised platform facing the *vedi* was lined with a number of silver thrones and one golden throne for King Dhritarashtra. Bhishma was seated next to the king on his right and Balarama on the left. When Vyasa arrived, he was taken to a wooden bench covered by a deerskin. Krishna occupied the seat next to the great sage. On the platform to the right of the thrones, sat Shukadeva, the son of Vyasa, who was a great ascetic.

Separate enclosures seated the Pandava brothers closer to Krishna's silver throne, whereas Dushassana and his other brothers sat on the opposite end. After a while, Yudhisthira and Duryodhana were ushered in, with the blowing of trumpets, and were seated next to the king's throne.

The priests, at the appointed time, raised the pitch of Vedic chants and showered grains of rice on those seated on the thrones. When the chanting got over, Yudhisthira and Duryodhana got up from their thrones, walked up to Vyasa and prostrated themselves before him. Then Bhishma, followed by Dhritarashtra, came forward to receive his blessings. Bhishma then spoke:

> Respected rishis and *munis*, learned brahmanas, noble kings, and the best of the Kurus and citizens! I speak with the blessings of the gods, and the permission of the venerable master, Veda Vyasa. I would like to announce the agreement that the noble King Dhritarashtra and I have reached, which affects the future of the Kurus and the empire they govern.

Bhishma then addressed Duryodhana, 'Suyodhana, my son, in the best interests of the Kurus and the empire, we have decided to give half the kingdom to the Pandavas. The king will announce the details of the division.' Dhritarashtra collected himself to speak coherently, for he was afraid of what his son would say.

> Yudhisthira, my son, listen to my words. The kingdom of Kurus owes its existence to your dear and illustrious father. You are entitled to rule this kingdom too, and, therefore, I suggest that the kingdom be divided between you and my son, Duryodhana. I have decided to make you the lord of Khandavaprastha.

Bhima was furious and hissed like a cobra, but Krishna cautioned him to be patient.

Yudhisthira replied, 'Whatever you say, I will obey.'

Dhritarashtra called Vidura to his side and asked him to initiate the coronation of Yudhisthira as the king of Khandavaprastha.

Kripacharya, Bhishma, Drona, Dhaumya, Vyasa and Krishna blessed Yudhisthira with the words, 'May you conquer the world as your forefathers did before you! May your fame spread to the four quarters like the perfume of flowers carried by the breeze and may you establish a kingdom of dharma.'

Dhritarashtra then spoke to the Pandavas:

> Yudhisthira, you are now the lord of Khandavaprastha. It is but proper that you should go to your kingdom and begin your rule as early as possible. It was Khandavaprastha that our ancestors Puruvavas, Nahusha and Yayati ruled. It was the capital of the Kuru kingdom for a long time. I hope you will have a happy life there.

Yudhisthira, with all humility, took leave of the king. Vyasa told Yudhisthira about the land:

> The country called Khandavaprastha was once the capital of the Kurus, but it was later destroyed due to the curse of the rishis. This was to punish the misdemeanour of the son of Buddha, and the capital had to be abandoned. It is now a barren waste where wolves and other wild animals rule. As it is, no one could live there. Nothing grows there despite its proximity to the sacred river, Yamuna. But you can turn the land into heaven with Krishna by your side.

Krishna then got up and addressed Dhritarashtra, 'Noblest of Kurus, your decision has been just. In the spirit of righteousness, Yudhisthira and his brothers should share, with your noble sons, all the grain, gold, cattle, horse chariots, elephants and arms of Kurus equally. Is it not?'

As Duryodhana grasped the price of division that he would have to pay, he wanted to protest, but his voice failed him. 'Perhaps the venerable grandfather would approve of this accord?' continued Krishna, turning to Bhishma, who nodded and said, 'Indeed,' as the possibilities of the situation dawned on him slowly!

Dhritarashtra had never thought of the implications of his decision, but he maintained his composure and said, 'Of course! Thank you, Vaasudeva, for reminding us that the division has to be equitable and just.'

Krishna asked Bhishma, 'Noble grandfather, perhaps some of the brahmanas, Kurus and kshatriyas, Mahajans, craftsmen, and others, together with their families, would like to accompany the five brothers to Khandavaprastha?'

The silence, which had descended upon the assembly like an ominous cloud, disappeared. Most of the gathering felt that there was now a way out from Duryodhana's rule; they cheered at the thought of building a new life under Yudhisthira.

Bhishma Pitamah looked at Krishna and smiled. What was, in fact, the banishment of the five brothers into the wilderness was being transformed by Vaasudeva into their triumph, for they would go forth to establish a new empire of the Kurus. He said, 'I give you my word that everyone in Hastinapura, who wants to go to Khandavaprastha, will be free to do so. They can take all their wealth with them and also their cows, horses, chariots and other belongings.'

Balarama then stood up and addressed the assembly in his resounding voice.

> Noble son of Shantanu, we, the Yadava *atirathi*s, had only come to Kampilya to take part in the *swayamvara* of the princess of Panchala. We had no idea that Arjuna would win her hand. We are happy that two auspicious events have occurred while we were in Aryawartha. It is therefore our privilege that we, the Yadavas of Dwaraka, should make a suitable present to our *Bhagineyas* on this occasion. My brother Krishna will make the announcement on behalf of King Ugrasena, the lord of Dwaraka, and our esteemed father, Vasudeva, and all the Yadavas of Dwaraka.

Concluding his address, the elder brother looked at Krishna and sat down.

Krishna then addressed Yudhisthira, 'Noblest of the Kurus, by the permission of my brother, the noble Balarama, the Yadavas of Dwaraka will give you and your brothers a small gift of one fifth of the gold, cows, horses and chariots that they possess.'

A stunned assembly cheered. Krishna also informed them that he, along with his brother and some Yadava *atirathi*s, would be accompanying the Pandavas to Khandavaprastha to help them build a city. Then, in the same breath, he turned to Vyasa and said, 'May I beseech you, best of *muni*s, to bless the five brothers and come with us on our journey to Khandavaprastha?' Vyasa promptly agreed.

Once alone, Krishna spoke to the Pandavas:

> If Yudhisthira was made the king of Hastinapura—the seat of *adharma*, imagine how helpless he would be. He would have to deal with Shakuni's scheming, his spies tarnishing your and Panchali's image. Her very honour will be at stake with people like Dushassana around. Karna would be plotting to kill Arjuna out of sheer envy. Even Sage Vyasa was taken aback when he heard of Khandavaprastha. Do you know, Vyasa's father, Sage Parashara, had lost his legs near Khandavaprastha, where Kartavirayarjuna ran his chariot over his legs? Khandavaprastha may be a wilderness at the moment, but remember that the beautiful Yamuna passes through it. I have already asked Maniman to clear the scrubland and bring Naga craftsmen to help build your city.

The Pandavas felt much better seeing Krishna's optimism, and grew eager to start their new life.

The division of the kingdom and the crowning of Yudhisthira occurred peacefully on an auspicious day. The next day, Bhima was crowned as the crown prince. Jalandhara attended the great event. Bhima was overwhelmed with joy when she was around.

Two weeks later, the five brothers, accompanied by Krishna and Balarama, offered their parting salutations to the Kuru elders. Veda Vyasa then proclaimed, 'I shall lay the foundation of the empire of dharma at Khandavaprastha. This new city will be an eternal one; empires may come and go but Indraprastha would remain forever.'

INDRAPRASTHA

It was not unlike an exodus from Hastinapura. Bhima and Krishna led the caravan and were followed by the *atirathi*s and *maharathi*s in their chariots. Some Kurus were also in the crowd. Finally, the travellers reached the Yamuna river. Its vast expanse and torrential flow fascinated everyone. Shouting in great ecstasy, most of them rushed to take a bath in the river.

When they arrived at Khandavaprastha, King Maniman and the Nagas had already cleared a vast space in the wilderness where the city was to be founded. With the help of city planners, especially sent by Bhishma, streets and squares were laid out. Sites for royal mansions and private houses were earmarked for development. The expert Naga architects consulted the Kurus and, together, they prepared a master plan for building the city. The plan was approved by Yudhisthira and other Kuru elders. Sahadeva took keen interest in setting Vastushastra principles that would create harmony amongst the citizens.

There was no shortage of land. Krishna, with Yudhisthira's consent, created a land guild that allotted land to the poor and professional farmers for farming. Sacred rituals were performed, with master Vyasa presiding, to make an offering to Indra—they prayed to Indra to not overwhelm the new city with torrential storms. Indra seemed to have heard the prayers. The monsoons came, but there was no flooding.

Vyasa also invoked the divine architect, Vishwakarma, to aid the craftsmen and architects in building the city. Krishna advised Yudhisthira to rename Khandavaprastha as Indraprastha, which he said would become the most wonderful place on earth. Within a year, the city rose as if by magic; people from distant places came to see its wonders and settled there.

Yudhisthira had completed his one-year tenure as Draupadi's husband. Shortly after the next full moon, she would be the wife of Bhima.

KRISHNA REMINISCES

It was a full moon night; the moon's reflection on the placid waters of the Yamuna was breathtaking. A cool breeze was blowing from the east; people in Vrindavan had named it *purvaiah*—the eastern breeze. Drawn by the mesmerising scene, Krishna left his apartment and walked to the sandbars of the Yamuna.

He heard the gentle flute music being carried by the breeze and grew sentimental and pensive. His heart was pining for his eternal love—Radha. He wondered if he had been cruel to her and asked himself: Would she have fitted into the whirlpool of his life? He had not had a moment to himself since leaving Vrindavan. Radha would never have been able to bear the separation, which his dear Rukmini had gotten used to, from their very first night; Rukmini was a jewel of a wife whereas Radha was a tender flower. She would have withered away if she had come with him to Mathura.

Krishna Yashodanandana was happy and carefree, whereas Krishna Devakiputra's life was that of concern and strife. Krishna sat on the riverbank in a yogic posture to meditate and regain his inner tranquility.

Draupadi had just completed her Chandrayana Vrata and, from the next day, would be the wife of Bhima. She wanted to meet Krishna before she started on the next milestone in her life. Being around him, she automatically felt all her worries drifting away. She saw Krishna beautifully silhouetted against the full moon and went to meet him.

Krishna felt her presence and turned around and asked, 'My Sakha, what brings you here?'

Draupadi replied, 'Your sweet flute music, Govinda. I have heard that, on such a full moon night, you used to play Rasa with your *gopi*s of Vrindavan. I hear that music now, but where are your *gopi*s?'

'Yonder. Do you not hear them playing Rasa? Do you not hear their anklets jingling? They think I am still playing Rasa with them; such is their devotion to me.'

'Vaasudeva, I no longer remember the reason I wanted to meet you; but I felt I must, before you return to Dwaraka. Whenever I am in doubt or in distress, I think of you and you seem to respond, leaving me happy that I have spoken to you.' She saw a luminous glow surrounding Krishna and felt the presence of true divinity.

'Princess,' said Krishna, 'you and I are made for each other—we are the *samidha*s of this mission to establish dharma.'

Draupadi then said to Krishna:

> I just saw you enveloped in a beautiful blue haze. You wanted me to be sure of myself and the path I am on! I am aware that I am a *samidha*—the dry grass twig of the fire pit over which the *arghya* ghee is poured so that the twig will burn for a longer time. I am aware that I have to bear the pain and distress that comes with it for as long as I live. You have only reminded and assured me that you will watch over me.

Such was the draw of Krishna's personality that no one could resist it. Draupadi, who had many misgivings about his intentions at the beginning, was now his ardent devotee.

When the city settled down to its normal life, Krishna and Balarama decided to leave for Dwaraka. The Pandavas bid them a teary farewell. In all, the Yadava brothers had been away from Dwaraka for more than two years.

Krishnaaya Hariye Paramatmane
Pranata Kle'sanaasaya Govindaaya namo namah!

Krishna, You are Hari, the Supreme Soul, God, benefactor,
The dispenser of gloom and despair. The sublime Govinda,
I salute you.

*****

Episode 4

Dwaraka: Krishna's Dham by the Sea

Jaidash vardha Kivardhita kausalam
Tridasadatta samastavi vibhutimat
Jaladhi madhyagatam twa mabhushayo
Navapuram vapurachitra rochisha

With thy charming bodily lustre, thou adorn the new city built in the middle of the ocean, with the skill displayed by the divine architect and with all the prosperity showered by the gods.

DWARAKA

Dwar, meaning door, and *ka,* implying supreme bliss, were the foundations of Krishna's city of dharma. He had conceived the city and built it with the help of Vishwakarma. Sthapatya Vidya—the science of aesthetic architecture in synergy with the forces of nature—was developed in India as Vastusashtra and Fengshui in China. Over a period of time, the science of architecture became one of the limbs of the Vedas, called the Vedangas and was codified by Veda Vyasa as part of the Atharvana lore.

Krishna wanted Dwaraka to be a place where people could attain knowledge of the Supreme Being and live in peace and harmony.

The Saurashtra region was part of a larger country known as Anartha, and in ancient times it was known as Kushasthali. The ancient rulers of this land were known as Sharyatas. Krishna and his Yadava clan from Mathura built their city on the ruins of Kushasthali, by the sea. It rose as the fabulous Suvarna Nagari—the golden city of Dwaraka.

The twenty-eight watchtowers, four in each of the seven concentric squares, were encrusted with golden mother-of-pearl shells, corals and other semi-precious stones. From afar, the ever-sunny Saurashtra coastline reflected the sunlight as if the city was lined with gold leaf. The weatherproof mother-of-pearl shells insulated the towers from corrosion by the sea breeze.

The terrain of Gujarat extends from the salt flats and marshes of the Rann of Kutch to the fertile banks of the Narmada river. India's coastline along the Arabian Sea begins here and its people have a tradition of maritime trade with the present-day Arabian Gulf and African countries, right from the times of Krishna.

Lothal, a part of the Indus Valley Civilisation, may have been a dry dock and port for shipbuilding. With the disappearance of River Saraswati, its importance decreased and it was ultimately forgotten—probably around 1900 BCE. It seems that Krishna adapted several features from Lothal in designing and creating Dwaraka as a deep-water port for the vessels going towards the ocean. In Krishna's time, the present-day port of Bharuch was famous as Bharukachha or Bhrigukachhapa (Bharuch). It formed the mouth for Madhyadesa states to interact with the outside world.

Dwaraka and Prabhasa Patan, where Krishna reigned, were very prosperous ports enriching the whole Saurashtra region. The maritime tradition has been sustained even now with Porbandar, Surat and Bharuch in the Gulf of Cambay, and Kandla in the Gulf of Kutch. Over a period of time, maritime trade helped people develop several talents. The region became famous for *silavats*—stone carvers—and their intricate stone carving; jewellers and textile weavers, known for their dexterity and penchant for colour and design. In subsequent centuries, these skills were reflected in Jain and Hindu temple architecture and Mughal monuments.

The most famous temple today, from that era, is of Somnath at Prabhasa Patan. Dedicated to Lord Shiva, it is the first amongst the twelve Jyotirlingas in India. Its wealth was fabulous and, hence, attracted Muslim invaders from Afghanistan, who looted and tried to destroy the Hindu traditions. Its wealth was plundered and carted off to Ghazni. People were enslaved and women were abducted, bringing untold hardships in the period from the eleventh to eighteenth centuries. The resilience of the Hindu populace was such that the temple was rebuilt every time it was destroyed.

Despite such resilience, time and tide have taken their toll and today, the ancient stones of Dwaraka lie fathoms deep, beneath the waves. Notwithstanding this, Krishna's undaunted and compassionate spirit beckons the faithful from every corner of the land even now.

Dwaraka is one of the places of pilgrimage which is twice blessed, as it is both *saptapuri* and one of the *chardhams*. No other holy place has that distinction in India. The *chardhams* are the sacred abodes of Vishnu: the other three are Badrinath, Puri and Rameshwaram. As the *dhams* are placed at the four cardinal points of the land, Dwaraka is known as Paschim *dham*—the lord's home in the west. Dwaraka is also the tirtha where Adi Sankaracharya established one of his monastic orders, known as Sarada Math, that continues to be one of the most important spiritual establishments for Hindus.

Dwaraka had beautiful gardens and orchards surrounding the palaces and mansions. The palaces of Krishna and his chief queens were built of marble and had silver doors. The pillars of Krishna's palace were intricately carved and embellished with coral, sapphires and emeralds. The canopies of silk were decorated with gold thread and edged with string of pearls. The furniture was made out of ivory, inlaid with gold and precious gems, and the rooms were lit by jewelled lamps.

Krishna's principal queen was Rukmini, and a beautiful palace was built at Bhet Dwaraka—island Dwaraka on the west side—for her. Satyabhama's palace was built near Satapura, Kutiyana, in the east;* and Jambavati's palace was near the Barda hills. Krishna's palace was in Mula Dwaraka, possibly where the present-day Dwarakadhish temple, also known as Jagat Mandir, stands.

The Mahabharata associates Krishna with Dwaraka, calling him Dwarakadhish. It also mentions Krishna's palace as Varidurga—a fortress in water—as it was built on reclaimed land. The fortress was impregnable. The Harivamsa furnishes lot of details (II 58, 59) with regard to the invincibility of this fort:

Kalpiteyam maya bhoomi…iyam Dwaravati naama prithibhyam nirmitam maya.

(My loving creation is this land and the citadel called Dwaravati, (Dwaraka) dear to me and built by the architect Maya Danava.)

The most important of all the mansions was the hall of dharma—Sudharma, Krishna's favourite building, symbolising Yadava democracy.

KRISHNA AND SATYABHAMA

Satyabhama was the daughter of Satrajit, son of Nighna. Satrajit had been Krishna's inveterate critic. Being a trader and moneylender, he was unscrupulous and had his own private army of unruly elements whose job was to make people suspect Krishna's actions and intentions.

Satrajit had three sons—Bhangkara, Vatapati and Tapabvanta. Satyabhama was one of his daughters and his favourite. She had lost her mother at a tender

*Kutiyana and Satapura were situated near Madhupura. The Harivamsa mentions Krishna's ancestor was one Madhu and hence he was also called Madhava.

age and had been raised by a maid. Satyabhama was a buxom and sprightly young woman, strong-willed, bold and beautiful. There was a voluptuous grace in her movements and a flashing brilliance in her dark eyes. She was enamoured by Krishna and was convinced that only she could bring happiness to his life.

She befriended Subhadra, Krishna's younger sister, and they would share their secrets and find succour in each other's problems. Subhadra was Balarama's blood sister, having been born to Rohini.

Satrajit had become a shipping magnate after reluctantly migrating to Saurashtra. His large fleet of trading ships brought untold riches. He was one of the merchants who would trade in horses and maintained a stud farm. He had a private army of *atirathis* and *maharathis*. Satrajit was a great devotee of the Sun God, Surya.*

Satrajit had built a temple for Surya near Prabhasa Tirtha and would offer daily worship. At the crack of dawn, during one of his early morning prayers in the sea, he found a beautiful crystal—a large pinkish-orange diamond. It had washed ashore from the depths of the Indian Ocean. He considered this to be a divine gift, blessed by the Sun God in appreciation of his utmost devotion to Him, the giver of light and life. It was his nature to flaunt riches, so Satrajit hung this brilliant diamond around his neck to proclaim his superiority. The jewel was known as Syamantaka and Satrajit told everyone that it yielded eight loads of gold every day.

He even harboured a desire to become a Chakravarti one day by conducting the Ashwamedha yagna, the highest sacrificial ceremony as ordained in the Rig Veda, performed by a king to attain the imperial status of an emperor.

Satrajit's arrogance and pride were rattled when he heard a voice cautioning him that, though the Syamantaka gem was an inexhaustible source of good fortune to the virtuous bearer, it was deadly to the wicked and who led a life of unrighteousness. This disturbed Satrajit, but he overcame his fear by chanting the sacred Gayatri Mantra 108 times, invoking the eternal glory of the Sun God. He also gifted cows and gold to brahmanas and preceptors of his Yadava clan to secure some mental peace. But he could not stop worrying that, some day, Krishna would hand over the jewel to Ugrasena for the common good.

Along the seashore stood Satrajit's mansion, painted white, with a verandah

---

Suryanarayana—sun worship—was the primeval worship of Aryans when they arrived on the plains of a land, sun-soaked and rich in the flora and fauna.

around it. Its extensive grounds also had small houses and huts for dependants and servants, a large stable for horses and a larger one for cows. Satrajit had built a temple in the courtyard of his mansion to honour his guardian deity, Surya.

One day, Satyabhama, or Satyaa as she was lovingly called, was returning to her father's mansion by the back door that opened into the courtyard. Her heart was singing as Krishna was coming back to Dwaraka after a long absence. She looked at the waves lashing against the seashore and felt that they were dancing in happiness. She was excited as she would also participate, along with other maidens, in welcoming Krishna, Balarama and other heroes returning from Aryawartha.

On the appointed day, Satyaa, carrying gold-plated pots on her head, joined the welcome procession to honour the victorious Yadava heroes; the others had only copper pots on their heads. When the entire city was out on the streets to welcome the heroes, Satrajit had intentionally called for a four-day sacrificial session in the honour of the Sun God in his mansion and excused himself from the welcome party. He had also prohibited his sons and other members from attending the ceremonies. As Krishna passed by her, he stopped for a moment to greet Subhadra and Satyaa got her chance to see him up close. Satyaki even introduced her to him; her joy knew no bounds.

When Satyaa returned, she stealthily entered the room in which the pots and vessels for water were kept, and replaced the ones she had taken earlier. She could not understand why her father had avoided the reception.

She was distressed by her father's hostile attitude towards Krishna. Her father held even the venerable Ugrasena in contempt and made no secret of his attitude. Perhaps the older Yadava chiefs were jealous of her father's wealth. In order to mollify them, he had offered her hand to Yuyudhana Satyaki, son of the prominent Andhaka chief, Satyaka, who was the most respected chief after Ugrasena and Vasudeva. Satyaa was glad that Yuyudhana's father, Satyaka, rejected her father's offer. Her heart was set on Krishna.

She decided upon a campaign to win Krishna's heart, unaided by the members of her family. When Krishna accepted Yudhisthira's invitation from Hastinapura and prepared to go north with most of the *atirathi*s, she confided in Kritavarma, the son of her mother's sister and Krishna's great friend. Together they supplied horses to Krishna's contingent, taking them secretly from her father's extensive stud farms.

After she had saved Satyaki's life from her father's goons, the two had become very good friends. Satyaa shared with him, her feelings for Krishna and earned his promise to help her win him. As Subhadra's friend, she would also visit Rukmini's mansion. True to a woman's nature, Rukmini treated her with guarded and distant cordiality.

Meanwhile, Satrajit completed the sacrificial offerings to the Sun God and asked Satyaa and the other children present there to seek the blessings of the priests. Satyaa was nowhere to be found and he immediately understood the reason. He was furious.

'She has brought disgrace to our house. Bhangkara, go and fetch her; tell her I will not touch my lunch till she returns.'

At this point, Satyaa stealthily entered and stood with her eyes lowered and arms folded, the very picture of humility. Satrajit was very fond of his child and could not scold her. 'Satyaa, my darling child, I know you had gone to the reception of our Yadava heroes, but it is an insult to the house of Satrajit when we learn that you went to see that beggar, Satyaki.'

'No, father,' she replied. 'Subhadra pressed me to go with her.' This admission was not correct, but she felt she could not reveal the truth. Satrajit gently explained to his daughter:

> Satyaa, you can never understand how a man's world works. You are infatuated with someone who is a tool in his proud father's hand. Remember, when I offered your hand to Yuyudhana Satyaki, his father called me names. He called me a traitor to the Yadavas and portrayed me as a shameless wealth-monger who flaunts his wealth by showing off a white stone. You know Satyaa, this stone is the gift from Surya himself.

Satyaa interjected, 'Father, I heard that the possessor of the jewel has to be righteous and benevolent to get the benign grace of the Sun God or else it will invite harm and disaster for the owner.'

'Who says so?'

'Gargacharya, the preceptor of Yadavas.'

For a moment, Satrajit was speechless and stared at his daughter.

Satyaa lovingly cuddled her father's feet and timidly said, 'Father, as it is, we are very wealthy; your ships bring large crates of gold from far-off lands. Why do you not give this jewel to the king, as it would benefit the poor and needy Yadavas?'

Satrajit lost his temper when she dared to advise him regarding his prized possession. 'Who has tutored you to say all this? From today, I will restrict your wanderings. I should have gotten you married by now.'

'Yes father, but not to Satyaki. He has already rejected me once,' replied Satyaa.

Satrajit asked, 'Who do you want to marry then?'

'I shall tell you, when the time comes. I have decided to marry someone else and I shall succeed,' said Satyaa with firm determination.

Later in the day, she met Subhadra at the shrine of Mahadeva, their usual rendezvous point. A very ebullient Satyaa asked Subhadra to arrange a meeting with Satyaki immediately!

'Satyaki and Krishna will be very busy meeting the elders today,' said a stunned Subhadra. 'I heard, my brother is briefing the noble king, Ugrasena, and Vasudeva on Hastinapura. He briefly visited mother Devaki to pay his respects. You know, Krishna is yet to meet Vaidarbhi.' Subhadra teased Satyaa, 'Can you not wait for a day?' She then pinched Satyaa playfully.

'Subhadra, you are a fool if you think that the noble Satyaka would accept me as his son's wife. Am I that desperate to be after a man whose father insulted mine in the most derogatory terms?' replied Satyaa.

'Then why do you want to meet Satyaki?'

Satyaa became coy and said, 'Subhadra, I have selected my husband already and I am going to win him! Please help me.'

'But who is this man?' Subhadra became more curious and asked Satyaa. 'You seem to have an eye on my brother, Govinda, do you not?'

Satyaa parried a direct reply and remained mum. 'Satyaa, you are impossible!' Subhadra raised her voice a bit and said, 'I could see this morning when you met Govinda; I could see the emotions in your eyes, you cannot deceive me. Tell me the truth, do you want to marry him?' asked Subhadra.

'Subhadra,' Satyaa said in all brevity. 'You are my best friend and confidante. Will you not promise that you will help me marry the man of my choice?'

Subhadra moved over and sat on a stone platform holding her head in her right palm. 'Do you think that Vaidarbhi would allow my brother to marry you, Satrajiti? Your father considers Krishna his enemy!'

'I know the situation,' replied Satyaa in exasperation. 'I am Satrajit's daughter and I have no choice in the matter. My father hates Krishna, but

I have been in love with him from the time I saw him challenging Kamsa.' She started crying and became inconsolable.

'All right, all right,' said Subhadra, patting Satyaa on the back. 'Keep your secret to yourself and let us go to Kritavarma's house; Satyaki will be there.'

She whispered to Satyaa to go to the verandah where Satyaki was waiting for her.

Satyaki was glad to meet her and after exchanging a few pleasantries, he said:

> Satyabhama, I have kept my promise to you. Time and again, I tried to get him to be interested in you, but I have failed. All that he said at the procession was that he was disappointed looking at our womenfolk. They were bare, could afford no ornaments and were carrying copper pots, except you, who showed off your wealth with your gold-plated pots. When I told him you were Satrajit's daughter, Krishna, who usually keeps his poise, looked pained and muttered that Satrajit is a blot on the Yadavas, and the girl with the gold pots has no feeling for the plight of her Yadava sisters. I tried to mollify Krishna by saying that you were innocent and were raised by a Naga foster mother. I spoke in your favour and told him that you are a fine girl, though impudent at times, and that you are a friend of Subhadra.

Satyaa slapped her palm on her forehead and said, 'Oh Satyaki, I am ruined; Govinda is angry with me. I will drown myself in the sea near his mansion.' Satyaki reprimanded her, 'Satyaa, stop this drama and have patience. Govinda is upset because he feels that he has been the cause of the destitution of the Yadavas today! Let us help him to find a way out.'

Crestfallen, Satyaa returned to her room and started sobbing uncontrollably. Bhangkara heard her crying and came in to console her. 'Sister, you are living in a dream world. Even if everyone agrees to this marriage, father would not. Forget him, and marry Satyaki.'

'No, never,' replied Satyaa burying her head in the pillow. 'Krishna, help me please! I love you so dearly; please forgive me. I shall never wear any jewels till all my sisters in Dwaraka start wearing gold ornaments. This is my pledge.'

KRISHNA AT RUKMINI'S MANSION

At long last, Krishna found the time to meet Rukmini, who was waiting with an affectionate smile and carrying Pradyumna. 'Vaidarbhi, forgive me. I have been away for a very long time.'

'I am going to bathe you, Govinda. After that, I have kept aside some fresh butter just for you.' Krishna also visited the cowshed. He was, at heart, still a simple cowherd. The cows and calves started mooing, welcoming their best friend! He picked up some fresh grass and fed each one of the cows. Rukmini felt that her lord was at peace here and had forgotten the troubles of the past two years.

Once he had a chance to sit back, Krishna said to Rukmini:

> Princess, you look more beautiful without your ornaments. Gold and wealth seem to be the cause for so much *adharma* in this world. My world at Vrindavan was simple, where the *gopi*s wore no jewels, except ornaments made of beads carved out of wild seeds; how happy they were with the simple pleasures!

Krishna reflected on his childhood. 'Vaidarbhi, this morning in the welcome function, I noticed one maiden bedecked with ornaments and carrying gold-plated pots, the other women had no ornaments at all! It is all because of me that they have reached such a state of impoverishment.

'Lord, the golden doll would have been none other than Satyabhama, that impudent daughter of Satrajit,' replied Rukmini in one breath. 'She was to marry our Satyaki. His family is impoverished today. Noble Satyaka had to give twice his share to make up for the lapse of that proud Satrajit, who repudiated your request to help the five brothers in setting up their kingdom in Aryawartha,' replied Rukmini.

'Vaidarbhi, it is not just a kingdom, but will be the empire of dharma,' said Krishna.

RAJYA SABHA OF THE YADAVAS

The Rajya Sabha was convened by Ugrasena the next day. He had summoned the Rajya Sabha with the view to not only welcome the heroes, but also to hear first-hand accounts of their achievements in Aryawartha. Now that all the heroes were back, the king wanted to fix the date for the chariot race.

Under the leadership of Krishna, Balarama and Satyaki, the Yadavas had transformed themselves into a martial clan from an agrarian one. The ruling hierarchy of the Yadavas comprised heads of clans and *atirathi*s. These ranks were filled by men who attained the highest proficiency as chariot warriors and emerged as champions in horse races. An *atirathi* was the head of a self-sufficient battalion of *maharathi*s and *rathi*s, mostly recruited from a batch of promising youngsters.

The Yadavas specialised in breeding horses of the Kathiawad breed, which, apart from being a symbol of status, were indispensable in war. Their strength and vigour were maintained by frequent wrestling bouts and horse races in times of peace.

Trade and commerce with foreign lands and cities along the west coast of India was growing at an amazing pace, so was the opulence of the city. When Krishna and Balarama had gone to Aryawartha with fifteen chosen *atirathi*s and their respective battalions, two *atirathi*s had not accompanied them: Bhangkara and his friend, Shatadhanva, for obvious reasons, as they were under Satrajit's influence. Satrajit, despite his formidable wealth, had risen only to the rank of *maharathi* and could never attain the status of *atirathi*. He wanted to buy his way up, but all his efforts were in vain.

The Rajya Sabha in Dwaraka lacked the pomp and pageantry of Hastinapura. With the king were seated Vasudeva, Akrura, Yuyudhana Satyaka and Gargacharya. Krishna, Balarama and Satyaki were sitting on seats of prominence in the hall. They were the heroes of the day.

When Satrajit arrived with his sons, Bhangkara, Shatadhanva and Tapabvanta, they were received and seated according to their ranks, but their reception was cold. The magnificently bejewelled Satrajit felt slighted, but there were no sympathisers.

When the chamberlain announced the arrival of King Ugrasena and chief Vasudeva, all the chiefs, except Satrajit, stood up as a mark of respect and obedience to the king. As they settled down, King Ugrasena looked at the *atirathi*s who went to Aryawartha and said, 'My sons, let me welcome you back. I am proud of your achievements in Aryawartha. Let the Rajya Sabha know how you have fared and what you have achieved.'

Krishna requested his elder brother to speak. The formidable son of Vasudeva stood up and spoke:

> Respected elders, we have brought glory to the Yadavas of Saurashtra. First, we went to Pushkar and restored it to one *atirathi*, Chekitana, without even twanging our bows.
>
> Then we heard that the Pandavas and their mother Kunti had been burnt

> alive at the insistence of Duryodhana. The yaksha, who was engaged by Duryodhana for the gruesome act, confessed his guilt to Drupada, the king of Panchala. Our brother, Uddhava, traced the Pandavas to the land of the demons. It so happened that this adventure fetched him two wives, Naga *kanyas.* They are identical twins and Uddhava was at a loss to distinguish between them.

Balarama paused and had a hearty laugh and then continued:

> The most significant event that has happened so far, though, is that the five brothers have got married to the princess of Panchala. Today, Panchala is our ally, thanks to Krishna. Our brother, Bhima, also married a Rakshasi in the land of the demons, where he was made the king of Rakshasas, King Vrikodara. Bhima begot a son, who is named Ghatotkacha, and is the first claimant to the throne of Santanu.

Balarama regaled everyone with the rest of the details of their two-year adventure.

'But what did you do, other than enjoying your drink?' asked Satrajit, with a sneer.

Balarama looked at him with scorn and shouted, 'We have not been living ingloriously at Dwaraka, hiding behind our womenfolk; we challenged the God of Death every moment of our lives and have been busy building new citadels of dharma, instead of decorating ourselves with golden ornaments like the womenfolk.'

There was unanimous approval from the assembly and Bhangkara and Satadhanva, the two *atirathi*s who remained in Dwaraka, were embarrassed and asked Satrajit to keep silent.

Balarama continued:

> My young brother, who has not even completed forty years of his life on earth, dreams of a world of dharma where men and women, rich and poor, can live in harmony. We, the Yadavas, should be proud that we have also contributed to Govinda's dream kingdom. It is true that most of us are impoverished after we parted with part of our wealth. This is a small price we have paid to stabilise the noble Pandavas and to help them continue their journey on the path of dharma. We are kshatriyas and we have tried to fulfil our kshatra dharma.

Satrajit got up once again and said, 'I still do not understand why such lavish presents were given to the five brothers, to the ruin of the Yadavas? In my opinion, we need not be so generous to a kingdom so far away in Aryawartha.'

This time Krishna couldn't control his emotions and replied, 'It is the price that we have paid for being accepted as the architects of dharma in Aryawartha.'

'By doing so, you have crippled us. If Shalva invades us, we will be crushed and will have no place on earth to hide ourselves.'

Krishna replied, 'My dear sir, wealth is not an evil, if it is the product of virtue, properly earned and used. Not willing to part with one's wealth, for dharma, is evil.'

Satyaka, the veteran chief, stood up. Till this time he had been patient but felt that, now, he should definitely express his opinion: 'Krishna, I have learned by bitter experience that wealth and virtue never go together. Venerable Yadavas, I speak for all of us who left Mathura and came to Saurashtra with nothing, to escape Jarasandha's wrath. Thanks to Govinda, we are now a powerful and prosperous society and a power to reckon with in Aryawartha.' Satyaka paused and then, pointing at Satrajit, said:

> What would you call this man, who thinks himself equal to gods because of his vast possessions, not all acquired by virtuous ways? What would you call such a man who did not part with his share of wealth when Govinda sent a request to help establish a kingdom of truth and virtue?

There was a chorus from the assembly calling Satrajit an asura.

Krishna interceded at this stage and said with a charming smile, 'Noble chief, Satyaka, I understand your feelings and your loss, yet I beg to state that whatever wealth we gave to the five brothers is an investment in righteousness. Noble sir, we are now their partners in whatever they do to vindicate dharma.'

Satrajit was perturbed; his status amongst the Yadavas was threatened. 'What have we to do with the Pandavas? We have earned our wealth ourselves and we should enjoy it as we like.'

Krishna replied, with a trace of sternness in his voice:

> Noble Satrajit, wealth used to inflate one's importance or provide pleasure, is theft. I will now answer your earlier query about the resources in case Shalva invades Dwaraka. Shalva dare not attack as long as Balarama, Satyaki and I live and, if he does, we shall appropriate your wealth to save the Yadavas.

'Hear! Hear!' there were shouts of joy from the assembly.

Satrajit panicked and shouted insolently, 'I will not permit anyone to sit in judgement on my conduct. Krishna, we can discuss the issue at some later date.'

Krishna replied, 'What else have I been doing all the while, if not discussing it? But I understand that you do not want me to talk to you in public. I shall meet you tomorrow, at your mansion.'

The chamberlain pounded his standard on the platform and announced that it was the king's wish that the chariot races be held on the day of the full moon in the coming month.

THE SYAMANTAKA GEM

Satyabhama learnt what had happened at the Rajya Sabha from Kritavarma. She could feel that the rift between her father and the man she loved was increasing. Anxious, she sat with her cat, Uri, hoping for the best, when Krishna would visit her house.

Satrajit boasted about his performance, in the Rajya Sabha, to his family. His family was hopeful that the meeting would bring about an understanding between Satrajit and Satyaka.

On the day Krishna was to arrive, Satyaa dressed in white and waited in an anteroom for her Govinda. Her father and brother went to receive Krishna at the gate, though their welcome was very formal. Just then, Satyaa's cat jumped from her arms and ran to where Krishna was standing. It purred at Krishna's feet. This gave her the excuse to rush to Krishna's side. As she lifted Uri, Krishna looked at Satrajit and asked, 'Is this the young lady meant for Satyaki? He is a lucky fellow; she is beautiful, noble chief.'

Satrajit rolled his eyes and said, 'That proud old chief rejected my proposal. My Satyaa is a precious jewel meant for someone very special.'

Satrajit led Krishna to the rear of the verandah, which was his favourite place for meeting people. The haughty chief was wearing the Syamantaka jewel around his neck, as always.

Satyaa followed the proceedings through a chink in the door. Satrajit made a sweeping gesture with both his hands to boast of his vast possessions. He told Krishna with pride that he would be performing the Ashwamedha someday. A surprised Krishna asked, 'Are you aspiring to be a Chakravarti? Whose?'

'Such has been the mandate of Lord Surya,' replied Satrajit. 'I am rearing a couple of horses, which are consecrated and will be ready for Ashwamedha in a couple of years. They will lead me to power greater than that of a Chakravarti.'

Krishna smiled at Satrajit's foolishness and asked, 'That means you have to challenge the might of the Kurus, Panchala and Magadha. Can you face them, noble sir? Would the Yadavas lend support to your ambition?'

The chief replied:

> They have to. Vaasudeva, I want to ensure that the Yadava chiefs and I share a harmonious relationship. They are jealous of my wealth and influence in Dwaraka. You see, I have a large fleet of trading ships; some of them have two or more sails to make them move faster in the high seas. They are also envious of this jewel, Syamantaka, which is a gift from the Sun God. You know, Vaasudeva, the great god was pleased when I built a temple in his honour and chanted the Gayatri Mantra a million times. Look, how resplendent it is!

Krishna noticed the magnificent, scintillating diamond, roseate in colour, suspended by three gold chains from Satrajit's neck. Krishna, with his characteristic charm, said gently, 'Would it not be great of you to share your glory with the Yadava brothers, noble Satrajit? One of my reasons for meeting you was to talk about this jewel of yours.'

'I never give in; I shall never part with my wealth, never.'

'Suppose it is taken by force? It is a most unlikely contingency, of course! I know you are wise enough to avert such a situation,' said Krishna with a mischievous smile.

Satrajit now spoke in anguish:

> Why should I part with it? Vaasudeva, I welcomed you into my house today, even after you had threatened to take this jewel from me. How dare you take advantage of my hospitality? You may be a god to others, but not to me. In my opinion, you are an intelligent fraud; you brought disaster to the Yadavas.

Krishna said:

> Noble Satrajit, there is no need to lose your cool. May I ask why you ran away with your friends from Kamsa's Mathura? Kamsa had announced a price on your head, is it not? You could return to Mathura only after I killed Kamsa. Till we reached this land, you made your money in Mathura by lending at

> high costs—a terrible way to make a living as per our shastras. This jewel will bring disaster to you. You may be a devotee of the Sun God, but so am I. This jewel, if it is actually a gift from the Sun God as you say, should be put to use for the common benefit of mankind.

Satrajit said with a determined look, 'My possessions have been acquired by the grace of Lord Surya and I will not part with them.'

'Noble Satrajit, do you not ever think of anything, but yourself?' asked Krishna with a disarming smile.

'Why should I?' screamed Satrajit. 'I only think of my happiness; let others think of theirs.'

'Satrajit, you are a selfish coward. Please do not waste this life of yours. I am your well-wisher; it is still not too late to mend your ways. Your attachment to wealth will be your bane, I warn you.'

'Lord Surya gave me the Syamantaka to increase my prestige and my pleasure,' replied Satrajit in a rather low voice.

'I believe you, Satrajit. Such diamonds are washed ashore on our ocean beaches, but is it not a fraud to say that it gives you eight measures of gold every day? Is it not a lie? Gold cannot be made out of stones and diamonds,' said Krishna with a smile.

'What can you do if I refuse to part with it?' shouted Satrajit.

'I shall take that jewel from you before sunset tomorrow,' said Krishna and got up to leave the room.

Satrajit also got up and pulled Krishna's scarf and pushed him back into his seat. Satrajit wanted to throttle Krishna with his own scarf from behind; Krishna did not resist. Satyaa shrieked and rushed into the room. 'Father, what are you doing? You are choking Vaasudeva! Stop it at once!' She screamed and pulled her father away. In the scuffle, she lost balance and hit her head against the wall.

Krishna grew stern and said, 'Satrajit, you have invited your ruin.'

Krishna asked Bhangkara to look after his sister. 'Satyaa!' Krishna called her most endearingly and said, 'Thank you, young lady, for saving my life. It looks like you will have many opportunities to come to my help in future.'

After Krishna had gone, the whole family surrounded Satrajit and rebuked him for assaulting a guest of Krishna's stature.

A deep sense of remorse descended on the haughty Yadava; he had been indeed foolish to assault Krishna. The thought of Balarama sent a shiver down his spine; he sent for his younger brother, Prasenajit. Prasenajit was fun-loving and a good hunter. He had a hunting lodge in the forest, at the bottom of a cluster of limestone hills. It was rumoured that he had found the Syamantaka jewel by the seashore and Satrajit appropriated it.

'Prasena, when are you leaving for the forest to hunt?' asked Satrajit.

'One of these days, I would like to go for a wild boar hunt. This is their breeding season and they will be an easy prey,' he replied.

'Prasena, I want you to leave before sunrise tomorrow,' said Satrajit. 'You are fond of this jewel and I want you to hide it because Krishna wants to take it from me by force.' Prasenajit gladly agreed to hide it in a secret cave near the hunting lodge. 'Brother, I shall leave with my party tonight itself, when Dwaraka is asleep.'

Satrajit plotted to blame Krishna for the disappearance of Syamantaka, but he needed proof. Suddenly, he saw a shining object on the floor. It was part of Krishna's earring, which must have fallen down during the scuffle. This was the proof he needed.

While he was lost in thought, Satyaa came into the room in search of Uri. She noticed her father picking up something from the floor, but he would not show it to her.

'Father what happened to Syamantaka? Why are you not wearing it?' asked Satyaa. 'It is none of your concern, Satyaa. You did not want me to wear it, so I gave it to Prasenajit. Do not talk about the jewel to anyone, I warn you!' Satrajit was flustered, seeing that his daughter sensed something amiss.

'Satyaa,' he said to her endearingly, 'Krishna is very handsome. It seems a devil entered my head this morning and I regret my actions. I do not mind you choosing him for a husband,' he said, seemingly a changed man.

Satyaa laughed aloud. 'Father, you are already a changed man without the jewel! Of course, I love Govinda, but he may not be interested in me as a wife. I am a rich man's spoilt daughter and Govinda only likes simple girls who love him for what he is, a common cowherd.'

THE SCANDAL

Shortly after midnight, Prasenajit, accompanied by two armed guards, came on ponies to take leave of Satrajit. The shrewd Yadava whispered to Prasenajit, 'I shall see you in the cave on the next full moon night.'

Mugi, Satyaa's foster mother, saw the brothers whispering at such a late hour and casually mentioned it to Satyaa the next morning. Suddenly, she heard her father wailing and beating his chest, shouting, 'It is gone! The Syamantaka is stolen; a thief robbed it. I saw him running away.' Everyone gathered around him. 'Satyaa, you were a witness yesterday when Krishna vowed that he would take Syamantaka; and he did take it, like a common thief.'

'But, father,' interrupted Satyaa. 'I saw you giving Syamantaka to uncle Prasena, yesterday.'

'Yes, my brother was quite fond of the jewel and he wanted to wear it for a while, but he returned it in the evening. I had placed it in our puja room and slept,' said a wailing Satrajit. 'Oh god! I am ruined. What am I to do?'

Satyaa asked, 'How can you say it was Krishna who stole Syamantaka?'

'I saw him running and almost caught him from behind,' replied Satrajit.

'I have proof. In the scuffle, the thief dropped his earring.' Saying this, Satrajit showed the lower link of Krishna's earring.

It slowly dawned on Satyaa what her father was trying to insinuate. 'Father!' she screamed. 'You are a terrible crook. Krishna has not stolen Syamantaka and you will be sorry for your actions.'

'Who else can it be? I have proof. I shall go to the Yadava assembly and let them decide,' shouted Satrajit. 'I will seek justice from Ugrasena. Bhangkara, call for my chariot. Bring Satadhanva, Jayasena, Rudradaman and all our people as well. I need support to show my strength.'

Satrajit arrived at the palace fully armed with his *atirathi*s, Bhangkara and Shatadhanva; this was against the code of courtesy accorded to the king.

Brihadbala, who assisted the old king, announced Satrajit's arrival to Ugrasena. Satrajit barged in and without offering any salutations to the king shouted, 'My Syamantaka has been stolen by Krishna. I shall kill him if he does not return it immediately!'

'Noble Satrajit, take your seat,' said Ugrasena. 'What is the matter? You do not seem to be in control of your senses. You cannot kill Krishna or anyone else!'

'Noble king,' said the Yadava chief, still infuriated. 'Do you not remember that yesterday, Krishna threatened to take the jewel away from me? He has managed to steal it early this morning.'

'Can you prove that Krishna was the thief?' asked Ugrasena.

'Of course!' Satrajit replied, excited. 'He was running away and I could only see the thief's back. I tried to catch him and managed to get a hold of his waistband. In the scuffle, he escaped, but I found this link of an earring that Krishna had worn yesterday morning when he came to see me.' Satrajit handed the item to Ugrasena for inspection.

The king asked Brihadbala to summon Vasudeva, Yuyudhana Satyaka and Akrura immediately. In a short time, the three Yadava chiefs, along with Satyaki, arrived at the king's chamber. King Ugrasena explained the situation to them.

They advised that Krishna be called to court. Having heard Satrajit's tale, not everyone was convinced.

Satyaka spoke unsympathetically, 'Son of Nighna, I do not believe a word of what you say. Krishna would never stoop to steal your Syamantaka. Yesterday, we wanted to take it from you in the Rajya Sabha and he stopped us from doing so.'

'Son of Vrishni, you think I am lying about the whole issue. Are you accusing me of being a liar? Of course, I cannot expect anything else from you.'

Satyaka stood up and bellowed, 'Satrajit! I do not care what you think of me or what you propose to do with me, but I have known Krishna since he came to Mathura as a boy; he is the very embodiment of dharma and I cannot believe that he stole Syamantaka.'

'Noble king,' countered Satrajit. 'If that is the view of the elders, then allow me to deal with Krishna on my own terms. Bhangkara and Satadhanva, let us go and mobilise the chariots for a civil strife, a clash of arms, Yadava killing Yadava; that is what the elders desire.'

'Are you threatening us?' roared Satyaka.

Meanwhile, Brihadbala had reached Krishna's palace and informed him about the ruckus being raised by Satrajit. Krishna hurried to the palace and walked into the king's chamber. As soon as he entered, Satrajit shouted, 'Here comes the thief!'

'Thief! What have I stolen?' asked Krishna, amused.

'You stole my Syamantaka this morning from my puja room,' shouted Satrajit.

Krishna was unperturbed. 'You mean to say that, like a common thief, I stole your Syamantaka? You must be out of your senses! Why did you not catch me?'

'You were a hundred paces ahead, so I could not catch you.'

'How do you know it was me?'

'I guessed it was you.'

'If I was running away you could not have seen my face.'

'Who else would steal it? You threatened yesterday to take it from me before sunset today.'

'What time was it when you found that your jewel was missing?'

'Two *ghatika*s after midnight.'

'That means, it was still yesterday, whereas I had said that I will take the jewel from you before today's sunset.' replied Krishna. 'If I wanted, I could have snatched the jewel from your neck yesterday when you tried to choke me with my own scarf. You would have succeeded had your daughter, Satyaa, not interrupted you.'

Then he turned to the king and said, 'Noble sir, I request you to call Satyabhama; she will truthfully narrate what happened.'

Satrajit retorted, 'I call upon Lord Surya to bear witness that you, and you alone, stole Syamantaka.'

Krishna lost his temper. 'Satrajit, you are committing a sin by invoking Lord Surya regarding a crime that I know nothing of...this is perjury and our shastras condemn it!'

'It was you who stole the jewel and here is the earring you dropped when you were running away. I found it near the gate.'

Krishna glanced at the earring and said, 'Yes, it is mine. It must have fallen when I was at your house yesterday, possibly when you were trying to push me back on the bolster to strangle me with my own scarf.' 'That is a lie!' shouted Satrajit. Soon, Satyaki escorted Balarama and Uddhạva to the king's chamber.

Balarama was furious at the accusations. Krishna addressed the gathering:

> Noble king, elders and fellow Yadavas! I stand accused of being a common thief. I request my elder brother Balarama to allow me to vindicate this most serious accusation. The matter is between Satrajit and me, and I take a pledge in the presence of this august gathering that I will find the Syamantaka. If I fail to do so, I shall self-immolate before you, in this courtyard.

Krishna, still solemn in appearance, touched the feet of all the elders, embraced Balarama and asked their permission to allow him to redeem his name.

THE DISAPPEARANCE OF SATYAA AND SATYAKI

Bhangkara narrated the drama at court to his sister. 'Our father is a crook,' said a worried Satyaa. 'We are cowards to not stand up to him. I must help Govinda.'

She asked Mugi to deliver a message to Subhadra. 'Please tell Subhadra, in absolute confidence, that my father had given the jewel to Uncle Prasenajit for safekeeping.'

Mugi knew Uddhava's twin Naga wives, Kapila and Pingala, and she hoped they would help her reach out to Krishna. Satyaa went to Kritavarma's house and found Satyaki fretting and fuming. 'Satyaa, I am lucky that my father rejected Satrajit's offer and did not accept you as my wife; your father is a crook,' he chided.

Satyaa broke down in front of him. 'I have no part in my father's schemes. I know he has implicated Krishna and I am here to help Govinda recover Syamantaka with your help.' Satyaa told him what she knew of Satrajit's plan. Hearing this, Satyaki smiled at her: 'Satyaa, I am proud of you! Let us help Govinda in looking for the jewel.'

'Satyaki, I know where Uncle Prasenajit would have gone. It is a secret cave, deep in the jungle, where my father once took me when I was quite young. He worshipped the jewel in the cave and some wild creatures gave him a casket full of gold dust.'

Satyaki was hopeful of redeeming Krishna's honour. 'Meet me at midnight outside your house. Dress as a maid and take off these noisy jewels that cover your head.'

Meanwhile, Subhadra had passed on Satyaa's message to Krishna, who was happy with what he heard.

The next morning, Dwaraka woke up to the news that Satyaki had eloped with Satyaa. It was a terrible blow to both their fathers. Satrajit felt humiliated by the turn of events. There were rumours that they would marry according to the Gandharva way. On the other hand, Yuyudhana Satyaka's pride was hurt by his son's betrayal.

Rukmini got up, as usual, before dawn and was taken aback to find her husband's bed empty. It was unlike him; he would offer prayers at the Brahma Muhuruta* every day. Could he have gone to find Syamantaka? He had left behind his diadem, *chakra*, sword and even his *pitambar*.

'Govinda has been kidnapped by Satrajit!' said a worried Rukmini, running to Balarama.

---

* 3:30 am. As per Hindus beliefs, Lord Brahma created the world at this hour.

'Do not worry, Vaidarbhi. I will bring him back,' assured Balarama. People were surprised to see Balarama awake so early in the morning and on his way to Satrajit's mansion. Satrajit ran out with two of his sons, Vatapati and Bhangkara, and was shocked to see Balarama at his door, raging with fury. 'Where have you hidden Krishna?' demanded Balarama in a threatening voice.

'What do you mean?' asked a puzzled Satrajit.

'You had him kidnapped. Produce him, here and now, or I will set fire to your mansion, burn down your ships and appropriate your wealth for the citizens of Dwaraka,' roared Balarama.

Satrajit kneeled and started wailing:

> I am ruined. My life is done for. My daughter ran away, my jewel Syamantaka is missing, I do not know where my brother is for the past two days and now you threaten to burn down all that belong to me. I swear to you, I have no knowledge of the whereabouts of Krishna.

'Satrajit,' shouted Balarama. 'If what you say is true, then come with me to the noble king and present your case.'

Suddenly, Uddhava made his way through the crowd standing outside and whispered something to Balarama. Balarama burst into laughter when Uddhava informed him that, according to Vasudeva, Krishna had left of his own accord, after changing into a hunter's dress. Balarama chuckled to himself and enjoyed the chaos he had created.

Just then, a guard came rushing towards them, his hair dishevelled, feet bleeding, body bruised and eyes wild. He prostrated himself at Satrajit's feet. 'Lord, lord! Prasenajit has departed for the abode of gods,' he said and broke into sobs.

'What?' Satrajit collapsed.

'Lord, a…lion killed him,' continued the guard, still sobbing. 'I saw the lion jump on him with a frightful roar. The animal grabbed him from the pony and dragged him into the bushes. My pony, too, panicked, threw me on the ground and ran for its life and I ran for mine.'

Satrajit started wailing like a child. Balarama was enjoying the situation and he looked at Bhangkara and said, 'I am leaving now. Ask your father to come to the noble king as soon as he recovers. Do not make me come and fetch him myself.' Smiling to himself, he left Satrajit's mansion.

THE HUNTER

The strange happenings of the last three days were forming a pattern in Krishna's mind. The accusations made by Satrajit had disturbed him. That night, Krishna had gone into the kitchen and filled a small bag with a few *baati*s—dry, crisp bread, sweets and a small water jug made out of the shell of a gourd. He then left his mansion quietly in the night. As soon as he came out of the mansion, he heard footsteps and knew it was his bodyguard, Vainateya, the Garuda. Krishna whispered something into his ears and the Garuda vanished like a ghost into the jungle to scout ahead of Krishna.

He did not believe that the disappearance of Satyaki and Satyaa was a lovers' escapade. Satyaki had kept no secrets from him. Krishna was also aware that Satyaa wanted to marry him, not Satyaki. The only possible explanation of their simultaneous disappearance was that Satyaa knew where her father had hidden the jewel in a secret cave. The more Krishna thought about it, the more he was convinced that Satyaa had taken this suicidal step to find Syamantaka and save his honour. That was, indeed, the kshatra dharma, the code of heroic righteousness for a proud kshatriya girl!

Krishna looked up into the sky; the twilight of the dawn could be seen through the clouds. He had to find the cave before it was too late. As dawn broke, he came across some hunting lodges built by the Yadava chiefs, at the entrance to the dense forest surrounding Mount Ujjayanta.

A little further, Krishna came across three paths going up to the mountain. As the sun rose, the whole forest was tinted gold. He found a mountain spring and refreshed himself by sprinkling cold water on his face and had something to eat. Vainateya Garuda arrived after searching the dense jungle. He looked excited and told Krishna that he found vultures scavenging a human body and a dead lion nearby. He narrated that he had seen a young woman's body in a shallow gorge. Krishna wished to be taken there immediately. Vainateya carried him on his back and they set off.

Vainateya, with his swift leaps, brought Krishna into an opening in the forest where he had seen the skeleton of a horse and a gruesome carcass of a man. The vultures had made a meal out of him. Krishna found a girdle of gold, bearing the image of the Sun God. Krishna realised that this must have been Prasenajit. He then asked Vainateya to take him to the girl.

The Garuda guided Krishna to a thicket. With a scythe, Krishna made his way through the undergrowth into a little opening where he found the carcass of a lion on which the vultures were feeding. The stench was terrible. Garuda hit the vultures with his spear and scattered them.

Krishna found a piece of Prasenajit's scarf clinging to one of the lion's paws. Sticking to the nail of another paw was a piece of black hairy skin, probably that of a bear. All around, there were traces of a grim struggle between the lion and one or two powerful bears.

Krishna searched closely for the jewel, but found no trace of it. Garuda, with his acute vision, drew Krishna's attention to a piece of gold chain that was stuck in the lion's teeth. The jewel was not on it. As they were surveying the gruesome scene, they heard the meowing of a cat. Krishna recognised Uri, Satyaa's cat, and followed it. The cat led him to a ridge and meowed persistently.

Krishna looked down and found Satyaa lying on the ground. His heart missed a beat; was she dead? Immediately, he made a path for himself, climbed down the cliff and ran to where the body lay. A few strips of cloth, which had once been part of her skirt, remained attached to the string that fastened it. She was bruised all over and thorns had torn her skin in places. Her face was covered with streaks of dried blood that had flowed from a wound on her forehead. Krishna took her in his arms and checked to see if she was breathing; she was alive.

Vainateya brought some water from a nearby stream and placed it near Krishna. Krishna tore a piece of cloth from his headdress and bound the wound. With the rest of the cloth, he covered her modesty. He asked Vainateya to get some healing herbs to clean and dress the wounds.

Taking a piece of cloth, he started cleaning the wounds on her head tenderly. Satyaa stirred and it assured Krishna that she was regaining consciousness. He then crushed some herbal leaves and applied its juice on the wounds. The burning sensation of the leaves further stimulated Satyaa's movements. Krishna dripped a few drops of water on her lips.

Tenderness surged in his heart. This young maiden, brought up in luxury, had set her heart on winning him. She had risked her life only to vindicate his innocence. It also crossed his mind that, after the rumours surrounding her elopement with Satyaki had spread in the city, no family would accept her as a bride. Krishna carried her to the stream and waited for her to regain consciousness.

Satyaa came around bit by bit. Her body was aching and her head felt heavy as a stone. She could feel someone tending to her wounds and felt the warmth of a fire and a welcome smell of something being baked; she realised she was hungry!

She opened her eyes slowly and, realising who the man beside her was, started crying. Krishna consoled her and offered her some fruits and food that he had packed from his home. Once Krishna was satisfied that there was no immediate danger to Satyaa's life, he decided to get her out of the forest and into the cave they had come to seek, which was on a small hill before them. Vainateya found a place they could shift to, and cleared the path, which was full of thorny shrubs.

Krishna made her stand on her unhurt foot and walked with his arms around her shoulders. Satyaa went along, ecstatic at being so close to her beloved. When the mouth of the cave was in sight, the trio was delighted. A large boulder partially covered the mouth of the cave and, as the rays of the setting sun fell directly on it, it seemed as if it was the veritable house of the Sun God.

The cave had a variety of black granite with incrustations—this kind of granite has myriad micaceous grains that are embedded during its formation. A lateral reflection of the sun would emit a golden glow as if it was a wall made of gold; this was the plausible answer to Satrajit's cave of gold!

The cave was deep and there was a draft of cold air coming from deep inside.

'Lord!' Vainateya addressed Krishna. 'Please take the lady inside and wait for me. I shall make a fire so that she can be kept warm and then I will go and get some fruits.' Soon, the Garuda returned with some fruits and a large quantity of green leaves and set up two beds. Krishna gently lifted Satyaa on to one of the beds.

'Lord, I take leave of you now. I shall return before dawn,' the Garuda said and left.

Satyaa sat on her bed and sobbed uncontrollably. 'Please forgive me, Govinda. I am embarrassed at what my wily father did to you and, despite that, you put yourself through such inconveniences to save me.'

'Satyaa, you risked your life for me and that is proof enough of your faith in me. Now tell me, if this is the sacred cave and where is Satyaki?'

Satyaa replied:

> Yes. Once when I was a child, my father brought me here. The cave left such

> a vivid impression on me that I used to dream of it sometimes. I am sure that father performed his penances here to win the favour of the Sun God. Satyaki has been abducted by the bear people; I hid myself in a thicket. There was a violent fight between a lion and a fearsome bear. I also saw a man wearing bearskin who had a bear head as his crown. I almost fainted; I ran, but slipped and fell into the gorge below. I do not remember anything further, till the time you revived me.

'Poor Satyaki! It is my fault. I hope those beasts have not killed him already. I am afraid we cannot go further till the sprain on your foot has healed. If you permit me, I shall foment your sprain with a few more warm leaves.'

She started crying. 'Govinda, you are a God and I let you touch my feet; I am sinning.'

'Relax, Satyaa, I am only a cowherd, so you are free of sin. We must rest tonight because we will have to look for Satyaki tomorrow and also find who has the jewel.'

Satyaa, still recovering, fell asleep instantly. Some faint sunlight filtered into the cave through fissures and Krishna noticed an altar in one corner, with grains of gold. Krishna moved to the mouth of the cave to look at the rock. It had a carving of Surya, riding his chariot drawn by five horses, done with considerable skill. Perhaps Satrajit's claim, that Syamantaka was a gift from the Sun God for his ardent devotion, was true!

Krishna began to explore the cave and found that one end of the floor sloped down a couple of cubits to the mouth of a tunnel. Knife in hand, he entered and stepped into ankle-deep water. The narrow, winding tunnel was evidently the bed of a stream that flowed though the cave. He saw light coming through a tunnel at a higher level and realised that this was the source of the draft he had felt earlier. The upper cave shrank into a steep passage, possibly connecting to the upper plateau in this mountainous country.

It is possible that Satyaki was taken through this passage. Krishna returned to his bed and slept, mindful of the long day ahead of him. He rose before sunrise and saw the Garuda guarding the cave. Vainateya said in a low tone:

> Lord, above this cave, there is a plateau surrounded by several cliffs with caves. This is bear land. Sloth bears are very fond of ants. I have noticed the bear people, humans covered with bearskins. Women were scantily clad, long hair covering their bosoms. There was an altar with a fire pit, smoke

coming out of it; it had an unbearable stench of burnt flesh. The plateau leads to a high mountain and I heard some rumbling, perhaps that of a wild animal and, as if in response, there were some lions roaring once in a while. There was no sign of Satyaki, though.

Krishna bathed in the subterranean pool and then woke up Satyaa. Her ankle had healed completely. Suddenly, Satyaa screamed in fright, 'A ghost! A ghost!' and clutched Krishna tightly.

The Garuda informed Krishna that he had seen a strange-looking human girl flying from one treetop to another, playing some musical instrument. Suddenly, Krishna heard a melody from a wind instrument. Krishna pulled his *pillanagrovi*, flute, from his waistband and acknowledged the bird call. He got a reply; Krishna reciprocated.

Krishna asked Satyaa to follow him, and the bird-girl led them through the upper reaches of the cave into the plateau of the bear land. Suddenly, they were surrounded by strange creatures conversing in their own tongue. They took the intruders to their chief.

'Who are you?' asked one of them in the language of Aryans. Krishna introduced himself.

Satyaa was shivering with fright. Krishna whispered to her, 'Steady yourself, Satyaa. The real danger is now before us; stand behind me and do not expose yourself, whatever happens.'

As these creatures, resembling bears, came closer, they saw that one of them was actually a bear, lumbering on four feet. However, its companion, clothed in bearskin, which was kept in place by a foxskin tied over his loins, was human. On his head, he had a bear head, giving the frightful impression of having two faces. This was the chief of the bear world. He had a massive chest, a gaunt face with a stub nose, his arms were long and his hands were big and powerful. His grey beard almost came down to his waist. He walked as clumsily as a bear. He had a sling over one shoulder and a stone hatchet in his hand. Satyaa pointed out to Krishna that those were the two bears that had kidnapped Satyaki.

'Who is she?' asked the chief. Upon knowing her name and being informed that she was the daughter of a Yadava chief, the bear chief said, 'She is beautiful. I have a daughter too, Rohini; I call her the bird-girl. Ever since she lost her mother, Rohini lives on the trees, skipping from one branch to the other.

She mimics bird calls with her musical instrument. I think Rohini, in fact, speaks to the birds and squirrels. Is Satrajit with you?'

Krishna told him he was not. The bear chief then said:

> Satrajit cheated me. It has been two full moons since he has turned up. Satrajit brings Syamantaka and, together, we worship the Sun God in the cave. In return, I give him bushelfuls of gold dust, panned by my people, from the riverbed. I am known as Jambavan.
>
> Our race got trapped in this plateau many years ago while running from the wrath of King Kartaviryarjuna of Mahishmati. Rishi Jamadagni's son, Parashurama, was giving the king a difficult time and, ultimately, killed him. The whole country was in chaos. My father, the senior Jambavan, fleeing from the kingdom of Mahishmati, moved towards the west and we ended up in this world of wild bear men. In the last two generations, we have all become bear men and bear women. Our ways are wild and gruesome.
>
> I had one Aryan girl as one of my wives; Rohini's mother, who is now dead, was of Aryan descent. She never liked this bear world and when our daughter was born, she withdrew herself to live among the birds on the trees and, thus, Rohini had become a bird-girl. I was chosen as the bear king and had to marry a bear woman. These wild people have a witch doctor who is also a priest; he is very cruel and invokes their black god every full moon night, and takes a new wife on that night from among the bear women. Rohini has recently come of age, but has somehow managed to escape this ritual, but for how long I do not know. Rohini is very dear to me, a reminder of the civilised life into which I was born and into which I do want to escape someday, but my bear wife hates her.

Jambavan looked rather sad and crestfallen.

'How did you come to know of Satrajit?' asked Krishna.

> Satrajit used to come to the forest to hunt; he has a hunting lodge on the other side of this mountain. He would bring his Syamantaka jewel along with him. One day, he noticed a golden glow on the cliff near the mouth of the cave.
>
> The cave is our only line of communication with the forest, where rich wildlife is available. Our hunters hunt wild boar, deer and rabbits for feasting. This is the main source of our food in addition to edible roots and fruits.

Satrajit used to worship at this cave, wearing his jewel, sometimes for days, with great devotion. He had promised to get my daughter married to his son, once she came of age. Satrajit discovered that the stream in the cave washes gold dust from the mountain caves and asked me to collect the gold and offer it to the Sun God every full moon day, when he would come for worship. I have been doing this for a number of years. As time passed, I found that Satrajit became very greedy and demanded more gold. To meet his demands and for the sake of Rohini's future, I had to deploy more bear people to pan for the gold. Of late, they are reluctant and weary of panning for gold in the riverbed, under the hot sun.

Ever since I demanded that Satrajit take Rohini as a bride for his son, he stopped visiting the cave. Three days ago, when our hunting party went into the forest, we saw a lion feasting on a human; I noticed a gold chain, with the Syamantaka jewel, entangled in its forepaw. The powerful bear accompanying me then pounced on the lion and after a bitter fight, killed the animal, and I seized the jewel from its paw. At that moment, I saw a man and a woman coming up the mountain path, leading to our secret cave. We kidnapped the man, but the woman ran in panic and fell from the cliff. We left the woman for dead and took the man with us. He is our captive and Satrajit's Syamantaka jewel is with me. I have no use for it, but I will need it to redeem my Rohini from this hell.

'We came on a friendly visit to the king of bears, O noble Jambavan,' replied Krishna. 'As a token of our friendship, I offer you my arms.' Jambavan received the weapons with a smile on his face and handed them over to one of the bear men who stood by his side.

Krishna looked around and surveyed the plateau. It had about forty caves where bears roamed fearlessly. The plateau was a world by itself; on two sides, it was walled in by high peaks and on the third side, there was a sheer drop into the valley. The only access to it from the outer world was through the cave.

As they reached the centre of the plateau, they found gruesome-looking people seated around a community altar with a fire burning inside. The elders were draped in bearskins like Jambavan, the young and the middle-aged wore only a foxskin around their loins. All the women wore their hair long to cover their bodies, besides a foxskin tied over their loins. The children ran about naked, racing with bear cubs.

Pigs, foxes, rabbits and wild roots were being roasted on the fire and there was a loud chatter. They all fell silent as Jambavan raised his arms.

Krishna and Satyaa were both filled with joy at finding Satyaki seated near the altar. Krishna, by a meaningful glance, conveyed to him that they should not recognise each other.

Jambavan took them to a young man. He was short, but powerfully built, had a black beard and wore a heavy garland of bear's teeth. The tails of two bears were attached to his headgear, his eyelids were painted red and he had a small hand drum suspended from his shoulder, indicating that he commanded supreme sacerdotal authority over the community.

This was the witch doctor/holy man, Samba. Jambavan paid his respects by crossing his arms and slapping his chest in salutation. In reply, Samba grunted and, by way of blessing, sniffed the king's neck and patted his cheeks with two of his fingers. He recounted the story of the two strangers; the holy man was not happy.

Krishna thought it would be prudent to respect the holy man and touched his feet as a gesture of reverence. Samba forced a smile and sniffed Krishna's neck. When he tried to do the same to Satyaa, she stepped back in fright. The holy man's face turned harsh.

Jambavan invited Krishna to sit near him and Satyaa sat next to Krishna. The holy man grunted and a stout middle-aged woman took Satyaa to be seated next to her. The holy man stared intensely at Satyaa. When Satyaa was offered some roast meat, her displeasure at eating it angered the hosts. Krishna cautioned her that she should not offend these people and instead pretend to enjoy their feast. Then, from nowhere, Satyaa's cat meowed and jumped into her lap. The wild people tried to grab it as it would make a delicious meal, but Satyaa would not let it go. Samba asked his people to leave them alone for the moment.

Rohini, from behind the foliage of a nearby tree, began making bird calls. Krishna responded by playing on his flute. But Samba interrupted their duet and blamed Rohini for exposing their hideout. Then he turned towards Satyaa, who, he had been informed, was Satrajit's daughter, and said, he wanted to take her as his next bride.

'That might be difficult,' replied Jambavan. 'Her companion looks powerful and he will not allow it.' The holy man grunted his disapproval.

Rohini approached the holy man and saluted him by folding her hands over her chest and lowering her head. The holy man sniffed her neck and tapped her cheek with two of his fingers. Then she flung herself into the arms of her father who also sniffed her neck affectionately. The vivacious girl came and sat next to Satyaa and started speaking in the language of Aryans, though not so fluently.

The bear people went on with their feast and once they were all fed, Samba stood up and walked to the statue of their black god—an idol of a dragon-like animal carved out of black granite. The sight of this god, who instilled fear in his people, repulsed Krishna and he decided to put an end to this captive society. But for now, he watched the ritual.

Samba played the hand drum and performed a ritual dance. Then he shouted, 'Tonight, the Moon Bride will come to your bed, O ever mighty! I am your servant, bless me to take the bride on your behalf.' He then hurried towards the forest, leaving his bearskin, mask and hand drum on his seat. The young and the middle-aged women ran after him, shouting with joy. Then, all the bear men, except Jambavan and other old men, also ran into the forest. Krishna was told that they would have an orgy in the forest.

When the full moon had risen, Samba came back, caught hold of Satyaa's hand and began to pull her towards the forest. Horrified by his touch, Satyaa began to scream. Krishna pushed back the holy man's hand to stop him from dragging Satyaa. He was taken by surprise and lost his balance. Emitting a growl, the holy man rushed at Krishna in anger and, with all his muscular strength, threw both his arms around him, trying to break his ribs like a murderous bear.

Feeling choked, Krishna gave a sudden jerk and played the death trick with which he had finished Chanura a long time ago. Despite Samba's arms pressing down hard on his ribs, Krishna reached out to grasp his hair and pulled his head down. Then, with the edge of his right palm, he dealt a swift blow to the holy man's neck, breaking it instantly. The body of Samba slumped at Krishna's feet.

Not believing what they saw, the bear people stood transfixed, stunned and horrified; then they let out a fearful howl. Entrusting Satyaa to Satyaki's care, Krishna went to deal with the situation.

Jambavan walked up to the dead body of Samba and looked at Krishna in awe. He had never had the courage to fight the oppressive and brutal Samba who had his dissenters half-burnt at the community altar and then fed to the bears.

Krishna scanned the mountain peak for Vainateya, who was watching over the happenings on the plateau. The Garuda was to intercept and kill by an arrow, if Krishna's safety was threatened. Jambavan decided to take charge of the situation before Samba's followers let the bears loose on Krishna.

He tried invoking the black god by playing the holy man's hand drum and took a step or two of the ritual dance. All the bear people immediately bent their heads and crossed their hands on their chests. He then commanded five of his bear men to escort Krishna, Satyaa and Satyaki to an empty cave. Once there, the three of them sat down close to one another for the first time since they had left the city.

Krishna asked Satyaki, 'Did they try to kill you?'

'No. But the bear king had some motive in kidnapping me and, now, death faces all of us. They might hand us over to the bears or give us as an offering to their black god.'

'I think Jambavan is our friend, I do not think he wants to kill us so soon. The Garuda is also guarding us from the mountaintop. Do not worry, sleep now; we will have a busy day again, tomorrow.'

When dawn broke, Krishna was awakened by Rohini's music. When the sun rose, the guards rolled away the stone they had placed at the mouth of the cave and took them to a stream to get refreshed. When they had returned to their cave, the guards brought food for them, some wild roots and fruits.

At midday, Satyaki was summoned by Jambavan and Krishna cautioned him again to be calm and not reveal their acquaintance.

Later in the day, Krishna and Satyaa were also taken to meet Jambavan who sat with authority on a stone seat in front of his cave. The hand drum and two bear tails, which were the insignia of a holy man's sacerdotal authority, lay in front of him. Krishna and Satyaa folded their hands and touched Jambavan's feet in salutation. Jambavan asked them to sit near Satyaki, which they did.

'Son of Vasudeva,' the king addressed Krishna, and then spoke in the language of Aryans, 'do you know you committed a great sacrilege by killing Samba, our holy man?'

'Your holy man attempted to force an unwilling woman to be his bride and when I objected, he tried to kill me and, in self-defence, I had to hit him, which caused his death,' explained Krishna.

'The bear elders, as per their tradition, have elected you to now be the holy man and, also, to marry Rohini,' Jambavan proclaimed. Krishna refused to accept this dictate.

'All of you will be offered to the ever-mighty black god, here and now, if you refuse,' Jambavan said, raising his voice in authority.

Then, out of the corner of his mouth, Jambavan whispered to Krishna that he should accept this proposal and that he will try to save the three of them. Krishna asked for some time to think, so the bear king gave him time till next day afternoon. They were escorted back to the cave.

The next day, the three strangers were brought to the assembly of bear people. Jambavan asked again if Krishna had decided to accept the proposal. But the rest of the clan did not wait for his response.

Two elders brought the bear drum and the holy man's headgear, with the two bear tails fastened, was placed it on Krishna's head. There was jubilation in the crowd.

'Son of Vasudeva, now you have to marry Rohini,' commanded Jambavan, but Krishna refused. 'You have no other choice,' said the king and called the girl who was decked in flowers. She was carrying a crown made of flowers, in her hand, to put on Krishna's head. Krishna lifted his hand, indicating his unwillingness to go through the ceremony. Rohini started sobbing and was about to throw herself into the fire pit near the altar. Krishna, being ever alert, averted her attempt at self-immolation.

'This is sacrilege; I cannot save you now. Please marry Rohini or she will be killed by these cruel people. I shall help you escape with my daughter.'

Then, for the benefit of the people, he pretended to be in full command and asked for his daughter to be brought back. Rohini crowned Krishna with the floral crown, sobbing uncontrollably. Krishna, very gently, put his hand on her head and affectionately hugged the child in her. Satyaa, too, was inconsolable at this coup de grâce delivered by a stranger.

The couple was taken to their nuptial cave, Satyaa and Satyaki were taken to theirs. Krishna spoke gently to Rohini, 'Please listen, you need not accept me as your husband when we go to our land. I shall take you to my mother who shall also be your mother. Now, sleep with no fear, everything will be alright.'

A few *ghatika*s after midnight, Krishna heard some movement at the mouth of their cave. Jambavan called out his name and said:

> Please leave, right now, with Rohini and your friends. The bear elders insisted we close the cave, so there is no escape. However, there is a bear trail that takes you to the mountaintop—the house of the black god. If he allows you, you can escape into your world by the valley beyond. Take your weapons.
>
> Jambavan handed over Krishna's scythe, knife, bow and arrows.

Krishna smiled and asked, 'What about Syamantaka? If I do not return it to Satrajit, I will have to self-immolate myself as I have pledged. I am sure you would not wish your darling daughter to become a widow so soon.'

Overwhelmed with emotion, Jambavan handed over Syamantaka, saying, 'This stone has no value for me. My Rohini, the darling of my heart, will be leaving me forever. Now, call your friends and make a move. The bear people are drunk and will not come out of it till late morning. Take the trail along the cliff and vanish.'

They went to Satyaa and Satyaki's cave and woke them up. Satyaki got back his arms as well. The party hit the bear trail and, by morning, they had put quite a distance between them and the world of bears.

With great effort, they reached the summit of a rugged volcanic mountain—a basaltic plateau with scant vegetation. A wild growl alerted them and, from a distance, Krishna noticed the Garuda, his faithful guardian, guarding him from a vantage point. The growl emanated from a massive dragon-like reptile* that had its forked tongue out, sensing prey nearby. As it crawled, it left behind a trail of slimy liquid—this was the black god feared by the bear people. The Garuda cautioned them not to go near the beast or touch the slimy fluid of its underbelly. The beast grew aggressive and was about to pounce on Krishna's party when Garuda threw his copper-tipped spear; it pierced the beast's mouth and came out of its head. The beast instinctively leaped and, somersaulting, fell down the steep cliff into the valley of the bear world.

Twenty-eight sunrises had gone by since the day the trio had left Dwaraka. When Krishna reached the city, he walked into Devaki's mansion, prostrated at her feet and presented Rohini to her. 'Mother, she is an innocent girl from a strange world. Look after her,' said Krishna.

---

*We now know them as Komodo Dragons.

Vasudeva heard of his son's arrival and rushed to meet him at Devaki's chambers. 'Bless you, my son. I knew you would return with glory.'

'Father, please take me to the king,' requested Krishna. 'Satrajit's daughter and Satyaki are at Kritavarma's mansion. The Syamantaka is with Satyaa.' Krishna reached Ugrasena's palace along with Satyaa and the jewel. Krishna, Satyaa and Satyaki prostrated before the king, and Satyaa handed over the jewel to Ugrasena. 'Vaasudeva,' the king tenderly addressed Krishna, 'I never doubted your integrity. Where did you find Satyaa and Satyaki?'

'Lord, she is the one who found the jewel along with Satyaki, and they risked their lives trying to retrieve it. I am grateful to them,' replied Krishna.

Kritavarma told the king that Satrajit has disowned his daughter and has taken a pledge to never see her face again. Ugrasena called his minister and issued a command to bring Satrajit forthwith. He also asked for Satyaa to be produced before him. Satyaa's face flushed with fear, uncertain of her fate.

Ugrasena smiled and, calling Satyaa nearer, blessed her by keeping his right palm over her head and said, 'Heroine of Dwaraka, may you soon belong to the hero of your choice.'

Satyaa looked embarrassed. The king continued, 'That hero would be your Govinda! My dear girl, I have been told about your love for him and you have proved yourself worthy of this match.' Satyaa was speechless.

Meanwhile, Satrajit arrived, frowning and fuming, and stood before the assembly. He did not bother to pay his respects to Ugrasena and arrogantly asked why he had been called.

'Satrajit!' Ugrasena said sternly. 'You are charged with perjury. You wanted to hide Syamantaka and blamed Krishna for stealing it; this is a serious offence. However, we are pardoning you this time.' Then he panned all over the assembly hall and said, 'Citizens of Dwaraka, the Syamantaka jewel was found and now, I intend to restore it to Satrajit. Krishna Vaasudeva had not stolen it; Satrajit wanted to implicate Krishna. I am glad the honour of our hero is vindicated.'

When the king tried to hand over the jewel, Satrajit refused to take it, and arrogantly replied, 'Keep it! It no longer belongs to me and neither does Satyaa. She has brought disgrace to my family.'

'The jewel should be in the king's treasury; give it to noble Akrura', was the verdict of the people. They also deemed it best that Ugrasena himself should become Satyaa's godfather and marry her off to Krishna.

Krishna whispered to the king, 'Noble sir, I have yet to meet Vaidarbhi. I cannot take another wife without her consent.' The king called for his chariot and Krishna was taken to his mansion.

With a sweet smile, Vaidarbhi ceremonially welcomed Krishna. As he alighted from the chariot, Rukmini was amused to see Krishna holding a stick, which he had picked from the king's chariot. He had wound his scarf into a turban, which used to be his attire at Vrindavan. Rukmini remembered seeing her Krishna in this attire for the first time in the streets of Mathura a long time ago—a cowherd.

Krishna freshened himself and asked for his baby son. Then he sat down with Rukmini and recounted the events of the month gone by. Before he could tell her about Satyaa, Subhadra came bursting into the room and announced it for all to hear.

Rukmini was not surprised and kept her cool. 'Subhadra, you mean Satrajiti is going to be my co-wife?'

'*Bhabhi*, Satyaa was disowned by her father. She is now the foster daughter of the king. Satrajit also refused to take back the Syamantaka jewel; surprising, is it not!' said Subhadra.

'Satyaa is a very simple girl, credulous and pampered, being a motherless child. Her stepmother, Mugi, reveals that she is a very honest girl, but strong-willed,' Krishna turned to Rukmini, smiling:

> Vaidarbhi, I have never taken the lead in these matters. Do you not know that I rejected Drupada's daughter outright? Satyaa is too young and pampered, but staked her life for my honour. Vaidarbhi, what do you want me to do? Give me a solution. I find myself at a loss to carry such extra baggage in life.

Rukmini, the proud princess, had a quick repartee. 'You mean your son and I are a load and a drag? I have had enough of your sermons on dharma,' and she walked away in a huff.

Vaidarbhi had borne his life with great forbearance and incredible patience. Krishna became pensive; he had no one whom he could ask for counsel. He entered Rukmini's bedroom and said:

> Vaidarbhi, do not lose faith in me; I am also human like you. You are my anchor and my rock of support. I refused kingship, power and pelf, but they chase me. At one point of time, when I was a captive in that bear world, I

thought I would never see you again. I did all this to vindicate my honour and for our happiness. I never had any other motive, except the happiness and prosperity of Dwaraka and the Yadavas.

Rukmini was moved to tears and she fell into his arms and said:

Govinda, I understand; I have not lost faith in you. I know you are the saviour, the chosen one. I am only worried about domestic strife because Satyaa is a very possessive and stubborn girl. But as your wife, I shall try my best to circumvent unhappy situations! I only request you to keep her mansion far away from ours.

KRISHNA WEDS SATYABHAMA

The next day, Krishna, along with Rukmini, called on Balarama and Revati. The brothers rejoiced on meeting after a month. Balarama raised his glass to his brother's safe return and his new wife-to-be.

In the meantime, Ugrasena sent for Krishna's father and Gargacharya. On an auspicious day, Krishna Vaasudeva and Satyabhama exchanged garlands to be man and wife. The petite Satyaa could not believe her luck! The moment she saw Rukmini, Satyaa became unsure of herself and fell at her feet. Rukmini lifted her and hugged her, welcoming her into the family.

Soon after the wedding formalities were over, Krishna took Satyabhama to Uddhava's mansion. Mugi, along with Kapila and Pingala, ceremonially welcomed the bride. As per the Naga custom, Satyaa was changed into a colourful bridal dress and her hair was done in the Naga fashion, tucked into a bamboo crown with black and white beads. The bashful Satyaa was nervously waiting for the man in her life.

Her Govinda, who had Naga blood, entered the room dressed as a Naga chief, with headgear made out of beads, two horns of ox and ram's wool. The peacock plume was tucked into the bamboo headband. He wore white bead amulets on his arms.

Satyaa dissolved into Krishna's arms and the night passed in bliss.

The morning after, Uddhava called on Krishna and invited him to come to a place called Satapura. Krishna asked Satyaa to accompany him and visit the site where a palace would be built for her. 'Satyaa, you said that you were very fond of horse-riding and that you learnt it in your childhood. I want you to become an ace horse rider and, also, a champion in archery. Your features convince me that you can be a sharpshooter who will not miss her mark,' said Krishna.

Krishna kept extremely busy directing the master builder, Viswakarma, to execute his dream city. He had also requested his dear friend, Satyaki, to train Satyabhama into a warrior princess. He hoped that would keep her possessive mind channelised and she would not miss him too much in his absence. He prophetically told Satyaki, 'Who knows, some day I will take her into real battle; she should also play her role in my mission, brother Satyaki.'

One day, Satyaa ushered in a messenger from Indraprastha with a request from Yudhisthira, requesting Krishna to visit the Pandava court as early as he can. Krishna had no choice, but to continue on his path. Satyaa realised how difficult it would be for her to stay away from her husband; but she had no choice.

NARADA MUNI

Narada, the celestial *muni* from the Himalayan region, belonged to a Gandharva tribe. Traditionally, Gandharvas were singers who sang about the lives and times of great Aryan leaders as Aryan civilisation spread across the length and breadth of Bharatvarsha.

Narada was a *tapasvin* and a musician par excellence. He was a great devotee of Narayana and was familiar with almost all the clans and tribes of the Himalayan region, namely, the Deva, yaksha, Kinnara, Gandharva and Kimpurusha. He knew the vales, streams and mountain passes that take one beyond the Himalayas into the Trivishtapapitha—Tibet, known as the seat of Indra. Indra was an institution that governed and nurtured the Aryan civilisation during the period of the Rig Veda. These tribes formed the uppermost clan of Aryans and were called Devas; their spoken language was the refined tongue, Sanskrit, termed as Deva Bhasha; and the generic name of the people were Devatas or Devas—the cultured and enlightened civilisation.

Narada knew the region of Mount Kailash and Manasarovar, considered the abode of the Supreme Spirit—the universal Shiva, esoterically called Purusha, and his consort Prakriti, Nature or Creation, and Shakti, the altruistic Energy, the dynamism of the cosmos and its forces.

During the spread of the Aryan way of life, there was a clash of civilisations—the Vedic Aryans versus the original tribes of our land, possibly the ones that were associated with the Indus Valley Civilisation. Their generic name was Asuras, almost like today's *kafir*s—non-believers. The Asuras would have been the ruling class, because Nagas, Nishadas and Dalits were part of the lower strata of society. In addition, there were Karkotas or cruel people and Rakshasas or cannibals.

Narada Muni, owing to his intellectual prowess, was much sought after by all the tribes mentioned here. He was a great communicator and possibly knew the tongues and dialects of native societies. Hence, he had access to the corridors of power and influence of non-Aryan kings, besides the Aryan civilisation.

Narada was an itinerant traveller. In one of his visits to Sage Vyasa at Kurukshetra, the veteran of the Vedas told him that he should meet Krishna Vaasudeva. Vyasa advised Narada to spread the message of Krishna: Dharma, the righteous way of living.

Narada was also familiar with the house of the Kurus and the conspiracies that had transpired there. He was also intrigued by Draupadi's stature as a wife of five brothers. To find out more, he took the liberty of visiting Indraprastha and, by happy coincidence, it was around the same time as Krishna's visit to the city.

NARADA AT INDRAPRASTHA

The Pandavas had arrived at the decision that Draupadi would spend one year at a time in the house of each of the five brothers and, should any other brother intrude into their privacy, he must retire into the forest for twelve years, passing his days as *brahmachari*. They all agreed to this, unanimously. But, one day, Arjuna was forced to breach Yudhisthira and Draupadi's privacy by bringing in his bow and arrows to save a desperate brahmana. Therefore, he decided to live like a celibate in the forests for twelve years, even though Yudhisthira condoned his transgression.

It suited Arjuna's temperament, as he had not yet reconciled to the fact that the bride he won in the *swayamvara* had to become the wife of all the brothers. Yudhisthira was upset due to his brother's resolve and wanted Krishna's counsel. He had urged Arjuna to wait for Krishna's arrival.

Yudhisthira received Narada with all the honour that was due to great rishis. Having settled himself in royal comfort, Narada advised Yudhisthira on ruling a kingdom wisely, elaborating on examples of great and just rulers of Aryawartha. Yudhisthira then sent for Draupadi to meet the *muni*. The queen prostrated before the sage and received his blessings, after which she retired to her apartments.

Narada then said:

> Dharmaputra, the princess of Panchala is the wife of all five brothers. You must be careful that there is no dissension amongst yourselves because of her. I am reminded of a story of two brothers who were inseparable, yet became bitter rivals over a woman. The two brothers, Sunda and Upasunda, were most devoted to each other. One day, while they were travelling through the beautiful valleys of the Himalayas, they met an Apsara of exceptional charm, named Tilottama. Both of them fell in love with her and, in a bid to win her over, they destroyed each other. You and your brothers should not let anything come between your unswerving loyalties to each other. Once your team is broken, the sons of Dhritarashtra will find it easy to defeat you.

'Maharishi,' replied Yudhisthira, 'we are aware of this truth; however, we feel greatly honoured by your advice in this regard. Rest assured that my brothers and I will follow it in word and spirit.'

Krishna reached Indraprastha in about a fortnight. He was received by all the brothers and Draupadi. He also learnt about the incident and Arjuna's resolve to leave for exile. Later, when Krishna was sitting with the Pandavas in the palace he decided to speak to Arjuna about it.

'Partha!' Krishna, with his charming smile, rebuked his friend, 'You need not punish yourself for this so-called indiscretion, unless you need an adventure.'

Arjuna still did not relent. Finally, Krishna said:

> Dharmaputra, let it be so. But what is this talk about observing celibacy for twelve years? Partha, this is irrational! I strongly advise you against it. Remember, you are a kshatriya. I am happy at your resolve; make good use of your self-imposed exile to elevate your spirit, and acquire Divyastras. I advise you to go to the north-eastern lands. Good luck Mahaabahu! On your way back, please cross the great southern rivers, especially River Cauvery and visit Gokarna Kshetra in the west coast, hugging the ocean. There you will see Parama Shiva's Atmalinga; and, finally, visit Dwaraka.

ARJUNA'S EXILE

During his twelve years in exile, Arjuna visited many pilgrimages and religious centres, overlooking his resolve to remain celibate in this period. He married

Ulupi, a Naga damsel from Manipur, who gave birth to his son, Iravan. After spending a couple of years there, he turned south towards the Godavari and Cauvery regions.

He reached a place called Manalur, on the way to Cauvery. The king of the place, Chitrasena, had a daughter called Chitrangada. Arjuna married her under the stipulation that neither the daughter nor their offspring would leave the kingdom. A son was born to them, whom they named Bhabruvahana. From there, he visited Gokarna Kshetra and proceeded towards Prabhasa to meet Krishna.

As a cadet learning archery from Drona at Hastinapura, Gada, Krishna's cousin, had become a good friend of Arjuna. Through him, Arjuna had come to know about Subhadra, the blood sister of Balarama. He had heard that she was beauty personified, and Krishna's favourite sister. Without even seeing her, he had fallen in love with her image.

As Arjuna reached Prabhasa Tirtha, he looked forward to meeting Krishna with great anticipation. He had grown a beautiful beard and looked handsome and pious, carrying a trident that he had acquired at Gokarna. As night fell and it started raining, he sat under an ancient banyan tree in deep meditation.

SUBHADRA

Krishna had already heard about the arrival of a handsome holy man at Prabhasa. He guessed that it was none other than Arjuna. That night, Krishna was with Satyabhama. He told her about Arjuna, meditating under a tree, thinking of Subhadra.

'Is it alright with you if I bring him here? It is raining heavily,' asked Krishna. 'Of course, Govinda, your cousin will be my brother and dear guest. But how did you know that he was in Prabhasa getting wet in the rain?' asked Satyaa, amazed.

'Satyaa, my cousin was meditating on me and called for my help. It is my dharma to reach my devotees in their hour of need.'

Krishna reached Arjuna and the friends met with great warmth. Satyaa personally welcomed him with a cup of warm milk, laced with *kesari* and *kasturi* spices.

Once he was refreshed and relaxed, Satyaa told Arjuna that he looked very forlorn, longing for someone. He blushed and turned to Krishna, 'Vaasudeva, you know everything. Our minds become transparent before you.' Satyaa was amused and whispered into Krishna's ears, 'Your cousin is smitten. Shall I tell Subhadra?'

'Satyaa, not so soon. They should find each other,' replied Krishna. With a cool smile, he assured Arjuna that nothing would please him more than to see his sister as the wife of his dearest friend.

The next day, Krishna took Arjuna to Mount Raivataka and asked him to spend some time there, while he returned to Dwaraka. A few days later, a festival was about to begin on top of the hill. The Vrishnis were to celebrate the Katyayini festival, worshipping the mother goddess for a good harvest and good husbands for their daughters. Arjuna, as a *tapasvin,* spent his time in a remote corner under a tree. He looked pious and respectful. One day, he saw Subhadra surrounded by several maids. Krishna was also there. He came up to his cousin and cheekily said, 'Partha! What are you doing...your expression betrays the attire you are now sporting. Remember you are a *tapasvin* and not a prince anticipating romance.'

'She is such a beauty. Can I take her as my wife?' Arjuna dared to ask, at last.

Krishna replied:

> My dear Arjuna, you know that marriages are of many kinds and the most wonderful of these is the meeting of two minds in love. If you can make my sister fall in love with you, then you can carry her away to Indraprastha and marry her. For the present, you must go and sit in the temple's courtyard. It will look better if you are absorbed in meditation. The rest shall follow and I advise you not to lose your nerve.

Arjuna did as he was told. Krishna joined the crowd worshipping in the temple. As soon as the rituals were over, Subhadra left with her maids. Balarama, Kritavarma, Samba, Sarana, Pradyumna, Gada and others were going around the temple and saw a Yati, sitting in deep meditation, under the tree in the courtyard.

Balarama was impressed by the gaiety of the young Yati, who looked pure and unearthly, his body covered by holy ash. When Arjuna opened his eyes, he found Balarama standing in worshipful attire and, to his surprise, the mighty man prostrated before him and offered his salutation, 'I welcome you to Dwaraka. Where are you from, Your Holiness?'

Arjuna replied:

> Noble sir, I have no place. I belong to the entire world. I have been to many places and have never spent more than three nights in any place. Because of the rainy season, I have to spend these four months here. This hill and its environs are so exhilarating that I chose this temple grove for the time being.

Balarama wanted to be the Yati's host for the entire duration of his stay. Just then, Krishna came towards them and Balarama asked him to suggest a suitable place for the Yati's dwelling. Krishna diplomatically replied that he would agree to whatever Balarama decided. A delighted Balarama said:

> Our tradition calls for *kanya*s to attend to the service of saints and Yati. I feel that the best place will be the gardens above the apartments of Subhadra, and I will ask her to attend to all the needs of this great man. His blessings will ensure a happy future for her.

Krishna smiled to himself and mischievously added:

> I do not think it is advisable to let him stay in such close proximity to our Subhadra. We know nothing of this young Yati. He looks handsome and athletic. His limbs are so shapely; they suggest that he has not been observing severe austerities for long. This holy man seems to be endowed with all the qualities that are sure to attract and charm a young girl like our Subhadra. But, of course, you are wise and far-seeing, and I am sure you must have considered this before coming to such a decision.

Balarama was upset with Krishna for doubting the very credentials of the young Yati. 'Govinda, sometimes we must evaluate persons more charitably.'

Krishna took Arjuna by the hand and introduced him as a Yati to Rukmini and Satyabhama who were amongst the pilgrims. The ladies agreed to delegate Subhadra to his service. Arjuna spent several happy days in the gardens of Subhadra's palace; she followed her elders' commands religiously. Arjuna was astounded by her looks and felt guilty about duping her like this.

In the city of Dwaraka, Arjuna was well known as a brave and handsome warrior. Subhadra had also heard tales of his bravery and was keen to meet this Pandava hero, whom everyone seemed to be talking about with gusto. She was enamoured by him without having ever met him! Subhadra had, many times, wanted to confide in her best friend Satyaa, but she dared not, lest someone come to know about it. Satyaa noticed her friend becoming reserved and moody as the days rolled by and finally asked her what the matter was.

Subhadra innocently asked, 'Dear Satyaa, have you ever seen Arjuna, have you ever met him?'

Satyaa got the cue which she had been waiting for and replied:

> No, but I have heard about his good looks and heroic acts; they say he is as handsome as Govinda and more athletic, almost like your Yati. Who knows, perhaps Arjuna could be this Yati? Why do you not ask your Yati about the whereabouts of Arjuna? Yatis are supposed to know everything in this world.

The next day, Subhadra thought of following her friend's advice, but she was overcome by shyness and the decorum of a girl brought up in a noble household. During one of her meetings with the Yati, she noticed that both his shoulders were scarred. She had heard that Arjuna was adept at using both his hands to wield the bow; could he be Arjuna? She wondered that perhaps Arjuna might have lost all interest in life, having lost Draupadi to his brothers. She was intrigued by this holy man. His every move and gesture was as precise and regal as if he had been a prince.

She finally dared to ask him, 'Noble sir, they say that you have travelled all over Bharatvarsha. Tell me about the beautiful spots you have visited.' Arjuna was only too glad to speak to the object of his affection. Their conversations became a daily routine. One day, Subhadra broached the topic of Indraprastha. She asked him if his travels had taken him to Indraprastha and if he had met her Aunt Kunti and the Pandavas. Arjuna replied that he had indeed met them and had been their guest.

Subhadra, gaining confidence, asked, 'I have heard that Arjuna has been away from Indraprastha. He too must be wandering all over Bharatvarsha like you. Have you met him?'

Arjuna was elated by her curiosity in him and replied, 'Oh yes, I met him and I know where he is at present.'

'Where?'

'Arjuna has fallen in love with the most beautiful woman in this world. To get near her, he is wearing the garb of a Yati and is here, right before you. How come you do not see him?' Subhadra blushed and ran to her chambers, highly embarrassed.

Subhadra, then, went to Rukmini's apartments and started crying and laughing at the same time and told her about the Yati's identity. Rukmini, who was not aware about anything, was as elated as Subhadra.

As they were talking, Krishna arrived at the palace and Subhadra ran towards him and started pounding his chest with her fists in jest. 'Brother... you are a trickster!'

Krishna pretended he did not know what she was talking about. Rukmini intervened and said, 'Bhadra says that the Yati is Arjuna himself and he would dare not play this joke without your consent, Govinda.'

'Now, come on Bhadra; do you like him or not? If you say 'no', I will ask him to leave Dwaraka immediately,' said Krishna, winking at Rukmini.

Subhadra blushed and nodded in agreement. She was indeed in love with Arjuna! 'From tomorrow, I am not going to look after that Yati. I feel sick, I am going home,' she said and left for her apartments.

The next day, Rukmini took fruits and milk to the Yati. Seeing his discomfiture, she said, 'O noble soul, it seems you are not pleased with my coming?' Arjuna looked sheepish. 'Subhadra is unwell; the cause is beyond the reach of physicians. Only a Yati would know the cure!' saying this, Rukmini left.

The whole household was upset about Subhadra's illness, as she had shut herself in her apartments. Krishna assured Devaki that everything would be alright. Meanwhile, he suggested to Balarama and his father that they should all participate in a very auspicious Rudra worship on a nearby island. Subhadra would be under the care of Rukmini and Satyabhama. The credulous Balarama was happy to leave Dwaraka for a while.

Krishna managed to spend a few moments with his sister before their departure. 'I have told the Yati that you like him too and twelve days from today is an auspicious day. Get married to him and I will take care of the rest.'

Twelve days later, Arjuna spoke to Subhadra, 'Your brother must have told you that today is an auspicious day when we can marry.' Subhadra was apprehensive and said, 'No elder is in Dwaraka to bless us. What will Balarama say when he comes to know? You cannot stand my elder brother's wrath, O Pandava prince!'

Arjuna replied, 'We are kshatriyas and we are allowed the Gandharva form of marriage. Do not be afraid. I will take you away to Indraprastha.

I am told that you are proficient in driving a chariot. Krishna asked me to take his chariot and leave at the earliest.'

Subhadra manned the reins and the chariot left Dwaraka, even as Arjuna discarded his ochre robes for princely ones. The guards at the gates were alerted and they tried to stop the chariot, but in vain. They recognised the miscreant as the Yati, and Subhadra driving Krishna's chariot. The guards were terrified and tried to chase them, but their horses could not keep up.

The commander of the palace guards was shocked and immediately set off for the place where all the Vrishnis had assembled for the festival. Frightened, the commander informed Balarama that the Yati had abducted Subhadra in Krishna's chariot.

Balarama was furious and looked at Krishna, who stood silent. He said, 'You are quiet; this must be your doing. Why did you allow this to happen?'

'It was I who warned you about this possibility. Perhaps you do not remember.' Krishna replied in an unusually severe tone. Balarama was taken aback; Krishna never rebuked him like this.

Balarama smiled and said, 'Krishna, you are dearest to me and I know you. You have a hand in this. Please let me know who that Yati was.'

Krishna revealed that it was Arjuna. 'He was on his way back to Indraprastha after his self-exile of twelve years, and was visiting Dwaraka at my invitation.' Balarama was furious and said he would destroy the Pandavas for this breach of trust. Krishna tried to mollify his brother.

'Let bygones be bygones. After all, Subhadra went willingly and, in fact, drove the chariot herself. This is no insult to our family. He is our cousin and belongs to the great House of Kurus.'

'Govinda, I am now certain that you planned it this way, but look at it from my point of view. We are Vrishnis; how dare our cousin make a hole in the same vessel from which he has taken his meal; he was my guest.' Once again, Krishna could not contain his laughter and said:

> He did not get time to shave his beard as he had been wandering for nearly twelve years. He told me that he had heard about Subhadra's charms from brother Gada. Brother, Arjuna is the brightest star in the galaxy of the Kuru clan. Let us follow him to Indraprastha and, as elders, help them become husband and wife.

Balarama relented at last and returned to Dwaraka along with Krishna and their entourage. Devaki also consented and even suggested a grand bridal dowry to be sent, befitting the Vrishnis of Dwaraka. Arjuna reached the gates of Indraprastha and halted at a nearby grove; he was afraid of Draupadi's wrath. He looked at Subhadra and said:

> Draupadi is a very temperamental woman. When she comes to know that I have married you, she could become very angry. You must win her affection first. Dress up as a *gopi* and go to her; she is fond of *gopi*s because she admires your brother, Krishna. Tell her you are Krishna's sister. She will be pleased.

When she reached the gates of the palace she requested the guards for an audience with their queen. Looking beautiful in her rustic dress, Subhadra went to Draupadi's apartment and announced herself as the sister of Krishna, and prostrated at her feet. 'Oh! You are beautiful; so much like him. Where is your brother?' asked Draupadi. The two women talked for a long time as if they were long-lost friends. By evening, a messenger brought the news to the queen that Arjuna has returned and was now with his brothers and mother. Arjuna informed them of his marriage with Subhadra and told them that she was with Draupadi as they spoke.

Arjuna reached Draupadi's chambers and was received by his smiling queen: 'Aryaputra, do not worry, I have already met the *gopi*. She is very beautiful. Who can resist her?' She took the shy and beautiful Subhadra in her arms and said, 'You have won my heart already. Where is your trickster brother? Sakha would be most happy to accept Partha as his brother-in-law.'

She then looked at Arjuna and said, 'Aryaputra, I congratulate you and welcome you to Indraprastha. I hope new relationships would not weaken old ones!'

A few days later, the Vrishnis arrived in Indraprastha with expensive jewels, precious diamonds and cartloads of gold as dowry for Subhadra. An expansive Balarama announced that they had come to celebrate the wedding of Arjuna and Subhadra. All of them stayed in Indraprastha for a few days after the wedding and Balarama, with all his attendants, soon returned to Dwaraka. Krishna, however, did not return with them. He stayed back at the request of Yudhisthira.

KHANDAVAVANA

Khandavavana was a primeval forest, stretching from the eastern banks of the Yamuna to the dense forests along the Ganga, going up to the foothills of the Himalayas, known as the Shivalik range of mountains. The terrain was treacherous with wild animals, and was home to unruly tribes such as Rakshasas and Karkotas. In the Mahabharata, this land is referred to as Varanavata. The land was harsh and infested with insects and mosquitoes, thriving under the sunless marshy swamps. The tribes had cannibalistic tendencies.

The period now being discussed can be construed as post-Indus Valley Civilisation. The Vedic Age and Indus Valley Civilisation could have been contiguous periods in the history of Bharatvarsha. Historically, the Indus Valley Civilisation vanished by 1900 BCE, after about six hundred years of taking great strides in human development. The main reason for the demise of this civilisation could have been the result of the disastrous drought that lasted three hundred years, from 2200 to 1900 BCE. During this period, the glaciers of the Vedic rivers, Saraswati and Dhristadvati, dried up due to the global warming cycle of that age.

By the time of Sri Rama and Krishna Vaasudeva, Saraswati had ceased to be a river. Instead, the Ganga and the Yamuna played a prominent part in creating another civilisation—the Indo Aryan. The Saraswati river turned into five lakes, known as Samantha Panchaka, in Kurukshetra—present-day Haryana, where Veda Vyasa had his ashram.

Survivors of the Indus Valley Civilisation migrated eastwards towards the Ganga-Yamuna *doab*—land between two waters—and established settlements away from the Aryan world, in the dense forests of these rivers. Thus, Khandavavana became home to non-Aryan tribes comprising Danavas, Nagas, Nishadas and other Dalits.

Yudhisthira's Indraprastha prospered and the population almost doubled during the fifteen or twenty years of its formation. Indraprastha was getting congested, therefore, Yudhisthira requested Krishna to suggest an alternative.

Krishna was making the most of his time at Indraprastha by relaxing and reliving memories of his childhood. Time passed by and one summer evening, when Krishna went for a swim in the Yamuna with Arjuna, he noticed vast tracts of forests on the other side of the river. He thought of an idea and shared it with Arjuna, 'Why do we not reclaim the land from those forests and build new townships for the people of Indraprastha?'

'Not a bad idea, Krishna...but I am told that the forest is impenetrable and infested with serpents and wild beasts. A Naga king called Takshaka was reportedly the chief of the principal tribe there.'

Crossing the river, they settled themselves under a tree in a grove located on the fringe of the forest. Krishna, with his keen sense of observation, scanned the forest and found that it was not only dense, but also deep. He could hear lions roar and sense other creatures in the forest.

A brahmana came out of the woods and approached them. He seemed to glow like molten gold. His beard and eyes were red. The brahmana resembled *Udayabhanu*—the just-risen sun.

'Who are you noble sir, and what can we do for you?' asked Arjuna.

'I am Angara Varma, also known as Pavaka and Hutasana,' he replied.

Krishna was surprised at the names, and their meaning, and introduced himself. He asked, 'O noble one, you said you are called Hutasana. Does that mean your food is sacrificial butter?'

The brahmana replied:

> Yes, the age of sacrificial fires has ended with the death of King Svetaki. During his time, this forest used to reverberate with the Vedic chants of brahmana priests. The fire-worship was so intense that the priests fell sick and their eyesight got affected by the constant exposure to the smoke and flames from the ghee. The priests then refused to participate in worship anymore and left the forest. However, King Svetaki wanted to continue the sacrifices with non-brahmana priests, mostly from local tribes, ruled by the chief Takshaka Naga. King Svetaki, too, passed away some years earlier and, since then, I have been starving. Indra and other deities were upset at the termination of the ritual sacrifices.

Krishna looked at Arjuna and said, 'Your godfather was upset, Partha; he had been annoyed once before, when I defied him at Govardhana. I think the time has come to put an end to this ritual worship and consequent sacrificial practices.'

'You want to set fire to this forest?' asked Arjuna with great consternation.

'You cannot do it,' said Hutasana.

'Why?' asked Krishna.

'...Takshaka is a friend of Indra and whenever there is a fire in the forest, Indra summons Varuna, the rain god, to extinguish the fire,' replied Hutasana.

'Is it so? Indra has set himself to perpetuate archaic ideas of worship, god and religion. My dharma preaches that god is love and not fear! I have decided to challenge him and tell him that the age of reforms has been ushered in,' said Krishna with great conviction.

Arjuna reasoned with Krishna, 'If the forest is set on fire, many tribes will be exterminated, along with the wildlife that reside here. We will create a holocaust, is it not a sin?'

Arjuna was astonished to see, for a brief moment, Krishna's transformation into his true form—he was enveloped in a divine glow and looked like Rudra, time eternal—Kala, the destroyer. The moment lasted a few seconds, then Krishna regained his human form and said:

> To bring about social change, and to usher in new rationale, we have to make drastic changes—old order must yield to the new. That has been the nature of Time, it is ever-changing. Change brings turbulence and, hence, violence will be inevitable. Besides, we have to quench the hunger of this brahmana, as kshatriyas it is our dharma to do so.

Arjuna, I am sure you are aware of the Vayuvya Astra. Invoke Vayu such that it will excite the fire as well as deflect the rain. Let us work simultaneously from opposite sides of the forest.' He then looked at Hutasana and said, 'I shall invoke Pavaka—the celestial fire—so that you will never suffer from hunger again.

Krishna asked Arjuna to invoke Agneya Astra and Vayuvya Astra and said that he would take care of the rest.

The Khandava *dahana* continued for fifteen days and nights. The hot air from the fires, being lighter, rose to heavenly heights and sucked the cold moist air into the smoke; dark clouds enveloped the forest and precipitated heavy showers, dousing the fires. Krishna would then light the fires all over again and so, it went on for a fortnight till only the charred remains of the forest were left.

As foreseen by Arjuna, most of the tribes and wildlife perished. Many exotic plant and animal species became extinct. The ancient civilisation of Danavas—remnants of the once great Indus Valley Civilisation—was burnt. Those who tried to escape were struck by Arjuna's arrows. Takshaka's son, Asvasena, escaped from this holocaust and survived to tell the story to his father, who was visiting Takshashila in north-west India. Takshaka took revenge at a later date, when Arjuna's grandson, King Parikshit, was killed, after being bitten by him.

According to the Mahabharata, only two birds of the Sarangka species survived. Likewise, the Danava chief Maya, who was an outstanding architect, survived by seeking refuge with Arjuna, who then prevailed upon Krishna to spare his life. The grateful Danava prostrated at their feet and said:

> I belong to a great civilisation that had knowledge of advanced technology in almost all fields of engineering and architecture. Our great and ancient king, Vrishasirpan, died of old age, but his kingdom and civilisation were superior and prosperous. I can be of immense use to you in this new age that you are ushering in.
>
> Our civilisation had remarkably organised cities and superior weaponry. We had huge harbours and were shipbuilders. Our trade used to take us to far-off lands. King Vrishasirpan had a great armoury of weapons and battle cars. These fine chariots travelled almost at the speed of wind and ensured that our king never lost a battle. I belong to a race of people who were master wielders of mace and sharpshooters. Our king had a divine bow called Gandiva, which was a gift from the celestial god, Agni. Gandiva has a complement of two sheathed quivers that supply endless arrows when you invoke a mantra. I shall teach you the invocation and you will become invincible, O prince. As a token of my gratitude, I shall also present you the battle conch of my late king, that he had named as Devadatta. Lord, please accept my humble gifts.

Maya presented them with a sleek chariot that had belonged to the late King Vrishasirpan. It had a light canopy and a flagstaff on which an ape-like figure was carved. Maya said:

> This was the insignia of my noble king. That ape was his signature and a witness to the glory of our king. As a token of my gratitude, I would also like to present you a very heavy mace, made out of heavy metal alloys. This can only be handled by a man who has the strength of the Wind God.

Krishna would later give that to Bhima, his *atmabandhu*, soulmate. Krishna asked Maya, 'You mentioned that you were a great architect. Can you plan and design the city of Indraprastha?'

'Noble sir, it will be my honour and pleasure.'

Krishna then said:

> The world we live in is the present, but your magic should take us into an

> illusive world, where reality is far from truth! The palace should have a Hall of Illusions that would be a blend of the real world and that of the imagination. I want posterity to know what we have lost because of the human violation of nature and spirit.

'I can do it, my lord, but it would need exotic materials for which will I have to travel to the Himalayan terrain.'

'So be it.'

Maya addressed Krishna and Arjuna:

> Noble lords, I come from the family of magic builders called Maya. We are Danava kings, and we were good at creating make-believe worlds. Our ancestor, who was the king of the lands deep under the southern ocean, was a contemporary of the famous Ravana, the King of Lanka. Ravana married Mandodari, the most beautiful daughter of my ancestor. We were also masters of exotic *vidyas* that have now become extinct with time. Stay assured that you will see a city, the like of which no one has ever seen before.

KRISHNA'S FAREWELL

Krishna told Arjuna that it was up to him and rest of the Pandavas to organise the relocation and reconstruction of Khandavaprastha. He would soon leave for Dwaraka. As they reached Indraprastha, Krishna told his brothers about the reclaimed land of Khandavavana and introduced Maya to Yudhisthira.

> Dharmaputra, the great god of gods has gifted Maya to us. He says, he is a great architect belonging to the dynasty of the Maya Danavas. He has promised Arjuna and me that he would assist in building a most beautiful city for you, including an outstanding assembly hall. We will call it Maya Sabha!

A grateful Yudhisthira embraced Krishna. 'Krishna, I do not know what would have happened to us without you; you are our guiding light.' Krishna then requested them to give him leave and reassured Yudhisthira that he would be always at their service and, in the service of dharma, he can be called upon whenever required.

Krishna turned to Subhadra with a mischievous smile and asked, 'Sister, can I take my chariot now? It has served its purpose here.' With these parting words,

Krishna ascended the chariot. Yudhisthira himself took the reins in his hands and, as was the custom, drove the vehicle till the outer gates of Indraprastha. Arjuna and Bhima stood on either side of Krishna with *chamaras*—fly whisks—in their hands. Nakula and Sahadeva held the umbrella over his head.

Maya started his preparations in right earnest for reorganising the layout of Indraprastha and for building his fascinating *sabha*, as promised to Krishna. He approached Arjuna and said, 'Lord, near the great mountains of Kailash and Mainaka, there is a lake called Bindusaras. In that lake, I have buried vessels filled with many precious gems. I want to go and fetch them for using in the Maya Sabha.'

Maya took leave of Arjuna and went to Mount Kailash. Bindusaras was the sacred spot where the Ganga was released from the matted locks of Lord Shiva. She had to flow drop by drop to avoid a deluge, thus giving the name to the lake. From this lake, she flowed as seven streams. Three towards the east, three towards the west and the seventh stream followed Bhagiratha. The place was holy because it was in the neighbourhood of this lake that the sages Nara and Narayana performed their penance.

Maya wanted to build the most unique creation that had ever been conceived and built on earth. It took him fourteen months to complete and the end result was remarkable, exceeding Sudharma of Dwaraka and the Indra Sabha of Amaravati, in its splendour.

Flowers bloomed in and out of season—lotuses, jasmines, *kuruvaka*s, *sirisha*s, *tilaka*s and *kadamba*s; the walls of the hall gleamed and glistened with embedded precious gems, camouflaged so cleverly that one could see only the glow from the gems and not the gems themselves, unless one looked keenly. Maya invited the Pandavas to assess for themselves, the magic of his creation. The *sabha* had a thousand pillars, a mosaic ceiling, crystal flooring, a magical lake, delusive towers and enchanting fountains. The brothers were astounded and stared at each other in disbelief. Maya took leave and retired to the Himalayas to spend his days meditating on God Pashupati. As he was leaving, Maya turned to Arjuna and said:

> Noble lord, the chariot of yours is as powerful as the Sun and Agni. These noble steeds are unrivalled in the entire world. Your chariot has the monkey crest; it belongs to a great civilisation of the past. You will be as famed as Kapidhwaja hereafter and, because of your white horses, you will be

famed by the name, Swetavahana. The twang of your bow will send shivers of fear through your foes and you will be called Bibhatsa—the terrible. May you always be victorious and happy!

Arjuna embraced Maya, tears welling in his eyes, as he bid him farewell.

On an auspicious day, the Pandavas entered the new city and the *sabha*. Kings and rishis from all over, except the sons of king Dhritarashtra, visited the *sabha*. Satyaki had also been around during the building process and was overjoyed at the effect.

After leaving Indraprastha, Krishna halted at Pushkar for the night. He was the guest of Chekitana, where a letter from Satyaa was delivered to him, asking for his immediate presence at Dwaraka. She informed Krishna that her father Satrajit had been killed by Shatadhanva. After losing Syamantaka as well as Satyaa, Satrajit had turned desolate and become even more quarrelsome. Shatadhanva had confronted him for failing to keep his promise and give Satyaa to him in marriage. Going wild, Satrajit had hit his crony and Shatadhanva, in turn, stabbed Satrajit, who died instantly.

On his return to Dwaraka, Krishna chased Shatadhanva and killed him. Meanwhile, Akrura silently slipped to Kashi, taking the Syamantaka with him. Akrura was, by nature, a diplomat and a survivor, unlike Vasudeva. He was not as saintly as he pretended to be and had his own axe to grind. Therefore, he shifted to Kashi along with the jewel. He performed several yagnas and distributed gold in charity during the sacrificial ceremonies, earning many accolades for his piety and generosity. Shrewd as he was, he observed a vow of silence so that nobody could question him about the source of his opulence.

Krishna understood Akrura's intentions. Out of guilt, and fear of Krishna, the wily Vrishni chief returned to Dwaraka. Krishna addressed Akrura in one of the meetings of chiefs, 'Uncle Akrura, you were made the custodian of Syamantaka for safekeeping on behalf of the king. Its benefits must reach the citizens of Dwaraka and not be used for pilfering by any individual. It is the property of the state of Dwaraka.' Akrura surrendered the jewel to Krishna. However, Krishna handed it back and advised him to desist from temptations for the sake of personal glory.

Time passed by with happy tidings. Subhadra was now the mother of a son, whom she named Abhimanyu. Draupadi bore five sons, one from each of the five brothers. Yudhisthira's son was Prativindhya, Bhima's son was Sutasoma,

Arjuna's son was Srutakarman, Nakula's son was Sataaneeka and Sahadeva's son was named Srutasena.

Yudhisthira had earned fame as a just king, honest and upright; the kingdom was prosperous and the people were happy and contented. Vedic schools, under preceptor Dhuamya, were functioning in the line suggested by the great master, Veda Vyasa.

Krishna became a father of twins by Satyaa. The boys were named Bhanu and Subhanu, in deference to her devotion to the Sun God. Pradyumna grew up not only to be to be extremely handsome, but also a formidable military general and war strategist. In tribute to his prowess in battle formations, a formation was named after him—Pradyumna Vyuha.

Years rolled by...and peace prevailed for nearly two decades.

RAJASUYA—THE IMPERIAL QUEST

A royal sacrifice—Rajasuya—became one of the defining moments in Krishna's life as well as in the history of Bharatvarsha, the impact of which was felt for the next thousand years.

Rajasuya was a great sacrifice performed during the coronation of a king: It was religious in nature, but political in its operation. It implied that he who instituted the sacrifice was a king over kings—the emperor, and his tributary princes were required to be present at the rite. In short, it represented an imperial ambition to dominate and rule a number of kingdoms.

The peace and calm reigning for nearly two decades seemed to be only a lull before the storm. Duryodhana's network of spies had been active and informed him of the prosperity of Indraprastha. He was smitten by jealousy and storm clouds were gathering, slowly but surely.

Krishna was busy consolidating his Yadava state and there were frequent skirmishes to subdue arrogant kings. He paid occasional visits to Indraprastha to spend some time with his cousins.

One day, Narada Muni came to the court of Yudhisthira and was welcomed with reverence. He had heard of Maya Sabha, the Hall of Illusions, and desired to see it himself. An impressed Narada said, 'Dharmaputra, your Sabha outshadows even Indra's Sabha. What next?'

Yudhisthira, with great reverence, asked the sage, 'Is there anything else you are expecting from me, O divine one?'

Narada smiled and said, 'You deserve to be a Chakravarti. Dharmaputra, a king like you should support the ancient traditions and extend the order of dharma to the whole Bharatvarsha and, only then, dharma can be established on a macro level in this world.'

'O divine one, please order me and I shall obey your commands.'

'Dharmaputra, perform Rajasuya Yagna. Your noble father passed away without performing it and could not find a place amongst the great kings of Bharatvarsha.'

'That could mean war and I abhor violence.'

'Dharmaputra, with your four brothers by your side, and Krishna as your guide, you can conquer our known world with the least bloodshed, I assure you,' countered Narada.

Yudhisthira was confused and remained silent. Narada, looking at Yudhisthira's dilemma, suggested, 'Consult your brothers, mother and take the counsel of Krishna and Sage Vyasa.' The sage then blessed the brothers and continued on his journey.

Since that day, Yudhisthira had become solemn. The Pandavas had never troubled their neighbours with conquest and domination. It was not the nature of Yudhisthira to nurse grievances. He and his brothers were happy with their lot. Yudhisthira was aware of the portents and consequences of the yagna. Before coming to any conclusion, he wanted to consult Krishna and he sent a formal invitation to the Yadava brothers through Nakula, requesting them to visit Indraprastha. Krishna and Balarama had not seen the transformed Indraprastha. Balarama declined the invitation, as he was needed at home, and requested Krishna to return soon as well, for they were in the process of consolidating Dwaraka.

Krishna brought with him Uddhava and several *maharathi*s in chariots. Indraprastha wore a festive look as Yudhisthira had also invited Veda Vyasa for consultations. Yudhisthira narrated Narada's visit and sought his advice about performing the Rajasuya.

Kunti, who was also present, was apprehensive of the whole episode; yet, she had faith in Krishna's guidance. Yudhisthira also mentioned a dream that had been bothering him; in his dream, his father urged him to do something. Shortly after this dream, Narada Muni had arrived and given his suggestion.

Dharmaputra urged Krishna to help him:

> I am nervous about this whole business of Rajasuya; I am against any form of violence. However, Arjuna and Bhima are advocating it vociferously. I beg for your counsel, Vaasudeva! You are beyond the reach of desires and attachments; your keen intellect can discern the complexities of the event, please advise me.

Krishna weighed the pros and cons of the situation:

> I am not worried about other kingdoms, except that of Jarasandha. He will be a formidable foe. His allies include the Chedi Raj, Shishupala; Dantavaktra of Karusha; Rukmi, the son of Bhishmaka; and Paundraka. He has friends in all the four quarters and is the sworn enemy of the house of the Vrishnis. Dharmaputra, before you embark on the Rajasuya, you must get rid of Jarasandha. The rest will fall into place with no significant resistance, except your cousins, the Kurus of Hastinapura.

Arjuna asked how they could get rid of Jarasandha and Krishna replied, 'By personal combat. He is a great wrestler and, when challenged, he would oblige us with a one-to-one combat. Would you like to become a wrestler, Partha, and face Jarasandha?'

Bhima said vigorously, 'Atmabandhu, do you not consider me fit enough to face Jarasandha?'

Yudhisthira put in, meekly, 'Bhima, I do not want to lose anybody on my account; let us abandon the idea and enjoy Krishna's stay.'

Krishna knitted his eyebrows and said with gravity:

> Dharmaputra, Jarasandha is *adharma* personified. His grandson, Meghasandhi, sent a message to me in Dwaraka that Jarasandha has imprisoned several Aryan kings—*rajanyas*—and when he has imprisoned a hundred, he would offer Nara Medha to Lord Rudra. He is in a hurry as he is getting old and wants to attain immortality before long. His grandson heard the emperor telling the high priest that he would not mind adding his own grandson to the list of prisoners if there is a shortage in numbers before the coming solar solstice. Rajasuya or no Rajasuya, Jarasandha has to go!

VEDA VYASA: THE MASTER

The next morning, after the rituals were over, a conclave was held in Acharya

Dhaumya's ashram, around the Vedic altar in which the sacred fire had been lit. Besides Vyasa and Acharya Dhaumya, Krishna, Uddhava, the five brothers, mother Kunti and Draupadi were also present. It was an informal event, without diadems and arms. Krishna just tied his favourite headband with a bunch of peacock plumes tucked into the folds. Yudhisthira explained his dilemma to Veda Vyasa and asked him for guidance. Vyasa said:

> The Rajasuya would ensure your status as an emperor and I will have the pleasure of meeting many *srotriya*s. This will enable me to find out how the *rita* is propagated. I want the Vedic *rita* to be spread to the whole of Bharatvarsha. The ordinary men and women should also realise that dharma alone will bring happiness and rejuvenate the Aryans.

Vyasa then turned to Krishna: 'Let us hear what Krishna has to say on the event.'

Krishna panned his eyes over the assembly, smiled and offered his greetings to the master and asked Dharmaputra, 'Am I to take it that our military strength is adequate to win a war? Our strength should infuse confidence in the *rajanyas* that righteous living can always overcome wickedness.'

Vyasa also pitched in. 'Vaasudeva, I agree with you. The one who undertakes Rajasuya has to undertake military campaigns not to subjugate, but to ensure moral and political guardianship and authority.' The brothers replied that their forces were 'battle ready' and can face any adversary.

'How about Jarasandha?' queried Krishna.

'We can face him too. This time I will break his skull with my mace,' boasted Bhima.

Krishna just smiled and asked, 'What about his allies: Shishupala, Dantavaktra, Bhagadatta, Rukmi and Paundra Vasudeva? I am certain Duryodhana will join this league against you.'

'With the Yadavas of Dwaraka, Panchala Naresh and Virata of Matsyadesa, we can defeat them,' replied Bhima.

Krishna was lost in thought for a while and then said, 'We must destroy Jarasandha first.' Yudhisthira agreed and said, 'Krishna, I know Susharma of Kashi, Jalandhara's brother is mortally afraid of him. All the kings, from Kashi to Madhyadesa, were afraid of Jarasandha for that matter.'

'You are right,' said Krishna. 'When the sun comes into the constellation of

Makar—Capricorn—Jarasandha will begin his preparations to hold his human sacrificial session. This message was brought to me by Acharya Indrapramad, the disciple of Acharya Shvetaketu who has an ashram in Kashi. It was from prince Meghasandhi.'

'I know the acharya well; can I meet him?' asked Vyasa.

'Master, he is on his way to Girivraja to request Sahadeva and Meghasandhi to prevent the sacrifice,' replied Krishna.

'This ritual is archaic,' said Vyasa. 'Many ages ago, an Aryan king, Harischandra, attempted the human sacrifice of Sunahshepa and Sage Vishvamitra prevented it with his Brahma Tejas.' Vyasa looked at Krishna and suggested, 'Vaasudeva, the time has come for you to act.'

Krishna repeated his strategy of challenging Jarasandha to a one-on-one wrestling combat. 'Yudhisthira,' said Krishna, 'No army, no battles. Jarasandha will be eliminated without spilling innocent blood. I need Arjuna and Bhima to accompany me to Girivraja."

THE END OF JARASANDHA

Magadha was a fertile land watered by several rivers, including the Ganga. The fertility of its soil and its hot water springs attracted people from neighbouring areas. Its people were prosperous and Girivraja, the capital city, was a sprawling settlement around the rocky hill which served as a citadel. King Brihadratha, Jarasandha's father, had been a benevolent monarch and under his rule peace had prevailed between Magadha and its neighbours, Mithila and Kashi.

When he succeeded his father, Jarasandha moved his residence from the royal mansion to the citadel and employed *mull*s—a network of spies who were trained wrestlers. Jarasandha was a formidable wrestler himself. The Mahabharata mentions four formidable wrestlers—Jarasandha, Keechaka, Duryodhana and Bhimasena. He was also a great wielder of a mace.

Jarasandha raised *baahuvidya* and *mullavidya*—body combat—to the status of an esoteric cult. The *mull*s were invested with priestly authority, with him as the pontiff and Lord Rudra as the presiding deity. The sacred *mull*s served as an instrument for enforcing Jarasandha's commands; they lived in the foothills with their families, but thrice a week, each one had to serve the emperor in the citadel.

Jarasandha's family lived in the royal mansion in the centre of the settlement, but his son, Sahadeva, and three grandsons, Meghasandhi, Marjari and Somahji, had to wait upon him every day in the afternoon. Jarasandha was a known womaniser; if he took a fancy to someone, she would be the queen for the period he desired her to be. He was a sadist, but could be gentle and genial when he chose. Jarasandha wanted to be the master of the world, the overlord of all kings and wished to conquer death to become immortal, a characteristic typical of a dictator and tyrant!

To realise his obsession, he would march out with his massive army, defeating kings or taking them captive, looting their wealth and insisting on unquestioned allegiance. He kept the captured *rajanya*s—most of them from Aryawartha—locked up in the dungeons of the citadel, so that they could be offered in sacrifice to Rudra at the appropriate time.

The citadel of Girivraja had an open-air shrine of Lord Shankar as Rudra. Dressed in a lion's skin, Jarasandha would sit in the courtyard of the shrine to pray. Surrounded by the *mull*s on duty there, he would conduct tantric rituals.

Jarasandha was a giant of a man and his massive strength did not diminish even as he aged. At the moment, his eyes were pinned on the face of his grandson, Meghasandhi, who stood in front of his grandfather. Being in charge of Girivraja, Meghasandhi could bear arms in the presence of Jarasandha. 'Fool,' shouted Jarasandha. 'Why did you allow strangers to come into the town? What sort of men are they?'

'Lord, there are three of them, and they want your audience. One is a giant, looks like an expert wrestler and has a broad chest. The second one is of medium size and the third has a charming face with sparkling eyes,' said Meghasandhi. 'They said they are *srotriya*s and had come to Girivraja to pay respects to the lord.'

Meanwhile, when the strangers reached the outer entrance of the citadel, they were stopped by the *mull* guards. Bhima cracked the skulls of the *mull*s with his bare hands and broke the two huge drums at the main gate. As the main gates were closed, the three travellers entered the citadel from the rear, a gesture of an unfriendly act.

Jarasandha was busy with his worship and asked Meghasandhi to look after the visitors; he would grant them an audience at midnight. Jarasandha met them at the appointed hour and honoured them as he would all brahmanas.

You seem to be s*nataka*s, but your dress belies it. You are using flowers and

> perfumes, which are against the tenets of *snataka*s. I understand you entered my palace in the manner of enemies; friends enter from the *simhadwara*—lion gates. You look more like kshatriyas; your shoulders are scarred and broad like those of fine archers. I have a feeling that you are kshatriyas in disguise and, if that is so, what can I do for you?

Krishna replied, 'Jarasandha, your guess is correct. We are kshatriyas and have come here as your enemies. We have trespassed into your palace like adversaries and have come to challenge you.'

Jarasandha laughed loudly, 'You are challenging me in my own house? No one has ever dared to do this; I am intrigued. I do not know you at all. What have I done to earn your enmity?'

Krishna replied, 'O mighty emperor, it is unbecoming of Magadha Naresh to unlawfully imprison the *rajanyas* for sacrificing to Lord Rudra. Human sacrifice is a heinous crime, improper for an emperor of your stature. It is against the established norms of Kshatra.'

'Who are you to teach me Kshatra Dharma? How dare you?' frowned Jarasandha.

'I am Krishna, your old acquaintance. We have come to challenge you to single combat. You can choose anyone of us to fight.'

Jarasandha looked at Krishna and said with utmost contempt, 'You are a coward who fled from me eighteen times. I will not fight with you; you are inferior to me in all respects. It is beneath my dignity to fight with you. Who are you young man?' he asked Arjuna. 'You look so delicate and childlike. Are you sure you want to get killed by me? No, I shall fight with my equals,'

Bhima chuckled; Jarasandha stared hard at him, 'How dare you heckle me? I think I will fight you; you look like a wrestler. Young man, say your prayers and enter the arena.' Jarasandha looked around, clapped and handed over his diadem and armbands to a waiting *mull*.

Jarasandha paused, looked at the sky and called for Sahadeva. Placing his diadem on his son's head, he kissed him and said, 'Be a good king, in case something happens to me.'

The fight was on. The two were equally matched. Both were thumping their thighs, challenging each other. No one could say who was the better fighter. The fight went on for fourteen days and fourteen nights, relentlessly. As per the rules, the only break that was allowed was to attend calls of nature and for drinking water.

Neither of the two would give in, but slowly Bhima had begun to gain the upper hand. Age was taking its toll on Jarasandha.

'Atmabandhu!' cheered Krishna for Bhima. 'You are the strongest and most powerful of all kshatriyas.' Hearing this, Bhima prayed to his father for strength, took two deep draughts of air and thumped his thighs vigorously, fighting with new vigour. He lifted up Jarasandha and, grasping his legs, one in each hand, tore him up into two. Bhima felt that he had won at last. But he watched as the two halves of the body crept nearer and joined together to form a whole once again. The emperor rose as though nothing had happened. The king roared and challenged Bhima again.

Bhima glanced at Krishna who smiled, picked a blade of dry grass, tore it vertically into two halves and threw the right half on the left, and the left half on the right. Bhima understood the significance. New enthusiasm surged through Bhima's body. He repeated the trick and tore apart the body of Jarasandha. This time, the right half was thrown on the left side, and the left half on the right side. Each of the halves lay inert in pools of blood. The halves did not join again.

Bhima felt sure that Jarasandha, the favourite of Lord Rudra, was now dead. Perspiration ran down his body. He climbed out of the wrestling pit and collapsed with exhaustion. Panic gripped the crowd. The *mull*s could not believe that their master was dead; they were also frightened that the suppressed wrath of the people of Girivraja would fall on them.

At a signal from Meghasandhi, the kshatriyas sprang into action. With swords in their hands, they surrounded the *mull*s. The crown prince, Sahadeva, fell at Krishna's feet and hailed him as the saviour of Magadha. Krishna lifted Sahadeva and said, 'Your father was a great man, but he did not use his greatness to uphold dharma. Combine your father's valour with devotion to dharma. Your first act as the King of Magadha should be to release the *rajanya*s.' He then invited Sahadeva to attend the ceremony of Rajasuya at Indraprastha.

Bhima had achieved the impossible and become synonymous with immense strength. As they returned to Indraprastha, everyone's happiness was beyond comprehension. Krishna now looked at Yudhisthira and said, 'The one thorn in the path of dharma has been removed. You can now perform the Rajasuya uninterrupted. Get busy with the preparations and ask your brothers to seek allies and wealth by fanning out in the four directions. They should conquer the heart and soul of Aryawartha and beyond, and strengthen the idea of the ideal Kingdom of Dharma.'

Krishna then went to meet Veda Vyasa, at the ashram of Dhaumya, to recount the outcome of his mission to Magadha. Vyasa instinctively sensed that Krishna had become the architect of a new age for Aryans.

Krishna departed after partaking honey and fruits from the hands of the master. Vyasa bid farewell to Indraprastha and went to meet his mother at Hastinapura. Upon reaching her mansion, he prostrated at her feet and said, 'Mother, I had promised to seek the redeemer and I am glad that I have finally found him.'

'Who is he, my son?' asked Satyaki.

'My namesake, mother—Krishna Vaasudeva. He is the essence of the Supreme Being, living in our midst. My search for Sasvata Dharmagopta has ended. I will be going to Badarika to meditate upon the lord and realise bliss. Mother, when you need me, just think of me and I shall be by your side.'

JANARDANA

Veda Vyasa moved on to Badarika Vana with his principal disciples: Vysampayana, Paila and Jaimini. His ashram was in a deep cave below the snow-clad mountain range, now known as Nar Narayan peaks. The cave was called Vyasa Guha and is now known as the famous Badrinarayana shrine, the temple abode of Mahavishnu.

After his ablutions in the nearby Alaknanda river, Vyasa sat in meditation. He was transported to a blissful state by divine music and realised that the music was not his imagination; it was being played, in reality, by Narada.

Vyasa welcomed the itinerant Narada who greeted him while playing his veena.

Narada asked, 'O great master, so you found him, your Sasvata Dharmagopta?'

Vyasa replied that he felt blessed at having met Krishna. 'O great *muni*, your time has now come to spread His message of dharma. He is in Dwaraka; seek Him. He needs you,' Vyasa also told Narada. '*Krishnastu Bhagavan Swayam.*' (Seek Him and you shall become immortal.)

Narada then said:

> Oh great master, I have just returned from Trivishtapapitha, the seat of Indra. They are in great peril from the asuras of Kiratadesa. Their chief is Bhaumasura, whose mountain fortress is called Pragjyotishpura. He and his commander, Murasura, practice occult worship of Goddess Kamakhya. Their form of worship is witchcraft and they have converted Indra's land into *naraka*.
>
> The beautiful and peace-loving people of these hills are subjected to inhuman violations of their body and spirit. Brahmanas and young *kanya*s are their target. Bhaumasura has imprisoned several hundreds of young girls, destroyed all the *vedi*s and converted all brahmanas into his slaves. Narakasura has not even spared Aditi, Indra's mother. Not only has he stolen Indra's royal umbrella, but also plucked the earrings from the elderly Aditi, leaving her bleeding in pain. He also invaded the settlements of yakshas, Kinnaras and Gandharavas. Had I been in our country, I, too, might have been harmed for I belong to the Gandharva clan.
>
> O great one, I was on my way to Kurukshetra and when I sat in deep meditation, I felt your vibrations and came here. Help the king of Devas. Krishna must finish off Bhaumasura without any delay. The hill habitats and civilised settlements of Aryans are in great peril. I beg for your intervention!

Vyasa replied, 'Why do you not meet Vaasudeva personally? You have to seek him and he will help you. Krishna will welcome you with open arms. He loves men of god!'

As guided, Narada reached Dwaraka. Krishna received him with great devotion. Narada was housed in the ashram of Sandipani. Acharya Garga took care of the divine sage.

Krishna visited Narada at the ashram, the morning after his arrival. Narada was playing his veena and Krishna was enchanted by the divine music. Krishna bowed and said, 'O divine sage, you seem to be concerned about some urgent matter. Can I be of any service to you?'

Narada replied:

> Indeed, Vaasudeva. There are many more Jarasandhas to be eliminated before a semblance of dharma can be established. I speak of the powerful king of Pragjyotishpura, who calls himself Bhaumasura—son of the Mother Earth.

Perhaps, he means that he belongs to the ethnic race and is, therefore, against Aryans and their civilisation.

We can trace him to Kapalikas, the aboriginal people of Kamarupa who worship the fierce form of Shiva. They indulge in occult practices and fearsome witchcraft, and their land is also known as Kiratas. It is a mountainous, marshy land that gets heavy rains. This asura's tyranny has reached such an oppressive state that his kingdom is an embodiment of hell. Let me brief you about this land.

Due to heavy rains and the marshlands of the mighty Brahmaputra, which overflows its banks annually, the country is slushy and filled with cattle dung and other filth. The land is full of insects and reptiles, all products of the earth. The activities of these animals make the country an inhospitable land. Bhaumasura is like a demon living in his mountain citadel, cruel and tyrannical; hence, he is called Narakasura. His commander, Murasura, is worse than his king.

The city has fortified concentric walls and any invader must face the formidable commander, Murasura, before reaching Naraka's fort complex. The hill forts are accessible only by narrow winding passages. It is almost impossible to attack him, whereas his armies, at regular intervals, invade and plunder the Aryan settlements in the Himalayan vales and plateau, including Trivishtapapitha.

The collective civilisations of the Himalayan region pay obeisance to Indra. Indra's capital, Amaravati, is a beautiful city; his palace is exotic and so are his queen, Sachidevi, and the courtesans known as *apsara*s. They practice Vedic rituals and offer their sacrifices to Agni and Indra, who is the chief and mentor of this heaven-like region called Swarga.

The sage continued:

Narakasura is irreligious, unethical, immoral and cruel. He is dead against the new civilisation and the intellect of Aryans. He, thus, plunders Himalayan settlements, torments its people, abducts beautiful maidens for his harem in Pragjyotishpura and robs the jewels of women, not sparing even the old. Recently, when he attacked Swarga, he did not hesitate to tear the earrings of elderly Aditi. He is following the tradition of Lanka's Ravana, who was vanquished by Sri Ramachandra.

Sage Narada requested him to end the menace of Narakasura. Satyaa was also present and told Krishna that it was their dharma to restore order in this region. Krishna took leave of Narada, promising the sage that he will act against Narakasura right after the end of rainy season—Kartik month. Narada blessed him and departed, singing the praise of Narayana.

Krishna summoned Vainateya and asked him to survey the mountain kingdom. He asked him to take all able-bodied Garudas on this reconnaissance mission and report a strategy for a siege. As the season of clear skies descended on Aryawartha, Krishna, accompanied by Garudas and a few of his *atirathi*s, along with Satyabhama and Uddhava, besieged Naraka's mountain stronghold at Pragjyotishpura.

The city was fortified on all sides by ramparts of mountain ranges; traps of water, fire and smoke had been laid by the commander, Murasura. Krishna and Satyabhama were transported over the mountainous terrain by Garudas. Krishna shattered the ramparts of the mountains with his mace, Kaumodaki. With the aid of his sword, Saranga, and discus, Sudarshana, he shattered all other impediments. Then he blew his conch, Panchajanya, and its thunderous sound bewildered the defenders who ran helter-skelter.

A fierce battle took place with Murasura, who used his occult practices in an attempt to frighten Krishna and his regiment of Garudas. Murasura began attacking from his underwater fortifications by simultaneously releasing five sequential *astras*. He aimed his trident with enormous force at Vainateya, but Krishna intercepted the weapon and split the trident in transit. In rapid succession, Krishna whirled his shafts at Murasura, who, in indignation, hurled his mace at Krishna, which he thwarted with Kaumodaki. Krishna then destroyed his foe's weapon. Finally, he beheaded the commander with his discus, the severed head falling into the moat.

Murasura's seven sons now took to the field. After a fierce battle fought with shafts, spears and pikes, the invincible Lord Krishna severed the heads of all of the asura's sons.

END OF NARAKASURA

A furious and frightened Naraka retaliated with an army of elephants, and Daitya warriors equipped with several types of mountain warfare weapons such as rolling and hustling stone boulders called *sataghni*s. Krishna, with his sharp arrows, made up the entire force against Naraka. The Garuda warriors confused the war elephants with their shrieks and spears such that the beasts trampled over Naraka's own army, crushing them completely.

Now, Naraka was left alone in the battlefield. Perched on an elephant, he threw his javelin at Garuda, which Krishna intercepted, and retaliated by whirling his discus. The demon's head, with the diadem and Aditi's earrings, rolled on to the ground.

Not a soul wept for the deceased king. Naraka's son, Bhagadatta, too, detested his father and was himself a refugee. Bhagadatta, then, came out of hiding and paid obeisance to Krishna. He also prostrated before Satyabhama, addressing her as Mother Earth.

Krishna said with great compassion, 'Satyaa, Bhagadatta respectfully addressed you as the Mother of the Daityas, thus accepting you as their provider. Welcome him into our fold and let us install him as the king of Pragjyotishpura.'

Bhagadatta was then crowned the king of Kamarupa and Krishna blessed him. 'Be virtuous and rule your people like a benevolent father. On behalf of Yudhisthira, I also invite you to come to Indraprastha for the Rajasuya. Your kingdom shall serve as the outpost of Arya Dharma in Prachidesha—the north-east.'

THE DILEMMA

Kind Bhagadatta regretfully informed Krishna that his late father had imprisoned thousands of Aryan girls in harems. These unfortunate girls must be returned to their families.

Even the usually calm Krishna was moved to tears when he saw the deplorable condition of these girls. Thousands of women of different age groups, mostly young, wailed helplessly in their confinement. Krishna ordered Bhagadatta to immediately vacate the premises, seal the cave, and set fire to the evil chambers. Next, the girls were bathed, clothed and fed sumptuous food. Krishna asked Bhagadatta to send them back to their parental homes.

The sixteen thousand women were in a more precarious state than ever before. They had neither shelter nor succour. There were not enough resources to manage the basic requirements of all of them and, if left astray, men would exploit them. Krishna spoke to Uddhava, 'Given the grave dimensions of this problem, I think you should escort them to Saurashtra for eventual rehabilitation, and ensure an honourable place for them in our society.'

Krishna requested Bhagadatta for suitable transportation to shift the women to Dwaraka. He also called Vainateya Garuda and asked his Garudas to scout the path and assure the safety of the caravan, which proceeded under the leadership of Uddhava.

There was jubilation in Pragjyotishpura; the citizens and the rescued damsels wanted to celebrate their liberation in the form of a festival of lights and they asked Janardana, as they called Krishna, to lead the celebration.

Meanwhile, Indra came to know of the events at Pragjyotishpura and was eager to welcome Krishna and Satyabhama to Swarga. He sent an advance welcome party with a golden palanquin to transport the couple to his kingdom. Indra and Sachidevi met the two at Sambhala, an astral world known to be the land of Manes. Krishna was amazed to see this ethereal world where peace reigned supreme.

They reached Amaravati, which was located on a vast plateau surrounded by snow-clad mountains. The people looked serene and peaceful, chanting the sacred Panchakshari—*Om Namah Sivaya* and *Om Namoh Narayana*. The sanctity of the land pleased Krishna and Satyabhama.

They were transferred from the golden palanquin to a bejewelled *houda*—king's mount of a massive white elephant known as Airavata. Floral welcome arches and beautiful women greeted the guests.

Satyaa returned to Aditi, the pair of earrings recovered from Naraka. The umbrella and Mani Parvata—Indra's seat—were restored to him. Indra then paid homage to Sri Krishna by chanting the sacred mantra: *Namoh Narayna Devaki nandana Janardana*!' Satyabhama was honoured with a garland of Parijata flowers, which had a bewitching fragrance. Satyaa expressed her desire to have such a tree in her palace at Dwaraka. Krishna pointed out that it would not survive in their hot country, but Satyaa insisted.

Indra reiterated Krishna's concern, 'Our plants and animals, and even our people cannot survive in your air. If you still insist, I agree to give, though reluctantly, one Parijata plant, out of sheer gratitude to Lord Krishna for having saved my honour.' Krishna wanted to see the array of weapons Indra had, especially his Shakti—thunderbolt. While leaving, Krishna asked Indra, 'One of my cousins, Arjuna, is your godson; are you aware of this?'

Indra replied:

> I know, Vaasudeva. I have also come to know that he is an outstanding archer. Vaasudeva, please send Arjuna to us and I shall present him with my choicest weapons. If Arjuna is an intellectual as you say, he should earn the Pasupata Astra from Mahadeva through devotion, austerities and penance. As a godfather, it is my dharma to ensure that Arjuna excels in all walks of life.

As a parting gift, Indra gave them a seedling of Parijata. 'It will bloom in your land also, provided it is protected from direct sunlight. It has been conditioned such by our medicine men, the Aswin brothers.'

Indra then called Mathali, his charioteer, who escorted them to the plains of Aryawartha.

THE CONQUEST OF BHARATVARSHA

After Jarasandha's end, the way was clear for the conquest of all the four corners of Bharatvarsha. Thereafter, began the systematic annexation of the various kingdoms. All the kings who refused to recognise Yudhisthira as emperor and to abide by the codes of dharma had to be subjugated by force. Those who agreed were asked to offer gifts as a token of their submission and were invited to attend the grand coronation.

To subdue recalcitrant kings, Arjuna was deputed to the northern regions of India; Bhima's army was deputed to the east, in the rainforests of the Ganga and Brahmaputra delta; Sahadeva and his army went to the south, accompanied by Ghatotkacha; and Nakula left for western India with his contingent.

The kings of the outer and inner Himalayas and the famous Uttar Kuru, present-day Garhwal, readily agreed to align with Yudhisthira. Arjuna brought back enormous quantities of gold that filled the treasury of Indraprastha.

When Bhima confronted Chediraj Shishupala with the proposal of Rajasuya, he also promptly agreed. Shishupala looked at the towering personality of Bhima and was intimidated. He offered many gifts as well and promised to attend the Rajasuya.

The kings of Kishkindha, Mainda and Dwivida fought Sahadeva as they objected to Yudhisthira's Rajasuya, although they had no problem in following dharma. They claimed to be familiar with the codes of dharma; they claimed to adhere to it as their forefather, Sugriva, was a friend of Sri Ramachandra. There was a brief skirmish in which they were defeated by Sahadeva and Ghatotkacha. In the end, they agreed to pay homage to Yudhisthira.

Sahadeva also went to the southern kingdom of Pandya, which was famous for its elephant cavalry. The Pandya king was known as Gajendra—the king of elephants. Sahadeva reached the city of Melnur and met Chitrangada, wife of Arjuna. Gajendra was more than glad to pay allegiance to Yudhisthira and promised to gift many war elephants to Indraprastha.

Nakula found no serious opposition in the west, where Krishna's influence prevailed. The whole of Bharatvarsha agreed to acknowledge Yudhisthira as emperor and follow the Bharata Dharma laid down by the sages. This conquest of Bharatvarsha lasted for about eighteen months.

RAJASUYA: THE CORONATION OF YUDHISTHIRA

Nakula was sent as a special envoy to invite the Kuru house of Hastinapura. Bhishma received him with affection and Nakula invited him personally on behalf of Yudhisthira. The grand old Pitamah, Dhritarashtra, Acharya Drona, Kripacharya, Aswathama, Baahlika, Somadatta, Bhoorisravas, Duryodhana, Radheya, Shakuni and his seven sons, Subala, the king of Gandhara and Shakuni's father, Dushassana and his brothers were affectionate and cordial.

Krishna arrived at Indraprastha with Vasudeva, Balarama and other Yadava chiefs. He brought many gifts to honour Yudhisthira. Krishna and Vyasa supervised with meticulous care, the intricate arrangements for the ceremony, and Vyasa performed the preliminary rites.

Sahadeva was sent as a messenger to invite *srotriya*s, *rajanya*s, leading traders, agriculturists and shudras to attend the Rajasuya. Susharma, the best of the *srotriya*s, took charge of the ceremonies connected with the Sama Veda. Yagnavalkya, who was the best ritualist in Aryawartha, was nominated the *adhvaryu*—presiding priest—Dhaumya and Paila, the disciples of Vyasa were named *hota*s—priests who offer oblations.

Yudhisthira had decided to make the Rajasuya an occasion for fostering harmony between the Pandavas and the Kauravas. To show confidence in the members of his family, he appointed them to key positions. He pleaded with his grandfather, Bhishma and guru, Dronacharya, to oversee the arrangements.

Aswathama was asked to receive the *srotriya*s and look after them.

Duryodhana was requested to receive the presents from the guests, a position implying great confidence. Dushassana and the minister Sanjaya were to look after the royal guests. Kripacharya, the revered teacher, was entrusted the task of evaluating the gold and jewellery presented. Vidur, who was wise and far-sighted, was appointed to oversee the disbursement of valuables.

Krishna took upon himself the sacred duty of washing the feet of the learned *srotriya*s. He was the cynosure of all eyes at the event and participated in intellectual debates, enthralling the learned brahmanas with his acute grasp of *rita* and dharma. Yudhisthira, though nervous at times, was happy with the progress of the events preceding the main ceremony.

Shishupala was most difficult to please. He had never forgotten that Krishna had carried away his bride-to-be. He had been a close associate of Jarasandha and had never considered Krishna to be a threat. With Jarasandha gone, Krishna seemed to be the power behind the kings of Aryawartha. Shishupala also remembered that his birthmark had disappeared when Krishna touched his feet at his Upanayanam.

When the planets were auspicious, Yudhisthira was ceremonially initiated as the Yajamana (head) of the sacrifice. Accompanied by *rajanya*s, he entered the hall of sacrifice where hundreds of brahmanas were chanting the Vedic verses under the direct supervision of Vyasa. On the first day, at the end of the ceremony, Yudhisthira was crowned the king of Indraprastha. On the second day, with the *srotriya*s and *sajanya*s gathered in the hall of sacrifice, the sacred fire was worshipped ceremoniously.

Next was the important ritual of offering *agrapuja* to a *muni* or king of the highest distinction, appointing him the guardian of the sacrifice. *Agrapuja* honoured the first among equals. Such a person was to excel in all fields of life and was to be the best amongst men. Yudhisthira was in a dilemma as to whom to choose, and the assembly was obviously tense. Yudhisthira looked at Bhishma as the rightful choice, but he politely declined the offer. Yudhisthira nervously paused for a moment and asked, 'Pitamah, who else, but you, can I choose? You are the greatest human being I have known, but you are reluctant. I, therefore, would like you to suggest the person fit enough to be called first among equals.'

Bhishma smiled and, with great dignity, replied, 'The person greatest in valour, learning and wisdom, who recently saved dharma from collapse, would be Krishna.' There was spontaneous applause in agreement. Sahadeva approached

Krishna with offerings, washed his feet, placed a tilak on his forehead, performed the *aarti* by waving the wick lamp before him and offered him *agrapuja*. Led by Vyasa, there was a chorus of blessings as the *srotriya*s began chanting.

When the rituals were over, Vyasa stepped forward to where Krishna was seated and, placing his hands on Krishna's head, said, 'You are Purushottama, the foremost amongst men; may the gods help you to be the *Sasvat Dharma Gopta*.' Following his lead, the *srotriya*s chanted Vedic mantras for peace. Then, just as everything was going smoothly, Chedi Raj screamed, 'I will not be a party to this sinful affront!' Consumed with rage, Shishupala started abusing Bhishma using foul language.

> Son of Shantanu and Ganga, in worshipping the cowherd, you have been subservient to the Pandavas. You have forsaken the righteous path for selfish ends. Krishna is not a king; if you wanted a suitable Yadava, you could have selected his father, Vasudeva. If you wanted a king old in years, King Drupada is here. If you wanted a hero who is a master of both intellectual excellence and martial arts, Aswathama is here. If you wanted to honour a venerable sage, Muni Dwaipayana is here.

Meanwhile, Krishna began counting areca nuts by dropping each nut from a plateful kept nearby as part of the worship materials.

Shishupala turned to Krishna, 'Son of Vasudeva, you are greedy, ambitious and deceitful. The five brothers, out of cowardice, have paid you an undeserving honour. If you are an honourable man, you would refuse this honour that you do not deserve at all.'

Saying this, Shishupala and his friends walked away. Yudhisthira went after the Chedi king and tried to reason with him. 'Valiant son of Damaghosha, is it fair to abuse the revered Bhishma, so noble and so valiant, who has been the living embodiment of Kshatra Tej?'

But Bhishma restrained him, saying, 'Enough of it, Yudhisthira. If Shishupala thinks that we have wrongly honoured Vaasudeva, he is at liberty to leave the assembly and we can go ahead with the ceremony.'

The usually reticent Sahadeva spoke, 'Shishupala, please do not interrupt the *agrapuja* proceedings. Those who oppose *agrapuja* to Krishna Vaasudeva may stand aside and allow us to proceed further; we respect their opinions and I salute them.' Except for a handful of Shishupala's cronies, the rest of the *rajanya*s agreed to the decision of honouring Krishna. Shishupala was enraged further by this turn of events and, once again, directed his anger at Bhishma. 'You, son of Ganga, who received men indiscriminatingly, your words were all false. Your vow of celibacy was false, made to cover your impotence. Today, your end is inevitable, you wretched old man.'

Krishna moved near Bhishma and apologised with folded palms. 'Grandfather, forgive that imbecile. I will take care of him.'

Shishupala then poured his venom on Krishna, 'You cowherd, you will also meet a similar end. You started your life with the murder of your uncle, Kamsa; you prompted Bhima to butcher Jarasandha by trickery. Why are you here? You have no place among the *rajanya*s.'

Bhima shook with rage and was about to pounce on Shishupala, when Bhishma intervened. 'Hold your temper, Bhima! Let us not spoil the occasion. We have offered *agrapuja* to Vaasudeva. He is now the guardian of Rajasuya and it is up to him to deal with the situation.'

Shishupala continued to seethe. 'To you, Krishna may be the ultimate reality; but to me, he is a fraud, cheat and trickster. I will deal with that cowherd and the five brothers, you senile old man. Mark my words!'

Krishna stopped counting the nuts as he reached the hundredth count and then, he roared. Shishupala unsheathed his sword to attack. Krishna and the Pandavas were unarmed. But, all of a sudden, a sharp, whirring noise could be heard in the assembly. Like the shining sun, the Sudarshana discus began chasing Shishupala, who, in deathly fright, took to his heels; the discus sliced Shishupala's neck and returned to Krishna. The beheaded trunk of Shishupala fell to the ground, defiling the sacred precincts of the sacrificial hall.

Friends of Shishupala then rode out of Indraprastha, dazed by the overwhelming power of Krishna. The assembly sat stunned, for they had never witnessed Krishna's wrath.

Vyasa and the other *srotiya*s started chanting, *'Purusha Suktam'*—the verse of the lord, praising, 'Who He is and what He is. He is the pivot on which the entire universe revolves, He is the sun, the moon, the stars the very cause of life—the eternal time-space continuum.'

At the end of the chants, when peace was invoked, 'Shanti...shanti...shanti,' Krishna regained his composure and helped in his cousin's cremation rituals as per the shastras. He requested Yudhisthira to crown Shishupala's son as the next king of Chedi.

The Rajasuya was resumed after a break of fifteen days. Vyasa blessed all the *rajanyas*, *srotriyas* and the general polity with his healing presence and advised them to follow the path of virtue and righteousness.

AFTER THE RAJASUYA

When the Rajasuya was concluded, the sacred fire was ceremonially extinguished and Vyasa retreated to Dhaumya's ashram for a few days.

The *rajanyas* who had accepted Yudhisthira as a Chakravarti were presented with valuables and the brothers escorted them to the frontiers as they returned to their kingdoms. Vasudeva and Balarama, along with some of the Yadava *atirathis*, departed for their homes soon after. Krishna, Uddhava and Satyaki stayed behind for a few days. Everyone was apprehensive of the consequences of Shishupala's death. Grandfather Bhishma and other guests from Hastinapura too stayed behind to see the incredible Maya Sabha that had astounded everyone. Duryodhana wore his best smile through all the time that he was in Indraprastha. Yudhisthira misunderstood it to be genuine and when his cousin requested for a tour of the Maya Sabha, he promptly asked Bhima to escort him to there.

During the tour, in the company of Bhima and Draupadi, Duryodhana walked into a pool that he had mistaken for solid floor. He also hit a wall in which an illusion had been created of a doorway. Bhima and Draupadi laughed uproariously. Duryodhana was deeply mortified and took this as an affront, especially a remark allegedly made by Draupadi, 'A blind man's son will also be blind, after all.'

Yudhisthira was most upset once he learnt of the fiasco, but could not rebuke anyone. How could he disown responsibility?

The Rajasuya was performed to bring peace and harmony, but ended up increasing hatred between the two clans of the Kurus, who now pledged to destroy one another. He could not believe that his own wife and brother had affronted Duryodhana, an important guest. Bothered by such distressing thoughts, Yudhisthira collapsed on his bed in sheer fatigue and, at last, sleep overtook him. It was a disturbed sleep and he dreamt of a battlefield, clash of swords and maces, broken chariots, blood and vultures and, at the same time, he heard the distant refrain of the invocation to peace, 'Shanti...shanti...shanti.'

He woke up very agitated. The next morning, a distraught Yudhisthira visited Vyasa at his retreat, who was preparing to leave in the afternoon for Kurukshetra.

Yudhisthira narrated his nightmare and asked him what he foresaw. Vyasa closed his eyes and, after a while, said, 'My son, Shishupala's death was not the end, but the beginning of a carnage involving the massacre of kshatriyas. The ghosts of Kamsa, Jarasandha and Shishupala will stalk the earth, and will continue to do so till their bloodlust is satisfied. An apocalypse is in the making!'

'How can I prevent this disaster, master? I am ready to do anything to avoid it,' said Yudhisthira.

The master's eyes were fixed on the future. 'Yudhisthira, you will become the centre of this carnage; you cannot avoid it. That is the way of *vidhi*! This holocaust cannot be stopped even if you renounce the world and Vaasudeva unfurls all his divine powers!'

Yudhisthira slumped to the floor and fell at the feet of the master, who lifted the king and, caressing him very tenderly, said:

> Son, you know, this has to happen for Krishna to spread the message of dharma. Dharmaputra, this is the meaning of his sojourn, on this planet, amidst us. Surrender before him and he shall come to your aid. This is ordained by Lord Shiva, the Great Destroyer! Son, a new age will be ushered in and Krishna Vaasudeva will lead it; you, your brothers and I are, but, mere instruments. The age of dharma will be called the Yudhisthira era and it will be born from the ashes of this holocaust.

A few days later, Krishna departed for Dwaraka. Before leaving, he said to Yudhisthira, 'Follow your own conscience and strengthen Indraprastha. Duryodhana will never forgive his humiliation and, moreover, your prosperity will continue to sting him...do not get trapped.'

Krishna halted for couple of days at Pushkar on his way back, where he was the guest of Chekitana. Krishna took a ceremonial bath in the Pushkar Lake and worshipped Brahma and Savitri, the Great Mother Gayatri. He remained rather solemn and pensive as he knew that Shishupala's death would have serious repercussions.

After a few days of journeying through the desert, Krishna was informed that Shalva had raided Dwaraka and kidnapped Vasudeva.

Krishna sent messengers to all friendly powers to join him in fighting Shalva. Krishna now wore the crown of *Dharma Gopta*—Guardian of Dharma. When *agrapuja* had been accorded to him unexpectedly, even he had felt the burden of far-reaching responsibilities. His empire of dharma did not have visible boundaries, yet, he felt more powerful because it was founded by willing hearts and included everyone—Yadavas, all Aryans, Nagas, Rakshasas and even Nishadas.

A ghastly scene awaited Krishna upon his return to Dwaraka. Houses had been burnt down, charred remains of men, cattle and horses lay everywhere. Taking advantage of Krishna's absence and that of the leading *athirathi*s, Shalva had descended upon Dwaraka. After destroying it, he had returned to his homeland, the barren desert and salt marshes.

Krishna blew his conch to announce his arrival and so did the other *atirathi*s and *maharathi*s, to challenge Shalva; but the enemy was gone. The Yadavas who had valiantly tried to defend Dwaraka but had been forced to take refuge in the dense forest, now came out to meet Krishna. Some of them fetched Pradyumna, who arrived with some warriors and prostrated himself at his father's feet. The contingent camped along the seashore and began setting up huts and equipment was necessary for the refugees. Pradyumna narrated to his father how Shalva and his camel warriors had crossed River Lavanika and overrun Saurashtra.

Pradyumna was Rukmini's firstborn. She had nine other sons and one daughter: Charudeshna, Sudeshna, Charudeha, Susena, Charugupta, Bhadracharu, Charuvinda, Sucharu, Charu and Charumati. Pradyumna said:

> Our warriors bravely resisted Shalva's forces. Uncle Uddhava sent two *maharathis* to bring you back to Dwaraka. The wounded were removed to the citadel in the forest. The able-bodied Yadava chiefs and their followers hid themselves in the jungle while pursuing Shalva's men. Father, Shalva's forces were barbaric and he himself looked like an uncouth demon with big teeth.

'I had seen him many years ago,' replied Krishna. 'I thought he would not attack us after we restored Pushkar to Chekitana. Shalva hates the Yadavas. Now, tell me, how did he manage to capture my respected father?'

'By sheer accident, father! I do not know why Grandfather joined a reconnaissance party of Yadavas, but it was then that some Saubha warriors captured him. We tried to pursue them, but they had fast-moving camels and we had none. I am worried about Grandfather's safety.'

Krishna stared far into the horizon and then, looking into Pradyumna's beautiful eyes, said, 'Do not worry. Father is still alive; if Shalva kills him, he would have to pay a severe price. Where is Satyaki?'

'He had gone in search of you, to warn you that Shalva's men might ambush you. Have you not met him?'

'No,' replied Krishna. 'I hope he was not captured too.'

Krishna pondered over the situation and said:

> It is difficult to resist Shalva when he invades our lands. Now we will have to fight him on his own ground protected, as it is, by River Lavanika and the long stretch of desert beyond. We cannot destroy Shalva by running away from him; we shall fight him and destroy him on his land. Let us regroup our warriors. Inform our chiefs to assemble as soon as they can.

Krishna then walked among his people to assess the chaos and their distress. The shrine of Lord Somnath had also been destroyed by the raiders. 'We shall build a new temple in silver,' said Krishna and promised that Dwaraka will rise once again to greater glory.

'Father, why does Shalva hate the Yadavas? I heard he considers you the foremost enemy of Danavas. Why is that?' asked Pradyumna.

Krishna smiled and said:

> It is a long story son. The Aryan way of life is *rita*, dharma. Danavas were opposed to it and they had Asuras on their side. Both wanted dominance of Aryawartha but, with Aryans gaining the upper hand, Danavas and other aboriginal races had to surrender or retreat into the forests and wastelands of this vast continent of Bharat.
>
> Shalva, who now calls himself Rajadhi Raja—the king of kings—is a Danava king; and Saubha is a desert city to the west of River Lavanika, close to the ocean. Their civilisation is a remnant of the Indus Valley Civilisation, which is now extinct. The population is mixed, comprising members of the ancient Pashupati cult of Shiva worship, Semitic Siddhis and peoples of Negroid and Arab descent from the nearby gulf of Pancha Jana—Aden in the present Arabian Peninsula. Danavas hated Aryas and their refined civilisation.

> Along with Jarasandha in the east, Shalva wanted to take control of Aryawartha and destroy the new enlightened way of life based on dharma.
>
> Shalva's animosity began with the *swayamvara* of the three princesses of Kashi. Esteemed Bhishma kidnapped the princesses to marry them off to his brothers. One of them, Amba, had fallen in love with Shalva. When Bhishma came to know of this, he released Amba, but Shalva refused to marry the princess, having lost her in fight. Amba, desperate and desolate, offered herself in marriage to Bhishma, who refused, owing to his pledge of celibacy. Amba committed herself to extreme austerities in the worship of Lord Shiva and, over a time, passed away.
>
> Shalva, in alliance with Jarasandha, wanted to destroy the kings of Aryawartha. This grand alliance was organised to meet the danger of Aryan supremacy. Kamsa also joined this confederacy and seized control of Mathura from his weak father, our King Ugrasena.

Krishna then narrated to his son, the circumstances surrounding his birth to Devaki.

> Every time Shalva joined Jarasandha in alliance, they failed miserably. So, out of contempt for my brother and me, Shalva instigated an animal of a Mlechha—Kalayavana to kill me. I tricked this Mlechha and he was killed. Today, we are a powerful and formidable force and can save Dharma and the Aryan way of life. That is why Shalva attacked Dwaraka when I was away at Indraprastha. He would have come to know that Shishupala was also killed, and, hence, wanted to destroy Dwaraka, the citadel of Yadava power and influence. I am his enemy, but he cannot fight me on my land; therefore, he abducted my father, knowing that I would meet him on his land. The time has come for us to get rid of this tyrant, once and for all; we must make our western borders secure.

Patting Pradyumna with affection, Krishna asked, 'And now, tell me son, how did you fare in your first battle with Shalva?'
Pradyumna replied:

> Father, he had come by sea and hurled firebomb missiles at the city. Within a short time, the city was in flames. But the attack was repulsed, after the initial setback. The Saubha fleet had two swift, high-mast ships. At each level, they had lookout platforms from where they targeted us with arrows

that were soaked in oil and set ablaze. The lead ship belonged to Shalva and, from a distance, you would have thought that it was a flying fortress. Shalva was directing the attack from the topmost platform. Father, these Danavas outperformed us technologically.

Krishna smiled and said:

Yes, it was a great civilisation at one point of time, but has now become extinct. That is the nature of time—it fosters change. The Danava civilisation was a materialistic one. It was technologically advanced, yet, had a stunted mindset. They worshiped Mahadeva as Pashupati. Despite their material advancement, under peculiar circumstances and adverse climate, the civilisation collapsed. Shalva is last of that lost generation. They shun the Aryan way of life—our language, customs and our enlightened rishis and *munis*; they abduct our fair-skinned and delicate womenfolk.

Shalva is a despotic ruler, and his society is licentious; he hates me and all that I stand for. His allies, Jarasandha and Shishupala, have been eliminated by me and now, the last of the devils must be finished.

Pradyumna revealed:

Father, we gave a good beating to Shalva's forces. We slew his trusted lieutenants, Vegavan and Vivindha, and also his minister, Kshemavriddhi. Shalva fled when I was on the verge of killing him. He boarded his ship, Viman Saubha, and left the field of battle. Kshatra Dharma required that I should not fight a foe who is no longer in combat.

Krishna appreciated his son's intentions. 'Son, not always; adversaries like Shalva and Jarasandha are to be killed even if Kshatra Dharma is violated; that is an exception to the rule!'

Pradyumna continued, 'Father, you have been saving the Yadavas single-handedly for so long. Now, it is my turn to put an end to this danger once and for all. Now that you are here, may I go in search of noble grandfather, Vasudeva?'

'It is indeed noble of you to undertake this task on your own, and my blessings are always with you,' said Krishna. 'I would have restrained you from undertaking this hazardous mission, but I also realise that you would be happier if you can perform valiant deeds, all by yourself.'

Krishna hugged his son and asked where Mayavati was, 'Is she with the other ladies of the royal family, taken to Bhrigukachhapa or Girinagar? What is all this mystery about her? Your choice of a wife was so unfortunate. Your mother was miserable for fifteen years when you were kidnapped by that Danava, Sambara.'

Pradyumna had been kidnapped by Sambara when he was just five years old. He was brought up by Mayavati, a servant girl of Sambara, who was fifteen years senior to Pradyumna. At the age of twenty, Mayavati brought him to Dwaraka. Rukmini did not relish the affair between a young man and a much older woman. She rejected them as man and wife and, hence, Mayavati lived in the forest.

Sensing his father's discomfiture, Pradyumna replied:

> She is staying all by herself in the forest, as the other ladies of the family would not accept her. My mother avoids me in disgust. It was a quirk of fate that I lived with her for the past fifteen years. She raised me from an infant into a man, and shared my bed as mother and wife. Circumstances were extraordinary. The world in which we lived, that of Danavas and Asuras, was different.

'Can I meet her?' asked Krishna. 'Of course! You are the only person who she may not object to meeting, besides Uncle Uddhava, who has been very kind to us.' Later in the day, Pradyumna led Krishna into a cave, deep in the forest, where she was busy preparing food.

Seeing Krishna, she prostrated at his feet. Krishna lifted her up and noticed tears welling in her proud eyes. Krishna smiled with great compassion and said, 'Daughter, why did you not go to Girinagar with the other ladies of the family?'

'O noble father, do you expect me to be with those proud ladies of your family? They do not approve of my relationship with your son and I do not accept them. Pradyumna is going alone to challenge Shalva, so I have decided to accompany him.'

'Daughter, will you not be an encumbrance to him when he ventures into that lion's den?'

'Encumbrance! But for me, where would he have been? He was about five years old when he was kidnapped. He did not know from where he came from or who his parents were. Had I not been there, he would never have survived.'

After a brief pause, she continued:

> One night, when the barbarians had gone out on their expedition, we went

> to sleep as usual. However, I woke up in the middle of the night, perturbed. I realised that Pradyumna was no longer a child, but a young man craving for partnership in life. I was half awake and debated the situation. He put his hands on me softly, perhaps in sleep. I felt ecstatic at his touch. Pradyumna was also shivering with excitement. Since that moment, we became partners in life. We had no feast to celebrate our wedding and no *srotriya*s to bless us. I lit the fire, both of us went round the sacred fire seven times and the gods made us one.
>
> Vaasudeva, since then, Pradyumna has played a significant part in my life. I decided that I would not leave Pradyumna at the mercy of Sambarasura and his tribe of barbarians. He had become my love, my heart and my salvation. With the help of some friends, I taught him body combat and archery. One day, we met Uncle Uddhava, who was on an unrelenting search for Pradyumna. Seeing his handsome features, he realised that it must be your son.
>
> Uddhava was kind enough to give us a house and a small entourage to protect us. Uddhava shaped Pradyumna into a *maharathi* and he has vindicated his lineage by driving Shalva out of Dwaraka. Your son has also killed Asura Sambara in body combat and, from then on, asuras are scared of harming him. I want him to be the great son of a great father. My life is bound with Pradyumna's. If Shalva does kill Pradyumna, I shall jump into his funeral pyre.

Krishna was delighted at the forthright confidence exhibited by this valiant woman in his son's life. 'Daughter, you have my blessings.'

JOURNEY THROUGH THE DESERT

Pradyumna crossed River Lavanika and entered the desert on foot. During the day, when the sun blazed, they rested in a small oasis where there was ample water. The next morning, they halted at a tiny village where he met some soldiers of Shalva's army who were on camels.

Pradyumna signalled who he was and declared that, at the insistence of Krishna Vaasudeva, he would like to meet their king. The soldiers laughed aloud thinking it was a joke, but Pradyumna insisted that they should believe him.

The soldiers of Saubha provided camels and riders for Pradyumna's party. After an arduous journey, on the fifth day, Pradyumna's party arrived at Matrikovata, the capital of Saubha.

'Young Yadava,' the head of the soldiers, Vajranabh, addressed Pradyumna. 'We have reached your destination. I saw you in the battle at Dwaraka; you fought well. Our king of kings would welcome you, valiant Yadava.'

Pradyumna was stunned when he reached Matrikovata. He was taken to a huge house with goatskin walls. They were escorted to a luxuriously furnished chamber and several servitors were placed at his disposal. Vajranabh clapped and half a dozen women servitors came into the chamber and took Pradyumna to a pool for bathing. At dinner, Vajranabh joined Pradyumna. Before parting for the night, Pradyumna asked the head of the soldiers, 'Do all your servitors provide all amenities of life?'

Vajranabh said with a laugh, 'It is scarce to find a woman who is chaste in this land. We are not Aryans; do not be shocked. Our women do not like to be condemned.' Then he lowered his voice and said, 'Be careful, the king is watching you. These servitors are his spies. Do not fall for their charms; they have a weapon more powerful than the weapon which we possess.'

'What is the weapon?'

'Poison. Men, after enjoying our women, are murdered as they sleep, with their heads in their lap. Control yourself and tell the same to your companions.'

The next morning, Pradyumna was informed that the king would receive him in the afternoon. When he entered the king's chamber, Shalva looked at Pradyumna with a smile. Pointing to a seat near him, he asked him to sit down. Pradyumna responded with a boyish smile of disbelief.

'You are the young warrior whom I would have finished at Dwaraka, but spared. You fought bravely. I have no quarrel with you; only with your father.' At his command, a slave girl came in, followed by musicians. 'She is a wonderful girl,' Shalva said, 'You can have her after the entertainment.'

'Thank you, noble king of kings, I have vowed not to touch a woman unless she is married to me. This is part of Kshatra Dharma.'

Pradyumna then enquired about his grandfather. 'Oh, do not worry about him; he is comfortably located. We shall deal with him after we meet your father,' replied Shalva.

Pradyumna dared to say, 'Just now, you said you have no quarrel with me; then, please release my grandfather. In fact, my visit to your court is to seek his release. He is an old man, respected greatly by the Yadavas. Please release him,and I shall leave immediately. You can see, I am unarmed.'

'Of course, you can take your grandfather. I will release him after I meet your father. I am waiting for him,' replied Shalva.

MUGG FORT

Shalva could not forget the devastating defeat of his forces at Dwaraka. This young boy and other *maharathi*s had defended well and he had lost three of his great commanders. He had, himself, narrowly escaped. He had to retreat hastily, leaving behind Vajranabh. Shalva called Vajranabh and said, 'I now place all my powers in your hands. You are as dear to me as your father, Vegavan.'

'Your commands shall be obeyed, lord,' replied Vajranabh. 'We have to deal with our enemies as they deserve,' said Shalva, and paused for a moment. He did not trust Vajranabh's loyalty to him but, under the circumstances, he had no options. Shalva continued:

> You have to play host to Pradyumna. Mugg Fort is placed at your disposal. I have already given instructions to shift your family there. Remember, I have also lodged Krishna's father there. Take care that no one learns about this. Krishna is bound to come to rescue his father. I hold you responsible with your life.

As Vajranabh was leaving, Shalva called him back, 'Vajranabh, how many daughters do you have? What is the age of your eldest daughter?'

'Sixteen, Your Majesty,' replied Vajranabh, in great fright.

'Why do you not give her hand in marriage to this handsome Yadava?' asked Shalva. Vajranabh hesitated for a moment and said, 'I have to check with Prabhavati if she will be willing to wed or not.'

Shalva laughed. 'I will be delighted to celebrate the wedding of Prabhavati with Pradyumna. It will be a great occasion; the meeting of two cultures—Danava and Aryan. Think it over, Vajranabh.'

'Lord, I will be delighted to convey your proposal to my daughter, but I need some time…I request you to please give me a month.'

'But, take care that you play no games with me,' said Shalva, dismissing him for the day.

PRADYUMNA

Pradyumna's life in Mugg Fort was filled with constant joy, but he was also in equal agony. He had promised his father that he would find Vasudeva. So far, he could see no trace of the Shoora chief. He realised that Shalva was holding him hostage.

The Mugg Fort was a prison of rosebuds; he had resisted the advances of many a voluptuous beauty. Then Prabhavati tried to attract him. She was aggressive in her approach. It was very difficult for Pradyumna to overcome his desire for her, yet he managed—a trait he seemed to have inherited from his father.

Vajranabh arrived in his chamber one morning, to convey Shalva's proposal. Pradyumna flared up and said, 'Impossible! I have come here to find my grandfather. I will not accept your daughter as my wife.'

Vajranabh was cautious in choosing his words because Shalva had placed his spies all around. He lowered his voice and said:

> If you refuse this proposal, Shalva will kill you, your grandfather and me. Buy time and agree…marry my beautiful daughter, Prabhavati. Please do not worry; she will not kill you on the wedding night. That is what Shalva wants, but it will not happen, I can assure you!
>
> However, be on your guard. I have a hunch that your grandfather is a prisoner in this fort. Shalva does not trust me and would not mind killing my entire family. Give me some time to find out more. Marry Prabhavati; she loves you.

Pradyumna pondered over the situation and replied, 'Give me a day or two. Meanwhile, let me speak to your daughter.'

Prabhavati and Pradyumna were married, with Shalva presiding over the ceremonies. On the wedding night, Prabhavati tried to obey her king's command to kill her husband, but her heart was not in it, and Pradyumna easily wrenched the assassin's knife. She feared the wrath of Shalva and wept for having failed in her task.

Two days later, Vajranabh returned from Matrikovata. He summoned Pradyumna and was glad to see him alive. 'The king had to leave for Pushkar all of a sudden. There were some incursions, so he left in haste with some camel cavalry. This is the moment I had been waiting for; both of you can leave immediately for your lands. I have kept a couple of trusted camel riders ready to help you make a quick escape.' Prabhavati, who was also present, started crying, 'Father, I cannot leave you and mother alone, that demon will kill you…'

'Prabhavati, do not be stupid. I will take care of the situation.'

‘What about my grandfather?’ asked Pradyumna.

‘He is in the prison inside Mugg Fort,’ replied Vajranabh. ‘Threatened by Chekitana, the king rushed to Pushkar. I think it is a diversionary strategy by your father, who would be arriving soon at Matrikovata to attack Shalva. Shalva’s days are numbered. Please leave now and, if you can, help your father, Krishna.’

Suddenly there was a commotion in the courtyard! Vajranabh came rushing with a naked sword in his hand and screamed, ‘Prabhavati, stop wherever you are, and if Pradyumna is with you, ask him to stay where he is. His days are numbered.’

Pradyumna did not know what to do. He had a small knife in his waistband, which would be of no use. Two servitors blocked Pradyumna’s path. Vajranabh had Pradyumna in his grip, but did not use the sword against him. Vajranabh whispered, ‘You fool, catch hold of me and throw me down, now!’

Vajranabh let the sword fall to the ground. Pradyumna understood his tactic and caught hold of the sword as it fell to the ground. Vajranabh fell and Pradyumna sat on his chest. The two servitors, with half swords in their hands, made no serious attempt to run to the defence of their master; instead, they ran away.

Vajranabh said, ‘Do not kill me, but tie me up with the rope I have around my waist.’ Pradyumna tied up his father-in-law to a pillar and made a few cuts on his hands and face.

‘Run away on the camels that I have stationed for you at the foothills and ride as fast as you can. Shalva is too busy defending his territory in the north,’ Vajranabh urged Pradyumna.

‘Krishna has already sent some tribals who look like wild eagles. The Yadava is not far away.’

After riding for about two days on a camel, Pradyumna and Prabhavati reached the Lavanika estuary and witnessed a strange scene. There stood an army of Garudas and, frightened by their headgear and bird noises, the camels ran away into the desert. The Garuda chief bowed before Pradyumna and introduced himself as Vainateya, Krishna’s guardian. He told them that his lord was not far away and was coming with *maharathi*s who are familiar with these lands.

Pradyumna and Prabhavati were fed fish and kakadas. They rested in a shelter shaped out of soft bird feathers; the newly married couple slept, carefree.

When they woke up late in the morning, the Garuda chief called Pradyumna and informed him that Krishna had arrived and was waiting for him.

Pradyumna narrated his adventure and also informed Krishna about Shalva being in Pushkar to fight Chekitana. Krishna met Prabhavati and gave her his blessings. He asked them to leave for Dwaraka while he took on Shalva.

Pradyumna fell at his father's feet and pleaded, 'Father, please forgive me...but I have to keep my promise...please let me be with you, I would like to help you in rescuing Grandfather.' Krishna agreed and allowed his son to participate in the final battle against Shalva.

Meanwhile, Shalva's guards rushed to inform him that the Yadava army was marching towards Matrikovata. Shalva panicked and instructed one of his trusted lieutenants to inform Vajranabh to hold the fort. He rode with his army to the Lavanika river to intercept Krishna's forces. He could use his ships to damage the invading Yadava *maharathi*s.

When he reached the river, Shalva switched over to his ship, Viman Saubha, while his camel riders clashed with the Yadava forces. They faced stiff resistance from Pradyumna and both sides suffered many casualties. Shalva's Siddi—Negroid soldiers, led by lieutenant Duman, attacked Pradyumna and knocked him unconscious. However, his charioteer, Daruka's son, took him to the Yadava camp; after some first aid, Pradyumna recovered and, in a fierce battle, he killed Shalva's general, Duman.

At this moment, Shalva entered the battle arena, blowing Danava trumpets, and his ship entered the bay area of the river. Shalva's archers rained arrows on the Yadava forces. He discharged a deadly arrow at Krishna that made him drop his bow. Shalva roared in joy and jumped from his ship to deal a death blow to Krishna. Krishna retaliated with a hefty strike to Shalva's chest from his club. Shalva vomited blood and swiftly retreated to his ship. Using occult tactics, Shalva, as a defensive measure, created an illusion wherein it appeared that he was carrying a beheaded Vaasudeva.

For a moment, Krishna was nonplussed. Then, regaining control, he blew his divine conch. The resonance of the conch disrupted the deceptive magic of Shalva. Krishna now aimed his club at Shalva's post and, as it fell, the beam's weight shattered the ship. Panicking, Shalva ran to deboard from the damaged ship but, just then, Krishna's discus sliced through Shalva's neck, ending another savage realm.

Shalva's friend and ally, Dantavaktra, was the king of Karusha in the east. He was the son of Vriddha Sharma, the old king of Karusha. When he heard of Shalva's death, Dantavaktra attacked Krishna to avenge his friend's end. But Krishna delivered a fatal blow with his club, and Dantavaktra died soon after.

JANARDANA—THE REFUGE OF THE DISTRESSED

Once Krishna came back to Dwaraka with his contingent, he summoned the council of Yadava chiefs and apprised them of the momentous events that had been occuring during that year. Krishna also introduced Vajranabh as the new king of Saubha.

With the neighbourhood finally peaceful, they could now rebuild Dwaraka. Krishna spoke:

> Noble Yadava chiefs and revered King Ugrasena! The evil foursome of Jarasandha, Shishupala, Shalva and Dantavaktra has been vanquished at great cost. From now on, it is the duty of every Yadava to rebuild Dwaraka and transform it into a citadel of dharma. I am directing Pradyumna to assist his father-in-law, Vajranabh, in consolidating our victory in the western frontiers and establish dharma among the people of Saubha.
>
> O noble king, there was a massive social and humanitarian problem after vanquishing the evil of Narakasura; at my behest, Uddhava brought several thousand Aryan girls to Dwaraka. They have to be rehabilitated by suitably marrying them to our Yadava men, such that the unit of family and the fabric of dharma are protected for posterity.
>
> I had seriously pondered over this matter at Pragjyotishpura, when their parents refused to accept them into their fold. I concluded that this would be the best we could do. Having agreed to be their guardian, I am also aware that history might project me as their de facto husband. I have borne many insults and insinuations in my life and I do not mind another one. However, I seek your wise council; we must find proper husbands for these girls.

Balarama was vociferous in his support for this proposal. Vasudeva, who had just been released from Shalva's prison, joined the crowd and said, 'My son, from now on, you will be known as Janardana—the refuge of the distressed.'

Tvamaksharam paramam veditavyam
Tvamasya visvasya param nidhaanam.
Tvamavyah sasvatadharmagoptaa sanaatanam
Purusho mato me...Janardana!

Purushottama, you are the primordial Omkara, focus of this Universe, Supreme Soul, repository of eternal Truth, Wisdom, the Indestructible, our ancient refuge. O God, I salute you! O Janardana!

*****

Episode 5

Mahabharata and Its Effects

Sri Krishna kamalanadha Vaasudeva Sanatana
Vasudevatanaja punyo lilamanusha vigraha
Srivatsa Kausthabhadharo Yasoda vatsalo Hari Jagatpata

—A traditional prayer

This is the final and most important segment in the Krishna saga. The canvas of the story spans over fifty years of tumultuous events and includes the catastrophic Mahabharata War. An entire civilisation was decimated, culminating with the departure of Krishna. The prelude to the holocaust was a simple game of dice—a royal game, which was a vice among all the kings of Aryawartha.

The part played by Krishna in the Mahabharata War was enormous. The original story, in 10,000 verses as *Jaya*, was written by Veda Vyasa and has been told and retold over several thousand years; in the process it eventually became 1,00,000 verses known by the name of the Mahabharata.

As we see in this chapter of his life, Krishna gradually becomes a pale shadow of his earlier self and, after the war, he turns into a philosopher and mystic.

The highlight of this story is the Bhagavad Gita, which contains Krishna's message to mankind and the very purport of his incarnation. The Gita has a unique status among all scriptural texts, as it is the teaching of truth by the lord Himself. Unlike other scriptures, the Gita was taught in the battlefield, highlighting the fact that it is a text that has relevance to humanity in the thick of worldly life.

This is the central theme of Sanatana Dharma, wherein the creator often takes many forms with human qualities and is born in this world. In each incarnation, he has destroyed evil and established dharma—the righteous way of living, which is the bedrock of Hindu philosophy.

THE GAME OF DICE

After attending the Rajasuya at Indraprastha, Duryodhana had been smitten with jealousy, having seen the prosperity and popularity of the Pandavas.

The honour and love they got from their people was something unheard of in the Kuru kingdom. And, above all, he had been ridiculed by Draupadi. By the end of his tour of Indraprastha, he had been seething with anger and sought revenge. He was aware that he could never defeat the Pandavas in fair battle, with Drupada on their side.

On his return, Duryodhana and his evil trio—Shakuni, Karna and Dushassana, began plotting against the Pandavas, seeking ways to humiliate them. Shakuni suggested a game of dice as he was confident of defeating Yudhisthira in it. According to Aryan tradition, kshatriyas invited to a game of dice had no choice but to accept the invitation. Moreover, Yudhisthira was fond of the game, although not adept at it. Shakuni, on the other hand, was known to cheat with the help of a loaded dice.

The dice were made of ivory or animal bones and Shakuni fraudulently loaded them with lead in the hollows, making them heavy, so that they yielded to expert players like him. Yudhisthira assumed that the game would be played in true professional spirit, but it was full of intrigues with political overtones, and the loser would have to face disastrous consequences.

Duryodhana sought his father's permission and convinced him of their plan. Dhritarashtra, the doting father, agreed to send Vidura to invite Yudhisthira. Vidura sensed a conspiracy and tried to prevail on the king to desist from this fraud as it might lead to a war and the ultimate decimation of the Kauravas, but to no avail.

Yudhisthira was reluctant to accept the invitation as a game of wagers would end up in more enmity. However, he could not violate the code of Aryans and, besides, Yudhisthira was fond of the game. He accepted the invitation with a sense of fatality.

As per their plan, Shakuni rolled the dice on behalf of Duryodhana and, with his loaded dice, kept winning game after game against the king of Indraprastha. This being a game of bets, Yudhisthira was tricked, ultimately, to stake all his wealth, jewels, kingdom, servants, gold and silver from his state treasury. After forfeiting all his material wealth, he dared and wagered his brothers one by one and, in the end, lost himself too. In a state of trauma and despair, with nothing else to give, he wagered Draupadi and lost her.

Duryodhana was drunk on arrogance and *madira*. Intoxicated, he ordered his charioteer, Pratikami, to bring Draupadi to the assembly hall as she was no more the queen of Indraprastha, but his slave. Pratikami was shocked at the command and reluctantly went to the women's chambers, apologetic and weeping. Draupadi was aghast at the turn of events and asked Pratikami whether Yudhisthira wagered on her after he lost his kingship or before. When Pratikami replied that Yudhisthira had put her on stake after losing his kingship, Draupadi asked him to tell Duryodhana that she was not bound by this wager and would not obey the command.

Pratikami conveyed this to Duryodhana, who, by this time, was shamelessly inebriated and ordered the equally drunk Dushassana to bring Draupadi as she was, even if he had to drag her. Dushassana brusquely rushed into Draupadi's room, caught her by her hair,and dragged her into the Kuru assembly. Duryodhana told her that she was now his slave and, in an obscene manner, invited her to sit on his right thigh. Even Karna shamelessly remarked that Panchali, the common wife of five men, need not feel shy about Duryodhana's proposition.

The shocked Draupadi appealed to the Kuru elders, including Bhishma and Drona, to stop this heinous and dishonourable act from occurring in their presence. The spineless elders hung their heads in shame and did not intervene to help the woman wailing in deep distress. Bhima could not contain his anger and wanted to set fire to Yudhisthira's hand that had cast the dice, but Arjuna prevailed upon his brother to control his temper. Bhima vowed that he would, one day, tear apart the right thigh of Duryodhana to avenge this indecent proposal.

At this point, Duryodhana let go of all decency expected in a kshatriya prince; he commanded Dushassana to strip Draupadi of her sari and make her stand naked in front of the assembly. Dushassana started pulling the sari of the helpless Draupadi. When no one came to her rescue, she thought of her Sakha and prayed to him to save her honour. All this time, she was holding the last fold of her sari with her left hand, while with her right, she was appealing to her lord, Sri Krishna. Seeing no help forthcoming, in despair and absolute surrender, she left the fold of her sari. Just then, a thunderous flash of light blinded everyone present in the hall; the shaft of unearthly brightness stunned everyone and plunged the assembly into a stupor. Dushassana fainted instantly. Drona and the other elders swooned; only Bhishma remained conscious, but motionless, as he chanted '*Vaasudevaya Namo Namaha!*' and meekly asked

Draupadi to leave the assembly. Draupadi ran into Gandhari's room, wailing pitiably at the outrage.

The Pandava brothers were the first to regain consciousness. Arjuna swore to kill Karna for his indecent remarks on Draupadi's chastity. Draupadi was furious at Yudhisthira and his brothers, and vowed that she would not tie up her hair till the wild wretches who dishonoured her are killed and her hair is smeared with Dushassana's blood. Bhima roared and promised to break Duryodhana's thighs and tear open Dushassana's heart, drink his blood and anoint Draupadi's hair with that blood.

After comforting Draupadi, a troubled Gandhari went to the blind king who, being blind to truth and justice, was rejoicing at the fraudulent victory of his sons. Gandhari severely reprimanded him, 'Are you blind to the consequences of dishonouring the noble daughter-in-law of the family? O Aryaputra! You are inviting the decimation of the race!' She pleaded with him to set things right and disclaim the illegal gains of the game of dice.

'Set the Pandavas free and return their kingdom. Let peace prevail,' she implored. Taken aback by this rebuke, Dhritarashtra ordered that the Pandavas be set free from their bond and their kingdom returned.

The Pandavas returned to Indraprastha, traumatised by the events of the previous day.

Duryodhana, upon recovering from his stupor, learnt that his father, at the behest of his mother, had returned the kingdom to the Pandavas who had then left for Indraprastha. He was furious; goaded by Shakuni, he convinced the wicked king to invite Yudhisthira for another game of dice.

Yudhisthira, to the chagrin of Draupadi and his brothers, submitted himself and his family to the hand of destiny once again and returned to Hastinapura. This time, the wager was that the defeated party would go into exile with his brothers, staying in the forest for thirteen years and in the last year, they should remain incognito. If they were recognised during the thirteenth year, they would have to repeat the term of exile all over again.

With stoic fatalism, Yudhisthira lost the game once again and immediately departed to the forest along with his brothers and Draupadi, all wearing austere clothes, leaving Kunti with Vidura.

Thus, the Pandavas began the long ordeal of forest life and severe hardships. Some citizens, brahmanas and holy men from Hastinapura also joined them, in protest against Duryodhana's evil rule. Dissuaded by Yudhisthira, most of them returned home, but some still remained.

AKSHAYA PATRA

Yudhisthira and his party went westwards beyond Kurukshetra, across the rivers Yamuna and Drishtadvati; they crossed the desert country and finally reached the Kamyakavana at the source of River Saraswati. Yudhisthira's immediate problem was to feed the retinue that followed him. He took the counsel of Dhaumyacharya who asked him to pray to Surya for help and succour. After a purificatory bath and meditation at sunrise, Yudhisthira, along with his brothers and Draupadi, invoked Surya, the giver of life and sustenance on this planet, chanting the Gayatri Mantra. Lord Surya responded by presenting an earthen cooking vessel to Draupadi; the vessel would provide an endless supply of food as long as she was the last person to eat for the day. They thanked the lord and continued on their journey.

When the game of dice was being played, Krishna had been fighting Shalva. Only on his return did he come to know about the events at Hastinapura. The news of the exile stunned him and he, at once, set out for the forest where the Pandavas were living. Krishna was accompanied by many from the Bhoja and Vrishni clans.

Draupadi, seeing her Sakha, fell at his feet, weeping inconsolably. She narrated the atrocities and indignities she had suffered in the Kuru court in front of her five husbands.

> Sakha, they remained silent with shame; it was disgraceful of the great heroes to let it happen, in the name of dharma. Even the great Kuru elders remained mere spectators. I was scantily dressed and dragged by my hair by that beast, Dushassana. Then Duryodhana bared his thigh and that Sutaputra called me a prostitute to five men. No one said a word, not even noble Pitamah! When Duryodhana ordered that I be disrobed, you should have seen the glee of the Kaurava brothers, with the exception of Yuyutsu. Govinda, it was terrible, it should never happen to any woman in any age. This act shall be a curse on mankind.

Krishna replied:

> What happened was unthinkable. I can help only when one trusts me without any reservation, which is how you were saved from the ordeal,

when you let go of your garment and put your faith in me. Those who tormented you will be stricken to death, including Pitamah and Drona! Wipe your tears and bear your grief. I, Krishna Vaasudeva, solemnly promise to avenge the grievous wrongs done to you. I shall stand by your husbands and regain their kingdom and establish an empire of dharma in Aryawartha.

Krishna left for Dwaraka after a few days, taking with him, Subhadra and Abhimanyu. Draupadi's sons were sent to Kampilya with Drishtadyumna.

VYASA'S ADVICE

Soon after Krishna's departure, the Pandavas decided to leave Kamyakavana. Dhaumya advised them to move to Dwaitavana, a beautiful forest with placid lakes and flowering trees. Holy sages had been living in harmony with wild beasts in these forests for ages.

Bhima sulked at their mundane routine, which was without any action or excitement. At the behest of Draupadi, he reminded Yudhisthira that they should plan to hit back at Duryodhana for the injustices done to them.

Yudhisthira asked them to be patient and said:

> Today, Duryodhana has become powerful with a large army and many allies on his side. His commanders are none other than Bhishma, Drona, Karna and Jayadratha. They have formidable resources to fight us and can easily kill us all. Karna has acquired powerful weapons and is blessed with an invincible armour. We have only Panchala's army on our side. It will be suicidal to attack them at this point of time. I feel that Arjuna, with his prowess for excellence, should acquire divine weapons and invincible *astra*s. For this, we should perhaps seek the guidance of venerable Muni Vyasa.

While the Pandavas were debating the best course of action, Vyasa arrived with his pupils. After giving his blessings, he looked at Draupadi and said, 'We are all hungry and famished. Will you not serve us some food?' Draupadi touched his feet as a mark of respect and asked Bhima to attend to the ablutions of the sage's entourage. Refreshed after the repast, the sage reflected on the predicament of the Pandavas and advised Arjuna to visit the Himalayas and secure divine weapons from Indra, Varuna, Kubera, Yama and Shiva. He peered into Arjuna's eyes and said:

> Kuntiputra, with dedication and devotion, acquire Pasupata Astra from Mahadeva and the thunderbolt, Shakti, from your divine father, Indra.

Yama would be pleased with you and bless you with an exceptional weapon. By nature, you are humble; this will please the pantheon of Vedic gods. My blessings are with you always.

He then spoke to Draupadi, 'Victory is yours; Narayana is with you, daughter. We are all bound by destiny. Presently, I advise you all to go back to Kamyakavana till Arjuna returns.' He looked at Bhima and said, 'Vayunandana, you are destined to meet your ancestor, a wonderful soul.' He then continued on his journey with his disciples.

ARJUNA'S DIVINE WEAPONS

The Pandava brothers and Draupadi were uncertain of surviving in the forest for twelve years and then remaining anonymous during the thirteenth year. Even if they were to survive it, there was still no guarantee that Duryodhana would return their kingdom without a fight. As they were reflecting on their desperate situation, Sahadeva interrupted, saying:

> I have heard that a highly disciplined community lives on the other side of the Himalayas, Trivishtapapitha. They are reported to be under the spiritual guidance of holy men and rishis. They have practically no dealings with the people of the plains of Aryawartha. In other words, they live beyond the limit of our known world.

Sahadeva looked at Arjuna and said, 'Falguna, you always try to mould yourself as Indra, whom you regard to be your spiritual father. He is said to be the leader of this community. Veda Vyasa knows about this world and chose you to contact them in the Himalayas. The sooner you depart, the better it would be for us.' Arjuna was only too happy to leave their desolate surroundings, and soon departed on his Himalayan odyssey.

When he reached the Gandhamadana mountain range near Mount Kailash, an old brahmana approached him. He asked Arjuna, 'Young man, your demeanour speaks of a noble descent. Who are you and what brings you to this cold country?'

Arjuna introduced himself and narrated the sequence of events that had taken him there. The brahmana replied:

> I am immensely pleased to meet you; I feel as if I know you. I belong to the village of Swargadwara—the last outpost of the inhabited world.

Beyond this, begins the unexplored holy land—the land of the Universal Spirit, Lord Shiva. Your mission will be fulfilled if you please Him with intense devotion and penance.

Arjuna found a cave and commenced intense penance with great determination and forbearance. Pleased with this, Lord Shiva appeared before him as Kirata—the savage hunter—and decided to test his skill and courage by provoking him to fight.

After putting in his best effort, Arjuna realised that he was up against a much superior force and surrendered. The hunter spoke to him, 'I am no one; I belong to none; I listen to the faithful; I am everywhere.' Arjuna understood who the hunter was and, with great affection and devotion, fell at His feet. 'Lord, forgive me. I was impudent to fight you. Please forgive me and punish me for my ignorance,' cried Arjuna.

'Nay my son, do not apologise. I am pleased with your devotion and know your mission; I grant you a weapon of immense power—Pasupata. Use it only in dire need,' so saying, the lord disappeared.

Soon after, Varuna, Yama and Kubera materialised and blessed him with exceptional weaponry. Kubera, the god of wealth, said to him, 'You will be known as Dhananjaya, as you have conquered the desire to pursue wealth. I present you with a divine weapon, which would bring immense wealth in due time.'

Varuna said, 'By your valour, you will bring comfort to the oppressed and help to the righteous. I present to you, the Varuna Astra; it will ensure that wherever you go, that land will be *subiksha* and *sasya shyamalam*, prosperous and plentiful.'

Yama, when he appeared before Arjuna, was beaming with joy and said, 'Son, you are very noble and you are not afraid of death. I watched you duel with Lord Shiva and, therefore, I present you with the divine weapon, Anjalika. Use it in the defence of dharma.'

Indra heard from his brahmana messenger, how Arjuna had impressed the four gods. Indra, being the chieftain of all the Himalayan communities, was eager to meet his spiritual son. He instructed Mathali, his charioteer, to go towards Swargadwara and bring Arjuna across the seemingly inaccessible mountain passes.

The way beyond Swargadwara was known only to a select few among those who lived in the village. No other contact existed between this exclusive civilisation and the rest of the world. And because of this, people living elsewhere believed that Swarga was a place beyond the earth.

Mathali was an expert guide and escorted Arjuna through the high mountain passes with ease. They were at such heights that dense clouds almost completely covered them. They could barely see the ground below their feet and all that was visible were clouds all around; Arjuna felt as though he was suspended in mid-air, between earth and heaven.

At last, he reached Swarga where he was welcomed by Indra; the holy men present there blessed him. The *apsara*s were attracted to Arjuna and tried to entice him with their sensuous appeal, but he ignored their charms. Arjuna's demeanour pleased Indra, so he gifted him new weaponry. These weapons were specially designed to fight against specific enemy tribes such as Daityas and Danavas—referred to as Asuras, who lived in the high mountainous country below Swarga. Arjuna was warned never to use these sophisticated weapons against a lesser enemy.

At the request of Indra, he undertook several expeditions in the surrounding areas. Arjuna's mission was to destroy Daityas and Danavas who harassed the residents of Swarga while they performed their religious rites.

When the time came for Arjuna to return to his brothers, everyone, including Indra, tried to persuade him to stay. Indra tried to get Urvashi, one of the most desirable *apsara*s, to entice Arjuna to prolong his stay, but Arjuna remained steadfast in his goal. A jilted Urvashi cursed him; she said he would become impotent and a hermaphrodite—eunuch. Arjuna was aghast and pleaded his spiritual father to intervene. Indra could not negate the curse, but reduced its severity to one year instead of a lifetime. He also told Arjuna that he could choose when he wanted the curse to take effect.

As he was leaving, Indra presented Arjuna with a rare conch, Devadutta. It had been obtained from an ancient seabed, Thetis, in the Gandak Valley of the Himalayas. Indra also bestowed upon him, his powerful weapon, Shakti. With a heavy heart, Indra, once again, ordered Mathali to lead Arjuna out, safely, to be reunited with his brothers.

When Arjuna rejoined his family, everybody was surprised to see him. Arjuna had acquired a beatific glow during his stay in Swarga. He told them about his journey and the weapons he had acquired. Everyone was glad that Arjuna had returned successful.

BHIMA MEETS HANUMAN

The long absence of Arjuna had left the already desolate four brothers and Draupadi, dejected. They wanted to go on a pilgrimage and visit the great shrines in the Himalayas, hoping it would take their minds off their hapless state. At the Gandhamadana Mountain, they took a sacred dip in the Rakshas Tal near Manasarovar Lake. They felt so exuberant that they lost any desire to return to the mundane world of Aryawartha.

Brahmana priests guided them to the sacred shrine of Narayana at Badrinath at the foot of the snow-clad Nara-Narayana peaks. Aeons ago, on these peaks, the great rishis Nara and Narayana had performed penance for the welfare of mankind. Led by Draupadi, the Pandavas worshipped Lord Narayana with great devotion.

They moved to the charming forest of Narayanashram for rest and recuperation. One day, while Draupadi and Bhima had gone for a stroll along the forest meadows, a beautiful breeze from the east brought with it a fragrant flower. The fragrance was so sweet that Draupadi desired to get the plant for her garden. Bhima was only too willing to attend to her wishes.

He left to find where the flower grew and came upon a beautiful garden where an old monkey sat blocking his passage. The monkey said that he was old and indisposed and, if Bhima wanted to go across, he should jump over him. Bhima replied that it was improper to jump over elders and, once again, prevailed on the monkey to move his tail. The monkey meekly replied that he was too weak to do so himself and Bhima was most welcome to do it for him.

Bhima tried to lift the tail but it did not move; it did not yield even an inch despite Bhima's great effort. Amazed, he looked at the frail old monkey, who had a smile on his face, and asked, 'What are you made of, O Kapiraj, that I, Bhimasen, cannot move your tail?'

The monkey laughed and replied, 'I am an old monkey and you are called a Simhabala. It is a pity that you cannot recognise me.'

Bhima scratched his head for a moment and said, 'You seem to be the guardian deity of this mountain range. Forgive my impudence and reveal yourself.'

In that moment, the monkey transformed himself into his legendary form of Hanuman—Vayuputra, the son of Vayu and the devotee of Lord Sri Rama. The mighty Bhima fell at his feet, asking for his pardon. Bhima remembered being told by his mother that he too was a Vayuputra, therefore Hanuman was his elder brother.

'What brings you here?' asked Hanuman.

Bhima replied, 'I seem to have forgotten after meeting my mighty brother!'

Hanuman smiled and reminded him, 'I know...your wife Draupadi wants the Saugandha flower and this valley is full of them. We call them Brahma Kamal.'

Bhima told Hanuman that his mother would narrate his story with a prayer: *Manojavam Marutatulyavegam, Jitendriyam Buddhimatam Varishtam, Vatatmajam; Vanarayutha mukhya, Sri Rama dootam sirasa namami.* (A verse from the Valmiki Ramayana in praise of Hanuman.)

Pleased with Bhima's disposition, Hanuman said:

> Bhima, my younger brother! Not only is your strength like that of an enraged lion, but your roar in the battlefield would scare the wits out of your enemies. I feel lonely these days and I long for some fun and excitement. Your brother Arjuna passed my cave dwelling near Yamunotri and did some penance. I am pleased with his devotion and shall guard him in battle by mounting myself on the flagpost of his golden chariot.

Bhima was perplexed at the mention of battle, but Hanuman did not elaborate. Hanuman personally picked the best of Saugandha flowers for Panchali and disappeared.

The Pandavas then returned to Dwaitavana.

DURYODHANA DISGRACED

Duryodhana, prodded by his evil trio, wanted to add to the miseries of his cousins. His spies had informed him that the Pandavas had recently arrived at Dwaitavana, located between the Ganga and Yamuna rivers. Under the pretext of visiting the Kurus' cattle, the four of them pitched their camp near that of the Pandavas.

They erected pompous tents and canopies to show off their wealth. Duryodhana's hunting party penetrated into the forest and reached a beautiful pond where the Gandharva king, Chitrasena, was relaxing with his wives and other womenfolk. Seeing that the privacy of the ladies was being flouted, Chitrasena requested Duryodhana to leave the precincts. Instead, the arrogant Duryodhana challenged the Gandharva king to a fight.

The tough and hardy tribal king soon inflicted a crushing defeat on Duryodhana and bound him like a caged animal. Karna abandoned his friend and ran away on a horse, an act of cowardice that further embarrassed the great prince. A captured Duryodhana was left to fend for himself.

When Yudhisthira came to know of Duryodhana's discomfiture, he sent Bhima and Arjuna to his help. An irritated Bhima asked, 'Shall I dump the baggage in the Ganga?' Yudhisthira reminded them that the honour of the house of the Kurus was at stake.

Chitrasena recognised Arjuna and embraced him. Arjuna said, 'Please accept our apologies; I request you to please release that arrogant fool.' Chitrasena released the crestfallen crown prince and, upon his return, Duryodhana was reprimanded by Shakuni for not observing royal etiquette.

JAYADRATHA HUMILIATED

Jayadratha, the son of Rudrakshatra, king of Sindhudesa, was passing by the ashram of the Pandavas when the brothers were away hunting. He was Duryodhana's brother-in-law, having married his sister, Duhsala. He happened to see Draupadi waiting for her husbands' return. He stopped to greet her and, as courtesy demanded, Draupadi served him food. The uncouth Saindhawa remarked, 'You are such an outstanding beauty! Are you not wasting your prime in this forest by being the wife of penniless husbands? My palace is the right place for you; I shall make you the chief queen, if you come with me.'

Draupadi rebuked him, so he forcibly abducted her. One of the disciples of Dhaumya, who saw this terrible incident, ran into the forest and informed Bhima. The Pandava brothers chased the chariot and overpowered Saindhawa. Bhima was about to break his skull when Yudhisthira intervened and reminded him that their cousin would become a widow if he did so.

Instead, Bhima shaved Jayadradha's scalp into five locks—Panchasikha, and shaved half his moustache—a disgrace considered worse than death. Bhima apologised profusely to Draupadi for leaving her alone in the cottage and promised her it would never happen again!

YAKSHA PRASNA

The Pandavas' twelve years of exile was nearing completion. While walking along the forest, Yudhisthira felt thirsty and asked Nakula to fetch water from a nearby lake. As he was about to collect some water, he heard a voice address him, 'This lake is mine; you cannot drink the water till you answer my questions.' Nakula did not heed the warning, drank the water and immediately fainted. When he did not return for quite some time, Yudhisthira sent Sahadeva to look for Nakula.

He saw Nakula on the bank, unconscious. When Sahadeva tried to fetch water from the lake, he suffered the same fate. Bhima and Arjuna followed, they too disregarded the command, drank the water and fell to the ground, unconscious.

Yudhisthira was astonished by their disappearance and went to the lake himself. He was shocked to see his brothers lying there, lifeless. When the yaksha spoke, Yudhisthira agreed to answer his questions.

The yaksha asked thus:

'What is virtue and what is sin?'

'Doing good to others is virtue and doing bad is sin.'

'Is a man called a brahmana because he is born to parents learned in the shastras or because he has got the qualities of a man of God?'

'Good qualities associated with a man of God alone make a brahmana.'

The final question was, 'How can dharma, *artha*, *kama* and moksha be combined?'

Yudhisthira answered with a smile, 'They can be combined by marrying a chaste woman of noble qualities and enjoying *artha* and *kama*, while following the path of dharma with her.'

The yaksha was pleased with the responses and told Yudhisthira that he could ask for the life of one of his brothers. Yudhisthira asked for Nakula's life. He explained his choice, 'My mother has a son left in me; I want mother Madri to have a son alive as well.' The yaksha was amazed at the generosity of Yudhisthira and revealed himself as Yama Dharma Raja, who was his spiritual father and the God of Death. He restored all the brothers to life and granted Yudhisthira a boon.

Yudhisthira smiled and asked, 'May our identity not be revealed during our last year of exile.'

VIRATA PARVA

After the period of twelve years in exile, the Pandavas moved to Matsyadesa. As they had to live the next year without being recognised, Yudhisthira disguised himself as Kanakabhatta, an expert advisor in the game of dice and told the king, Virata, that he served in the court of Yudhisthira. Bhima joined the palace as Valala, the head cook. Arjuna decided to invoke the curse of Urvashi and turned himself into a eunuch named Brihannala, who was an expert dancer and musician—he had learnt these skills in the company of Kinnaras in the Himalayas. He was to train Uttara, the princess of Matsyadesa, in the fine arts. Nakula, as Dharmagrantha, introduced himself as the stable-keeper of Yudhisthira; Sahadeva, as Tantripala, became the keeper of the king's cattle. Draupadi introduced herself as Sairandhri, the wife of five Gandharvas, who had worked as a lady-in-waiting for Queen Draupadi. Virata's queen, Sudheshna, developed a liking for this exceptionally good-looking Gandharva woman.

Virata was an eccentric and weak king. Being fond of the game of dice, he found Kanakabhatta an amiable companion and began spending a good part of his time in play. Yudhisthira, being an embodiment of peace and tranquillity, would suffer many an insult from him during the game.

Draupadi would sing for the queen, who was amazed by her melodious voice. She told the queen that Gandharvas were natural singers and were teachers of divine music. Since polyandry was an accepted practice among Gandharvas, Sudheshna readily accepted Draupadi's tale of being married to five Gandharvas.

Bhima turned out to be a great cook and the king relished his preparations. Arjuna became the favourite of the royal womenfolk. His dancing prowess enthralled everyone who saw him perform. The adolescent Uttara desired to learn the Natya Shastra. She asked him if he entertained Arjuna, along with *apsaras*, when he visited Swarga. Brihannala replied in the affirmative. Innocently, she enquired if Arjuna was as handsome as everyone said he was. 'He was so handsome that the best of *apsaras*, Urvashi, wanted him to take her as his wife,' said Arjuna.

Sudheshna's brother, Prince Keechaka, was the commander-in-chief of the Matsyan army. He was the power behind the throne and a wrestler of repute. Keechaka was startled to see a voluptuous and attractive woman in the queen's chamber and asked Sudheshna about her. When told she was already married, Keechaka reiterated that he had a weakness for beautiful women and wished her to be sent to his chambers.

Sudheshna cautioned him that she was a virtuous woman, so he should not meddle with her and invite her husbands' wrath. Keechaka roared with laughter, 'I shall take care of them. Send her to me now. This is a command, sister!' Sudheshna was in distress, yet she had to obey her brother as he was the keeper of her kingdom and the chief of its army. When the queen confided her brother's outrageous wish to Sairandhri, she was terrified. A stunned Draupadi informed Arjuna and Bhima, who laid a trap for Keechaka. Bhima asked Draupadi to invite Keechaka to the dance hall in the night, requesting him to keep their rendezvous a secret.

With great anticipation, Keechaka stealthily entered the dance hall where Bhima, dressed as a lady, was waiting for him. Only one lamp burned in the large hall. The dark shadow on the couch resembled a lady-in-waiting and as Keechaka advanced, Bhima pounced on the semi-drunk Keechaka. By the time Bhima was through, Keechaka's body was grotesque and unrecognisable.

DURYODHANA—THE CATTLE RUSTLER

When the Kauravas came to know of the death of Keechaka, they suspected that to be the work of Bhima since there were not many who could have defeated him. Duryodhana suspected that the Pandavas were living somewhere in Matsyadesa and therefore conspired to surround the kingdom, which was renowned for its cattle wealth. He planned to steal the cattle and provoke the Pandavas out into the open. Though Karna tried to dissuade him from this cowardly act and refused to play his hand, he accompanied him nevertheless. Prince Susharma, now the ruler of Kashi, agreed to be a part of this plan.

Virata panicked when people approached him, complaining that their cattle were being stolen. He felt helpless after the murder of Keechaka. His aid, Kanakabhatta, counselled him to seek the help of his cook, Valala, who was a wrestler; the stable-keeper, Dharmagrantha; and the keeper of cows, Tantripala. Yudhisthira told him that they had been in the service of the Pandavas for a long time and were familiar with wielding arms.

The prince of Matsyadesa, Uttarakumara, then bragged about his valour and wanted to meet the challenge of the Kauravas, if only he had a reliable charioteer. With a gentle smile, Yudhisthira replied that the dance master, Brihannala had been, at one time, Arjuna's charioteer. Uttarakumara felt affronted at the suggestion that a eunuch should be his charioteer, he being a valiant kshatriya. However, when his sister taunted him saying that he was just finding excuses to avoid fighting Duryodhana, the prince's pride was hurt and he consented to go to battle with Brihannala as his charioteer.

Virata led the attack, confronting Susharma in the south. But Susharma soon captured and imprisoned the king. Bhima attacked Susharma's forces and liberated Virata, sending Susharma scampering back to his country in defeat.

In the meantime, Duryodhana captured the cattle ranches on the outskirts of Matsyadesa and was about to breach the fortifications. Uttarakumara had to reluctantly advance to face Duryodhana. He was shivering with fright, and when all courage left him, he alighted from his chariot and started running back to the city gates. Arjuna caught hold of him and put him back on the chariot, revealed himself as Arjuna and assured him that he would help fight Duryodhana's contingent. He blew his conch, Devadatta, that reverberated in reply to Duryodhana's challenge. Soon, Arjuna dispensed of the Kaurava forces single-handedly, using the Sammohana Astra—the weapon released a gas that made everyone faint. The *astra* had no effect on Bhishma, who recognised Arjuna and blessed him.

After regaining consciousness, Duryodhana was jubilant that the Pandavas had been exposed and hence would have to go into exile all over again. However, Bhishma and Drona told him that as per the astrological calculations, the thirteenth year had been completed the previous day and the Pandavas could now return to Indraprastha.

Duryodhana arrogantly replied that he would never part with Indraprastha. Bhishma warned him that a war would ensue and this fight to the finish would annihilate the Kauravas from the face of the earth.

When Yudhisthira disclosed the identities of his brothers and himself to Virata, the king was overwhelmed with gratitude. He offered the hand of his daughter Uttara in marriage to Arjuna. However, Arjuna declined the proposal saying that as he was her teacher, the princess was like a daughter to him. Instead, he offered that the princess marry his son, Abhimanyu, thus forging a formidable alliance between the Pandavas, Panchalas and Matsyadesa.

The Pandavas then moved to the Upaplavya region of Matsyadesa. Krishna, Balarama and Subhadra along with the bridegroom, Abhimanyu, arrived at Upaplavya from Dwaraka. The wedding took place in the presence of King Drupada, Drishtadyumna, Shikhandin, Srijit and Draupadi's five sons.

After the wedding celebrations were over, a grand banquet was held, followed by the assembly of kings and elders. Krishna, with great brevity and concern, narrated the gross injustices suffered by the Pandavas for thirteen years for no fault of theirs. He looked at Draupadi, who sat across with Subhadra and other ladies of the royalty and said, with a frown on his face, 'The noble queen Draupadi was humiliated grossly in the Kuru assembly and that needs to be vindicated. The ghastly affront to the daughter-in-law of the family cannot be overlooked. The insult is an affront to womanhood and, to restore her honour, I am not against the clash of arms.'

While Yudhisthira was bewildered, Bhima and Arjuna were jubilant. Alarmed at the prospect of imminent war, Balarama urged Krishna to look for an amicable settlement. Krishna was bemused and said, 'I would be the last person to support a war, but if dharma demands it, I will not shy away from fight.'

Satyaki supported Krishna's views and said his armies were ready for battle. Drupada announced that in the event of hostilities, he would put the armies belonging to him and his allies at Yudhisthira's disposal; however, he wanted to, first, send a learned brahmana as an envoy of peace to the court of Hastinapura. Krishna nodded his consent for this proposal.

Soon after, Krishna and the other Yadavas left for Dwaraka, and Drupada sent his emissary to Hastinapura. Meanwhile, the Pandavas also sent messages to their allies to be prepared to come to their aid in the event of a war.

Duryodhana learnt from his network of spies that the Pandavas had started mobilising support. At the instance of Shakuni, he sought the help of Yadava armies, having learnt that Balarama had differed with Krishna at the parleys. Duryodhana went to Dwaraka to meet Krishna. Arjuna had also decided to go to Dwaraka on a similar mission.

Both Arjuna and Duryodhana reached Dwaraka almost at the same time—at noon, when Krishna was taking a nap in his chambers. The imperious Duryodhana, in the manner of a king, occupied a high chair at the head of Krishna's bed; while Arjuna stood at Krishna's feet with folded hands and waited for his friend to wake up. When Krishna woke up, his eyes fell on Arjuna, standing near his feet, 'Partha, what brings you here, at this time?' Arjuna touched Krishna's feet. Krishna clasped Arjuna in a warm embrace and was surprised to see Duryodhana also, in his bed chamber.

'What a surprise! Raja Duryodhana in my humble chamber. Welcome, my good friend. What can I do for you?' Duryodhana said, 'War seems imminent among the Kuru cousins and I have come to seek your help.'

Krishna smiled and said, 'Of course! I am at your service.' The impatient Duryodhana added further, 'I was the first to come here, hence, you should give me precedence.'

Krishna paused and, with a smile, said, 'I seem to have a problem here. You might have come first, but I happened to see Arjuna before you. We are both older than Arjuna and, as per our traditions, the younger one gets to talk first. I hope you will bear with me if I ask Arjuna the purpose of his visit.' Duryodhana conceded and Arjuna echoed his request.

Krishna looked around and, with a meaningful smile, said, 'The highly trained Narayana Sena of my clansmen are my equals in battle. In my distribution of assistance they will be on one side; and I, as an individual, on the other, wielding no weapon; and I shall be a non-combatant.' Arjuna was quick to grasp the purport of Krishna's rationale and, with least hesitation, announced, 'I opt for you, Krishna, and you alone. I have no preconditions.'

Duryodhana was surprised and very happy at the turn of events. He knew the immense advantage he would reap with the Narayana Sena on his side. He thought Arjuna had been foolish to ask for Krishna as a non-combatant on his side. Pleased with his successful mission, Duryodhana returned to Hastinapura.

Krishna asked Arjuna the reason for his seemingly imprudent choice, and Arjuna replied, 'I have great faith in you, and with you as my charioteer, we cannot lose the war. You are Vaasudeva; wherever there is Krishna, there is dharma and dharma always wins.'

When Balarama came to know of this, he said, 'Krishna will be on the Pandavas' side alone, and I do not want to fight my brother. I would prefer neutrality and go on a pilgrimage instead.'

SALYA OF MADRA

King Salya of Madra was the maternal uncle of Nakula and Sahadeva. When he came to know that the Pandavas were camping at Upaplavya and preparing for a war against the Kauravas, he gathered his army and set off to join them. Duryodhana intercepted Salya, without revealing his identity, and offered his hospitality to Salya and his large army. Overwhelmed by his host's attention and hospitality, Salya wanted to repay him.

Duryodhana introduced himself and paid his respects. Salya was caught unawares and asked Duryodhana how he could repay him for his hospitality. The sly prince had been waiting for this and lost no time in requesting Salya to fight on his side against the Pandavas. Salya was shocked at the treachery, but he could not go back on his word.

Salya hurried to Yudhisthira and told him about Duryodhana's trickery, but also said that his forces would try to help them in their own way. Delegations in support of the Pandavas had started arriving at Upaplavya and soon, they had a mighty force of seven *akshauni*s—divisions. The Kauravas too had mobilised an army of eleven *akshauni*s.

At this juncture, Drupada's messenger arrived at Hastinapura, walked into Dhritarashtra's court and addressed the assembly:

> Kauravas and Pandavas, being the sons of brothers, were entitled to share the great kingdom of Kurus equally. But it was not to be. Time and again, the Pandavas were cheated and deprived of their share. There is no justification for this. Now, they have acquired the support of many rulers and are very strong. Yet, they do not want war and are ready to let bygones be bygones. They only want their kingdom to be returned to them without delay.

Bhishma advised Duryodhana to return Indraprastha, but he refused. Dhritarashtra intervened and sent the brahmana, along with Sanjaya, back to the Pandavas, saying that he could not convince his sons against war and, hence, requested the Pandavas not to lose their patience and swerve from rectitude.

Yudhisthira replied that he, too, was averse to war and knew that rectitude was the best of possessions, but he would abide by Krishna's suggestions as he was the one who knew best, the intricacies of dharma.

Krishna, on his part, said that he was close both to the Pandavas and Kauravas and, therefore, desired the welfare of all; he offered to go to Hastinapura in person and try to settle the matter peacefully, as far as possible, and see to it that the Pandavas got back their kingdom. But if justice was denied to them once again, then, like true kshatriyas, they would prepare for a war. In order to prevent terrible carnage, Yudhisthira told Sanjaya that they are ready to make peace with the Kauravas, if they were given at least five villages for the five brothers.

Dhritarashtra was filled with anxiety; he tried talking to Vidura, but was advised that the only way to avoid war was to prevail upon his son to give back the Pandavas their share of the kingdom. Bhishma also supported Vidura, but Duryodhana was as adamant as ever; with eleven *akshauni*s of army at his disposal, along with Karna, Bhishma and Guru Drona as his commanders, he was sure of victory.

Before he set out on his peace mission to Hastinapura, Krishna had a long discussion with the Pandava brothers and found that all of them favoured a peaceful settlement, if possible. Only Draupadi could not forget her humiliation in the Kuru assembly. Holding her long tresses, she spoke to Govinda with great passion:

> Govinda, look at these tresses of mine and do what honour requires to be done. There can be no peace without honour. If Arjuna and Bhima prefer peace, my five sons and Abhimanyu will go to the battlefield, supported by my father and my brothers, Drishtadyumna and Shikhandin, and fight for my honour. I have suppressed my anger and grief for thirteen years, for the sake of Dharmaputra, and I cannot restrain myself any longer.

Krishna consoled her, saying that he was sure Dhritarashtra's sons would never opt for a peaceful settlement and, also, he was certain that there was going to be a terrible holocaust in which the Kauravas would perish.

Hastinapura was lit up to welcome Krishna and Dushassana's palace was prepared for his stay. Dhritarashtra asked Vidura to offer Krishna elephants, chariots, jewels and other valuable presents, but an amused Vidura told the king that he cannot bribe Krishna with riches. He was as an ambassador of peace and, to please him, he would have to heed his advice and offer to return Indraprastha to the Pandavas.

When Krishna arrived at Hastinapura, its citizens thronged the streets eagerly to catch a glimpse of the Yadava hero. He first went to King Dhritarashtra to pay his respects, then visited Vidura's modest house to meet Kunti.

From there, he went to Duryodhana's palace, where he was welcomed and invited to a banquet held in his honour. Krishna politely declined the invitation citing diplomatic etiquette. Till his mission was fulfilled, he would not accept Kuru hospitality. Duryodhana felt slighted when Krishna refused to stay in Dushassana's palace and, instead, went to Vidura's house for the night.

Vidura warned Krishna that the Kauravas were not to be trusted. Krishna assured him that he would try his best to bring about a peaceful settlement, and no one could say that he propagated war.

KRISHNA—THE PEACEMAKER

The next morning, Krishna went to the court and after paying respect to the elders, addressed the assembly:

> The Kuru dynasty was one that had no blemish. In the past, its rulers were endowed with all the noble qualities of truthfulness, generosity, love of justice, kindness and compassion; they never left the path of dharma. But now, everything has changed. Dhritarashtra, for the love of his own sons, was selfish, causing injustice to his own brother's sons. He deprived them of their own kingdom. His sons are treading the path of sin and they have no respect for their elders. They will bring destruction on to themselves and their kith and kin. The king should control his sons, who sow evil, but he is not able to do so because of his excessive love for them. Unless he interferes and stops the treachery against the sons of Pandu, there is going to be a great holocaust. The Pandavas are not helpless; they have gathered enough strength from friendly kings and are ready for war, but they would still prefer to avoid it and make peace with the Kauravas.

Dhritarashtra told him that he was aware of all the facts that were stated, but was helpless. He begged Krishna to talk to Duryodhana and advise him to make peace with the Pandavas. Krishna turned his attention towards the Kuru prince, 'You belong to the great dynasty of the Kurus, but your behaviour is most unbecoming. You should stop being greedy and avaricious; you should not cheat the Pandavas of their kingdom. Please listen to me and make peace with them.'

An arrogant Duryodhana replied that he did not owe the Pandavas even a single penny and will not part with anything:

> I am the king's eldest son and the kingdom is rightfully mine. The elders had made me part with a portion of my kingdom earlier, and the Pandavas lost it to me in a fair play of dice. Now, under no circumstances, am I willing to give it back to them. I was never unfair to the Pandavas and have never wronged them. The misfortunes of the Pandavas are because of their own doing.

Krishna laughed in contempt at Duryodhana's words and said:

> You have never wronged them, indeed! So, you think it was proper to deprive and cheat them of all their riches and their kingdom? It was right to try and burn them alive, along with their mother, in the house of lac in Varanavata?

When you were a kid, was it right to have tried to poison and drown Bhima? Was it right for you to drag Draupadi and insult her in front of the court?

Krishna's eyes were red with fury, but he had a smile on his lips. He looked at the people assembled in the court and said:

> You were all present when the treacherous and infamous game was played, when the Pandavas were wrongly robbed of everything, out of jealousy of their prosperity. In spite of all the injustice done to them, they never fought back because Yudhisthira would never overstep the bounds of dharma. The time has now come when Duryodhana cannot have his way any more. If he refuses to return Indraprastha, he will be forced to part with his kingdom and wealth, eventually. Duryodhana, you are the most sinful man on earth and your actions will not go unpunished.

After hearing Krishna's reproachful words, Duryodhana was furious and walked out of the assembly hall. Krishna was sombre and reprimanded the elders in the assembly for letting the matter reach such a state; they should have put a stop to the evil before it got out of hand. He beseeched them to take matters into their hands and bring justice to Yudhisthira, even if it meant arresting the perpetrators of *adharma*. Dhritarashtra was alarmed and asked Vidura to fetch Gandhari to the court, and asked her to convince their son to come to his senses and make peace with the Pandavas.

Duryodhana was also summoned. Gandhari tried her best to convince him that what he was doing was *adharma*. But the stubborn prince, once again, walked out of the assembly hall in a huff, making it clear that he was not willing to step back.

Duryodhana went to his palace and had a conference with his accomplices; they decided to bind Krishna and take him prisoner, forcing the Pandavas to surrender. Satyaki got wind of their plans and sent Kritavarma to assemble the army and return to the court. He himself hurried to inform Krishna of Duryodhana's plans. The assembly was aghast, but Krishna only laughed and said that he was in no danger, as there was no one born yet, who could bind him. Dhritarashtra was in a state of panic and sent for Duryodhana again.

VISWAROOPA

Duryodhana returned to the court and was reprimanded by his father, yet again.

> I am aware of the sin that you are steeped in, but I never expected you to

> stoop to such madness as to arrest Krishna! Even gods cannot capture him; he can be won over only by love and devotion. Suyodhana, you are foolish, like an obstinate and ignorant child, you are trying to hold the Sun with your bare hands.

Krishna looked at Duryodhana and smiled. Meanwhile, the court started filling up with the army that Kritavarma commanded. Krishna was glowing, and a bright light began emanating from Him, blinding everyone except Bhishma, Vidura, and the rishis. Only the wise and the enlightened could see His Viswaroopa—the divine form. Devas materialised from His body, and He assumed an awe-inspiring form; everyone else seemed to be smaller than His thumb! On His expansive chest, were the eleven Rudras; on His shoulders, were the lords of the four quarters—Indra, Varuna, Kubera and Yama; Agni was glowing from His mouth; the twelve Adityas, the Vasus, the Aswini twins, the Maruts and all the gods of the heavens were all within Him. On His left, stood the heroes who favoured the Pandavas. Balarama emerged from His left arm, and on His right, was Arjuna with His Gandiva. Behind Him were Bhima, Nakula, Sahadeva and Yudhisthira, along with the heroes of Vrishnis and Andhakas. Krishna's many arms held His weapons—Panchajanya, Sudarshana, Kaumodaki and Nandaka. He looked as devastating as death itself. In the illusion, the earth shook and the terrified congregation begged Him to return to His human form. Krishna the compassionate, consented and walked out of the assembly hall with Vidura and Satyaki.

Before he got into the chariot, he told all those present there that he had tried his best to avert war and bring peace, but to no avail. 'Duryodhana was adamant and his father was helpless; hence, war is inevitable.'

As soon as Krishna left, Duryodhana roared and gave orders for the preparations to start immediately. The eleven *akshauni*s were ordered to proceed towards the battlefield of Kurukshetra.

Balarama left on a pilgrimage; Rukmi was not welcome to either side. Apart from these two, everyone else fought the Mahabharata War, resulting in an apocalypse.

KRISHNA AND KARNA

Before going back to Upaplavya, Krishna went to meet Karna, without whom Duryodhana would surely lose his self-confidence. Radheya was surprised by his unexpected visit.

Krishna asked Karna, why he, being a noble person with knowledge of the Vedas, supported Duryodhana, a symbol of *adharma*. Karna replied:

> It is true Duryodhana is a sinner, but he is also my friend and mentor, and I love him more than my life. When the whole world was insulting me because I am a Sutaputra, only Duryodhana stood by me and offered the kingship of Anga Desa. Even Guru Drona refused to be my teacher; and under the tutelage of Sage Bhargava Rama, I was cursed, when he came to know that I was not a brahmana. Arjuna and Bhima insulted me, time and again. Only two people in this world love me as I am, my mother Radha and my friend Duryodhana.

Krishna then asked him if he knew about his birth and who his real mother was. Krishna told him that his mother was a princess of high birth, but he had been born when she was still a maiden, so she had to abandon him. 'Not a day passed when she did not think of you and grieve for her beautiful child born with *kavacha* and *kundala*s (armour and earrings).' Krishna told him that his mother was Kunti and his father the god he worships daily, Ishtadevata Surya, which made the Pandavas his younger brothers. 'The son born to a maiden, becomes, by law, the son of the man she marries; so, by law, you are the eldest Pandava and, when the Pandavas win the war, you will be made the king of Hastinapura, provided you leave Duryodhana and join them.' Karna was despondent and asked:

> Why are you telling me about my unfortunate birth now? You have destroyed my resolve. I know Duryodhana is pursuing *adharma* and will lose in the end, but he has affection for me and has pinned great hopes on me to win the battle. How can I leave him now? It will be treachery to join the Pandavas. I am aware we will all perish because you are on their side. I cannot kill my brothers, but I had promised that I will fight Arjuna to the finish. I know I will meet my end in that conflict because you are with him, and not because of his prowess.
>
> I would like to make just one request, please do not disclose my identity to my brothers and make it difficult for them to fight too. This is a war of dharma and Yudhisthira will abandon the war even before it starts; if he comes to know that I am his elder brother, he will refuse to become the monarch.
>
> I know the end is near. I will be killed at the hands of Arjuna; Dushassana will be lying on the field bleeding; Drona and Bhishma will perish; Duryodhana

> will be killed by Bhima. I am tired of this wretched life and am waiting for the end. I long to reach heaven, which holds all that I crave for.

Krishna was filled with compassion and admiration for the valiant warrior.

KARNA AND KUNTI

Kunti was distraught at the final declaration of war. She was terrified at the thought that her sons will be fighting against the combined force of the mighty Bhishma, Drona and Karna. Bhishma Pitamah and Guru Drona may not intend to kill the Pandavas, but Karna had no such scruples. In fact, he had made it clear that he planned to defeat and kill Arjuna in a one-on-one combat. Worried about the safety of her sons, she decided to meet Karna and disclose the identity of his birth to dissuade him from fighting the Pandavas.

Kunti found Karna on the banks of Ganga, offering his evening prayers to Lord Surya. It was a hot day, so she covered herself with Karna's upper cloth and stood patiently behind him. After he finished his prayers and turned around, he was startled to find Kunti waiting for him.

Kunti narrated to him, the story of his birth: how he was born with a full panoply of armour and gold earrings and she had to abandon him as she was afraid of censure. She told him the same thing as Krishna had, that being the eldest, Yudhisthira would not hesitate to crown him the king, and that he should join them instead of Duryodhana. Listening to his mother, Karna was filled with mixed feelings of sadness and anger. He felt the Sun God was testing his resolve, character and loyalty. With a great effort, he controlled the urge to give in to the temptation of power and said:

> Dear mother, what you want me to do is against my dharma. If I swerve from my duty and loyalty to Duryodhana and join the Pandavas, as suggested by you, I will be harming myself more than what my enemies might inflict on me.
>
> When you abandoned me to the river, you deprived me of my birthright as a kshatriya and also of a mother's love, which Radha, my foster mother, gave me in ample measure. I have eaten Duryodhana's salt and now, I cannot desert him. There cannot be a bigger treachery and ingratitude for me, and if I do so, my life will not be worth living. I cannot join your sons and will never fight against Duryodhana. But mother, I have my scruples and will not send you back in vain. I promise that you will be left with five sons. Except Arjuna, I shall not fight with your four other sons, no matter how much I am provoked to do so.

Her heart was full of contrary and tumultuous feelings: sadness at the outcome and joy at seeing Karna. Kunti embraced her firstborn and left quietly, saying a silent prayer for him.

THE BEGINNING OF THE END—THE MAHABHARATA WAR

The great battle was about to begin. The eleven *akshauni*s of the Kaurava army faced the seven *akshauni*s of the Pandava army on the battlefield of Kurukshetra. The commanders of the Kaurava army were Kripa, Drona, Salya, Jayadratha, Sudakshina, Kritavarma, Aswathama, Karna, Bhurisravas and Baahlika, with Bhishma as the supreme commander of the forces. Sudakshina and Kritavarma were from the Yadava army, fighting for Duryodhana, while Baahlika and Bhurisravas were the commanders from Bahlik country, bordering north-western Kashmir, known by the name of Bactria in later times, famous for their double-humped camels. Sanjaya, blessed with the faculty to see all proceedings on the battlefield, would narrate it to Dhritarashtra. Sanjaya was a sort of war correspondent and was given a special boon of divine sight and perception by Vyasa to narrate, in great detail, the conduct of the war, including the Divinity of Krishna as revealed to Arjuna.

Before the war commenced, Yudhisthira led his brothers to Bhishma Pitamah and sought his permission to fight against him. As ordained by the ancient rules of chivalry, Bhishma readily gave his consent and asked them if they wanted anything more from him. Yudhisthira then requested him to reveal as to how they could win this war. Without mincing his words, the grand old sire declared that as long as he was alive it would be impossible for the Pandavas to achieve success. Yudhisthira then enquired how he could be killed. Bhishma replied that the time for his death had not yet arrived. Then, after a pause, he said, 'Where there is Krishna, there is dharma and, hence, your victory will be certain!'

Yudhisthira then went to seek Drona's permission and asked him the same question. Drona replied that no one could kill him as long as he stood on the battlefield, armed and ready to fight. He could be killed, only if he threw down his arms; the one thing that would provoke him to disarm would be if he heard some dismal news, which would prompt him to enter *prayopavesa*, the yogic state for attaining death by dejection.

The brothers then met Kripacharya, who told them that he would outlive the battle and granted permission to fight with him. Salya was the last person whom the Pandavas met and he too gave them his approval.

Duryodhana consulted Bhishma and Drona about the appointment of a commander-in-chief for his army. He was hoping to give the coveted position to Karna, however, Bhishma shot down the proposal. Karna, though brave, was haughty and arrogant, and was easily carried away by his hatred for Arjuna. A commander-in-chief should be cool-headed, free from conceit and irrational enmity and should not underestimate his opponents. Enraged by Bhishma's words, Karna told Duryodhana that he would not enter the battlefield as long as the old man was alive. The prince had no choice but to appoint Bhishma as his commander-in-chief to initiate the battle.

Meanwhile, Yudhisthira proclaimed that he would welcome with open arms, any person in the Kaurava army who wanted to join his camp and fight for dharma. Yuyutsu, Dhritarashtra's son by a Vaisya woman, opted to walk over to the Pandavas.

As both armies waited for sunrise to commence warfare, a great storm erupted; a blinding sandstorm, unusual for that part of the year in the Kurukshetra region. The dawn was darkened by dust clouds; visibility dropped due to a series of tornado-like dust storms. A heavy shower of red-coloured rainwater fell from the sky, jackals howled in panic, birds fell dead in hundreds in that raging storm and vultures were seen hovering in the high skies above the dust blanket. The earth shook with mild tremors, peals of thunder and lightning raged through the skies. These were all ominous signs indicating the imminent *pralaya*—Armageddon.

When Vyasa was consulted by his disciples, he predicted a great cataclysm and *yugaantara*—the change of an age.

DAY ONE ON THE BATTLEFIELD

Arjuna's chariot, steered by Krishna, was in the forefront and, on it, fluttered the Kapidwaja banner—a monkey, representing the warrior scholar and Vishnu's devotee, Hanuman. Arjuna could see the sons of Dhritarashtra and their army divisions in the *vyuha* formation set up by Bhishma Pitamah. In the deafening noise of several conchs, war drums and trumpets, Arjuna took the Gandiva in his hand and said, 'Krishna, set my chariot right in the midst of the two contending armies. I want to see all the heroes who are arrayed against us. I want to have a good look at these men who are so eager for battle and, against whom I have to fight this war.' Krishna took the chariot a few yards ahead and placed it in front of Bhishma, Drona and the other elders. He said, 'Look Arjuna, look at this great army. Look at all the Kauravas assembled, who will die at your hands.' Arjuna was stunned at this statement. Arjuna cast his eyes at the grand spectacle. He saw the heroes ready for battle and all those who were dear to him, on the other side. They were his grandfathers, teachers, uncles, brothers, sons, dear friends and comrades. He was overcome with immense compassion for each of them. His voice shook with grief as he said:

> Krishna, I feel an awful weakness stealing over me. My mouth has gone dry all of a sudden and I am trembling all over. My head is reeling and I feel faint, my limbs refuse to bear me up. My form burns, as if with fever; and my Gandiva is slipping from my grasp. These are all my kinsmen and I feel I cannot fight them. Is there any meaning in killing them? I do not want to win this war. I do not want any kingdom nor do I want all the pleasures in the material world. I find they are futile and meaningless. These heroes, whom I am to fight, mean so much to me; I could never bring myself to kill them, not for the lordship of the three worlds.
>
> For the transient pleasure of ruling a kingdom, why should I attack the sons of Dhritarashtra? I agree that they have been avaricious, covetous and unjust, but the fact remains that they are my cousins and the murder of one's kinsmen is an unforgivable act. I would rather turn away from the war than commit this grievous sin.

Arjuna collapsed on the seat of the chariot and threw his bow and arrows on the floor, his heart laden with misery.

Krishna paused for a moment and said:

> Partha, how did this uneasiness sneak over you? Can you not realise that the situation is critical? You seem to have reached a crisis in your life and have allowed yourself to be swayed by these feelings that are anything but noble. You are courting ignominy. Get over this momentary weakness of your heart and get up. Do not fail in your Kshatra Dharma.

Arjuna, still despondent, was not to be shaken out of his fatalistic state.

> How can I aim my arrows at my grandfather, the noble Bhishma, and my revered guru, Drona? They...whom I worship, how can I kill them? I cannot do it, Krishna. You know that I am not a coward and this is not weakness, but

> compassion for the enemy. I do not know what to do. I leave it in your hands; do with me what you will.

Saying this, Arjuna went silent, refusing to fight.

Krishna, with a glum smile, said, 'Arjuna, you are grieving for those who do not deserve your compassion. You talk as though you are wise, yet a wise man never weeps; he weeps not for the dead, nor for the living.'

Krishna drove the chariot away from the battlefield, into a secluded place, and started his sermon that would become a testament of faith for mankind, for times to come, popularly known as the Bhagavad Gita—the celestial song.

Krishna declared:

> Arjuna, let me tell you the secret of our existence. It is only our bodies that are impermanent. We pass through different stages in our lives: childhood, youth and old age. These are but natural phases, and death, the fourth stage, is natural too. Once the body dies, the soul passes on from one body to another. Contact, of the senses with their object, generates cold and heat that affect the body, and pleasure and pain that affect the mind. These are but passing clouds and they do not last forever. You should learn to bear with them, for when you learn to be unaffected by them, you become fit for immortality.
>
> This entire universe is pervaded by the Eternal, which can never be destroyed. You think that you have killed and your victim thinks that he was murdered. In reality, you are both wrong; you do not kill and your victim is not killed—he cannot be killed. What was not born can never die. The soul is not slain when the body is destroyed. Once you know that it is imperishable and eternal, once you realise that it has no birth and no change, you will know that you cannot erase it.

Confused by this concept, Arjuna asked, 'What is the nature of the imperishable subject you talk about?'

Krishna smiled, because only an intellectual thinker like Arjuna could have such analytical discernment.

> Arjuna, it is called the Self—the soul and the divinity in you, the spark of energy in you. It is an ancient concept and a dimensionless quantity. One cannot quantify it distinctly, yet it is the thing that resides in every living being. It is not different from the Supreme Spirit, as you are part of that spirit. It dwells in your body, but it is not responsible for your actions. Have you never noticed that the drop of water on a lotus leaf never wets the

leaf and is independent of the leaf? Similarly, this soul is not accountable for any of your actions, yet you are part of it. When it leaves, your body perishes. It is the source of your life's energy; it is infinitely small, yet it occupies the whole universe.

Once a garment is old and torn, we throw it away and take up a new garment. The same is with the soul; when the body becomes old and worn out, it abandons it and takes up a new body. We cannot harm it, because it is beyond all concepts of this mundane world.

You know, a man's death is decided the moment he is born. Whenever anything is born, it is certain to die, and wherever anything dies, it is sure to be born again, so there is no point in our grieving for this imperishable truth!

How things and beings come into the world and how they end is a mystery. We know only the portion that is intermediate, this transit on earth. Even if you do not comprehend this, being a kshatriya, you have to fight. It is your duty. This Dharma Yuddha is the greatest good that can happen to a kshatriya. You have been chosen to fight in this war and, if you do, the gates of heaven are opened to you. But shirking your duty will make you a sinner.

If you die fighting, you are assured of a place in heaven. If you win the war, this world is yours. Make up your mind and rise up, O son of Kunti! This is not the time for timidity. You are afraid that you are sinning. Let me tell you the means to escape sin. Treat pleasure and pain alike, treat gain and loss alike, loss and victory alike. Let not your mind be troubled by thoughts of these. Get ready to fight and I can assure you that you will not incur sin and regret your actions!

Let me explain more about this rule of conduct called Buddhi Yoga—Sankhya. If you follow it, you will escape the bondage of karma: the bondage following action, which seeks results, benefits and fruits. This is not like the Karma Kanda of the rituals where there is the danger of incurring sin because of a single lapse in procedure. This is different and no effort is ever lost, no harm is ever done. Follow it, but a little, and you will be free of the great fear that grips you.

Arjuna, try and rise above the three Gunas. Try to be unaffected by the pairs of opposites. Think only of purity. Do not think of possessing anything. Think only of the soul. Your right is only till the action and as for the fruits of the action, you have no right over them; do not think of that at all.

> When you perform an action, do not think of the results or rewards. But also do not delude yourself into thinking that inaction will help you. No, you have no right to be inactive. Do not attach yourself to anything. Conduct your actions with an evenness of mind. You must be unaffected by both success and failure. It is this evenness or equality of mind, which is called Yoga.

Arjuna interrupted and asked, 'Krishna, tell me more about the man who has the equanimity of mind and whose intellect is steady and unclouded. How does one become such a perfect man?'

Pleased that his pupil was coming out of his stupor of self-negation, Krishna replied:

> Arjuna, I am called Sthitaprajna. Such a person has cast off all the desires of the mind and his spirit finds comforts in itself. His pulse does not fail when sorrow approaches him, it does not beat faster when joy approaches him. Three things have no place in his mind: desire, fear and anger. He is never attached to anyone or anything. Good and evil are treated with the same equanimity by him. A man with balance of mind withdraws his senses into him as a tortoise does its limbs.

> It is very difficult, yet possible, that once the senses are withdrawn, the soul loses the appetite for the objects of the senses. Even the taste for them, which may linger on, will drop away when the Supreme is realised. O Son of Kunti, it is by no means easy. The wisest of men will find that, sometimes, the senses will rebel and sweep the mind in its current and, then, the mind will be like a boat, tossed to and fro in a gale. The senses should be controlled and this is possible only if you meditate on me.

> Partha, once attachment for the objects of the senses is given a place in the mind, it will be disastrous, because attachment gives rise to desire, and desire breeds anger; it makes you lose your ability to understand. Destruction follows in its wake; therefore senses should be controlled at all costs. A man attains peace when he is conscious that desires are like the floodwaters of rain that enrich the ocean, yet it remains unconcerned. That is the divine state and this is the bliss of Brahman, the Ultimate Spirit, from where no man can ever fall again.

A keen listener, Arjuna intercepted and said, 'If the state of realisation of Brahman is the highest, then why are you advising me to kill? Is it not contradictory?'

Krishna replied:

> Partha, there are two paths to attain that state. One is knowledge by meditation, and the other is work for men of action. Remember, no one can remain still, even for a moment; it is not possible by the nature of things in our universe.
>
> It is the law of nature that man should work. You may find a man who sits still without doing anything, but his mind is still engaged in the world of the senses. He is a hypocrite. There is the other type of man, the *sthitapragna*, who has controlled his senses along with the mind; when he works, he does so without attachment and is infinitely superior to any other kind of man. Action and duty are essential to humankind. By not acting, you cannot live; even the bodily functions need work to sustain them. Action is an essential part of existence.

Arjuna was amazed by Krishna's articulation. 'How, then, can one escape the bondage of action?' he asked.

> By performing action as a sacrifice. Give up your attachments and work as though you are performing a sacrifice for the general good. Work should be done so that others, not you, may benefit from it. Dedicate all action to me, and fight! Fix your mind on the Eternal Spirit. Detach your mind from all traces of desire and self-benefit. Then, when you do your duty for its sake, the sin or the benefit, as the case may be, does not cling to you, and you are free.

'Krishna, I am beginning to comprehend what you say. But man is sometimes driven to commit sin, in spite of himself, despite his best intentions and against his better nature. Why does it happen?' asked Arjuna, his interest rising. Krishna replied:

> It is wrath, which prompts man to commit sin. Consider lust and anger, the two direst enemies of man. True knowledge is hidden inside and enveloped by these. A flame is enveloped by smoke and mirror is covered by dust. The unborn child is hidden in the womb. Even so, the soul inside you is not seen by you because of such obstructions. A breath of air is enough to clear the smoke hiding the flame; for a man of *sattvic* disposition, a slight effort is enough to reveal the God in him. The mirror has to be wiped by a cloth for it to become clear; a slightly greater effort is needed by a man of the *rajasic* nature to realise the Supreme. The child has to wait for months before it

can free itself of the womb which holds it; even so, it is harder for a man of *tamasic* character to free himself from the senses and realise Brahman.

'Who is Brahman?'

'The spirit in you, the goodness in you, is Brahman.'

Arjuna was confused and wanted to know who Krishna really was:'The one who is my charioteer, is he a virtual person and, if so, who is the real person in you?'

> Partha, see the divinity within you, and you will come to know who I am. Maybe, I am that divinity within you! I taught this yoga to Vivasvan, who spoke about it to Manu, who then told Ikshvaku about it. This has been passed on from generation to generation. It has been eclipsed in recent times and, now, I am going to reveal to you, the secret science.

Arjuna asked, perplexed, 'Vivasvan is an ancient art. How could you have told him this secret science? Please explain to me, this riddle.' Krishna smiled and said:

> Arjuna, I have passed through many births and so have you. I know all of my births, but you do not know yours. I am the Unborn and Eternal; I am the lord of everything. When there is dearth of righteousness in the world, when there is danger of lawlessness becoming prevalent in the world, I appear and incarnate myself. I am born, era after era, to protect the good and destroy the wicked, to establish and propagate dharma. It is not given to everyone to know the divinity that is me; but the chosen few who try to reach me, can see me. It is very rare and, unless I ordain, they cannot realise me. Such persons will have no fear, no anger and no passion, Partha.
>
> They seek refuge in me and are lost in me. Their quest and the passion for knowledge and the Ultimate Reality are realised, when they become one with me. It does not matter in what manner they approach me or in what form they worship me; all paths lead to me and I accept them with no reservations.
>
> Arjuna, knowledge of the Divine reduces all work to ashes and man is free of all bondages. A man prompted by selfless action and knowledge has all his doubts destroyed and he becomes one with me. When you renounce the fruits of action to me, you attain a disciplined state of mind and peace. But men prompted by desire, who are not selfless, become attached to

the fruits of their action. A sanyasi, a real yogi, is one who does the work he ought to do and does not seek the fruits thereof. Renunciation is selfless work. True renunciation is renunciation of desire and nothing else. Work is the only means to attain the yoga of renunciation. Once it is attained, serenity is achieved of its own accord.

Arjuna, the pleasures that arise from attachment are only sources of pain. They have a beginning and an end; and anything which has a beginning and an end, is never a source of eternal joy. A wise man should avoid them. When a man reaches the stage when cold and heat, pleasure and pain, honour and dishonour, seem alike; he is ever-serene. A clod of earth, a stone and a piece of gold, will all look the same to him. He can see no difference between friends and foes. Such a man is supreme and attains the Ultimate Bliss!

I have assumed a human form and, so, fools do not recognise me as the lord of all beings. I am the One! Worshipping me will lead one to the Supreme State, which is myself. I am Pita—the father of the Universe, the goal of all meditation and worship. Those who meditate on me, and worship me and only me, will reach me in the end. It is very easy to win my grace… anything you do and anything you eat, anything you give away, any sacrifice you perform; dedicate it all to me. You will then be free of the bondage of karma, from the good and evil fruits of your work; you will be free to come to me.

Arjuna was thrilled at Krishna's affirmation of himself. Arjuna asked, 'Tell me, how I can know you by constant meditation? I want to know all about your power and grandeur. I want to know where I should look for you. Where do you dwell?' Krishna replied:

I am Vaasudeva Sarvamiti—the Soul dwelling in the hearts of every living thing. I am the Beginning, the Middle and the End. Of the Adityas, I am Vishnu, the all-pervading entity. Of the lights, I am the Sun. Among the stars, I am the Moon. Of the Vedas, I am the Sama. Of the senses, I am the Mind and, in the living beings, I am the Intellect. Of the Rudras, I am Sankara. Of the mountains, I am the Meru. Of the words, I am the AUM. Of the weapons, I am the Thunderbolt. Of those that measure, I am Time. I am Death that destroys all, and I am the origin of things that are yet to be born, the Germ of all living beings is me. *Krishnasya sacharacharam*—there is nothing moving or unmoving that can exist without me. All things endowed with grandeur, beauty and strength have sprung from the spark of my splendour. *Mama Thejonsa Sambhavam*—I stand, pervading the Universe, with a single fragment of myself.

Arjuna was ecstatic at the revelations and urged Krishna, 'I desire to see your Divine Form. If you think I am fit enough to behold it, reveal to me your true form.'

A brilliant light shone and an astounding form manifested. Krishna granted Arjuna *divya chakshu*—the divine eyes—and revealed to him His Divine Form. Like the light of a thousand suns, the splendour of the Mighty One was seen by Arjuna. He beheld the entire Universe with all its myriad manifestations within Him, all gathered together as one. He bowed his head before the lord and, with his palms together in incessant salutation, he said:

> Lord of Lords! In thy body, I see all the gods and all the varied hosts of beings as well. You are Infinite in form. There is no beginning or middle or end. You are a glowing mass of light. You are the Imperishable, the Supreme that has to be realised. You are the home of this entire Universe—the Guardian of the Eternal, You are the Primal Being. Your eyes are the sun and moon, Your face glows with the radiance of fire. The universe is being devoured by the fire that is You. You fill the spaces of Heaven and Earth, the sky. Looking at You, the world trembles, and so do I!

An awestruck Arjuna continued:

> I see all the sons of Dhritarashtra and the many warriors and heroes on our side too, rushing into your fearful mouth which is all fire—like mountain rivers rushing in tumult into the great ocean, they are rushing into your mouth. They seem like a flight of moths that rush towards a burning flame, perishing fast. Have mercy on me and tell me who you are. What is the purpose of this destruction that strikes terror in to me?

Krishna replied:

> Can you not recognise me? I am Time, the great destroyer. I destroy the mightiest in the world. I began to slay these heroes here, who will all die anyway, every one of them. Arise now, Arjuna, and win fame and glory; these men have already been slain by me. You are just the instrument with which I will destroy them.

Arjuna was choking and his words were faltering. He folded his palms together and said:

> O Parameshwar, the infinite Lord of the Lords! You are imperishable—the being and what lies beyond. You are first of the gods and the Supreme Treasure of the world. You are the knower, and You are what is to be known. You are the abode of everything. This entire universe is pervaded by You; You are Vishnu; and infinite is Your form, Your power and Your might. You pervade everything and You are everything. Nothing can equal You in the three worlds. I prostrate before You and seek Your mercy. Unaware of Your greatness, I called You Krishna and a friend. Forgive me and my ignorance. Bear with me, as a father with a son, as a lover with his beloved. Please assume Your human self. I find, I cannot bear to see this form of Yours.

The lord transformed into a humble charioteer once again.

'Krishna, having seen your cosmic self, I still have a few doubts. There are devotees who worship you and, again, there are others, who worship the Absolute. Which of these two is the better yogi?' asked Arjuna. Krishna replied:

> Both of them reach me. Some worship the Absolute, the Imperishable. They have subdued all their senses. They are even-minded under all conditions and are engaged in doing good to all beings—they contemplate on the Absolute and they come to me. Those who fix their minds on me, worship me with supreme faith and remain steadfast in their devotion to me, are considered by me to be perfect yogis. It is a hard path, which the worshipper of the Absolute treads. The goal is harder to reach. When all actions are dedicated to me with single-hearted devotion, I save them soon from death, and from the ocean called *sansara*—the mortal life. Fix your mind on me alone and let your thoughts rest in me, then, without a doubt, you will live in me.

Arjuna then asked, 'I want to know the true nature of *Sanyasa*. Is it resignation or renunciation? Pray tell me.' Krishna replied:

> The sages say that relinquishing all actions that are prompted by desire is renunciation. Surrendering the fruits of action is called *tyaga*. Some say that all action should be abandoned as they may lead to evil, while others say that works of sacrifice, gifts and penance should not be given up. But I will

> tell you the truth of the matter; action of any kind should not be given up. Duty has to be performed, but it should be done by surrendering all attachment for its fruit. One should perform one's duty, and only the fruits and attachment should be renounced.
>
> The doer who is free from attachment, who has no feeling of 'I' and has subdued his self and his desires, is worthy of becoming one with God. Endowed with a clear vision, firmly restraining himself; turning away from the senses and the objects of the senses; casting aside likes and dislikes; dwelling in solitude; restraining his speech, body and mind; ever engaged in meditation and concentration; cultivating freedom from passion; casting aside conceit, violence, pride, desire, wrath and possession; and tranquil in mind, he becomes worthy of becoming one with God.
>
> Having become one with God and tranquil in spirit, he neither grieves nor desires. He regards all beings alike and is devoted to me. He may be always engaged in all kinds of action and, yet, having found refuge in me, he reaches the Eternal and Indestructible by my grace.
>
> Surrender all duties and come to me alone for shelter. Have no grief. I will release you from all sins. I have declared to you this wisdom, so consider it in totality. Review it in your mind and then, act as you will.

Arjuna was at peace with himself and said, 'O Krishna, my lord! My misconceptions have been dispelled. I am no longer in doubt. I will act according to your command!'

Arjuna then took up his Gandiva; the lord took the reins of the white horses in his left hand and whip in his right hand. The golden chariot of Arjuna began to move towards Bhishma's silver chariot.

THE BATTLE BEGINS: DAY 1

The battle began with the two commanders-in-chief, Drishtadyumna and Bhishma, blowing their conchs. Shouting with defiance, the brave men on either side clashed in a terrible fray. Swords and maces were wielded, javelins and darts were hurled and arrows whistled past. Duryodhana fought Bhima, Yudhisthira with Salya; Drishtadyumna fought Drona and Drupada; with Jayadratha—Saindhava, Bhishma inflicted terrible blows on the Pandava army.

Abhimanyu attacked Bhishma, who checked his advance, but declared that he had not beheld such a mighty young hero before. Salya killed Uttarakumara, son of Virata. Bhishma advanced again, but Arjuna charged against him and fought his grandfather and teacher, somewhat unwillingly. At sunset, the hostilities were ceased, according to the agreed rules of war. The day had been distinctly favourable to the Kauravas and Yudhisthira was dejected.

DAY 2

The Pandava army was drawn up in Krauncha Vyuha or the heron formation, but Bhishma attacked, along with Drona and broke through. Yudhisthira rebuked Arjuna that he was not fighting Bhishma with all his might because of which the Pandava army had serious casualties. Arjuna looked at Krishna and said, 'Bhishma is playing havoc with the Panchala army. Drive the chariot up to him. I shall kill him for the sake of our allies and friends.'

Duryodhana informed Bhishma and Drona that Karna was not participating in the battle after being slighted by them and, it was now up to them to kill Arjuna and win the war. The battle ended for the day with the prodigious valour of Bhishma, Bhima, Abhimanyu and Drishtadyumna.

DAY 3

The Pandava army was arranged in an Ardha Chandraakar—crescent formation—to match the Kaurava's arrangement—in the form of Garuda with extended wings on both sides to a central column. Bhishma fought like a whirlwind. Krishna goaded Arjuna to checkmate Bhishma's terror. Arjuna cut Bhishma's bowstring with three arrows discharged in rapid succession. Bhishma cried out in admiration, 'Great Partha, I am pleased by your skill,' and reached for another bow. Arjuna cut this bowstring too.

Bhishma took up another bow and Krishna upbraided Arjuna, saying, 'Partha, this is no time for games. Attack Bhishma mortally. Look how he is annihilating the Pandava army. You are endangering the victory of dharma by shying away from killing your grandfather. I shall have to get down from the chariot and kill Bhishma myself.' So saying, he jumped from the chariot and rushed towards Bhishma with a fallen chariot wheel and was about to whirl a discus to kill Bhishma.

Seeing this, Bhishma dropped his arms on the chariot floor, hands outstretched, saying, 'O Govinda, nothing would please me more than death at your hands; it will give me lasting fame in this world and bliss in the next.

Krishna, come and deliver me from this wretched life of mine.' In panic, Arjuna ran after Krishna and promised to fight Bhishma in earnest. Krishna relented and resumed his role as a charioteer.

DAY 4

This was Bhima's day. He attacked fourteen sons of Dhritarashtra; killing eight of them, driving back the other six and wounding Duryodhana and Salya. He killed many elephants, but could do nothing to the mighty elephant of Bhagadatta, the king of Pragjyotishpura. Bhagadatta's elephant division was the most formidable offensive wing in the Kaurava army. To wreak havoc, Ghatotkacha met the monster and drove it back with his illusive contrivances.

DAY 5

The Kaurava army was in the shark formation and the Pandavas in a hawk arrangement. Arjuna and Duryodhana faced each other. Abhimanyu fought the Kaurava army, furiously and heroically. Lakshmana, Duryodhana's son, was wounded, but Bhurisravas slew the ten sons of Satyaki. Satyaki vowed to kill Bhurisravas, who was a great devotee of Krishna, in return. As the war progressed, in the blindness of animosities and desperation, both sides broke the agreed rules of war and indulged in many atrocities.

DAY 6

This was a day of great peril for Bhima. He advanced too far into the Kaurava army's formation and got cut off from his forces. Duryodhana hoped to catch him alive. Appalled by his reckless ways in the battle, Drupada saw Bhima in danger and rushed to his help. He too was surrounded and cut off. There was jubilation among the Kauravas. Abhimanyu attacked the Kaurava leaders fiercely and rescued Bhima and Drupada. Krishna and Yudhisthira greatly admired the valour of this young warrior.

DAY 7

This was Bhishma's day once again. He formed his army into the Mandala Vyuha and crashed into the Pandava army, which was assembled as Vajra Vyuha. Nothing that Bhima or Arjuna did could check his advance. Before sunset, the field was full of the slain and wounded. At night, wild beasts feasted on a rich harvest of corpses.

DAY 8

The tide of war turned the next day. Bhishma's charioteer was slain and the Kaurava army was in confusion for a while, but the Gandhara princes rallied the Kauravas and slew the Pandava warrior, Iravat. Ghatotkacha rushed against the Gandharas to avenge Iravat's death, and caused great damage.

DAY 9

Bhishma mowed down the Pandava army like a forest fire burning grass. Krishna reminded Arjuna that he should kill Bhishma if he did not want the Pandavas to lose. Krishna said to Arjuna:

> He has vowed that he will not fight against a woman or against a person who has been born a woman. Send for Shikhandin, who was born a woman and was transformed into a man by a yaksha, only to kill Bhishma, who had ruined her life in her former birth as Amba. Shoot your arrows at Bhishma, keeping Shikhandin by your side.

Arjuna was shocked at this suggestion and replied, 'I cannot fight behind another or achieve the fall of Bhishma by foul means. I loved him as a child and sat on his knee…he is my grandfather. I would rather die than kill the saintly hero in such a manner.' Krishna smiled and replied that this was war. 'It is fated that Bhishma will fall tomorrow, a victim of wrong in return for what he did to Amba. Look, he has fought, despite his love for you, and will kill you if he can, I cannot see why you should refuse to fight and kill him.'

DAY 10

Before daybreak, Yudhisthira, with his brothers and Krishna, went to meet Bhishma who told them he could only be defeated in the way suggested by Krishna.

So, the Pandavas put Shikhandin in front of Arjuna as the chariot advanced to challenge Bhishma. The advancing Bhishma suddenly stopped fighting, despite Shikhandin discharging three arrows at him. Bhishma said, 'I shall never fight you back, you were born a woman.' Taking advantage of the situation, Arjuna discharged two powerful arrows and Bhishma fell from his chariot, head foremost, exclaiming, 'These arrows that struck me like thunderbolts could never have been discharged by Shikhandin, but by Arjuna.' He said he had a boon from his father: *Svachhanda Maranam*—the power to postpone his death—and he would use that boon till the Uttarayana—sun entering the Makara constellation.

At his request, Arjuna formed a bed of arrows, and the grand sire lay on it stoically, awaiting the end.

Bhishma felt thirsty and asked Arjuna to give him some water. Arjuna discharged a *parjanya* or rain arrow and made a cool fountain gush out from the earth. Bhishma drank that water eagerly and said, 'I am glad to be freed from this slaughter of kinsmen. So far, I fought this internecine war out of respect for my duty. No more.' As a mark of respect for the grand old man, there was a ceasefire for fifteen days when all the dead were cremated and physicians attended to the wounded.

DAY 11

Both armies grieved at the fall of Bhishma. Arjuna's grief was immense and uncontrollable. Krishna consoled him saying that Bhishma was the ideal kshatriya who followed his kshatra dharma and, therefore, he need not grieve for slaying his grandfather.

After the period of fifteen days, Drona was made commander-in-chief of the Kaurava army and he promised Duryodhana that he would take Yudhisthira as a prisoner. Abhimanyu and Bhima fought so gloriously that all efforts by Drona to get at Yudhisthira were foiled for some time. But when Arjuna was drawn off to fight Trigarta, Drona rushed at Yudhisthira who escaped capture by riding away from the battlefield on a swift steed.

DAY 12

The next day, Abhimanyu's actions were nothing less than heroic. Drona had formed his famous Chakra Vyuha—spider's web. The Pandavas' attempts to break it had failed. It was vital to break the array if the Kauravas were to be defeated. The brave Abhimanyu fought and killed Lakshmana and advanced into the spider's web. He penetrated the array and advanced further. He was surrounded by Drona, Aswathama, Kripa, Karna, Brihadbala, Kritavarma and Jayadratha, all intent on killing him; the Pandava army could not reach him to help.

The seven *maharathi*s and a host of others shamelessly attacked the lone young boy together. He fought them bravely and killed Satrunjaya, Chandraketu, Meghavega, Suryobhasa and Suvarchasa and wounded Shakuni, but was finally thrown down from his chariot and killed while fighting weaponless, valiant against tremendous odds.

Great was the rejoicing among the Kauravas when Abhimanyu was slain. But it was against all rules governing the war, which had been ordained by Bhishma and Dronacharya. The event became a turning point in the war as thereafter, both sides conveniently broke rules.

When Arjuna heard the news he fell down on the ground, senseless. After he recovered consciousness, he vowed that he would burn himself alive, if he did not kill Jayadratha, who had brought about his boy's death, before sunset the next day.

News of this vow reached the Kauravas, who resolved to defend Jayadratha and foil Arjuna's plan. Jayadratha was quaking with fear and had no hope of escaping from Arjuna's arrow.

DAY 13

Arjuna, Bhima and Satyaki began the day with a firm resolve to slay Jayadratha. The Kauravas were equally determined to protect him. The day wore out, and sunset approached without Arjuna being able to get anywhere near Jayadratha. Everyone thought that, having failed, Arjuna would self-immolate and then, the war would be practically over.

The Pandava army was in despair and a spirit of fatality gripped it. Krishna noticed this sense of depression and decided to intervene, for he felt that *adharma* was holding dharma in a vice, trying to throttle the good in the world. He used his yogic powers to create an illusion in the minds of Kauravas that the sun had set. In reality, a dark cloud covered the sun and a pall of darkness descended on the battlefield, much to the delight of the Kauravas. Drona and Karna withdrew their protection from Jayadratha and brought him to the forefront to show everyone that the warrior was alive.

Just then, the cloud covering the sun passed away, revealing that the sun had not yet set. Arjuna shot a deadly arrow at Jayadratha and severed his head, which flew and fell on the lap of his father, Vriddakshatra, who was offering his evening prayers. In a reflex action, Vriddakshatra threw the ghastly thing off his palms and it fell to the earth; at once, Vriddhakshatra's head burst, in pursuance of his own curse—whoever causes Jayadratha's head to fall on the earth will have his own head explode.

On hearing about Jayadratha's death, Vidura said, 'The men who thought they could fight God were shown that they could not distinguish a false sunset from a true one!'

THE NIGHT BATTLE

The Pandava army was delirious with joy and the Kauravas were mad with rage. Contrary to the agreed canons of the conduct of war, the armies fought on murderously even after sunset. In the wavering light of the torches, men rushed madly at each other using swords, javelins, arrows, boulders and even cartwheels. Blood spurted everywhere. After several hours, a truce was called at midnight and every warrior slept where he was: the cavalryman on his horse, the elephant man on his elephant and the charioteer in his chariot.

Krishna was aghast at the sight and went into a trance. He warned Arjuna that Duryodhana was scheming a terrible massacre of the innocent. 'Sound caution everywhere and I shall keep guard on all of you.'

As Krishna predicted, Duryodhana confided in Drona that he had planned a treacherous attack that night on the sleeping Pandava warriors. Duryodhana told Drona that because they were not being able to kill the Pandavas in fair war, they should massacre them while asleep in their camp. Drona was aghast at the idea and wondered whether he was commanding an army of an immoral wretch who disregarded even the basic tenets of Kshatra Dharma. An enraged Drona replied:

> A descendant of Sage Bharadwaja and a disciple of Bhagavan Parashurama will never stoop to such a dastardly act. You are a vain fool, Duryodhana and you do not know who Krishna is. God never sleeps and you can never find him off guard; the world will consider you a fiend and a coward.

Grinding his teeth in despair, Duryodhana then said, 'You are like Bhishma, a lover of Pandavas and a stickler for dharma. Such people can never win a war. Your son, Aswathama, is made of sterner stuff. Give up your command to Karna, who will do anything I want.' Drona replied:

> Duryodhana! It is your pleasure to disband my command. But remember, though Karna might be a great warrior, he is easily frustrated and cynical. He does not see the right path in his insane jealousy against Arjuna and anger at the other Pandavas. Hate will consume him in the end. Despite all his valour and virtue, he will stand alone on the battlefield because his hate makes him forget all the invocations associated with the divine *astra*s he has

earned so far. When he presides as commander-in-chief, he will not take his orders from anyone, not even the king. I stick to my resolve not to stain my hands with blood through treachery. Being indebted to the house of the Kurus for my earthly comforts, I shall fight with greater vigour tomorrow. I shall kill Arjuna or get killed by him. This is my resolve. Let us get some sleep tonight.

NIGHT BATTLE RESUMED

Duryodhana left Dronacharya's camp in rage and ordered the night battle be resumed as soon as the moon rose. To the call of the trumpet, in the dead of night, all the warriors woke up and began fighting again. Karna charged at the Pandava army with deadly effect, sending its torchbearing soldiers running helter-skelter.

Krishna was enraged and told Arjuna that Ghatotkacha can stem Karna's fury. 'Remember, he is of Rakshasa descent, and they are very active during nights.'

Arjuna hesitated, but Krishna sent for Ghatotkacha and asked him whether he would volunteer to attack Karna. 'The son of Bhima is not afraid to fight for the Pandava cause,' said the young Rakshasa.

Krishna, Arjuna and Bhima warmly embraced Ghatotkacha; he set out to vigorously attack the Kaurava army. He adopted all the tricks of Rakshasas and frustrated Karna's efforts. He fought with Karna furiously and killed Alambusha, the son of Jatasura, who had been killed by the Pandavas earlier in the day.

Then Alayudha, another redoubtable Rakshasa, was sent against him. Ghatotkacha killed him, too, after a fierce fight. Karna was disappointed; in order to deal with Ghatotkacha, he had to invoke his ultimate weapon—Shakti, which he had reserved to slay Arjuna. The Shakti weapon is invincible and strikes the target without fail. In a moment of emotional weakness, Karna used this against Ghatotkacha and killed him instantly.

While falling dead, Ghatotkacha crushed several soldiers of the Kaurava army underneath him. The Pandava camp once again sunk into despair. Krishna addressed Bhima, 'Atmabandhu, your son is a martyr and a heavenly abode is assured for him. Ghatotkacha's fight with Karna has done immense good for us. He has exhausted his weapon, Shakti, from which even I could not have saved Arjuna.'

In another attack, Drona killed his arch enemy, Drupada, that night.

DAY 14

Furious at Drona for killing his father at night, Drishtadyumna decided to slay Drona before the day ended. Krishna was visibly annoyed with Drona for indiscriminately using weapons of mass destruction on ordinary soldiers; he was mowing down the Pandava army in thousands.

Krishna said, 'Unless Drona is killed, defeat is certain. But Drona can meet his end only if he disarms himself.' Arjuna pleaded with him, 'Please suggest a strategy, Govinda.' Krishna replied that, if Yudhisthira told Drona that his son Aswathama was dead, then he would lay down his arms and could be killed. Appalled by the idea, Arjuna said, 'Krishna, is it not *adharma*?' Drishtadyumna intervened to reply:

> Though it is a foul thing to do, we must remember that Drona was *adharmic* himself when he kept quiet while Draupadi was being humiliated in the Kuru court, when attacking Abhimanyu against the code of warfare, and for the indiscriminate use of Brahmastra against common soldiers. Therefore, Yudhisthira should not feel hesitant to tell a lie.

However, Yudhisthira declined to utter an untruth. Drishtadyumna taunted Yudhisthira:

> People call you Dharmaputra, but you use dharma for self-aggrandising your ego. Are you not heartless, O King? You kept silent when Drona used Brahmastra, killing thousands of your soldiers; you were indifferent when my sister Draupadi was dishonoured under your very nose; you never bothered about the grief of Subhadra when Abhimanyu was hunted and killed by Drona in the most *adharmic* battle. You maintained silence, thereby egging your ego and safeguarding your reputation. What sort of logic do you apply to these acts of *adharma*? Remember, by failing to act to establish real dharma, you are propagating *adharma*.

Drishtadyumna was greatly exasperated by Yudhisthira's stubbornness. Looking quite shaken, Yudhisthira asked Krishna, 'What should I do?' Krishna, as if approving Drishtadyumna's rebuke, said, 'Dharmaputra, announce that Aswathama is dead.'

Yudhisthira was still reluctant to utter an outright lie. Meanwhile, Bhima had killed an elephant named Aswathama and asked his brother to announce it loud enough for Drona to hear. Diffidently, Yudhisthira raised his voice and said, 'Aswathama is dead,' and, under his breath, uttered that it was an elephant.

A stunned Drona, believing that Yudhisthira would never lie, laid down his arms and squatted on the chariot floor in a yogic pose, chanting Aum and entered the state of *Prayopavesa*. Drishtadyumna caught him by his hair and cut off his head in a gruesome act. Sanjaya and Arjuna saw a light pass out of Drona's body and head towards the starry regions.

Arjuna and Satyaki rebuked Drishtadyumna for resorting to *adharma* to combat *adharma*. Drishtadyumna replied that he was ready to take any punishment from them. At this moment, Krishna intervened and asked Satyaki to take away Bhima and Arjuna to avert another gruesome murder.

Aswathama was furious at the cowardly way the Pandavas had killed his father. He went to see the severed corpse of his father and was filled with grief and sorrow. With terrible fury, he discharged the Narayana Astra against the Pandava army. The nature of the weapon was to kill anyone who resisted it; the more the resistance, the greater its power.

Being Lord Narayana himself, Krishna knew the power of that unique weapon and asked every man in the Pandava army to lay down his arms, lie down and allow the missile to fly past. With the exception of Bhima, everyone submitted to Krishna's command. Bhima exclaimed, 'I shall never lay down my arms and acknowledge defeat to Aswathama.' But the moment he wielded his mace, he fell down unconscious, struck by unseen forces—electromagnetic radiation causing high voltage shock.

At the insistance of Krishna, the Pandava soldiers standing near Bhima snatched his mace from him and made him lie low, unarmed. The terrible Narayana Astra whistled past the Pandava troops without causing any harm. All rose up, except Bhima, who was still in a swoon. Arjuna created a fountain by discharging a Varun Astra and revived Bhima with its life-giving waters.

Duryodhana was fuming at Aswathama's ignorance. 'What use is your technical victory? They have taken up arms again and you cannot use that weapon on them hereafter.'

'Do not worry, I have vowed to kill Drishtadyumna, by fair or foul means.' Duryodhana rebuked him, saying, 'You must also kill all the Pandavas, O brahmana, including the unborn child of Abhimanyu in the womb of Uttara. I want to rid this world of Pandavas. I had requested your father to do this, he refrained and paid with his life.'

DAY 15

Karna was made commander-in-chief and carried the war on the fifteenth day, with great credit. He slew countless warriors. Blood ran in streams and the dead and mangled bodies of men, horses and elephants lay chaotically, strewn all along the battlefield. The air was darkened with arrows and darts; it rang with the challenges of opposing warriors, moans and groans of the wounded and the dying. All the soldiers retired to their camps at sunset, afraid that, otherwise, they would be asked to fight at night, as on the previous nights.

DAY 16

Karna told Duryodhana that this would be the day he would slay Arjuna or be killed by him. But he wanted a charioteer to match Krishna's skills and suggested Salya's name. Salya was the only man equal to Krishna in manipulating the chariot and directing the horses. Karna asked Duryodhana to request Salya to be his charioteer. 'I dare not ask him, for Salya believes that he should have been the commander-in-chief instead of me,' said Karna.

Duryodhana pleaded with Salya to be Karna's charioteer for the day. Salya refused to play second fiddle to Karna, but Duryodhana's entreaties forced him to agree, on condition that Karna could not give him directional commands. A frustrated Duryodhana asked, 'How can that be possible, Uncle?' Salya, being eccentric, kept mum. He menacingly warned Duryodhana that, if forced, he would rather remain in his tent than suffer the disgrace. An exasperated Duryodhana consented to the demands of Salya, who became the reluctant charioteer for Karna.

SALYA'S CHARIOTEERING (SALYA SAARATHYAM)

Taunts and insults from an insolent charioteer did upset Karna, but he tolerated it, for his spirits were upbeat as he got into the chariot. He appreciated Salya's expertise in navigating the chariot and offered him lots of gold and elephants if he would take him to Arjuna in the battlefield. He would then slay him, without any further delay.

Salya retorted, 'Radheya, why waste gold and elephants? You will soon see Arjuna, but give up fighting him. Abhimanyu was brought down by seven *maharathi*s; his father would require seven more. Fight a lesser fry.' Karna felt slighted and replied in anger, 'I am a lion in war and no one can resist me. I have many divine *astra*s to fight Arjuna.'

Salya replied:

> A jackal living among hares considers itself to be a lion till it sees a lion and realises its mistake, only too late. A crow told a swan that it knew 105 ways of flying and competed with the swan in flight. Both began to fly across a vast lake. The swan went on gaily, but the miserable crow could not fly long and, after a short distance, fell in the water and struggled for life. The swan turned back towards the shore, saw the miserable crow struggling in shallow waters near the shore. The swan picked up the crow and put it on the shore, saying it had not revealed this 106th method of flight! My dear man, you ran away from Arjuna during the raid on the Virata country. How can you hope to defeat Arjuna when he is protected by Krishna Vaasudeva?

Salya had a long and loud laugh, heckling Karna, who was furious and muttered to himself, 'O, what a shame! I have to depend on this man as my charioteer!'

YUDHISTHIRA

Yudhisthira attacked Karna, but was soon defeated and thrown down from his chariot, wounded. Karna told him, 'You are fit only to lead a brahmana's life of prayer and sermonising truth. Why did you come to fight like a kshatriya?' Poor Yudhisthira retired to his tent, humiliated and wounded.

When Arjuna came to see him in his tent after sunset, Yudhisthira was smarting from the insult. He stared at Arjuna and said in reproach, 'Arjuna, you bragged that you would kill Karna. What use is your Gandiva when it could not kill Karna? You better give it to someone else!' Arjuna turned red, as he had sworn to kill anyone who insulted his Gandiva. Thus, he drew his sword to kill Yudhisthira. 'You are a coward and Abhimanyu died saving you,' said Arjuna.

Krishna prevented the slaying, telling Arjuna that addressing an elder brother in the singular was equal to killing him. A sobered Arjuna said to Yudhisthira, 'You, who could not stand one fight with Karna, are telling me this!'

Yudhisthira turned pale at this act of disrespect. Arjuna repented his outrageous behaviour towards his eldest brother and wanted to immolate himself in an act of expiation. Krishna upbraided Arjuna:

> Partha, what are you doing? You are a kshatriya, you cannot threaten to immolate yourself for trivial issues. Go and prostrate yourself at Yudhisthira's

> feet and seek his pardon. The prolonged battle and the senseless massacre must have frayed your brother's nerves. An apology will settle things.

Arjuna did as Krishna wanted and the incident was forgotten, with the brothers embracing each other.

On another front, Bhima had attacked Karna and a fierce fight had ensued. Dushassana went to help Karna, but Bhima left Karna the moment he sighted Dushassana, whom he had vowed to kill and drink blood from. After a fierce fight, Bhima crushed the chariot of Dushassana, pulled him out, held him helplessly and roared like a mad man, 'Come, Duryodhana or Karna or anyone else who dares, to his rescue!' All were terrified by the fearsome appearance of Bhima and refrained from responding to the challenge.

With his foot pressed against the chest of the Kuru prince, Bhima screamed, 'Dushassana, you rogue! You pulled the hair of Draupadi, you rotten wretch.' Perhaps in deep remorse, Dushassana stretched forth his right arm. Bhima tore off that arm in a trice, then cut off Dusshasana's head and, tearing open the heart, drank a few drops of his warm blood and rubbing his blood-soaked arms on his armour plate, laughed hysterically, 'I have not drunk anything sweeter!' Bhima then returned to his camp and, with his hands stained in Dushassana's blood, tied up the dishevelled hair of Draupadi, who was with the other ladies in a camp called Upaplavya. She was thus avenged.

KARNA'S DEJECTION

Karna was horrified by this gory scene. Holding his head in dismay, he approached Salya and told him:

> I do not fear death, however cruel. But on this battlefield, my heart is filled with utmost misery; and I remember the curse of my teacher, Parashurama, who took me as a disciple on my presentation that I was a brahmana. On discovering my fraud, he uttered the curse that my weapons will be useless at the time of my need! Now, when I need them the most, all these weapons seem powerless. These horses stumble along, helplessly driven by destiny; the elephants are trembling like aspen leaves; the conchs and kettledrums emit a dull and funereal sound, but I shall fight as best as I can. May I attain victory or death!

VRIHASENA KILLED

Arjuna advanced to fight Karna. But on the way, he found Nakula being chased by Vrihasena, Karna's heroic son, who had defeated him. Arjuna attacked Vrihasena, inviting Kaurava leaders nearby to come to the aid of the young man, if they could. No one dared to go to the aid of Vrihasena and the heroic youth was killed by Arjuna, after putting up a credible resistance.

KARNA AND ARJUNA

Karna heard of his son's death and screamed in fury, 'The sons have fallen, now is the turn of the fathers!' Exclaiming thus, he showered his arrows at Arjuna. They hit him like stinging snakes. Arjuna returned the offensive with doubled fury. One of Karna's arrows snapped the bowstring of Gandiva. Arjuna hollered, 'Pause till I string my bow; no Aryan ever fights a disabled man!'

Karna did not heed the cry and discharged the terrible Nagastra, intending to severe Arjuna's head. A Naga called Asvasena—son of Takshaka of Khandava forest, whose cannibal mother had been killed during the burning of the Khandava forest by Arjuna and Krishna—was guiding the Nagastra in his burning desire for revenge. Krishna deftly manoeuvred the chariot in the nick of time and the weapon simply carried off the priceless crown given by Indra to Arjuna, leaving his head unsheathed.

Asvasena begged Karna to discharge the Nagastra once again, revealing to him who he was, and promising to guide the arrow correctly this time, to finish off Arjuna. Karna declined the offer, saying, 'I will not use the same *astra* a second time; moreover, I want to kill Arjuna by my own skill, not with your help.' The disappointed Naga rushed at Arjuna menacingly, but was killed in no time by the Pandava prince, who had restrung his bow.

Arjuna resumed the fight with great vigour. All of a sudden, one of the wheels of Karna's chariot got stuck in the blood-soaked ground and Salya could not extricate it, however much he nudged the horses to move forward. Karna got down from the chariot to pull the stuck wheel out of the rut and cried out to Arjuna, 'Pause, O Arjuna, till I get my chariot out of the mud, no Aryan ever fights a disabled man. Remember our dharma and cease fighting for a while.' Arjuna hesitated and did not know how to respond to this demand, when Krishna intervened and said to Karna:

> Is it not fortunate Karna, that you remember dharma now? When you asked Dushassana to strip Draupadi naked in open court, where was your dharma? When you applauded Duryodhana as he refused to give back their

> kingdom to the Pandavas, despite his solemn promise to do so, where was your dharma? When you looked on approvingly when Duryodhana asked Draupadi to sit on his right thigh, where was that dharma? When you killed young Abhimanyu, fighting seven to one, where was your dharma? Cease to quote dharma when you have turned a blind eye to it all your life.

At the mention of Abhimanyu, Arjuna steeled himself and discharged deadly arrows at Karna. In spite of his precarious position while trying to get his stuck chariot wheel moving, Karna fought back with extraordinary dexterity. Arjuna's resources were being exhausted and, as a last resort, Arjuna used the powerful missile of Yama—Anjalika, the crescent moon, which was razor-sharp and clinical in precision, fixing it to his Gandiva. He invoked the mantra: 'If I have performed any penance, if I have served my gurus, if I have never betrayed friends, if I have any love of truth and dharma in me, may this missile go forth like the terrible Kritya and kill Karna!' The missile went unerringly and cut off Karna's head. There was consternation in the Kaurava army.

DAY 17

Salya was appointed the commander-in-chief of the Kaurava army. Yudhishthira resolved to salvage his tarnished image. He fought with Salya and finally killed him by hurling his powerful Shakti, that pierced the foe's heart.

Bhima killed Sudarsana, the sole surviving brother of Duryodhana, and Arjuna finally killed Susarma, the king of Trigartas, noted for his hit-and-run tactics. Shakuni attacked the Pandavas furiously, but was killed by Sahadeva, while vainly crying to Duryodhana for help.

DAY 18

On the eighteenth day, Sanjaya was captured by Satyaki. He was, however, released after the war was over, at the insistence of Vyasa, as he was only a war correspondent caught in the frontlines. All the warriors on the Kaurava side were dead, except Kripacharya, Aswathama, Kritavarma and Duryodhana.

Deprived of victory, Duryodhana hid in a cave behind a lake, waiting for better times to renew the war. Bhima discovered his hiding place and Yudhisthira challenged him to come out and fight. Duryodhana replied, 'All my brothers and friends are dead. Take the entire kingdom and rule in peace. I shall retire to a forest and do penance.'

Yudhisthira said, 'I am a kshatriya. I cannot accept a gift of a kingdom from you. Come out of your hiding and fight, and let the victor take the entire kingdom.' Krishna was startled at this wager. Duryodhana promised to come out and fight, if they fight him one at a time. It was agreed that Duryodhana and Bhima would fight each other with clubs and mace.

THE EPIC FIGHT

Yudhisthira requested Balarama, who had returned from his pilgrimage, to referee the combat. He chose a spot near the Samanta Panchaka lake, the holiest spot in Kurukshetra, for the fight and agreed to supervise it. Bhima was sure he would win easily, but soon found Duryodhana was more than his match. Krishna told Arjuna that, to defeat Duryodhana, Bhima must strike on his right thigh, which he had indecently exposed to Draupadi, thereby making himself vulnerable by this act of *adharma*. Arjuna said that it was against the Aryan code of war to hit a man below his belt.

Krishna exclaimed:

> That is so! But this is war and not a court of chivalry and, moreover, Duryodhana has never acted according to dharma. Was he an apostle of dharma when he insulted Draupadi, or wanted to burn you all in the house of lac, or when he asked Drona to murder you en masse treacherously while asleep, or when he asked Shakuni to cheat Yudhisthira in the game of dice? It is for you to consider whether one side alone can stick to dharma while your opponent flouts it blatantly and wins. Arjuna, I leave it to you!

Just at that moment, Duryodhana dealt a terrible blow to Bhima, who fell down and looked most unlikely to recover. When Duryodhana was about to give him a finishing stroke, Bhima rose, with blood streaming from his wounds, and rushed energetically towards his opponent. Arjuna made up his mind and patted his right thigh so that Bhima could see and understand the gesture; Bhima grasped the meaning and dealt a brutal blow on Duryodhana's right thigh. Duryodhana instantly collapsed and was unable to rise again. There he lay, like a serpent with a broken spine. Bhima kicked him on the head, as he lay helpless.

Yudhisthira was furious at this dastardly act and slapped Bhima on the face; Balarama too was full of rage and wanted to crack Bhima's skull, but Krishna intervened and reminded Balarama how he had never chastised Duryodhana for all his blatant acts of *adharma*, so why should he punish Bhima now?

Balarama frowned in disgust, but smiled with understanding, 'I know you cannot tolerate *adharma* and, now, it is your duty to establish dharma. Your time of reckoning has arrived, after all!'

MASSACRE AT THE PANDAVA CAMP

Kripacharya, Kritavarma and Aswathama were grieved to see Duryodhana on the ground, crippled and wailing for vengeance. They vowed to annihilate the Pandavas to avenge Bhima's *adharmic* act. Duryodhana appointed Aswathama as the commander-in-chief.

Aswathama, Kritavarma and Kripa crept into the Pandava camp stealthily that night. Aswathama kicked the sleeping Drishtadyumna, who woke up and begged to be killed with a weapon, as a kshatriya deserved to be. Aswathama said, 'No, you are the murderer of our Acharya and you deserve only to be kicked to death, like a worm.' That is exactly what they did till he breathed his last. The women woke up and screamed.

Uttamaujas hurled a missile at Aswathama, but was easily killed by the latter. Draupadi's five sons woke up and put up a fight, but Aswathama was a seasoned warrior and easily killed these boys without any mercy.

Kripa and Kritavarma wreaked havoc on the rest of the camp. Then the three, chagrined at not finding the five Pandavas in the camp, returned to Duryodhana and gave him the news of the holocaust. Duryodhana was much delighted.

DRAUPADI'S DEMAND

Drishtadyumna's charioteer went and told Yudhisthira and his brothers about the terrible attack at night and the slaughter of their sons born to Draupadi. On hearing this, Yudhisthira fainted with grief. Nakula was deputed to bring Draupadi from Upaplavya, where she was staying. Draupadi was inconsolable when she heard the ghastly news about her children. However, as soon as she recovered her composure, she demanded Aswathama's head in revenge.

Yudhisthira reminded her that Aswathama was a brahmana and should not be killed. Draupadi was furious and retorted that he was a murderer and no shastra absolved brahmanas of punishment.

Krishna said that it was not an ordinary murder, but murder in war, and that it would be enough if Aswathama's crown jewel was taken away and he was made to suffer the terrible consequences. He also reminded them that Aswathama had a boon to be a Cheeranjivi, meaning that he would never die.

'This punishment that I propose is worse than beheading him. Panchali, think of the prospects for a deathless Aswathama; his body and spirit decadent and suffering without an end; it will be terrible!' said Krishna. Draupadi understood and agreed.

Arjuna, Bhima and Krishna went in search of Aswathama, who had hidden himself in the ashram of Vyasa; the unrepentant brahmana invoked the terrible Brahma Sirsha missile, with the intention of terminating Abhimanyu's unborn child in Uttara's womb.

Arjuna also discharged a Brahma Sirsha to counter Aswathama's and the collision of the two deadly missiles was apocalyptic, with a column of fire rising high into the skies. Krishna asked Arjuna to withdraw the missile, which he did. But Aswathama could not withdraw it as he was ignorant of the procedure, and had Krishna not intercepted the missile, the weapon would have penetrated Uttara's womb, killing the unborn child.

Arjuna caught hold of Aswathama and cut off his crown jewel. He was left to wander in desperation, crying for water, but rarely getting any. The brilliance of a learned brahmana vanished from his face and Aswathama was despised and forsaken by the world. It was a punishment worse than death.

POST-WAR EVENTS

It was the practice that victors should enter the camp of the enemy, so the Pandavas proceeded towards Duryodhana's camp, blowing their conchs. The Panchajanya and Devadatta were blown with pride. The five brothers were sullen, owing to the events at Samanta Panchaka, where Duryodhana was dying. Even Bhima was filled with remorse!

As soon as they arrived at the camp, Krishna asked them to remain still and told Arjuna to pick up his Gandiva and quiver and alight from the chariot. Krishna was still in the chariot but, after Arjuna descended, the great Hanuman, who was on the banner, sprang up to the skies and vanished into thin air. Then, much to the shock of the brothers, Arjuna's golden chariot caught fire and burnt like a pile of wood and, in a matter of a few moments, was just a heap of ashes. The white horses of Arjuna were also consumed in the fire. Arjuna turned his tear-filled eyes to Krishna and asked, 'My lord, what is this I see? What is the reason for this?' Krishna's face was stern, as he said:

> Arjuna, its purpose has been served. The chariot has absorbed all the mighty

> *astras* thrown at you by your enemy. It should have been burnt long ago, but did not, as I was sitting in it, and I absorbed all the mighty energy by my Yogashakti. I have abandoned it now and you have achieved what you set out to do, hence, it has been reduced to ashes. Arjuna, everything in this world is created for a purpose and the moment it is served, it is not needed any more.

Krishna continued:

> Arjuna, it is even so with men; each man is set on this eventful journey called life. He comes into this world with a purpose. Once that is served, the earth has no need of him anymore. It applies to all of us, including me. I have manifested myself on this earth for a purpose, which is not over yet, something still remains and the moment it is completed, I, too, will die. Come on now, do not grieve. Let us set about our next task.

Krishna congratulated Yudhisthira formally for winning the war, addressing him as Dharma Raja. 'Yudhisthira, it is customary for the winners to sleep outside the enemy camp on the night of their victory. You must all sleep away from your camp tonight,' said Krishna.

'So be it. But Krishna, I am afraid to face Gandhari and inform her that all her sons are now dead. Once she knows that Duryodhana was killed by unfair means, she may curse us. I want you to go pacify her and we will follow later.'

Krishna smiled and said, 'I shall go at once. The curse of Gandhari should not fall on you, O king!'

THE BHIMA EPISODE

After Duryodhana died, Sanjaya lost his ability to see the battlefield. Yudhisthira, along with Draupadi and his brothers, called on Dhritarashtra at Hastinapura. This was to console the old king at the death of his sons and other kith and kin. Gandhari was also present. The wily king expressed a desire to hug Bhima out of affection. Bhima was about to oblige, when Krishna intervened. He pulled back Bhima and, in his place, pushed an iron statue that Duryodhana would use for combat practice. As the blind king embraced the statue, it crumbled into powder due to his ferocious embrace. He bled from gnashing his teeth.

Sanjaya rebuked Dhritarashtra, 'This anger is unbecoming of a ruler.' The king expressed his sorrow at having crushed Bhima to death with his embrace. Krishna said, 'O king, you need not be sorry as you have only crushed an iron statue of Bhima. Your sons have paid the penalty for their sins.' Dhritarashtra apologised and said that it was only out of great love for his sons that he acted irrationally. Krishna replied that a terrible fate awaited him at the end of his days. 'O king! You have no remorse even now, which is a pity! You will reap misery for your deeds!' Gandhari was also in great distress, but had known that her sons could not have been victorious as they were not on the side of dharma. She said sadly, 'Yudhisthira, you won because you are an incarnation of dharma. Be a good king.' She then turned to Draupadi and said:

> I am weeping for my sons and so are you, while Kunti weeps for her grandsons. Who among us shall console the other? We women give birth and bring them up with care for years and some wretched politician brings about a war and offers them as sacrifice to the god of war!

Gandhari then turned to Krishna and, unable to control her grief any longer, cried out:

> O Krishna! You had the power to prevent this fratricidal war and terrible carnage, but you did not. I pronounce this curse on you for allowing this apocalypse: your kith and kin, the Yadavas, shall also perish in internecine slaughter and you shall die at the hands of a low caste man.

Krishna smiled and replied:

> O deluded woman, all these calamities have still not chastened your mind; you have not yet come to recognise that all this was brought about by the wicked acts of your sons and the failure of yourself and your husband to prevent them. Why did you not insist on peace when I came as the ambassador of the Pandavas and begged for truce on honourable terms? Well, fate has worked itself out. Even this dreadful curse will take full effect, owing to your incomparable chastity and penance. You have acted only as my instrument and done what I had intended should come to pass. Your curse is a blessing!
>
> Listen, O Gandhari, the curse will take effect, but no one can destroy my body without my will. I have resolved to die in my hundred and twenty-fifth year* by the unwilling arrow of a humble hunter, one of my

*125 lunar years, equivalent to 81 years + 20 years of the solar calendar, centenarian. This gives the impression that Krishna would have been sixty-four years old at the conclusion of the Mahabharata War.

> Daridra Narayana. My kinsmen, the Yadavas, are so brave that only they can destroy themselves in war; that they will do. The last problem of this body of arrogant militarists will be solved before I depart. They are destined to die this way, and so shall it be. Noble Gandhari! In uttering this heinous curse on me, you have exhausted, in one stroke, the great merits earned by your lifelong penance and sacrifice.
>
> From now on, attune yourself to be calm, follow a higher path assiduously and prepare for the terrible end awaiting you and your husband—both your worlds have been devoid of light. What a pity!

Gandhari was visibly frightened and filled with endless remorse. She moved away from Krishna, feeling desolate. Thus, she forewent the grace of the compassionate lord who would have prostrated at her feet, asking her forgiveness for the tragedy of the war.

YUDHISTHIRA'S DILEMMA

Seeing the destruction of war, Yudhisthira wanted to go to a forest and become a hermit. He refused the coveted kingship. But Krishna told him that he had to work for *Lokasangraha*, (consolidator of dharma) and that, if he deserted his duty, he would incur sin. Vyasa, Vidura and others gave him the same advice.

Krishna suggested that Yudhishthira seek the advice of the noble Bhishma Pitamah who was about to depart to the world of Manes. There was none other more fit to reveal the duties of a king. Yudhisthira carried out the last rites of Duryodhana and other Kaurava heroes. He was shocked to learn that Karna was his elder brother and, at Krishna's insistence, Karna's funeral obsequies were performed on the sacred banks of Bhagirathi, near Badrinath, at the particular junction where Alakananda and Bhagirathi meet, now known as Karna Prayag.

At the end of the ceremonies, Yudhisthira remarked to Krishna, 'Out of the millions assembled on the field of Kurukshetra, only ten survived—seven on our side and three on the other. What a toll has the Great War taken!'

'That is so,' replied Krishna. 'It will continue to be so till humanity learns to do things according to dharma!'

PARIKSHIT—THE FUTURE

At Hastinapura, Uttara was in uncontrollable grief over the death of Abhimanyu. Kunti consoled her, saying that the time was not for mourning his death, but for caring for his baby, which was growing in her womb. Vyasa assured her that her son would be a great and successful king. However, he also cautioned Yudhisthira to conduct a Maha Mrityunjaya Yagna for the welfare of the mother and child. Krishna and Balarama, along with others, reached Hastinapura to await the arrival of the baby.

On the day Uttara was to deliver her child, everyone was excited in the royal household. But when the newborn showed no sign of life, Krishna rushed to the inner chambers. Kunti, in great grief, urged Krishna to save the child who was the last hope for the house of Kurus.

Draupadi and Subhadra lamented that the child was born dead, as Aswathama's curse to erase the Pandava dynasty on this earth was taking effect. At the behest of Duryodhana, his invocation had contained, among other incantations, a general induction on the Pandavas—*apandaviyam*—erasing their traces. Krishna transformed himself into his divine form. He did not tarry even for a moment and sipping holy water as a symbol of purifying his self, dispelled the injurious effect of Brahmastra on the child. Then, he started taking his affirmations before the assembled ladies and prayed:

> If I have never spoken the untruth, let the child be revived. If being ever-upright, I have never deserted any battlefield, then let that power revive the child. If I have never opposed Arjuna in his victory in life, by truth of this statement, let Abhimanyu's child, who is here born dead, be revived. If truth and righteousness are established in me as eternal foundations, then let Abhimanyu's child live. If Kamsa and Keshi met their death by my hands in a righteous manner, then by that power let this child breathe.

Nowhere does Krishna speak as a divine person performing miracles, but always as a human being, who has supreme confidence in his own righteousness and moral standing, having realised and experienced the enlightenment of the Supreme Divine Essence. The moment Krishna completed his affirmation, the child sprang to life; with joyous exhilaration, everyone present thanked him. Vaasudeva named the baby Parikshit—the one who responded to the supreme test of Divinity.

The child had been granted life by Krishna, but he felt limp with exhaustion. Sweat was pouring down his face in tiny rivulets. He came out of the chambers and could barely walk. He was tired and sat on a stone seat. Satyaki was waiting for him outside and saw Krishna emerging out of Uttara's chambers, dazed.

He did not want to disturb Krishna and waited for him to start the conversation. He had never seen his friend in such a stupefied state.

Slowly, the glow on Krishna's face was restored. Krishna recovered and came near Satyaki, his smiling face glowed with a new light. Satyaki said rather timidly, 'O lord! Abhimanyu lives again. Glory will be yours for this act. Govinda, you are God!'

BHISHMA'S EXIT

Uttarayana had arrived and Bhishma was ready to depart—an epoch was coming to an end. He sent forth a prayer for Krishna to meet him and give him permission to die.

Yudhisthira asked Vyasa to explain the tenets of dharma, especially Raja Dharma. Vyasa directed him to Bhishma, who was far more suitable to give this discourse. Yudhisthira felt guilty approaching the grandfather he had fought; however, Vyasa assured him that Bhishma was above such trifles and bore no grudge against anyone. Krishna said to Yudhisthira:

> Bhishma, lying on his bed of arrows and sinking like a dying fire, is meditating on me and fervently appealing to me for redemption. Dharmaputra, he is a warehouse of knowledge and the most virtuous man living now. He knows the past, present and future. He knows all about dharma. Go to him and learn all that you wish to learn from such a noble soul.

Yudhisthira requested his brothers and Krishna to accompany him. As they approached, Bhishma, in great pain, joined his palms and moved his lips to utter, 'Pranam,' to Vaasudeva. Krishna reciprocated by touching the feet of the great man and said, 'Pitamah, physical pain is more powerful than mental pain. Even if a little thorn pricks the body, we feel the discomfort. Your body has been pierced by countless arrows and yet, you lie as if on a bed of roses. O unconquerable hero! May your pain cease!' Saying this, he touched Bhishma's body. Bhishma exclaimed, 'Lord, my pain is gone! Krishna, you are Narayana, the all-pervading Vishnu Himself.' Krishna then requested, 'Grandfather, please explain the codes of dharma to Yudhisthira.'

Bhishma laughed and said, 'Is it not strange that while you, the citadel of dharma, is around, I am asked to talk about dharma? Krishna, you are dharma incarnate, and you should be the one to propagate it.' Krishna smiled and said,

'O noble sir, the world should hear from your own lips because you are the role model for human existence and its purport.'

Bhishma, being relieved of his physical discomfort by Krishna, folded his palms in great devotion and said, 'Vaasudeva, I am gratified and I have no desire to live anymore. With the Supreme Being Himself urging me to reveal the meaning of dharma, my life's mission is fulfilled.' Then, he looked up at Yudhisthira and addressed him:

> Dharmaputra, a king's duty is to work for the good of his people, ignoring his own selfish desires. Just as a pregnant woman cheerfully bears all pangs and privations for the sake of the child in the womb, a king should bear cheerfully all pangs and privations for the good of his people. A king is the root of dharma. Without law and order, no dharma can ever prosper; men will eat one another, like fish eating fish, and their lives will be spent in the mere act of self-preservation.
>
> A king should be ever-active. There is no sin equal to inactivity in a king. He should be vigilant and impartial; he should not be too sweet, lest people will swallow him up like a lump of sugar; nor should he be too bitter, lest people spit him out. If the women can go about fearlessly, unaccompanied by men, then that is the measure of a country that is well-governed.
>
> Of all fortresses, the human fortress is the strongest. Where men decay and society turns decadent, the country degenerates. Where brahmanas and kshatriyas cooperate, the country prospers; goodness consists in thought, word and deed being in a straight line. There are no friends or foes at birth. Friends and enemies are found by the identity or diversity of interests.
>
> A king makes the Time and not Time the king. Only a fool complains that the times are bad; the king is there to make the times good. There is no need for a man of self-control to go to the forest—whichever place he lives in, is a hermitage for him. All rivers are the holy Ganga and all mountains are Kailasa; the self is the holiest spot as the lord resides in the self.
>
> There is no eye equal to *Jnaana Chakshu*—the eye of knowledge, no penance equal to truth, no misery equal to greed and no happiness equal to renunciation. Lamentation never helps—it only adds one grief to another; the more cheerful a man is, the more his efforts succeed. Ignorance is man's chief enemy and knowledge his best friend. Energetic practice will yield

great results. As bodily ailments are cured by medicine, mental ailments are cured by knowledge. Let every man say to himself, 'The whole earth belongs to me, but it also belongs to all other living beings.' He will then realise that he is a son of Mother Earth and will work for dharma and *lokasangraha*.

Dharma is that which takes you to God or the Supreme Being

Dharma is God, Dharma is Duty

Dharma brings Peace, Dharma is Beauty

Uphold Dharma, it Upholds you

Destroy Dharma, it Destroys you!

Bhima interjected to ask, 'Noble grandfather, do you fear your approaching death?'

Bhishma replied:

No. I smile at it! You know, O mighty Bhima, that the great devotee of Narayana, Prahlada, asked Ajagara as to how he managed to smile through all his woes. Ajagara replied, 'I see all things coming to an end; things big and small, moving and unmoving, even stars fall down and have an end. Therefore, death does not worry me. One day I sleep on an expensive bed and another day on the bare ground. One day I eat a delicious meal and for many days I go without anything to eat. Such differences do not bother me. That is why you see me smiling always.' I remember that story and smile at my imminent death. Alone, a man comes into the world; and alone, he goes out of it. Alone, he enjoys the fruits of his merits; and alone, he suffers the fruits of his sins.

'Grandfather, do you prefer your country over others or is the whole world your motherland?' asked Yudhisthira.

'God gives all men the entire earth to love,' replied Bhishma. 'But man's heart is small, so he prefers a small spot over another. I chose Kurukshetra on the grounds of the great Parashurama.'

'Grandfather, do you prefer one form of god over another?' asked Yudhisthira.

'God gives Himself to all mankind to love,' he replied. 'Man's heart being small, he prefers a particular deity over others; *ishtadevata*—a personal god. I have chosen to love Krishna Vaasudeva as *bhagavan*.' Bhishma gave a devoted acknowledgement to Krishna, who smiled in great appreciation. Bhishma then spoke of Dhritarashtra:

> The king learnt the Vedas and shastras, the secret of gods and men from Vyasa and, yet, he was never wise. He lost his sons, kith and kin as a result of his imprudence. His son, Duryodhana, was advised many a time by his elders to take the path of dharma, but hate and jealousy consumed him. He justified it, saying: '*Janami dharmam na cha me pravarthi; Janami papam na cha me nivrithi.*'
>
> I know what the right thing to do is, but my nature does not allow me to do it.
>
> I know what a sinful thing is, but my nature does not allow me to desist from it.

Krishna looked all around and said:

> That is the problem with man in a nutshell, in that, he must not only know, but must also have the intelligence and willpower to do the right thing and avoid the wrong. The heart is more important than the mind. He must be pure at heart before he can be clear in his mind; he should get rid of selfish aggrandisement and the pursuit of maya, the virtual world of desire and possessiveness.

'Lord, it is my good fortune that I got to see you before the end. The sun has turned north and the Uttarayana has commenced. It has been fifty-eight days since I laid down on this bed of arrows,' said Bhishma. He spoke to Arjuna, who was weeping, 'Partha, it was your arrow that defeated me and, for that, I am happy.' He blessed the Pandavas and looked at Krishna and requested, 'The month of Magha has come. Lord, give me leave to go and let me not, by your grace, be reborn on this earth.'

Krishna replied, 'Go Bhishma, there has not been any fault in you. You were as devoted to your father as Markandeya was. Death waits on you as a servant. You will not return to earth. You will go to the world of Vasus.' As he departed, there was a smile on Bhishma's face.

Yudhisthira and Vidura covered Bhishma's body with silks and garlands. Yuyutsu held the umbrella; Bhima and Arjuna took the *chamara* and fan, Nakula and Sahadeva the headdress. Bhishma's body was taken in procession to Prayag, at the holy confluence of the Ganga, Yamuna and Saraswati. Krishna supervised the last rites of a heroic man.

By the end of the ceremonies, Yudhisthira became visibly dispirited. Krishna comforted him, 'This is unbecoming of a king, O Yudhisthira! Rise and look after your royal duties. Remember grandfather's advice. You have plenty of work to do, you have to rule your subjects well.'

Yudhisthira, once again, spoke of his desire to renounce the material world and spend the rest of his days in penance. Vyasa ridiculed the idea and upbraided Yudhisthira, 'Do not speak like a child. Take up your duties as a responsible king. First, we shall crown you and then, you shall perform an Ashwamedha Yagna as Rama and Bharata, sons of Shakuntala, your ancestors, once did, to cleanse yourself of all sin!'

Yudhisthira, having recovered his composure, asked, 'O great one, where would I get all the wealth required to perform the yagna?'

Vyasa replied, 'Maruta, a famous sage, had kept a great quantity of elemental gold, which he accidentally found, in a Himalayan cave, so that men may not be ruined fighting for it. We may use it for this holy purpose, and his soul will rejoice.'

Yudhisthira was crowned at Hastinapura and was anointed by Acharya Dhaumya with holy water from the seven sacred rivers of Bharatvarsha. Vyasa and Krishna were also present to witness the establishment of the kingdom of dharma. The kingdom rejoiced with great anticipation that Dharmaputra's reign would be synonymous with Ramrajya.

ANUGITA

A few days later, at Indraprastha, Arjuna asked Krishna, 'Lord, in the heat of the battle, I have forgotten most of the discourse you gave me on the battlefield. Please narrate it to me once again.' Krishna said:

> Arjuna, you should not have forgotten it so soon. But, I suppose Sanjaya remembers it and he will narrate it to Vyasa, who will record it for posterity. However, I will recapitulate what I said more succinctly and you may call this version the Anugita—a supplemental discourse between the self and the mind.

KRISHNA MEETS UTTANKA

A few days after the coronation ceremony, Krishna expressed his desire to leave for Dwaraka. He asked Arjuna to intercede with Dharmaputra, who would not permit Krishna to leave so soon. Yudhisthira had, very reluctantly, accepted the throne of Hastinapura and Govinda's absence would have driven him into greater despair.

With a heavy heart, Yudhisthira agreed to Krishna's request and honoured him with several gifts for the Yadavas. Krishna, Arjuna and Satyaki departed for Dwaraka.

As they were crossing the great desert, they came across the seer, Uttanka Bhargava, who, after honouring Krishna, enquired about the welfare of the Kauravas and the Pandavas and how he had solved their internecine disputes. Krishna replied that, despite his best efforts, he could not bring about a compromise between them and a terrible war ensued, that decimated the Kauravas, except for Dhritarashtra, Yuyutsu and Gandhari. At this, Sage Uttanka was livid with Krishna for having failed to prevent the apocalypse, despite having the power to do so, and was about to curse him, when Krishna interceded:

> O, venerable rishi, I beg of your wisdom, earned over long years of austerities and penance, before indicting me of inaction to prevent the terrible carnage. By cursing me, will you not lose all the spiritual powers you ardently earned, including realising the Supreme Self, Brahman, from a lifetime of devotion?

Uttanka relented and, instead, asked Krishna to reveal his supreme resplendent form. Krishna smiled and took the sage on a spiritual excursion, revealing the essential Krishna consciousness in his several descents. Krishna said to Uttanka:

> I am the repository of Satvas. In me is posited creation, and I in all creation. Men of wisdom accept me as the existence and non-existence; manifest and unmanifest; immutable and mutable; all these are verily my forms and so are the four fold stages in life, as well as the actions stipulated by the Vedic scriptures. Non-existence and existence and that which is beyond this universe, are nothing but my manifestations and not distinct from me. Sanatana Dharma is born from my mind and I dwell in everyone who has transcended from performance of actions. As a spark of energy that dwells within each one, I descend in the three worlds in many forms and aspects for the protection of righteousness.
>
> In my earlier forms, I was Vishnu, Brahma and Shankara; the creator and the

destroyer; acting as God in the godly forms, as Gandharva in the Gandharva forms, as Naga in the Naga forms and as yaksha, Rakshasa and others in their respective forms. In this present incarnation, I perform actions as a human being in the form of a human, pleading with the Kauravas for a negotiated settlement. When they did not listen, I even showed them my terrifying form, explaining to them the effects of dreadful war. But, being in attributes and inclination, unrighteous in their disposition, they refused to listen and died like kshatriyas, in the Great War.

Uttanka was amazed and folded his palms in great devotion and admiration for Krishna. Unlike the manner in which Krishna displayed his self to the Kauravas in the royal court to frighten them into submission, or to Arjuna on the battlefield, to show his essential reach, his discourse to Uttanka was rational and intellectual.

Uttanka begged Krishna to reveal his divine form as he had done in the Kaurava court and to Arjuna, and he obliged the sage with a divine revelation. Each one responded to his divine form according to their own attributes and predispositions. The Kauravas were stupefied and confounded, Arjuna was emotional and overwhelmed and Uttanka's response was intellectual, with supreme wonder at the magnificence of the spectacle.

Pleased with his adoration, Krishna gave Uttanka a boon to receive water in the desert at will. Bidding farewell, Krishna proceeded to Dwaraka.

On the way, Krishna halted for the night near the desert, at a waterhole. Having refreshed himself with the cool spring water, he had a quick repast of some fruits and warm camel milk affectionately brought by the villagers nearby. Soon Krishna and his entourage were asleep. Krishna's sleep was a state of awareness in reality—the yogi in him never went to sleep like an ordinary human being. Staring into the starlit desert sky, Krishna reflected over the events that had led to the terrible war and why he could not prevent it.

Dhritarashtra's love for his son, Duryodhana's arrogance and greed, Karna's pride and jealousy, Bhishma and Drona's failure to act, Yudhisthira's passivity and despondency and Arjuna's devotion and surrender to him.

He compared Sage Muchkunda, the liberated soul, to Sage Uttanka, a confused soul. He reflected on how every individual is unique, his nature determined by the interplay of the three *guna*s: *sattva*, *rajas* and *tamas*. These qualities are always in a state of flux and are responsible for his thoughts, actions and response to situations. When *sattva* dominates, it gives joy; while *rajas* impels one to action; and *tamas* clouds the intellect, thereby making the person lethargic.

These *gunas* also have a bearing on the spiritual progress of a person. The *guna* that prevails during the last moments of one's life, determines the state of the soul in the afterlife. If a human being dies when *sattva* is dominant, he attains higher worlds like heaven, which men of noble deeds reach; when *rajas* prevails, the person is reborn among those attached to action and its fruits; and if *tamas* is the governing *guna*, then the person falls from the privilege of human birth and is reborn as lesser creatures like insects and beasts.

The object of human birth being liberation from rebirths, it becomes incumbent on those who have been fortunate to be born as one, to make a conscious effort to put an end to rebirth. Abundance in *sattva* is essential for spiritual progress. Even if such a person is reborn after enjoying heavenly pleasures, the circumstances of his birth will be conducive for further evolution. In the case of a person under the influence of *rajas*, there is no guarantee that the environment in which he will be reborn will be favourable for spiritual progress. As for *tamas*, for those who yield to it, the loss of evolutionary status is irreparable as they have to plod again, from the very beginning.

Krishna placed Sage Muchkunda in the *sattva* state and therefore, the moment he saw Vaasudeva in him, the sage was liberated from the cycle of birth. Muchkunda had given all the merits earned by him, over long decades of penance, to Krishna, before leaving this world, never to be born again. The conceited Uttanka wanted to curse him for failing to prevent the war. His long years of penance did not make him wise enough to be a *sattvic* and it was his *rajasic* nature that wanted to see Krishna's divine form. Uttanka's self-realisation was far from comprehensive in essence, unlike Muchkunda's, because even after acknowledging and referring to Krishna as *Hiranyagarbharupaya*, *Samsorontharanaya*, *Avidhatimiraadityam*, *Nityaaya*, *Visvakarman*, *Visvaatman*, he could not experience Krishna's omnipresent personality.

Much later, when Uttanka had been thirsty and sought water, he was offered some water by a shudra. But he protested, saying that it was not proper for a brahmana to accept water from a shudra. As soon as he said this, the shudra disappeared. When he conferred with Krishna about this illusion, he was told that the water was given in a manner found necessary, and that it was not ordinary water, but nectar offered by Indra appearing as a shudra. The sage was remorseful that, in his ignorance, he had failed to recognise that the divine essence is in every form of creation. He had thus deprived himself of the nectar and immortality!

On reaching Dwaraka, Krishna found his people celebrating on Mount Raivataka. He went to meet his parents and offered his respects.

ASHWAMEDHA—THE HORSE SACRIFICE

A moon-like white horse with auspicious marks was found and turned loose on a full moon night in the month of Chaitra. An army led by Arjuna followed the horse to protect it from capture, to defeat those who resisted and to invite all the kings to the sacrifice. One of Yagnavalkya's disciples also accompanied Arjuna. Most kingdoms accepted the suzerainty of Yudhisthira.

Arjuna, after traversing the length and breadth of the country for a year, finally returned triumphant. Yudhisthira, along with Draupadi, was leading a life of purity, celibacy and prayer for that year. They would sleep at night with a sword fixed perpendicularly between them to prevent and punish carnal desires.

The Ashwamedha was celebrated with great pomp and ceremony. All the kings, learned men and men of repute from all over Bharatvarsha graced the occasion. Krishna and Balarama were also present. Yudhisthira and Draupadi performed the sacrifice under the guidance of Vyasa. Yudhisthira presented some earth to Vyasa at the end of sacrifice. Vyasa gave it back to Yudhisthira to rule over the kingdom as a trustee of God. At the end of the ceremonies, Krishna and Balarama left for Dwaraka.

Time passed by and, after about fifteen years of Yudhisthira's rule, Dhritarashtra, Gandhari, Kunti and Vidura retired to the forest as hermits; about two years later, Narada visited Yudhisthira to inform him that they had been consumed by forest fires. Sanjaya had gone into the heart of the Himalayas to do penance.

Presided over by Narada, Yudhisthira performed the funeral rites for Dhritarashtra, Gandhari and Kunti at Gangadwara, on the banks of the Alaknanda.

DWARAKA

Krishna's principal wife, Rukmini, bore him ten sons, the eldest being Pradyumna. His other sons were Charudeshna, Sudeshna, Charudeha, Susena,

Charugupta, Bhadracharu, Charuvinda, Sucharu and the very mighty Charu. He also had one daughter, named Charumati.

Satyabhama had also given birth to ten sons: the twins Bhanu and Subhanu, Svarbhanu, Prabhanu, Bhanumat, Chandrabhanu, Brihadbhanu, Atibhanu, Sribhanu and Pratibhanu.

Jambavati bore him one son, Samba. Ironically, this errant son later became the root cause for the demise of the Yadava race from Dwaraka.

Krishna busied himself in organising and rebuilding Yadava society, greatly relieved that the notorious Satrajit was dead in an internecine conflict. As Sangha Pramukh of the Yadavas of Dwaraka, he had his own share of problems. Narada Muni became a frequent visitor, offering pleasant company. A great entertainer, often intriguing and at times a practical joker, his visits were a pleasant relief for Krishna.

Narada was a keen student of Krishna and spread his teachings amongst people in the places he visited. He saw Krishna's different roles—the cowherd, the charmer, the warrior, the statesman and the empire builder. But the preceptor of the kingdom of dharma was gradually transforming into a mystic and philosopher.

Taking Narada into confidence, Krishna would often narrate his woes. 'You know, O Munindra, my great family consists of a large number of Andhaka Vrishnis who accepted me as their lord, but treat me even worse than a slave. The chiefs Akrura and Yuyudhana Satyaka, who occupied prominent positions in government, often quarrel with each other, causing great harassment to me.' Laughing it off, he would say to the itinerant bard, 'You know, people address me as their lord, but in reality, I am a veritable slave to them. I listen to their harsh words and constant complaints and, many a time, I remain in a helpless position. Perhaps, these are the hazards of a republican government.'

KRISHNA, THE GRANDFATHER

Krishna's most famous grandson was Aniruddha. He was the son of Pradyumna and Prabhavati. The boy was handsome and a formidable warrior. His looks and valour were so outstanding that his name Aniruddha, meaning irresistible, was synonymous with his personality.

Every young woman desired to be his wife. A Daitya princess named Usha, daughter of Banasura—an Asura king of present-day Assam in the north-east region—fell in love with him; she had him brought to her apartments by magic influence, in her father's city of Sonitpura—today's Tezpur. Banasura sent some guards to seize him, but the valiant youth slew his assailants with an iron club. The asura then used his magical powers to secure him.

On discovering where Aniruddha had been carried away, Krishna, along with Balarama and Pradyumna, went to rescue him. A great battle was fought; Banasura had formidable warriors who were worshippers of Rudra and they gave stiff resistance to the Yadava army. In the battle, Garuda and Pradyumna wounded Banasura, who was brought as a captive before Krishna. Banasura requested for peace and surrendered to Krishna; the compassionate lord pardoned him. Aniruddha married Usha and returned to Dwaraka. They had a son, named Vajra, who was later placed on the throne of Indraprastha by Arjuna, after Lord Krishna's exit from this world.

Rukmini was very keen that Aniruddha should remain within her parental family, thus safeguarding the interests of Vidarbha and Yadavas, which were broken at the time of her marriage to Krishna. Rukmi never forgave Krishna, even after the lapse of several decades. He had taken a vow not to enter his capital city, Kundinapura, in Vidarbha, and remained permanently at Bhojakota.

At Bhojakota, he conspired with the king of Kalinga and other like-minded cronies to kill Krishna and Balarama, or at least to humiliate them in revenge. Foreseeing her brother's inevitable doom if he indulged in any such manoeuvres, in an attempt at rapprochement, Rukmini suggested that Rukmi's daughter, Rochana, wed Aniruddha.

Rochana and her mother were eager, but Rukmi objected, saying it would be against the shastras as the bridegroom was the bride's paternal aunt's grandson. Krishna countered that the *dakshinatya*s—South Indians—freely contracted such marriages with the approval of the sages.

Rukmi's wife told her husband, 'Vidarbha and Bhojakota belong to the *dakshin* and we are *dakshinatya*s, therefore, such a marriage will be lawful in our tradition.' Rukmi had to finally consent to the marriage. Balarama, Krishna, Rukmini, Pradyumna and Aniruddha went to Bhojakota, and the wedding was celebrated with much pomp.

After the marriage, the king of Kalinga, a bosom friend of Rukmi, advised him to challenge Balarama in a game of dice with high stakes. The king said, 'The Yadavas know nothing of the game of dice and can be easily defeated by you.' However, the wily king of Kalinga cautioned Rukmi not to challenge Krishna, as he was too clever to be cheated.

Rukmi and Balarama first played with stakes of one hundred gold coins. Rukmi won, playing with loaded dice and the king of Kalinga laughed at Balarama. An infuriated Balarama then raised the stake to a crore of gold coins, but lost again. The king of Kalinga laughed uncouthly, displaying his protruding teeth. This time, Balarama suspected fraud and accused Rukmi of playing a dishonest game. Rukmi vehemently denied it and said, 'You cowherd, what do you know of war or dice, played only by kings and princes of blue blood? The gods will bear witness that I have not played with loaded dice.'

As the intoxicated Balarama planned his next move, he heard Krishna's voice prompting him, 'You are being cheated with loaded dice, punish him.' Balarama turned red and hit a petrified Rukmi on the head with his fists. Rukmi died instantly. He then caught hold of the king of Kalinga and pulled out his teeth, which had been on display when he had laughed derisively at Balarama. It was a tragic end to the marriage festivity. Krishna, Balarama, Pradyumna and Aniruddha returned to Dwaraka, along with the sorrow-stricken Rukmini and the bride.

Krishna consoled her, saying, 'Vaidarbhi, in this world there are obscurantists like your brother who would never learn the platitudes of life, and one should not feel sorry for them. Your great-grandson, son of Aniruddha, is destined to keep the line of the Yadavas alive in Aryawartha.'

KRISHNA AND SUDAMA

The move to Dwaraka symbolised the expansion of Krishna's mythic domain from the north and the east, to the west of Bharatvarsha. Dwaraka was built as a *Vari Durga*—fortress city, on a hilly perch overlooking the Arabian Sea. It was a well laid out city and the Bhagavata Purana speaks eloquently of its gold encrusted buildings and crystal balconies. This was the setting for a powerful king that Krishna was not; but as a poignant incident demonstrates, it was a power that was *saulabhya*—both accessible and human.

Once, Sudama, Krishna's childhood friend, came to see him at Dwaraka. Sudama was a very poor brahmana with many children by his wife, Sushila.

Yet, he had a glow on his face and was referred to as Brahma Varchas by some, owing to his vast knowledge of the Vedas, Vedangas and the tenets of Sanatana Dharma.

Sudama was never attracted to worldly riches and remained a detached soul. Tired of the constant nagging of his exasperated wife, he reluctantly agreed to visit Dwaraka and seek favours from his childhood friend. As he reached Dwaraka, he was assailed with doubts: Who would believe he was Krishna's friend? Would the royal guards even allow him to enter the city? Would Krishna recognise him?

Once in Dwaraka, Sudama was pleasantly surprised to find that he could enter the palace without hindrance. Krishna saw him approach and, from a distance, recognised him instantly. He clasped his friend in a tight embrace and seated him on his own couch.

With great reverence, he washed his friend's feet and served him food. All this while, Sudama tried to hide a handful of beaten rice tied up in a rag, which his wife had sent as a gift for Krishna. Sudama felt ashamed to gift it to a king so rich. Krishna noticed the little bundle and asked for it, opened it eagerly, and ate up the beaten rice with utmost delight. The next day, when Sudama left, Krishna saw him off in his personal chariot. Sudama had not been able to bring himself to ask anything of Krishna. It was more than enough, he told himself, that he managed to meet him and had been treated with so much love and respect. Sudama's spirit was elated in Krishna's presence and he forgot all his mundane worries while at Dwaraka.

A huge surprise awaited him when he reached home. His humble abode had been miraculously replaced by a glittering palace, Krishna having sent Satyaki to allot one of the palaces of Satyabhama while Sudama was in Dwaraka. Krishna had fulfilled his needs without his asking for it. The brahmana realised that his friend was indeed God in their midst.

This little story has come to be regarded as the definitive parable to emphasise the importance of human values in the conduct of those in high office. The Sudama episode reiterated Krishna's enduring links with his past. Sudama's journey to Dwaraka demonstrates the triumph of faith over doubt.

KRISHNA THE MYSTIC

The incident with Uttanka left a deep impression on the sensitive psyche of Krishna; his accusation that he did not do enough to prevent the terrible holocaust made a impact on Krishna's mind and he often wondered if he could have prevented the bloodshed.

His vision, of a kingdom based on dharma, had become an empire of orphans. In Dwaraka too, the sixteen thousand women, rescued from Narakasura's hell, had ended up as widows. Balarama was no longer his genial self; he had withdrawn into himself and had turned into an alcoholic. It was difficult for him to interact with his elder brother on matters of state; Balarama would agree with him on any subject, saying, 'Krishna, you are the best judge. You have my consent.' In fact, Krishna had no counsel to look to and often found himself alone at the apex.

Krishna had a perennial problem with the Vrishni and Andhaka chiefs, who were forever quarrelling on administrative matters. It was his lot as Sangha Pramukh to resolve differences on a day-to-day basis—a thankless job.

On the domestic front too, Satyabhama's possessiveness had become a point of contention with his principal queen, Rukmini. Jambavati, on the other hand, was docile and mild-mannered and had only wanted a son by Krishna, whom she named Samba. This came to pass only after she insisted Krishna go to the Himalayas to perform a penance so as to impress Lord Shiva. As a result, Krishna had the vision of the Mahadeva and his consort Parvati and later he was blessed with a child.

Gradually, Krishna withdrew into himself and became reticent and meditative. Krishna's constant companion was Uddhava, and Arjuna frequently visited Dwaraka, so that Parikshit could understand the intricacies of being a good kshatriya. Krishna would sit with Uddhava for hours, talking about the purpose of life, sermonising in depth on *jnana* and *vijnana*—knowledge and wisdom, quoting scriptures, narrating fables and the events of the land. Krishna was happy to leave the defences of Dwaraka to commander Satyaki, who was happily married and father of a valiant son, Yuyudhaneya.

Arjuna's visits were too frequent, for he could not stand the lacklustre reign of his elder brother. Draupadi bore with the regime, only with a stoic sense of participation and duty as the queen of Hastinapura. Bhima, who was always there to see the lighter side of life, had become her beacon of light in the dark chambers of Hastinapura. For rest and recuperation, she would visit Dwaraka as often as circumstances would permit. She was very fond of meeting her Sakha, for succour and solace. She was always the guest of Rukmini, who would address her as Vasudevasya Sakhi. Krishna enjoyed the company of two strong-willed women.

Draupadi noticed that Krishna was looking sullen and careworn.

Rukmini confessed to her that Krishna spent a lot of his time in meditation. 'A beautiful blue luminescence envelops him, and his face radiates; his lips pink, eyes like blue lotus buds and strange vibrations emanate from him that soothe you; a magnificent fragrance emerges from his room,' Rukmini explained to Draupadi.

Soon, days passed and years rolled by. Yudhisthira had ruled the kingdom for thirty-six years. Krishna had grown old—ninety-six odd years as per the present scale of time. Having assumed the mortal human form, he had become worn out over time. He was haunted by Gandhari's curse: 'You will die like a beast—alone, helpless and in agony. The way I lost my children, you, too, will witness the devastation of yours; your kith and kin will also suffer and die in front of your eyes!' Krishna often wondered whether she was the chosen one to curse him and free his spirit like only a mother can.

One day, Krishna confided in Uddhava:

> Uddhava, Gandhari's curse has become an apparition for me. I was never in favour of the battle or the bloodshed. You know, brother, I always professed acceptance and my entire life was a prime example of reconciliation; yet, the tragedy had to happen! Now, my time has come. I lived my entire life in detachment, never wavering in my focus to act in favour of dharma; I hope the future generations will treat me with compassion. The time has come to renounce this body; I owe it to the Universe!

Uddhava was anxious and could not imagine living without Krishna, who was his guide, philosopher and friend. Weeping inconsolably, he prostrated at Krishna's feet, 'Liberate me, lord, before you renounce this world.'

Krishna embraced him and said, 'I shall, my friend, when I ask you to leave for Badarika Kshetra, my place of penance, in a different age. Wait for your time. You shall reach me, I promise!'

Krishna, then, turned introspective and said:

> Uddhava, I am tormented by the decadence of Dwaraka and the Yadavas; the state is living in a drunken stupor, our Balarama is intoxicated all his waking time. The Yadavas have grown insolent by prowess, heroism and fortune and are now thirsting for the conquest of the whole world. You know, this celebrated race of Yadu has been held in check by me, as the ocean by its shore. If I leave the world without destroying this most powerful race of Yadus, they would overstep all bounds and consume the world.

> The disrespect to saints, sages and brahmanas by Yadavas has become intolerable and the curse of Gandhari has to take effect during my lifetime.

Uddhava's grief was doubled and he said:

> Govinda, after the Great War, the Yadavas brought plenty of war booty. Dwaraka has become a sin city; their desire for pleasure, wine and women is wreaking havoc on the citizens. Govinda, I cannot live without you. I know, having been too near you, I remained illiterate. I remain bereft of *jnana* and *vijnana*. Arjuna was fortunate to have heard from you, but I never had that privilege. If you think I deserve it, may I beg of you to please teach me?

Krishna laughed and said:

> You know, I could teach Arjuna the knowledge of the Ultimate Truth only when he was ready to receive the abstract teaching...when he had become a helpless child! You remember, I recommended Karma Sanyasa—the path of renunciation, which is a virtual sacrifice of all desires and expecting no returns for our actions. Such renunciation of the pleasures of the senses is well nigh impossible for those attached to sense enjoyment and more so for those who are not devoted to me.

Uddhava bowed with humility and, with arms folded, pleaded to Krishna:

> I am ignorant, O lord, being passionately attached to this body, wife and children, who are the creation of your Maya. I am immersed in the notion of 'I' and 'Mine'. I beg you to teach me the path of renunciation, the knowledge of the atma—the self, the only truth. Dispirited and afflicted by sins, I take my refuge in you.

Krishna was amazed at the transformation that came over Uddhava and decided to reveal to his disciple, the Song of Liberation.

UDDHAVA GITA

> Noble friend, in their pursuit of worldly ends, human beings invariably end up losing out on what really matters—a fruitful human life. The majority get caught in satiating their desires without knowing where to draw the line and, in the process, fritter away the golden opportunity to realise the goal of liberation from bondage.
>
> Uddhava, I have very little time left and, therefore, would highlight the

evanescence of worldly life and the need to strive for liberation by self-effort, through the dialogue between King Yadu and the immortal ascetic, Avadhuta, Lord Dattatreya.

Seeing a youthful and blissful mendicant roaming about fearlessly, the king asked him in wonder, 'Generally men strive after religious merit, riches and enjoyment, as well as self-enquiry, only out of the motive of acquiring longevity, renown and fortune. In the midst of people burning with the wildfire of concupiscence and greed, you remain unscathed by that fire!'

The ascetic gently smiled at the king and talked about what he had imbibed from the wisdom of many preceptors, by observing them during his peregrinations around the world. Then, he listed twenty-four points which were worthy of emulation. He said he had learnt what was good for him from their conduct.

- From Mother Earth, I have learnt forbearance, joy of sharing and universal love. I have imbibed the quality of remaining unperturbed even while being oppressed by others. Seeing the earth's endurance, man should not deviate from his course of righteousness and stay conscious of the fact of being subject to providence.
- From the air, I have learnt to be content with minimum requirements for sustenance. Though moving among all sorts of objects, an ascetic should not particularly get attached to them, any more than the air that flows freely. Contentment, non-attachment and reliance on one's own dharma are the lessons I learnt from air, both external and internal, which is prana or the breath of life.
- From the sky, I have learnt to remain detached even though covered by a body; a yogi should identify with the self, which is all-pervading like the sky. As the sky is not touched by the products of water and earth, or by clouds driven by the wind, so a man should not be touched by things, which are the creation of time. I learned to stand by Atma Dharma. A single Atman—Paramatma—pervades all things.
- From water, I learnt to sanctify the world, to be clean and transparent in thoughts and deeds; I learned to be pure and to purify others.
- From fire, I learnt to accept what is offered; and like the fire that devours everything, I learnt that I must remain unaffected by the impurities of matter. I also learnt that the body, which is subject to change, will perish any moment.

- From the moon, I learnt that the transformations of the body do not affect Atman: Meaning that birth, growth, decline and death pertain to the body alone.
- From the sun, I learnt the Atman is one and only one, complete and perfect, everywhere and in everything.
- From the ocean, I learnt not to be affected by gain or loss; to remain steady and calm in my single devotion to the lord.
- From the pigeon, I learnt not to be engrossed in family life, not to be forgetful of the supreme goal of life and get caught in the hunter's net.
- From the python, I learnt to be perfectly unconcerned about the needs of the body.
- From the moth, I learnt not to trust my eyes, which are carried away by attraction. The moth is attracted by the beauty of fire and, mistaking it for something edible, blindly rushes into the fire and perishes.
- From the bee, I learnt to receive alms, little by little; just enough for a time and not to cultivate the habit of hoarding. The bee collects little honey from different flowers and never stays long in the same flower.
- From the elephant, I learned to avoid women elephants. The elephant is the biggest land animal and roams freely in the forest. It values its freedom as much as its life. Usually, it is very careful in its movements and avoids pitfalls. But, it is easily trapped when its sexual instinct is roused at the sight of the she-elephant. Thus ensnared, it falls into a pit and gets enslaved for the rest of its life. Hence, a sanyasi should not touch even the wooden figure of a woman.
- From the honey gatherer, I learnt that it is unsafe to hoard wealth of any kind.
- From the deer, I learnt not to be deceived by sound. Spreading his net wide, the hunter lures the innocent deer, by means of music, into his snare.
- From the fish, I learnt to keep the organ of taste under perfect control. The fish is lured by the bait of food, attached to the hook. Of all the organs of sense, the tongue is the most difficult to conquer. When the organ of taste is controlled, everything else is controlled.
- From Pingala, the courtesan, I learnt that, to be desireless is the surest way to peace and happiness. Infatuation for women and yielding to the urge of procreation is the worst enemy of an ascetic.
- From the osprey, the hunter bird that feeds on fish, I learnt that the

high road to happiness lies in giving up all acquisitions. The source of misery and unrest is the acquisition of whatever men hold dear.

- From the infant, I learnt that if one is carefree, one can be happy always. A child is not aware of honour or dishonour and, hence, is happy.
- From the single bangle of a maiden, I learned to wander alone, keeping company with none, but the self.
- From the arrow-maker, who, with his mind absorbed in his work, did not notice the king with all regal pomp passing by his side, I learnt to concentrate and to live in single-minded devotion to the lord.
- From the serpent, I learnt to live happily in houses built by others or in caves.
- From the spider, I learnt how creation, preservation and destruction of the universe proceed from the incomprehensible lord, as mere sport.
- From the Brnga—king of wasps, I have learnt that it is possible for a high soul to attain the state of Brahman—godhead—by constant meditation on the Supreme Lord.

Krishna then continued:

Uddhava, having listened to the discourse of Avadhuta, King Yadu rid of himself of all attachments and gained the steady equilibrium of the mind.

This world is a theatre, *visvame vedam,* and we are surrounded by knowledge and wisdom that pours out from the lowly bee to the mighty elephant. Only humans are endowed with a mind and the sense of discrimination. Make use of it to liberate yourself from recurring births. The means to attain salvation is Bhakti—devotion to self and acceptance that a superior force controls our actions and nothing happens in our midst without the notice of the Supreme Soul.

Uddhava, the Supreme Being is resident in all of us, despite superficial differences. Belief in God has been the singular source of sustenance for mankind for eternity. Doubt and despair is removed by faith, as it satisfies a practical need in the lives of people.

Uddhava asked the lord, 'Kindly reveal, through what mode of concentration, which and what kind of siddhi can be acquired and how many siddhis there are.'

Krishna replied:

There are eighteen siddhis, as well as the modes of concentration leading to them, taught by those who have attained perfection in yoga. Eight of these, chiefly, abide in me and the remaining ten are attainable through perfection of *sattwa*—that element of the mind, which leads to illumination. The eight siddhis, which are natural to me and unsurpassed, are:

- Animaa—reducing one's body to an atom.
- Mahima—magnifying to a gigantic size.
- Laghimaa—extreme lightness of body.
- Praapti—establishing contact with the senses of the entire creation, in the form of deities presiding over those senses.
- Praakaamya—the capacity to enjoy pleasures through scriptures, as enjoyable in the other world, alone, and capable of being seen.
- Ishitaa—the capacity to impel maya and other subordinate potencies to function according to one's will.
- Vasitaa—absence of attachment to the pleasures of the senses.
- Kaamavasaayitaa—enjoying in the highest measure, whatever pleasure one seeks to enjoy.

These eight siddhis are my natural powers, found in me in infinite proportions, and conferred by me, in varying degrees, on the yogi.

Krishna continued:

My secondary powers are:

Absence of hunger, thirst and old age, in this very body.

The capacity to hear and see from a significant distance.

Locomotion at a speed, which can be increased at one's will.

Assuming any form at will.

Dying according to one's wish.

Participation in the pastimes of the gods with *apsara*s.

Attainment of one's desired ends.

Exercising authority, unobstructed everywhere.

Finally, my five petty powers are knowledge of the past, present and the future; to remain unaffected by pairs of opposites like: heat and cold, joy and sorrow, likes and dislikes; reading the thoughts of others; counteracting the influences of fire, sun, water poison, etc.; and to suffer no defeat at the hands of anyone.

> These are the siddhis that are the result of concentration in yoga. I am the Lord of the Powers, for I am their cause and maintainer. I am also the Lord of Yoga, of religion and its knowledge and of the teachers of brahmana. I am the self of all embodied souls, being their inner controller; I am also outside them, not being enveloped by anything. As the elements are both inside and outside the bodies of creatures, so also am I, the all-pervading. Devotion for devotion's sake is the highest of all yogas.
>
> Uddhava, when a man is wholly attached to me, he should control his speech, mind and the pranas by the intellect, endowed with devotion to me. Then he attains the goal. There is no difference between yoga and bhakti; both are directed towards the same goal, *Ekam*, *Akhandam*, *Anandam*—the attachment of bliss and beatitude.

Uddhava, with utter joy, said, 'Krishna, you are Anandaroopa. I am no longer grief-stricken at your imminent departure. I am liberated, my lord; it is my great fortune! I shall depart to your ashram at Badarika Vana.' Krishna embraced his childhood friend and whispered, 'We shall meet again.'

UDDHAVA'S DEPARTURE TO BADARIKA ASHRAM

Just before he bade farewell to Uddhava, Krishna instructed him to take the idol of Chaturbuj Vishnu—Lord Narayana, the Lord of Mind and Matter—to Parashurama Kshetra on the windswept Sahayadri range of mountains on the west coast and hand it over to the Garuda tribes who were his favourite devotees. Guided by the greatest of the sages, Parashurama, they would worship this idol as Narayana in the coming ages. Krishna said:

> Uddhava, this idol has been sanctified by me, as I offered it prayers. All of us are the products of Mind and Matter. Hereafter, I will be worshipped by the wise at Pavana Pura as the Father of Mind and Matter; Narayana will be known as Guruvayoorappa—Master of Mind and Matter. Brother, let this be your last errand for me before you are liberated.

Uddhava obeyed the command and, today, at Guruvayoor in Kerala, Narayana is worshipped as Guruvayoorappa—Pavanapurapati.

'Are we to worship Him in Absolute or Personal Form?' asked Uddhava, inquisitive to learn more. The lord replied, 'As you wish. The personal is easier to grasp and worship and the readier to respond.'

EVIL PORTENTS

When Yudhisthira had ruled for thirty-six years, nobly and justly, he began to witness portents of calamities to come. He was almost a hundred years old and his brothers had aged as well. Draupadi was a decade younger than them and yet, she looked as though she were middle-aged. Yudhisthira was longing to retire, as Parikshit had proved himself a wise and valiant prince who would take on the reigns of the kingdom.

EVENTS AT DWARAKA

Observing evil portents that manifest in the heavens, on earth, as well as in the air, Krishna cautioned the Yadus gathered in the Assembly Hall:

> I foresee terrible events; the forthcoming solar eclipse has the same potency as the one before the great Bharata War. Have you not noticed the strange happenings with the bird calls and animal behaviour? Even the rodent population has swollen to such an extent that all our foodgrains and crops are being destroyed. Yet, you are addicted to alcohol. The Yadava society has become a drunken cesspool.

Hearing a rumbling in the assembly, Krishna spontaneously reacted and said, 'I know you are pointing a finger at my brother Balarama. He should set an example by giving up drinking. That is my responsibility. He shall give up alcohol the moment I pronounce this ordinance—from this moment, I, as Sangha Pramukh, prohibit alcoholic drinks in Dwaraka.' There were protests from the assembly. Krishna spoke with great concern and said, 'As a token of expiation for all our excesses, let us all go to Prabhasa and atone for our sins by praying to Lord Somnath and seeking his forgiveness.'

Krishna asked Satyaki to enforce the ordinance and prohibition was introduced in Dwaraka. Krishna remained restless,and left for Balarama's palace.

DURVASA

In Pindara Tirtha, on a moonlit night, Rishi Durvasa was in deep meditation. The young and power-obsessed Yadavas had become notorious for their love of wine, women and gambling. They were arrogant, offensive and often intoxicated beyond all limits of decency. Inebriated, some of the youngsters got together and decided to play a prank on the sage. They disguised Samba as a pregnant woman and presented him before Durvasa.

They arrived at his cottage and, without greeting him, said, 'She is the consort of Babru Yadava and desires a child. What will she conceive?'

Just out of his meditation, Durvasa was affronted and enraged by their misconduct, 'She will conceive a *mashal*—torch—and it will destroy the entire Yadava bloodline.' The enraged sage cursed Samba.

Terrified by Durvasa's outburst, the Yadavas deliberately held back the information from Krishna. But true to the sage's prophesy, Samba conceived a *mashal* when he unbound his pregnant makeup. The young Yadavas conspired and crushed the *mashal* into powder, which they immersed in the ocean. The same powder sprouted into plants, in Prabhasa Kshetra, called Erka; every time the plants were destroyed, they rose higher and stronger, upright and sharp as iron weapons.

While these plants were mushrooming into lethal weapons for a battle, the Yadavas were ignorant about the event many miles away. A stray iron piece of the *mashal*, that could not be ground by the young Yadavas, was thrown into the ocean. It was swallowed by a shark, which was then caught by a fisherman. He extracted the piece out of the shark's gullet and handed it over to a hunter named Jara. Jara picked the piece, sharpened it and pasted it on his arrow.

Krishna, in one of his meditative sessions, sensed that His end was near, as the weapon for the exit of His human avatar was being readied.

KRISHNA AT BALARAMA'S PALACE

Revati was surprised to hear Krishna's chariot stopping before the palace gate. 'May I come in, please?' Krishna sought permission before entering Balarama's room. It was late evening and the cool breeze from across the river blew away the curtains over the doors. The setting sunrays filled the room like flames. The flickering sunlight on Balarama's fair body, spread out like a pinch of saffron sprinkled on milk. 'You, Kaanha, at this hour?' asked the elder brother.

'Can I really speak my mind?' asked Krishna, looking directly into his brother's eyes.

'I know what brings you here, Kaanha. I am aware of the ordinance. You had to resort to this extreme measure because of me.'

'The biggest problem with you is that you submit to your weakness easily.'

'Kaanha, if you have come to advise me, then please go away. But if you want to join me, you are more than welcome.' Balarama pulled out silver vessels and started arranging them over a nearby stool to pour out more *madira*.

'You are responsible for the prosperity and protection of the Yadava race,' Krishna said to him.

'Since when have I become the protector of this motley crowd?' roared Balarama. 'You are the king of Dwaraka, the provide, protector and caretaker of this land. I am your elder, yet everything in this land transpires according to your dictates.' Balarama pulled out an ornate bottle, poured some wine into the cup and relished a sip.

'Do I have a choice?' Krishna was fatigued and dejected. 'I have no freedom to dine, whenever I want; the option is never mine. I am a mere prisoner of time who has no right to express myself.'

'Is that so, Kaanha? Can you ever err? You are God, the infallible one and everyone bows to you,' said Balarama sardonically.

'You know very well they do not bow to me; they bow to my strength, my power and my strength that is you—the mighty Balarama,' said Krishna, gently.

A dejected Krishna was about to get up, when Balarama said with folded hands, 'Forgive me, Kaanha; I have let you down; I have wronged you.' Krishna helped Balarama rise and hugged him.

The brothers embraced; Balarama was still weeping on Krishna's shoulder. He had foreseen the future and made a decision, never again to reprimand his brother on his habit of drinking. 'I shall call on you tomorrow morning and we shall have morning repast together. Please wait for me,' Krishna said and left his brother to his woes.

KRISHNA'S LAST MEETING WITH BALARAMA

The next morning, when Krishna came into Balarama's chambers, his elder brother was in high spirits. 'Kaanha, I got rid of the bottle after it was emptied, and threw it out of the window. Now, tell me what I should do to please you?'

Krishna was looking at his brother with intense affection; an extremely handsome man, he now looked haggard due to regular drinking. His face appeared swollen, early in the morning; his eyes looked strained and red. 'Kaanha, why are you staring at this old man with a beard? Time has taken its toll, my little fellow. I had become a slave of wine since our Sahayadri days. Kaanha, let us not discuss my weakness,' said Balarama.

'You are still handsome as ever and I love you the same, my elder brother; you are my strength and support,' Krishna said lovingly. 'Kaanha, you are the lord of Dwaraka, spiritual guide of Aryawartha, the uncrowned king and emperor, you do not need my support,' a dejected Balarama replied.

'I desire that we accompany the Yadavas to Prabhasa Kshetra.'

Balarama, who was standing near the window, was aghast. He watched the sunrays dancing on the flowing water in the river. The golden waves rumbled all the way to the shore and quietly scattered amidst the sand. It was low tide and there were many hours to go before the tide changed. Still, one could hear the angry waves crashing inside Balarama's chamber. Balarama turned to Krishna and stared at him, unblinkingly.

For some time, the room was silent, except for the lapping of the waves against the palace walls.

'Prabhasa? Why?' There was a tremor in Balarama's voice when he spoke. 'Krishna, are you trying to tell me that the time has come for us to perish? Can we not postpone it?'

'Postpone time? Time listens to none.' Krishna rose from his seat, smiling, and clasped his elder brother in an embrace.

'When do we leave?'

'Tomorrow morning.'

THE FINAL JOURNEY

By afternoon, Dwaraka was in a celebratory mood. It was a marvellous spectacle—rows of elevated golden chariots, all looking glorious and elaborately decorated with jewels, accompanied by distinguished *sarathi*s, stood in line. It was a scene that spoke of a highly prosperous town.

Krishna had invited all the Yadavas for a carnival at Prabhasa Kshetra and they were all looking forward to the festivities. The Kurukshetra War had taken a great toll on Yadava warriors, as there was not a single home in Dwaraka that had not lost a life in the battle and the once happy town had been in mourning ever since. They had not even celebrated Krishna's birthday, on Janmashtami, after the war!

This day, Krishna had personally gone from door to door to invite the Yadava men, both old and young, for celebrations at Prabhasa Kshetra. The men could not wait to relish the euphoria that had come after such a long time.

From his window, Krishna looked at the carnival around him and sighed deeply. Did he take the right decision, he wondered. An enlightened soul, who had lived his entire life on the path of truth and justice, experienced self-doubt for the first time. The people of Dwaraka had implicit faith in him and to think that none of them were going to return home alive! Would this eventually destroy *adharma*?

'Let's go, I am ready.' Satyabhama's voice brought Krishna back to reality. He was gripped with fear as he came face to face with his moment of truth.

Beautiful and fragile as porcelain, wheat-complexioned Satyabhama was extremely sensual and characteristically well groomed. Krishna's eyes filled with tenderness and he pulled Satyabhama close to him. Satyabhama always basked in Krishna's attention.

'Where are you going, Satyaa?' asked Krishna. 'Would you enjoy yourself anywhere without me? The festival will be lacklustre without me by your side. I will go with you,' she said coyly. Krishna began to gently stroke her back. Satyaa sensed a different yearning in Krishna's touch today; it was not the touch of a lover, but the touch of a provider and a patriarch.

Krishna took a deep breath and, without saying a word, distanced himself from Satyaa. Satyaa was startled! After the war, he was frequently in a meditative mood and preferred solitude. Many a time, she found him wide awake at night, staring at the stars; and sometimes, he would go for days without speaking a single word. Satyaa was never found wanting of his love for her, yet she felt that there was a perceptible change in his personality. She always would try her best to draw Krishna out of his black moods. When his conflicts turned severe, Krishna visited Rukmini's palace to resolve them. This was unacceptable to Satyaa, a possessive woman.

Earlier, when Satyabhama was upset with him and sulked, Krishna would spend hours pampering her, but not any longer. Now, she would spend days standing on the verandah, waiting in vain for him to take her back.

Krishna knew his wife's feelings and gently said, 'Dearest, these celebrations are exclusively for the Yadava men. I want them to expiate their sins, for the excesses of life that they have committed, before Lord Somnath.' Satyaa said, 'They are arrogant drunkards. Lord, I cannot live without you. Take me with you.'

Krishna replied:

Ours is a karmic bond. You know, only the menfolk are going for the celebration. We are the sinners, not you women. You are noble and have tolerated us out of pure love. Beloved, even when you are not beside me, you are always inside me. You are my life, my better half and a part of you always resides in my heart, do you not agree?

'Swami, will I see you again?' Satya asked with moist eyes.

'Devi, you are forever and always within me.' There was gloom in Krishna's eyes. It was perhaps the pain of parting with such an extraordinary woman!

Krishna thought to himself as he left, 'The human bond is so strong that even God is unable to free himself from it.'

RUKMINI

After many nights of patient waiting, an exhausted Rukmini was happy when she saw Krishna enter her chambers. He handed over his diadem, armbands and sipped some cold water from the cup held in Rukmini's hand. 'Lord, am I married to the king of Dwaraka or to the beloved I eloped with? Are you the same person to whom I wrote a love letter and surrendered my life? Will you, for once, ponder what I desire or what my expectations from you are?

Krishna smiled in response, 'Vaidarbhi, the day I stop to ponder about myself, I will automatically worry about my better half. My beloved, I am not a king. But as Sangha Pramukh, my seat pierces my bottom painfully and I wear the crown of thorns. Dear, come near me. Vaidarbhi, I have neglected you. You have always been a pillar of strength for me.' Saying so, he enveloped her in a warm embrace.

That night, there was high tide and the waves roared and lashed at the shores. It was a still, dark night at Dwaraka. Seated in the queen's chamber, Krishna stared at the setting sun from the window—a distant, dull orange glow was still visible on the horizon.

Rukmini was known to be extraordinarily intelligent. She was well versed in both the art of weapons and in palace politics. Her father had brought her up like a boy, along with Rukmi, and she would have taken the responsibilities of a king, if such a need arose.

Krishna seldom spent any time with her and, when he did, he was more inclined to discuss state matters. She would often protest that she was not interested in his politics of Hastinapura. It was only yesterday that she had spent the entire night awake, all alone in her bed, yearning for Krishna.

Her lord, her beloved, her husband was not exclusively hers. His time and He were for everyone.

She was the wife of Krishna and the queen of Dwaraka and yet, Rukmini nursed a perennial sinking feeling. Fragmented moments from the past sprang up in her memory. Rukmini recalled that Krishna once promised to celebrate Janmashtami at her palace. After celebrating in the adjoining palaces, Krishna lived up to his promise and arrived in their bedchamber. As a birthday present, Rukmini gave him a flute. It was an excellent work of art, embossed with a peacock, beautifully crafted; the edge of the flute held silk strings attached to silk balls. When she lovingly placed the flute in his hands, Krishna surveyed it, then stared at Rukmini for a long time and finally looked away. He looked forlorn and he quietly placed the flute aside and picked up the Panchajanya. But when he blew it, it delivered the most mournful sound. That was before the war.

Was he crying at the ensuing calamity or his own vain attempts to prevent the cataclysm? She could never get over the haunting image of tears streaming down Krishna's cheeks as the sound of his conch reverberated in the Universe.

Krishna witnessed the fleeting expression of rejection in Rukmini's eyes. He drew her into him and stared into her beautiful eyes. Undoubtedly, the flute evoked turbulent memories within him. But his suffering was not restricted just to his pining for Radha, but the gloom of the tragedy to follow—the gloom of the forthcoming battle. In the festivities of Janmashtami, Krishna foresaw the shadows of the storm that was going to rage on the Kartik Purnima day. Krishna had caressed her and wondered about his innocent wife, who, in the midst of all this chaos, had thought of gifting him a flute, presenting him a new raga of life.

The memory of the incident consumed Rukmini with envy for Radha. She felt she was the last priority for Krishna. 'Yet he says that I am his *ardhangini* and the only *sahadharmacharini*, as he had wed me obeying all the strictures of the Vedas and other ordained scriptures, and swearing the Vedic affirmation, *naati charami*—until death separates us!' Thinking thus, Rukmini felt disheartened.

Rukmini turned to look at Krishna standing in the verandah. He appeared preoccupied. Rukmini wondered what worried him. The wedding vows described the wife as an equal partner. 'A deceptive description,' thought Rukmini, who was of the opinion that an equal partner was the one who matched her consort in every step.

His nightmare of the Kurukshetra War had not left Krishna. He had isolated himself from everybody, and Rukmini had got accustomed to his becoming an introvert. But today, she was ill at ease with his taciturnity. There was something ominous about his silence. His weary eyes seemed to say something, but his lips did not grant permission. At midnight, when Rukmini could bear his silence no longer, she sent her messenger to summon Uddhava to her room. Uddhava arrived immediately and, being aware of Krishna's quandary, remained silent. Watching his silhouette in the dark, Uddhava had a premonition of the events that were to unfold. Unable to hold back any longer, Uddhava fell at Krishna's feet. 'Oh lord! What are you up to? Why are you so restless?' Krishna caressed Uddhava's head gently and said:

> You are still here? I thought I had asked you to leave for Badarika Ashram. It is time for the extinction of the Yadava lineage! When the golden urn of the highest temple of Dwaraka is engulfed by the waves of the ocean, it is my wish that you find peace at the foot of the Himalayas.

Uddhava clasped Krishna's feet once again.

Rukmini could only see their figures in the balcony, but did not hear the words being exchanged. She watched Krishna's eyes sparkle in the small light of the solitary lamp in her room. Rukmini felt so pained that she could hear her heartbeats. What was it that her husband did not want to share with her, but confided to Uddhava? Uddhava continued to weep and pleaded, still clasping Krishna's feet, 'No, my lord, I will not go anywhere. Without you, there is no peace for me.'

Krishna then reminded his friend:

> Uddhava, have you forgotten my words? All of us who are born have to die. Accept your circumstances; accept your sorrows, the way you accept happiness. You have accepted birth, now be ready to accept death, for that is your duty, your dharma. Nothing is possible before time and without the lord's calling.

Slowly, Uddhava rose and left the chamber as if carrying the body without a soul. Rukmini looked dazed as he walked past her, without even a glance. It was almost dawn. The tide ebbed and the waters turned calm. The skyline had turned crimson and the changing hues of the sky reflected in Krishna's eyes. Rukmini hesitantly approached Krishna, stood beside him at the window and gently placed her arm on his shoulder. Krishna's eyes were moist and there was something unfamiliar about his expression. This was not Vaasudeva, her husband; he looked like a complete stranger. Rukmini was confused.

'Princess, do you wish to say something to me?' Krishna asked her in a deep, mournful voice.

'I am waiting to hear it from you,'

'What can I say to you?'

'Whatever you said to Uddhava?'

'So you want to know all that I told him?'

'Yes, of course, I am your wife.'

Krishna drew her closer and lowered his head and gently whispered, 'My beloved, these precious, intimate moments are about to end. I was destined to enjoy your commitment and companionship only till now. Time has, once again, beckoned me, and we will have to submit to Time. I will always cherish your presence and always miss your tender touch.'

Rukmini was speechless and nearly hysterical. 'What do you mean? Are you suggesting that your days as a human have come to an end?'

'Dearest Vaidarbhi, we are all committed to fulfil our duties; for, completion is truth and Krishna has never run away from the truth.' He continued to smile and said, 'As my *sahadharmacharini,* you ought to know that I have never expressed anything to you without meaning.' Rukmini's eyes brimmed with tears.

'And me?' Rukmini was unable to contain her sorrow. 'What happens to me? You are part of my body and soul. Is it ever possible for the other half to survive without the first?' It was difficult for him to tear himself away from her.

Krishna consoled Rukmini and said:

> Beloved, you know very well that you are not ordinary and can never be. How can Krishna's better half be ordinary? I do not say this out of pride. When I narrated the Gita to Partha, I said, "Among the elephants, I am Airavat; among trees, I am Peepal; among the cows, I am Kamadhenu; among the rivers, I am Ganga; and among the women, I am Rukmini"; I meant what I said. My beloved, you have played a vital role in my intimate life. Love is not at the mercy of reasons. It survives on a spiritual halo. The more enlightened you are, the more your love expands; the more you

spread your wings, the more you blossom and are enriched as an individual. The time we got to spend with each other was the best time of our lives. Our happiness was correlated and we relished many joyous moments; we have given a lot of sustenance and contentment to each other. There is a certainty that you have submitted more to me than I have to you, but it has been a fruitful marital life. It is better that you look at the positive side rather than repent and regret all that you could have got from me.

Unable to contain herself, Rukmini said:

It would have been a big loss, my lord, had I been deprived of this conversation with you today. I have, in all earnestness, tried to be an ideal wife. What I envisioned as your intrigue and mourned as the recurring reserve, was your caution to safeguard me from hurt; what I considered deprivation of time, was your commitment to the well-being of others. How superior and special you are from the rest of the men who treat women merely as objects of desire! You stand apart from the rest of them, because only you seem to endorse what our Vedas profess in the seventh step of the marriage vows, where the husband undertakes his wife as a friend. Please forgive me, my lord, for judging your magnanimity and suffering unnecessarily.

Krishna heard her, uninterrupted, and replied in the end:

My love, the mind is the male side of a human being while the heart is the female side; every time there is conflict, the mind reigns over the heart. Its only when the heart rules the mind that we make compassionate decisions. The best way to resolve conflicts between the mind and the heart is to remain alert. I have loved you intensely and valued your submission. It is my ardent wish that if I am reborn, I would desire you as my life partner and will pray for that to happen.

Rukmini sobbed, uncontrollably. Krishna tried to console her and affectionately said, 'Get rid of all your anxieties and liberate me now. Unless and until the heart sets me free from your attachments and your responsibilities, I cannot depart for my final journey and reach my home.'

'Home? Where is your home, my lord?'

'Dearest, Partha had asked me the same. *Natathbhasahito surya na sasanko napavakaha tattgatva na nivartante, tad thama paramamama!* Beyond the sun, beyond the moon, beyond all desires, that is where my home is...my beloved!'

'*Twadiyam vastu Govinda tawabhyhamev samarpyate*—my lord, Govinda, at this very moment I return to you all that you have showered on me.'

'We are together in my home, dear, as we are together in spirit. In times to come, I will be remembered as Srivallabha and Srikantha, and you are that Sri,' said Krishna. 'Among others you will be affirmed as *Krishnaya yadavendraya gnaanamudraya yogine; Naathaya Rukmineesaya namo vedanta vedine.*' (Krishna the first among Yadavas, the epitome of knowledge and wisdom, the yogi, the beloved of Rukmini, we salute you as the Ultimate Being in our Universe.)

As he left, he asked the palace guards to leave for Prabhasa Tirtha for participating in festivities. 'Prabhu, what about the security of Maharani?' asked one of the guards. He sternly replied, 'She is secure, you can go.'

HOLY PRABHASA

The ordinance prohibiting all consumption of alcohol was enforced in all seriousness by Satyaki. Drums of wine were drained into the sea. The Yadavas, deprived of drink within the city limits of Dwaraka, were happy to leave on a pilgrimage to Prabhasa, which would be a good diversion, they thought. They set out with numerous meats, wines and many dancing girls.

Their judgement having been vitiated by their destiny, they drank to their fill, a highly intoxicating and delicious drink called Maireyaka.

On the seashore, they indulged in further drinking, eating and dancing. Satyaki said, 'These are days when kshatriyas go at night and kill sleeping babies,' implicitly comparing them to Kritavarma, who had, along with Aswathama and Kripa, gone into the Pandava camp and slaughtered the junior Pandavas. Kritavarma retorted:

> Yuyudhana, you should be ashamed to have severed the head of Bhurisravas after Arjuna severed his arm to save you. You killed Bhurisravas when he was about to depart in the yogic way; it was an act of *adharma*. The great teacher of dharma, Krishna, was also a partner in this *adharma*. Perhaps one of his many *adharmic* acts.

Quick to react, Satyaki instantly severed the head of Kritavarma with his sword. Kritavarma's friends killed Satyaki. Pradyumna closed in on the fighting ground with Samba, Akrura with Bhoja. A free-for-all, indiscriminate slaughter began—of Dasarhas, Vrishnis, Andhakas, Bhojas, Sattvatas, the Madhus, the Arbudas, the Mathuras, the Surasenas, the Visarjanas, the Kukuras and the Kuntis. All clashed with one another and the fratricidal combat was total and complete.

After the arrows were exhausted, they plucked the iron-like Eraka grass and massacred each other. No kith and no kin mattered. Krishna was a witness to the death of Pradyumna and Aniruddha, Samba and Banu, his favourite, Charudeshna; all his sons were slain. Balarama, having witnessed the Yadava holocaust, decided to leave. He slipped out, without the knowledge of Krishna, to the confluence of Kapila, Hiranya and Saraswati, also known as Prak Saraswati.

At the seashore, resorting to yoga in the form of concentration of mind on the Supreme Person and identifying his self with the Supreme Self, Balarama cast off the human semblance and attained his realm.

Krishna looked stoic when Daruka questioned, 'Lord, why did you not prevent this destruction?' He replied after a pause, 'Because it was all destined. They had to pay the penalty of their karma. My friend, there was no reason for me to prevent it, anymore than I had, for preventing the Mahabharata War. Karma must work itself out. Let us go and see what has become of Balarama.' They searched and found Balarama lying dead in yogic samadhi, some miles away. They heard some cowherds saying that a huge serpent headed into the sea from him. Meanwhile, a massive wave carried Balarama's body into the ocean.

'Daruka, now it is my time to depart,' said Krishna in the most casual way. Daruka was grief-stricken and started sobbing. 'My friend, this is the inevitability of life,' consoled Krishna. 'You have served me so selflessly and did your duty, never complaining. You deserve no rebirth.'

'I never thought I was serving you. I was just happy to be a part of your mission to establish dharma. I was always at peace with myself, when you were around. Please forgive my lapses. O noble lord, please grant me liberation.' Daruka clasped Krishna's feet in overflowing gratitude and kissed the lord's lotus feet. Krishna said:

> Now, Daruka, I have yet another mission for you, the last one, perhaps. Please go to my father and inform him that the Yadavas have destroyed themselves—the curses of Gandhari and Durvasa acted, in letter and spirit. Tell him not to look for Balarama or me—our mission was over. He would understand and do the needful. Tell my father that Dwaraka will be under water, seven days from the time of my departure. Proceed to Hastinapura and

bring Arjuna to Dwaraka. He has to look after the obsequies of my parents and take the women of Dwaraka to Hastinapura. Please go now. We shall meet in a glorious world.

Krishna embraced Daruka for the last time. To the consternation of Daruka, Krishna's chariot, with his four white horses, departed skyward; so did his Sudarshana, Nandaka, Saranga and Kaumudi; his mace followed in sequence. Daruka saw an unusual glow leave Krishna's face and, much saddened, he left to fulfil his last mission.

THE LORD'S LAST HOURS

Krishna slowly walked to the bank of River Hiranya, near the great temple of Somnatheswar, and sat underneath a peepul tree. The clear water reflected the pristine moonlight. He watched the wave till he was lost in himself. The sun was about to rise. Krishna watched the three rivers—Kapila, Hiranya and Prak Saraswati—converge into each other. This was where his elder brother had entered his samadhi.

Tormented by watching his lineage decimate, Krishna did all in his capacity to bid them a dignified farewell. Krishna, the lord of the senses and the enchanter of the mind, appeared forlorn sans his crown and his signature ornaments. Though still alluring, his eyes were full of anguish, as if awaiting the inevitable.

Seated in a lotus position, his left foot upon his right thigh, Krishna slipped into a meditative state with his eyes open. It was almost as if he had transformed into a statue. The eyes that had once sparkled with mischief, today appeared vacant, staring into space. It was the dawn of Durvasa's victory; his curse to vanquish the Yadava bloodline and, with them, their leader Krishna. In anticipation of his end, Krishna waited beneath the tree at Prabhasa. The morning sun emerged pale without the halo, as if mourning in advance, the farewell of a divine presence on earth. It was during twilight, that the hunter Jara was on a prowl. In the darkness of the peepul's shade, Krishna's foot resembled a dormant deer.

Jara picked the arrow to which he had fixed the iron piece, a remnant of the *mashal* that could not be dismantled by the young Yadavas, who had flung it into the sea. Jara scrutinised the attached piece on his arrow and aimed his shot at the dormant deer. The arrow hit the sole of Krishna's foot and slit it all the way, like a lethal weapon. The curse of Gandhari was, at last, realised.

The hunter was aghast to find Krishna the target of his arrow. He tried to pluck out the arrow from Krishna's bleeding foot, but was unsuccessful.

'Let it be, my friend!' said a sinking voice, almost inaudible. 'Our scriptures define *niyati* as predestined. It means that we follow what is in store for us. Unless we do so, we cannot forsake our body when the time comes. Jara, you lived by your karma and did your duty as was predestined.' Jara could sense insurmountable pain in Krishna's voice. The hunter could not control his sobs. 'Lord! I have sinned. I have no means to expiate my sin. I have shot the Lord of the Universe.'

Krishna asked with a sympathetic smile, 'Who are you, my friend?'

'I am Jara, a hunter by profession and a sinner. Oh lord! What have I done to you?'

'Jara, I was waiting for you. Why did you delay, my friend?' asked Krishna, moaning as the blood flowed from the wound. 'You are the messenger of my freedom, Jara. You have done nothing to fear. You have relieved me of my human incarnation. You will go to heaven. I am indebted to you, my friend.'

Krishna folded his hands and shut his eyes; his face was brimming with pain and relief—pain that resulted from his bleeding foot and relief that he would be shortly detaching himself from this life. He felt dispassionate as he awaited his final journey.

He who had cured so many of their suffering, was today in excruciating pain. It was Krishna's destiny to witness and reminisce about his entire life. A vast canvas unveiled before him and Krishna was lost in innumerable memories from this life. Jara poured some water, carried in a mud pot, into Krishna's mouth. The hunter sensed relief on Krishna's face. 'One values water only when one is thirsty. Without thirst, we have no regard for it,' Krishna recalled his own words to Arjuna. 'Water is like knowledge—thirst for it and you will relish it when you receive it!'

It was Jara's voice that he could hear, calling him softly, 'I have brought the juice of a herb, which when applied, would reduce your pain.'

'Jara, I am beyond pain. Let me go, please.'

Slowly, Krishna lapsed into a trance as more memories flooded into his mind's eye. He thought about Draupadi, who had understood the meaning of devotion; he thought about Gandhari and her curse—the curse of a mother who had lost her sons in a war that she had requested him to prevent; he thought of his aunt Kunti's words when she said that her sons might have been victorious, but at the cost of too many lives.

He understood Gandhari's distress, but how could he explain to her that it was all predestined? He was destined to endure all he did, destined to witness the blood and destined to die, as he was now. There was just no way out for him without fulfilling his mission and it was to Krishna's credit that, through all this turmoil, he remained focussed, dispassionate and courageously faced the circumstances to fulfil his duties.

Abhyuthanamadharmasya Tadatmanam Srujamyaham—to protect and enrich dharma, the virtuous living: This promise had to be fulfilled. When a deity comes as an avatar among humans, he has to live like one; that is why, watching the suffering of his brethren, his friends and family, Krishna was in anguish.

River Prak Saraswati flowed gently, joined by the gushing waters of Hiranya and Kapila. It was as if the gushing Saraswati had transformed into River Ashva, with Karna standing at the shore, hands outstretched towards the rising sun and offering his prayers. Krishna envisioned Karna, accusing him of favouring the Pandavas and revealing his identity at a crucial point, to break his resolve and not fight his brothers.

He felt sorry for Karna and the circumstances that had led him to be who he was. He could have been a king. Many such memories haunted him towards the end, but he knew he had to take those steps to ensure the victory of dharma. He could not allow himself to regret what he had accomplished.

Suddenly, Krishna heard his flute playing the Mohana Raga, his favourite. 'Kaanha, you are leaving without me.' In his semiconscious state, he said, 'Radha, I may leave this world, but I am not leaving you. You are part of me and shall remain so in eternity. In times to come, I will be known as "Radhakanth". There would be no Krishna without Radha.'

'You are still tricking me, Kaanha. What about my solace now?' he heard Radha saying. Krishna replied:

> Radha, your soul is meant for spreading my message of love and devotion, without expecting anything in return. As you have been to me in this life, in the coming age of Kali, a time will come in Bharatvarsha, when the Mlechhas and the marauders will create havoc in our society. At that time, you will be reincarnated as a princess of great beauty and devotion. Spread my love by singing about our association at Vrindavan. Together, we shall

> become immortal and the most beautiful song—*Geet Govinda*—will be sung in every household. I know the anguish of my mother, Yashoda. Tell her, in the coming ages, the entire world will worship me as Govinda, and she will preside over my head as a beautiful garland of flowers; she will be the witness of the affection and devotion of my bhaktas.
>
> Radha, in this life of mine, I could not take you to Dwaraka, but you shall merge your soul into mine as Princess Meera at Dwaraka, in the age of Kali. Farewell, my love; you are the only one who knew me and my music.
>
> With those words, the lord breathed his last.

Jara was witness to a brilliant light taking flight into space. With folded hands, he left.

DRAUPADI'S CALLING

This was the year that Draupadi had to spend with Arjuna. It was late night and the fading lamps of the palace flickered in the breeze.

Arjuna woke up, startled from his sleep, and saw Draupadi standing in the verandah. He rose from the bed and stood beside her. She sensed his footsteps and turned around. Her usually fiery eyes were moist and had the dampness of clouds soaked in rain.

'Not able to sleep, Yajnaseni?' asked Arjuna.

'Sleep has deserted my eyes for many years. How I crave to get into a deep slumber.'

'So do all of us,' Arjuna replied with a deep sigh.

'Partha, I do not know why, but I have a sinking feeling that something is not right. My hands and feet tremble and I feel parched and anxious.' Arjuna pulled Draupadi close to him and said:

> It has been a recurring feeling for all of us. I have been frightened of the sunset ever since the battle of Kurukshetra. I am startled by the sound of the blowing conch, frightened of the screeching, rushing crowds, of the hungry vultures on the prowl for prey and of the wolves shrieking in the darkness of night. I am terrified too, Draupadi; terrified that it will soon be dawn, I will have to hold the arrow in my hand and, once again, fight my loved ones, once again be deafened by their wails. I am hounded by those nightmares and my heart feels gloomy.

'My fear is different, Partha.' Drauapdi stared at Arjuna, speechless for a while; then she said, 'I need to visit Sakha this very minute.' Arjuna was startled.

'What is the matter, my love?'

'I do not know. I have no logical explanation, but I know that at this moment, I want to visit him. My mind is restless and my heart is in despair. I feel that Sakha is calling out to me. I can hear his voice resounding in this room.'

'Why do you harbour such negative thoughts, Yajnaseni? He is the Almighty. Millions survive on his faith. How can anything go wrong with him?' Draupadi replied:

> I am aware that Sakha is a deity; indeed, he is the Supreme Spirit, the Godhead and, yet, he is a human being; in our midst, much superior, but still a man! I have seen in his eyes, all that you see in a living being. I have sensed his emotions and his experiences. It is the people around him who have given him the manifestation of a god but, in reality, he is just as flesh and blood as the rest of us.

Arjuna stared at Draupadi in disbelief. 'Yajnaseni, you have been the recipient of his miracles and have experienced his divinity. How can you still doubt that?'

'Nobody is better qualified, than me, to make this confession. What you describe as a miracle is, for me, his supremacy—a great power originating from a fervent desire to connect with other people; an unbelievable force that transforms him from the ordinary to the extraordinary.'

'You seem to have understood him better than me...' Draupadi's eyes brimmed over with tears, 'Take me to Sakha before it is too late.' Arjuna left the room and returned soon after, to inform that the chariot was ready.

'Are you not coming with me, Partha? You have to be by my side.' Arjuna was always accompanied by his *sarathi*. But today, he was in a hurry to fulfil Draupadi's wish and decided not to wait for his charioteer. In respecting Draupadi's instinct, he was inadvertently following the call of his destiny.

Arjuna's mind galloped in multiple directions and the racing chariot was unable to keep pace with his rushing mind. What could have made Panchali so restless? Was Krishna beckoning her? He had always remained his protégé, just a student who wanted to flee from the battlefield. On the other hand, Draupadi was the daughter of fire! She remained fiery till she avenged her wrath; she was ruthless and Krishna appreciated it. He thought Draupadi had to expiate the injustice and utter disregard for human dignity. When they were halfway to Dwaraka, just before sunset, they met Daruka's chariot racing through the desert. Daruka stopped when he saw them, looking desolate as he got down from his chariot.

'Arjuna, our lord wants you immediately at Dwaraka. He was all set to depart and was longing to see you. Please rush to Dwaraka and meet chief Anakabandhu and follow his instructions.' Then he collapsed with uncontrollable grief.

Draupadi collapsed in her chariot. Arjuna started his onward journey, with Daruka in the driving seat. When Arjuna's chariot entered through the gates of Dwaraka, it was mid afternoon. The horses were frothing at the mouth, after running for two days without a break. Draupadi's hair was dishevelled and her face covered with dust. When the chariot crossed the main entrance, Draupadi was surprised to discover the royal streets deserted. All the gates of the golden fortresses were firmly clasped. There was an ominous feel to the place.

Arjuna rode the chariot towards Queen Rukmini's palace and found it unusually quiet. Arjuna lent his hand to help Draupadi alight from the chariot. Both appeared weary after the long journey. Draupadi walked to the main entrance and met Rukmini, who told them about her conversation with Krishna. Draupadi stared at Rukmini with a blank expression. Arjuna waited, motionless, then, without exchanging a single word, went and stood at the verandah; far away, the sun was setting on the horizon. The orange skyline resembled a blood-splattered battlefield.

Rukmini had no more tears to shed. 'Time has spread its dragnet. The drinking sessions must have commenced at Prabhasa Kshetra and all would have been over.' Rukmini's voice was as cold as death. 'The Yadava carnival will be the end of the Yadavas and will mark the end of the golden era of Dwaraka,' Rukmini continued passively, her eyes were cold and her face was devoid of expression.

Meanwhile, Arjuna met Vasudeva, who had become old and forlorn. The moment he saw Arjuna, Vasudeva broke down in grief and said, 'I am now leaving, Partha; the kingdom of Dwaraka is in your hands. My sons are gone and you are my son-in-law; you can be the king of Dwaraka.' Arjuna refused the offer, saying he could never do so without Krishna. 'I have no life and am going in search of Krishna and Balarama,' and so saying, he started for Prabhasa.

Vasudeva passed away the next day. All his four wives: Devaki, Bhadra, Rohini and Madira committed sati on the funeral pyre. Dwaraka was plunged into utter despair; it had become a ghost town!

Arjuna, after reaching Prabhasa, searched for the bodies of Krishna and Balarama. But he could find only Krishna's body, serene, as if he was sleeping. Arjuna broke down and remembered his friend, philosopher and guide, telling him, *Jatasyi Dhruvo Mrityu*—the one that is born has to die one day.

Arjuna performed the funeral obsequies of Vasudeva and Krishna. Rukmini and Jambavati committed sati, while a remorseful Satyabhama was consumed with self-pity and preferred to enter a forest to do penance. She wished to get rid of her vanity and expiate her ego and, thus, become eligible to meet her lord in the other world.

DWARAKA GOES UNDER WATER

Vasudeva had conveyed Krishna's message to Arjuna: Seven days from the departure of Krishna, Dwaraka will go under the sea, taking everything with it; Arjuna should transport the womenfolk to Hastinapura.

Arjuna witnessed the catastrophic tsunami consume the beautiful city of Dwaraka, taking with it the grandeur and glory of the city of Krishna. Sad and stoic he stood, as he witnessed yet another cataclysm. He asked the Yadava womenfolk and children to accompany him to the safety of Hastinapura. While they were marching across the present-day Punjab, with long columns of refugee women and children, a horde of Abhiras and Vahikas attacked them and told Arjuna, 'Leave these pretty women for us and go.' Arjuna was astounded and said:

> You scum of the human race, what a request are you making and of whom? Do you know I am Partha, who fought in the Mahabharata War and won? Do you know that these are all Krishna's kinsmen and I am his friend? Do not unnecessarily trifle with me and rush into the jaws of death.

But the horde cried out:

> Stop that chatter, old fool! We have heard of you and we also know that, but

for Krishna, you would not have fought the war, much less won it. We heard he is no more and you are nobody without him. Hand over these young women to us. We shall not harm them. We shall marry them and bring into existence a fine race. This pretty lot of women will make our future race handsome and graceful!

How dare you provoke me?' said Arjuna in a rage. 'You will meet your end at my hands,' and tried to string his Gandiva, but found that he could not. He even failed to remember any *astra*s and the tribals seized the shrieking women and carried them all into the dense forest. Arjuna cried in anguish and, ashamed of himself, he reached Hastinapura with the remaining infirm and old refugees and told Yudhisthira about his journey. A crestfallen Arjuna rushed to Vyasa and fell at his feet. Vyasa consoled him:

The Vrishnis were under a curse and were bound to meet that dreadful fate, as the heroes of Kurukshetra did. As for Krishna, you need not mourn for him. He knew what he was doing. He could have prevented this holocaust, but he did not because he came to this world with a purpose, accomplished it and left. Why mourn for him?

'But Krishna is dead and I cannot bear it,' wept Arjuna like a child.

'Dead? What are you talking about?' asked Vyasa. 'How can the unborn and eternal die? Arjuna, he just finished the work for which he had come here and so, has left. Do not grieve, Partha. He still loves you and is watching over you with a deeper and more forgiving love.'

Arjuna asked, 'Why could I not save the Yadava women? Why could I not string my bow? How could I forget all the *astra*s? I sustained defeat at the hands of the Mlechhas!' The *muni* gently replied:

There is a time for everything to come and go. Krishna's Sudarshana went away from him before his departure, so, too, your weapon and the inexhaustible quiver of arrows. So went Sanjaya's divine sight the moment war was over. Come now, let us pray to him. Repeat his name and you will find solace.

Hey Krishna, Govinda, Hare Murare,
Hey Natha Narayana Vaasudeva

Say it three times and feel the peace, Arjuna!

Arjuna found solace in this prayer and took leave of Vyasa. He settled some of the refugees on the banks of Saraswati, at a place called Simhapura, and made Satyaki's son, Yuyudhaneya, their king. He settled Krishna's great grandson, Vajra, as the king of Indraprastha. Then, he met Yudhisthira, who installed Parakshit as the king of Hastinapura.

One fine day, the Pandavas and Draupadi recognised that it was all the work of the lord and that it was time for them to leave for the Himalayas. Thus began their Mahaprasthana.

Aakaashatupatitam toyam yadhagachhati sagaram
Sarvadevanamaskara kesavam pratigachhati

(As rains that descend on earth have their final destination—the ocean.
So, also, all prayers that we offer to different gods reach Keshava—Krishna.)

*****

ANNEXURE I

STRING OF MELODIES (KRISHNA AND HIS FLUTE)

Few people know that Guru Gobind Singh, the tenth guru of the Sikhs, has written *Dasham Granth*, which contains descriptions of twenty-four *satgun* avatars of Parambrahma. Sri Krishna is the twenty-first avatar and Guru Gobind Singh has written, in length, 11,092 *chhanda*s or verses on the life of this incarnation.

Guruji states that true beauty in *bhaktimarg* lies in transmitting the same in our daily affairs for the welfare of society. People following *bhaktimarg* should also fight against the evils prevalent in society and root them out as Guruji did.

He describes Krishna by saying that, till the age of twelve, he took out cows to graze. He was very handsome and attractive. Krishna's face was just like a lotus flower, eyes as attractive as that of a deer, waist as that of a lion, long arms like a lotus' stem, voice as sweet as that of a koel, nose as charming as that of a parrot's beak and eyebrows like a bow. Krishna was as sacred as the Ganga. He goes on to say that all the young girls of Vrij had termed Krishna's face as *sanwala*—dark, but attractive and cool like the full moon.

Guruji, in *Krishna Charitra*, writes that the darshan of Sri Krishna added to one's pleasure and the entire atmosphere swayed in harmony when he was present. In his flights of poetic ecstasy, Guruji states that the meandering

Yamuna, birds, reptiles, yakshas, Kinnara and wild beasts would all come to a standstill when Krishna played his flute.

Even Mother Earth was infatuated with him. Krishna would play his flute, rendering ragas: Sarang, Shuddha Malhar, Megh Malhar, Malasri, Devagandhar, Vibhas, Bilaval and enrapture all of Nature. Gods also joined in this Prem Astra, along with the living beings on Earth. The whole universe was enraptured by the divine melodies played by the Lord of the Universe—Jagannath.

Sri Guru Gobind Singhji stated that whoever sings songs of Krishna shall obtain moksha, all his sins shall vanish and he shall live free of worries.

Jo upma brijanath kee gaye
Hai aur kabitan beech karaiga
Pappan kee ten paavak mai
Kabi syam bhanai na jaraige
Chinta sabhai mit hai ju
Rajee chhin mai tinke adha
Bind taraige

—# 2483 Sri Dasam Granth

ANNEXURE II

KRISHNA AND GHORA ANGIRASA

Krishna had taken a great liking to Ghora Angirasa and the feeling was mutual. Angirasas are successors of Agni himself. The hymns of the Atharva Veda are called Angirasas and the descendants of Angirasa were specially charged with the protection of sacrifices performed in accordance with the Atharva Veda.

Ghora Angirasa was well-versed in the Sama Veda and Chhandogya Upanishad, as also the Kena Upanishad. Having gauged his divinity, the great sage gave special emphasis on Krishna in the Chhandogya portion of the Sama Veda. The doctrines enunciated by Angirasa greatly impressed Krishna and he appreciated the mystic interpretations of ceremonies of the Vedic sacrifice, as representing various functions of life.

Adi Shankara, in his commentary on the Chhandogya Upanishad, is said to have stated: 'Krishna never again thirsted for other knowledge and the desire for *vidya* was quenched in the mind of Krishna, after listening to the teaching of Ghora Angirasa.' At a later stage in Krishna's life, during the Gita's exposition to Arjuna, Krishna brought in these doctrines, in Chapter IV (1), chapter VIII (5, 10) and chapter XVI (3). One finds a distinct influence of the teachings of the great Ghora Angirasa, on account of his doctrinaire approach to Vedic scriptures and interpretations

1. Imam vivasvate yogam Proktava-nahamavyayam
vivasvaanmanave praha manurishva-kaveabraveet

(I taught this immortal yoga to Vivasvan—Sun God. Vivasvan conveyed it to Manu, who was his son, and Manu imparted it to his son, Iksvaku.)

2. Antakale ca ma-meva smaranmuktva kalevaram
yah prayaati sa madbhavam yaati nastyatra samshayah

(He, who departs from the body, thinking of me alone, even at the time of death, attains my state. There is no doubt about it.)

3. Praya-na kale manasa-chalena bhatya yukto yogabalena chaiva
Bhruvormadhye pra-nama-vesya samyak sa tam param purusamupaiti divyam

(Having the power of yoga, firmly held the life breath in the space between the two eyebrows even at the time of death, and contemplating on God with a steadfast mind, full of devotion, he reaches verily that supreme divine Purusha—God.)

4. Tejah kshama-dhritih sauchamadroho naatimanita
Bhavanti sampadam daivimabhijatasya bha-rata

(Sublimity, forbearance, fortitude, external purity, bearing enmity to none and absence of self-esteem, these are the marks of him, who is born with the divine gifts of Arjuna.)

Annexure III

When Lord Krishna came to Mathura, he was hardly fourteen years old. At this age, boys indulge in play and fun. For a lad in the early teens, he was charming, amorous too, and very much sought after by the girls of Vrindavan. His looks would mesmerise both men and women. His skin, though slightly dark, had excellent texture. His manners were impeccable. His smile would win even the wickedest heart. Above all, he had the uncanny intelligence to grasp the intricacies of statecraft.

Though not initiated into a regular school, Krishna possessed outstanding intellect for his age. He and his brother had a phenomenal memory. In Sanskrit, it is called *yeka samtagrahi*, or one with instant grasp of understanding and memory of any event. He knew that if an adversary is to be defeated, a sense of inferiority should be created in his mind. The psychological impact, of such a complex, on an adversary, would be immense and demoralising.

He employed this during the Kalia Naga episode. Once Kalia Naga's neck got caught in the lasso, he lost his power, became confused and ultimately submitted to Krishna.

Keeping this in mind, before visiting the royal court at Mathura, he went, first, to the armoury and picked up the powerful and anointed bow and broke it. When Kamsa came to know of the incident, he was truly frightened and lost his self-confidence. The incident with the elephant was also to serve this purpose. This was the stratagem of Krishna.

Krishna killed Chanura, using an intelligent stratagem—by hitting on the left heel of his weak leg, thus physically weakening the champion. After this, Kamsa sensed defeat and became desperate to save his life from certain death.

ANNEXURE IV

True to Sri Krishna's affirmation, in his last moments on our planet, the glory, love and romance of Krishna endeared the laity and the nobles alike. For aeons, the ballad singers have spread Krishna's story and glories among countless Indians of this blessed land. One of the famous ones was Surdas, who was born blind and, yet, sang the lord's glories as if he had witnessed them. His devotion to Krishna made him sing, '*Sur Kahe Shyam Sune*' (Surdas sings while Krishna hears with rapt attention.)

Meerabai, the princess of Mewar, immortalised Krishna. His Radha had been reborn as Meera and, in the end, she became a part of him.

Jayadeva, the court poet of the Pala kings in the twelfth century, deified the romance of Radha and Krishna in his *Gita Govindam,* in *ashtapadi*s—eight couplets, which formed the core of the Bhakti Movement in eastern and north-eastern India, and gave solace and succour to the people during a very difficult period of Indian history—the Muslim invasions.

Vallabhacharya, Leela Shuka, Paramananda Das, Madhusudhana Saraswati, Chaitanya, Kshetrayya, Kanakadas, Narayana Nambudiri, Annamacharya, Purandaradasa, Narayana Tirtha, Narsi Mehta, Sant Tukaram, Jnanadev, Namdev and a host of personalities sang Krishna's glories.

Indian classical dance forms—Kathak, Odissi, Kuchipudi, Mohiniyattam, Garbha and Manipuri—are all devoted to the Radha-Krishna theme.

Kuchipudi has an exclusive number for Satyabhama called Bhamakalapam. Bharatanatyam has numerous choreographed numbers on Krishna Katha.

A school of painting, exclusively dedicated to Krishna, had taken root in Kishangarh and Kangra valley in the Himalayan region.

The divinity of Krishna was expostulated by Adi Shankaracharya, Ramanujacharya and Madhavacharya—the trinity of Indian philosophical thought for nearly 2,000 years.

Krishna is the thread that holds together the vast multitudes in India, that is, Bharatvarsha.

BIBLIOGRAPHY AND REFERENCES

With the advice of Swamy Dayananda Saraswati, we have followed the footprints of Kulapati KM Munshi in the narration of our Krishna Katha.

1. Ayyar, ASP. *Sri Krishna: The Darling of Humanity,* Bharatiya Vidya Bhavan, Mumbai, 2001.
2. Dawson, John. *A Classical Dictionary of Hindu Mythology and Religion,* DK Printworld's, New Delhi, 2000.
3. Ganguli, Kisari Mohan. *The Mahabharata,* translated from the original Sanskrit text into English prose, Munshiram Manoharlal Publishers, New Delhi, 2000.
4. Goswami, Asha. *Krishna Katha and Allied Matters: A critical study of the life story of Krishna as narrated in the Mahabharata and the appended Hari Vamsa,* YR Publications, New Delhi, 1984.
5. Gopalakrishnan, TR. *Legend of Dwaraka*, Cover story, 'The Week', Malayalam Manorama Press, 1 June 2003.
6. Goswami, Asha. *In the Footsteps of Krishna: Researches in Krishna Love*, YR Publications, New Delhi, 2005.
7. Goswami, Asha. *The Krishna Legend: A New Perspective in Krishna Love,* YR Publications, New Delhi, 2005.
8. Mamtani, Madhardas. *Krishna Avtar in Dasam Granth*, 'Bhavan's Journal', Bharatiya Vidya Bhavan, Mumbai, 20 November 2006.
9. Majumdar, Ashok K. *The Hindu History*, Rupa & Co, New Delhi, 2008.
10. Mazumdar, Subash. *Mahabharata is Believable*, Bhavan's Book University, Bharatiya Vidya Bhavan, Mumbai, 1998.
11. Munshi, KM. *Krishnavatara* (Volume I to VII), Bharatiya Vidya Bhavan, Mumbai, 1973.
12. Kaushik, Ashok (ed) & Datt, Anak (tr). *Srimad Bhagavad Gita*, Star Publications, New Delhi, 2003.

13. Rajagopalachari, C. *Mahabharata,* Bharatiya Vidya Bhavan, Mumbai, 1996.
14. Raja Ram, NS. *Search for Historical Krishna*, Prism Books, Bengaluru, 2004.
15. Rev His Holiness Shastri Shri Pandurang Vathavale. *Life of Lord Krishna: A Glimpse*, Shrimat Bhagavat Gita Pathasala, Mumbai, 1975.
16. Sen, Makhan Lal. *Lord Sree Krishna: His life and Teachings* (Vol I, II & III), Oriental Publishing Co., Kolkata, 1955.
17. Sengupta, Subhadra. *Dwaraka…Krishna's Dhaam by the Sea*, Rupa & Co, New Delhi, 2003.
18. Somaaya, Bhaavana. *Krishna: The God Who Lived as Man*, Hindology Books New Delhi, 2008.
19. Sonde, Nagesh D. *Krishna: A Study based on Mahabharata*, Suman Art Prints, Mumbai, 2008.
20. Subramaniam, Kamala. *Mahabharata*, Bharatiya Vidya Bhavan, Mumbai, 1965.
21. Swami Ramakrishna Brahmanaanda. *Sree Mahabhagavatam: Message to Mankind,* Vanaprastha, Coimbatore, 2005.
22. Varma, Pavan K. *The Book of Krishna,* Penguin Viking, New Delhi, 2002.
23. Wison, HH. Joshi, KL (ed). *Vishnu Purana*, Parimal Publications, New Delhi, 2005.

Map:

Mukherjee, Radha Kumud. *Hindu Civilization: EPIC India*, Bharatiya Vidya Bhavan, Mumbai, 1989.

A TRIBUTE TO SRI KRISHNA

Yogindranam twadangeyshwadhikasumadhuram Muktibhajam nivaso
Bhaktaanaam kaamavarsha-dyutarukisalayam naatha Tey padamoolam
Nityam chittasthitam mey pavanapurapate! Krishna! Kaarunyasindho
Hritvaa nisheshataapaan—pradishatu paramaanandasandohalakshmim

O lord! Thy feet are the most beloved of all Thy parts to the Yogis
They form the abode for emancipated ones
For the devotees they are like the celestial tree, which yields them all their wants
O Krishna! O lord of Guruvayoor! O Ocean of Mercy!
May those feet of Thine ever rest in my heart, destroy all my sufferings and bestow on me the treasure of Supreme Bliss.

Govind Sharanam Iti

"Krishnapada Samarpanam"
1 July 2010

Glossary

Aarti: A Hindu form of worship, involves lighting of a lamp and waving it clockwise with the right hand, three times, while invoking one's prayers to the deity.
Abhijin Muhuruta: Noon or midnight.
Abhijit: Midnoon—12 pm, midnight—12 am.
Abhisheka: The ritual of sanctifying an idol with water or milk.
Acharya: Teacher or guru.
Adhyaryu: The presiding priest for the Vedic fire worship or yagna.
Agneya Astra: A fire missile.
Agnihotra: A special category of priests who are custodians of the sacred fire, in line with the ancient Aryan code.
Akshay Tritiya: An auspicious period.
Anandaroopa: Krishna's blissful personality, ever smiling.
Anakabandhu: Original name of Krishna's father Vasudeva.
Angirasa: A Rigvedic rishi—one of the seven rishis, *sapta* rishis of the Rigveda.
Angirasas: Descendants of Angirasa, supposed to have originated from Armenia near the Caspian Sea in Central Asia.
Apsara: A celestial nymph.
Arghya: Oblations to God, either offering water while taking bath or clarified ghee in fire worship.
Asura: A demon.
Asvayuja: October/November, during the time of Dussehra.
Ashwamedha Yagna: Horse sacrifice.
Atirathi: The captain of ten war chariots.
Atmabandhu: Soulmate.
Balbrahmachari: Young brahmana bachelor.
Bhabhi: Brother's wife.
Bhagineya: Father's sister's kin.

Bhaktimarg: The path of worship.

Brahman: The Supreme Soul of the Universe, self exultant, absolute, eternal—from which all things emanate, and to which all return.

Brahmana: The first of the four castes—the sacerdotal class, the members of which may or may not be priests.

Chaitra: The month of April.

Chakra: A discus. Krishna's secret weapon, the Sudarshana Chakra.

Chakravarti: An emperor or overlord of extensive territories.

Chamara: Palm-leaf fan.

Chandrayana Vrata: A lady's austerity.

Dahana: Cremation.

Daityas: Titans. They are the descendants of Diti by Rishi Kasyapa's race of demons and giants.

Danavas: Demons. They are the descendants of Danu by Rishi Kasyapa.

Dattatreya: The son of Atri and Anasuya. A brahmana saint encompassing the Holy Trinity of Brahma, Vishnu and Shiva.

Dham: Resident village or area of a deity.

Dharma: Translates literally as religion. But in traditional Hindu custom it means far more than that. The word encompasses holy, right knowledge, right living, following the tradition and natural order of the Universe and duty. It is essentially all that is good in the universe.

Dhobi: A washerman.

Divyastra: A divine weapon.

Diya: A clay lamp.

Dwaraka/Dwaravati: The 'City of Gates'. Krishna's capital in Gujarat, which is said to have been submerged by the ocean seven days after his death. It is one of the seven sacred cities—Abdhinagar.

Gada: Mace, the mighty weapon. Also a younger brother of Krishna.

Garuda: The king of birds—half man and half bird, the vehicle of Vishnu. Also, a mountain tribe that descended from Kasyapa and Vinata, therefore called Vainateya, or Krishna's bodyguard.

Ghatika: Twenty-four minutes.

Gopas: Male cowherds.

Gopis: Female cowherds.

Gotra: Lineage of a clan.

Gurudakshina: Offerings made to the teacher on completion of formal education.

Jyotishamyanam: Ancient treatise on astrology.

Kaka: Paternal uncle.

Kalia Naga: A serpent king who had five heads, and dwelt in a deep pool of the Yamuna, with numerous attendant serpents—the Asura Kalanemi is said to have been animate in him.

Kanya: An unmarried girl.

Kartik: The month of November.

Kasturi: Unguent.

Kula Kshayam: Decimation of a race.

Kula Vadhu: Noble daughter of the scion.

Leela: The divine play.

Loka: A world, a division of the Universe.

Loka Sangraha: Consolidator of dharma and protector of the virtuous.
Magha: February/March.
Maharathi: The commander of a hundred war chariots.
Mahout: A person who works with and rides an elephant.
Mandala: A period of forty days.
Mandapa: Platform.
Mangala Snana: Sacred bath.
Margasirsha: The month of December.
Mlechhas: Foreigners, barbarians, a non-Aryan race.
Moksha: Liberation from the cycle of births and deaths.
Mulls: Professional wrestlers who also worked as spies.
Naga Kanya: A snake maiden
Naraka: Hell
Naresh: The king.
Nishada: A mountain tribe dwelling in the Vindhya Mountains, outcastes.
Omkara: The sacred monosyllable—Om, akshara—indestructible.
Padma: Lotus.
Parama Purusha: The Supreme Soul of the Universe.
Paush: January/February.
Phalguna: February-March or March-April.
Prajapati: 'Lord of Creatures', a progenitor, creator, a term for Vedic Gods.
Prem Astra: Cupid's arrow.
Raja Dharma: Royal duty.
Rajanyas: A Vedic designation of kshatriya caste.
Rakshasa/Rakshasi: Goblins or evil spirits. The Rakshasas have many epithets describing their character and actions.
Rathi: A charioteer.
Rohini: Fourth of the lunar asterisms—Aalderban constellation. One of the wives of Vasudeva, daughter of Jambavan.
Sahadharmacharini: Better half.
Samidha: The sacrificial blade of grass.
Sanatana Dharma: The eternal and perennial virtue/order, bedrock of Hinduism.
Saptapuri: Name of a city.
Saropas: Turban.
Sasvata Dharmagopta: The saviour of the eternal dharma.
Satguru: The teacher of teachers.
Sharad Ritu: The month of autumn in India, when the sky is clear after the post monsoon showers, hence full moon is brightest in the sky.
Simhadwara: Lion gates. Entrance to the city or palace gates.
Snataka: A priest.
Srivatsa: A particular mark said to be a curl of hair on the chest of Krishna—a notation indicative of divinity.
Srotriyas: Well versed in Sruti or the Vedic mantras, learned priests.

Swayamvara: Selection of a groom by a princess.

Tirtha: Holy place.

Upanayanam: The sacred thread (*jahnau*) ceremony—a ceremonial thread tied from the shoulder across the torso, from left to right shoulder.

Uttarayana: The summer solstice.

Vaisakha: May/June.

Vedangas: Members of the Veda or six subjects necessary to be studied for the reading, understanding and proper sacrificial employment of the Vedas.

Vedas: Mean literally 'the root of divine knowledge'. The Vedas, four in number, are the holy books which are the foundation of the Hindu religion—Sanatana Dharma.

Vedi: The sunken altar in which oblations are made to Agni.

Vidhi: Destiny.

Vidya: Knowledge.

Viveka: Discrimination.

Yagna: Vedic sacrifice.

Yajamana: A brahmana of great sanctity, who presides over sacrificial oblations during yagnas.

Yodha: A warrior.

Yoga Nidra: 'The sleep of meditation.' Personified delusion—a state of wakeful awareness. The great illusory energy of Vishnu and the illusory power manifested in Devi as Mahamaya—Yogamaya, the great illusion.

Yogi: A school of philosophy generally accredited to meditation and concentration of mind for equitable state of mind.

Yojanas: A Vedic unit of distance. Its exact measurement is disputed among scholars with distances being given between six to fifteen kilometers (four to nine miles) depending on different standards adopted by various Indian astronomers.

Source:

A Classical Dictionary of Hindu Mythology and Religion by John Dowson

*****

ABOUT THE AUTHOR

Brahmanaanda Patro (JB Patro) refers to himself as 'Krishnapada'. He retired as a Deputy Chief Executive from the Nuclear Fuels Complex (Bhabha Atomic Research Centre), specialising in the production of fuel for nuclear power reactors. A member of Dr Bhabha's pioneering team, Mr Patro got to interact with Nobel laureates in Physics on many occasions. Drawn to the teachings of Lord Krishna in the Bhagavad Gita, Mr Patro was amazed to discover a strong scientific connection there. He viewed it as a treatise on the physics of energy—the Laws of Thermodynamics—the very cosmic laws that govern our universe and conduct our lives as the *rita* of the Vedas. Mr Patro firmly believes that Krishna's Karma Yoga and the Sankhya philosophy are not doctrinaire, but rationale and scientific.

The author has dedicated many years in correlating modern scientific theories to ancient Hindu concepts. He has also compiled and edited Swami Ramakrishna Brahmananda's *Sree Maha Bhagavatam* in English.

Mesmerised by Lord Krishna's personality, Mr Patro delved deep into ancient as well as contemporary literature, before conceiving *Krishna: The Life and Times of the Deity who Lived as Man*. Working round-the-clock for four years, he brought his passion to life in this book. In this wonderful journey, his wife, Kusum Patro, has supported and complemented his work at every turn.

Luminaries throughout history have inspired many myths and legends.

Lord Krishna was one of the most famous Indians, one whose tales have enchanted many generations. Over the past thirty years, the authors covered most of the places connected with their subject's life. They not only visited the prison cellar at Mathura, which is Krishna's *janmasthan*, but also Gokul, Vrindavan, Vrajabhoomi, Pushkar, Kootachadri in the Gomantak range, Jyotisaar in Kuruksetra—Karnal, the Jambavan caves near Porbunder, Dwaraka, Krishna's palace area in Bhet Dwaraka and Somnath. The Patros then went to Veraval—Balkaghar, where Lord Krishna was hit by a hunter's arrow and Dehatisarga, where Arjuna had cremated the lord. Their final destination was the point where the three rivers—Hiranya, Kapila and Prak Saraswati—met before emptying into the Arabian Sea. It is believed that this is the place where Arjuna had immersed the mortal remains of Krishna. Presently, a Gita mandir—run by the Hindustan Charitable Trust, stands there. Near the Gita mandir lie the ruins of an ancient Sun Temple, which was probably the site of the Ghora Angirasa ashram.

Mr Patro has also presented here, a rare map of ancient India, representing the kingdoms flourishing in Lord Krishna's era. The author acquired this map from his father's library.

In these pages, the Patros have tried their best to bring to life Lord Krishna, as he existed in and around 1500 BC. They aim to tell an eternal tale.

Index